You Have to Get Lost Before You Can Be Found
A Memoir of Suffering, Grit, and Love of the Himalayas and Basa Village

Jeff Rasley

You Have to Get Lost Before You Can Be Found
   A Memoir of Suffering, Grit, and
Love of the Himalayas and Basa Village

Jeff Rasley

ISBN: 9781696951869

Published by Midsummer Books
Indianapolis, Indiana, 2019

   Some names are changed to protect privacy, but all persons referenced are actual human beings (not fictional characters or artificially intelligent robots).

   Many more photographs, all in color, are in the e-book version of this book. The printing cost of so many photos in color was too expensive (for your literary budget, dear reader) to include them in this paperback.
   Additional photos of Basa village and other Himalayan expeditions may be viewed at the author's website: **http://www.jeffreyrasley.com**

"WE LIVE IN A WONDERFUL WORLD THAT IS FULL OF BEAUTY, CHARM AND ADVENTURE. THERE IS NO END TO THE ADVENTURES WE CAN HAVE IF ONLY WE SEEK THEM WITH OUR EYES OPEN."
– JAWAHARIAL NEHRU

"After you have exhausted what there is in business, politics, conviviality, love, and so on -- have found that none of these finally satisfy, or permanently wear -- what remains? Nature remains; to bring out from their torpid recesses, the affinities of a man or woman with the open air, the trees, fields, the changes of seasons -- the sun by day and the stars of heaven by night."
-Walt Whitman

Other books by Jeff Rasley

Island Adventures: Disconnecting in the Caribbean and South Pacific

Polarized! The Case for Civility in the Time of Trump

Hero's Journey: John Ritter, the Chip Hilton of Goshen, Indiana

GODLESS – Living a Valuable Life Beyond Beliefs

MONSTERS OF THE MIDWAY 1969 - Sex, Drugs, Rock 'n' Roll, Viet Nam, Civil Rights, and Football

False Prophet, a Legal Thriller

Pilgrimage: Sturgis to Wounded Knee and Back Home Again, a Memoir

Bringing Progress to Paradise – What I Got From Giving to a Village in Nepal

Table of Contents

The "midget priests" (father and son) of Boudhanath Stupa
and the author, Kathmandu, 2003

Shock and Awe: Two Hoosiers Experience Kathmandu
Everest Base Camp Trail 1995

I trekked the Nepal Himalayas for the first time in 1995. I was manifesting mid-life crisis symptoms after turning 40. My wife told me to go take a hike. She suggested I do it on the other side of the world. Alicia slapped a brochure about trekking the Mt. Everest Base Camp Trail down on our dining room table one evening, and said, "Go! Do it."

The brochure was from the adventure-travel company Snow Lion. The itinerary was a tour of the Kathmandu Valley, helicopter up to Lukla Village, and then trek part way up to Mt. Everest Base Camp and back to Lukla. To lay down the burdens I carried living the American professional-class lifestyle for a few weeks in order to pick up and carry a backpack up a Himalayan trail was appealing.

I told my friend Long John what I planned to do and why. He said he needed to get away from the office and home too and was coming with me. We signed up for the Snow Lion Base Camp Trek. After Nepal, we planned to fly to Jakarta, Indonesia to visit John's childhood friend, Gary, and then spend a few days in Bali. It would be a great adventure and a needed break from practicing law, building a business, being an involved dad with two young boys, coaching multiple youth sports, teaching Sunday School, serving as a church deacon and on several for-profit and three nonprofit boards, mowing the lawn, paying bills, and giving my wife a break from my bitching about this life not being the carefree life we expected to live when we were young and in love.

When John and I exited Tribhuvan International Airport we confronted a scene of human chaos. Hundreds of Nepalis were shouting and waving. Several young men tried to pull our luggage right out of our hands aggressively explaining that they would carry our bags and get a taxi for us. Three-wheeled tuk-tuks belching carbon monoxide chugged around with people hanging on and baggage spilling out. Out of the mass of confusion a little man appeared with a colorful topi hat on his head holding a "Snow Lion" sign. He led us to a cab.

The sights, noises, and smells we two Hoosiers experienced during the taxi drive across Kathmandu to the Mustang Hotel were exotic and astonishing. There were no traffic lights or street signs. Water buffalo, cows, dogs, goats, roosters, and chickens wandered across and slept in the streets. Masses of people – women in beautiful flowing saris with dabs of paint on their foreheads and men wearing clothes of every conceivable style from leather biker-jackets to loin cloths – walked, ran, pushed carts loaded with lumber, bricks, or raw meat. Street vendors pointed at their goods and shouted as we passed by. Shop owners gestured enthusiastically or dozed, and beggars held up withered limbs or a malnourished child. We passed men shaving and women washing their long black-hair in buckets of water right beside the street. Cars, busses, trucks, motorcycles, bicycles, rickshaws, tuk-tuks, and animal-drawn carts flowed chaotically through the streets. Road surfaces varied from stone, brick, pock-marked pavement, or rutted dirt. Odors of incense, spicy foods, diesel and auto exhaust, sewage, and body odor assaulted us. Horn blasts, shouts, conversations and arguments in a polyglot of languages, bleats, barks, bellows and clucks of animals, and the grinding gears and strain of rickety vehicles on the verge of collapse created a surround sound you'd never hear in Indiana.

Our car paused beside a bright red rickshaw. Its driver stared at us with dark perplexed eyes, then opened his almost toothless mouth and laughed as we pulled away. My first experience of Nepal was intimidating and captivating.

Now, almost 25 years later, a visitor to Kathmandu will still cringe away from or thrill with excitement to many of the same sights, sounds, and smells John and I experienced in 1995. The main streets have been paved. There are a few traffic lights and signs. Major retailers and international banks now line the King's Way, the downtown commercial area. But crowded local markets still thrive on the side streets. Unfortunately, the air pollution in Kathmandu is much worse because of the unregulated emissions of tens of thousands of motorized vehicles. Tourists and locals wear surgical masks or bandanas to cover nose and mouth trying to avoid wheezing and sniffling from the rancid air. Once you leave the city and can breathe the pure air of the Himalayan Mountains, this is the sort of reward you'll receive:

"All of a sudden a ray of sunshine touched the summit of Everest, and soon flooded the higher snows and ridges with golden light, while behind, the deep purple of the sky changed to orange. Makalu was the next to catch the first rays of the sun and glowed as though alive; then the white sea of clouds was struck by the gleaming ray of the sun, and all aglow with colour rose slowly and seemed to break against the island peaks in great billows of fleecy white. Such a sunrise has seldom been the privilege of man to see, and once seen can never be forgotten." (Written by Charles Howard-Bury, leader of the first British team to attempt to climb Mt. Everest in 1921; quoted from *Into the Silence, The Great War, Mallory, and the Conquest of Everest*, Wade Davis, Vintage Books, 2011.)

After my fourteenth visit to the Himalayan region, I do not expect to return. I have been blessed to experience the sheer majesty of nature's handiwork at its most extreme in the Himalayas. And I have been blessed to commune with the strongest and kindest people in the world.

Nepalese porter resting and gazing at the mountain called Ama Dablam, which means "mother's necklace"; Everest Base Camp Trail 1995

Along with those blessings I experienced much pain and suffering in the mountains, beginning with the very first trek in 1995. Why did I keep going back to the Himalayas knowing some degree of pain and suffering was bound to occur? ("Because it's there" is not the answer.) The short answer is threefold: 1. To break out of a too comfortable life and experience freedom, wildness, and a raw beauty beyond where the pavement ends. 2. To gain the sense of accomplishment by meeting and overcoming, in some cases just surviving, a test of physical endurance and mental toughness by force of will. 3. To develop a model of culturally sensitive tourism and infrastructure development in the Himalayan region.

Over time the third answer became more important than the other two. The joys and sufferings I experienced in the Himalayas were so searing the reasons I kept going back evolved as does the narrative arc of this book. What I labeled "philanthro-trekking" and involvement with the Basa Village Foundations became more meaningful than trekking or climbing. I have not lost my joy of adventuring, but the challenge of trying to find a way to make adventure travel compatible with respect for traditional cultures became a more interesting struggle than climbing a mountain.

This book is my fond farewell to the places, people, and cultures I came to love in the Himalayan region. It is not a lament. In this later stage of life that I find myself, it is time to step off the trail and let younger legs take over the mission of philanthro-trekking.

This book provided an excuse to relive the pleasures and pains the Himalayas gave me. I've reviewed thousands of photos taken and many journal entries written over a quarter century, as well as researched topics beyond my own scope of experience. I wanted to take on this project while the personal experiences related in these pages are still alive in my aging memory.

Memory is a tricky thing. When writing the book, *Hero's Journey*, I read up on the current research in the neuroscience of memory. I learned that each time a memory is accessed our brain chemistry is changed. So it's actually true that every time we remember something the memory is changed, if ever so slightly – because the brain chemistry in which the memory is expressed changes. With that in mind, I proceed with caution (an approach I did not always take in the mountains) in declaring the accuracy of this memoir. Some of the events described will be remembered differently by others involved. Some of the details in the stories are necessarily re-imagined, because of lapses in memory and lacunae in journals and photo albums.

In addition to the vagaries of memory, the challenge of trying to convey the meaningfulness of personal experiences to others through the written word can be frustrating; and sometimes satisfying. This sequential anthology of stories is my last attempt to describe a personal journey through the Himalayas, the strange and wonderful people I have encountered there, adventures had, lessons learned, and wisdom gained. The book conveys the perspectives and insights shared with me by people who live in, and others who have traveled to, the Himalayan region. You'll meet June and Peter Hillary, Sir Edmund's older sister and son, Lama Tenzing, the highest lama of the Sherpas, Gheylsan Sherpa, who helped Hillary and Tenzing Norgay summit Mt. Everest, and John Roskelley, the famous American mountaineer and author, who taught me how to use an ice axe and crampons. Readers will also meet a shaman and a village preacher, farmers and artisans, mountain guides and porters, Buddhist monks and nuns, gurus and saddhus, as well as elite climbers and novice trekkers, yaks, yetis, and a white lemur. There is a near encounter with a snow leopard, but only a photo of its paw tracks survived.

This book is not written by a great mountaineer who accomplished death-defying first routes on 8,000 meter (25,000 foot) peaks. The mountaineering adventures the author personally attempted were, for the most part, possible for anyone in reasonably fit physical condition. I was over 40, for god's sake, the first time I attempted to climb a Himalayan peak. The climbing and trekking adventures in the pages that follow are a travelogue for anyone who enjoys vicariously visiting exotic places. But the places and experiences described are within reach of many of you readers, not just supremely fit elite climbers and adrenaline junkies.

The book is more than a travelogue through the Himalayas. Woven into the tales of Himalayan trekking and mountaineering is the history I've learned about how local cultures and communities in the Himalayan region have responded to 100 years of contacts with Western explorers, mountain climbers, and tourists. Issues of global significance and perverse personal interest are addressed, including: a) Has tourism tipped a balance within Sherpa and other

5

indigenous Nepalese cultures so far that materialistic consumerism is now valued more highly than cultural traditions? b) Should outside "philanthropists" try to reduce infant mortality, pulmonary disease, and cataracts in remote villages, or should healthcare be left to traditional healers? c) Should the choice for infrastructural development, such as roads, water, electricity, telecommunications, and internet be made by the local community, a higher level of government, or by "do-gooder outsiders"? d) How is the caste system justified by local people in Nepal, and is it fading away? e) What will happen to people living in the Himalayan region, if glacier melting is not reversed? f) Is Himalayan mountaineering, when it puts the lives of local porters and guides in danger, ethically justifiable? And, can mountaineering be done in a "green-sensitive" way, so that Mt. Everest and other Himalayan peaks are no longer trashed? g) How much does it cost to go trekking in the Himalayas, and why is it so much less expensive than a Viking Cruise? h) What does it feel like to get altitude sickness, and how can it be avoided on a Himalayan trek? i) Why are Sherpas the best mountain climbers in the world? j) What is a sadhu, why do yaks only live in the High Himalayas, and do yetis really roam the Himalayan Mountains? k) How in the hell can Nepalese porters carry such incredibly heavy loads in wicker baskets strapped to their heads? And, what do they think about while they're carrying those loads? l) Are arranged marriages more likely to succeed than love marriages? m) What does it look and sound like when a Rai shaman sings? n) What does the High Lama of the Sherpas think about mountain climbing? Does he think mountain top experiences help or hinder the achievement of enlightenment? o) Which did Sir Edmund Hillary love more, mountain climbing or building schools for Sherpa children? p) How the deadly combination of ego and money kills people (mostly Sherpas) on Mt. Everest every year. And, q) Why the "simple people" of Basa Village have a better understanding of "God" and reality than theologians and religious scholars of all the major faiths.

I taught a course at Marian University and Butler University in international studies about culturally sensitive development. Readers will receive the benefit of the course without paying tuition, and no homework!

The photos included in this book were taken by me or a companion using my camera, unless indicated otherwise. People mentioned, described, or quoted are real, but several names and identities are changed to protect privacy. When a fake name is used, it is so stated.

[To view more photos, accounts of specific treks and mountaineering expeditions with Adventure GeoTreks, and for information about the Basa Village Foundation, check out **http://www.jeffreyrasley.com**.]

The first time I hiked in the Himalayas I was feeling lost. It took more than one trekking adventure to find my better self. But each of the fourteen times I went into the mountains, I came back a little further down the path and closer to home. Whether you are feeling lost or already found, I hope you will read on and share the trail with me.

Namaste, Jeff Rasley

Dedications

This book is dedicated to my wife, Alicia. We've been separated many times by our different travel adventures, but returning home is always a sweet reunion. Love sustains us.

To each of the mountain guides, camp cooks, and porters (many of whom will be named in subsequent chapters), who did the hard work and handled the many chores required of the crews on trekking and mountaineering expeditions I've experienced; thank you again.

To Niru Rai for his essential help in providing information for this book, and to his team members serving the Basa Village Foundation Nepal NGO.

To Joel Meyers and the contributors, members, directors, and officers of the Basa Village Foundation USA Inc. Everyone involved with the Basa Foundations in Nepal and the US have played a vital role in the success of our sister foundations to do culturally sensitive development projects in the Basa area of Nepal. The "BVF" has been a significant part of my life for the last fifteen years. I have received much in return.

To the memory of Ray Schaefer, whose generosity brought water to the homes of hundreds in Nepal and education to thousands in Palestine.

To the memory of Chuck Richmond, whose generosity with his time and legal talents helped to make the Basa Village Foundation USA a successful tax exempt nonprofit organization.

And with terrible sadness, to Jess Roskelley, who died "doing what he loved and what he lived for" on a mountain. Jess will be forever young and lives on in my memory and in the pages of the next chapter of this book as a beautiful boy of fifteen.

"There is something in man which responds to the challenge of this mountain...
The struggle is the struggle of life itself upward and forever upward..."
George Leigh Mallory

My First Mountain: "I'll never do that again!" Kanglachan Expedition with the Roskelleys
Ladakh, India 1997

It was a very cool experience touring the Kathmandu Valley and trekking the Mt. Everest Base Camp Trail with my friend, Dr. John Volbers, in 1995. Living in the flatlands of Indiana most of my life, I had little experience with mountains. The gigantic, shimmering white peaks touched a previously unknown place deep in my soul. The people we encountered on the Base Camp trek impressed and intrigued me. Our sirdar (chief guide), Nyima Sherpa, was highly intelligent and thoughtful, multilingual with excellent managerial skills. (The last name of all Sherpas is Sherpa. Among the people who inhabit the mountain villages of Nepal, a person's tribal-ethnic group is typically that person's last name.) Almost every local person John and I encountered up in the mountains, including our crew of porters, Buddhist monks at the Tengboche Monastery, yak herders, and potato farmers lived up to the description ascribed to Sir Edmund Hillary about the Sherpas. "They are the strongest and kindest people in the world". (For the sake of accuracy I would extend Hillary's description of the Sherpa people to all the tribal-ethnic groups that inhabit the high mountains of the Himalayan region, based on my experiences with Ladakhi, Rai, Tamang, Gurung, and Tibetan people. With few exceptions, I've found these folks to be exceptionally kind in their welcome of visitors and amazingly strong in their ability to endure hardship with a smile.)

As soon as I was back home in Indiana after the 1995 Base Camp Trek I began to plan a return to the Himalayan region. I wanted to touch and be touched by the mountains and local culture more intimately than what I'd experienced my first time over there. I wanted to learn how to climb mountains and join a mountaineering expedition.

In the summer of 1995 I took a beginner's course in rock climbing at Seneca Rocks, West Virginia. The following summer I enrolled in the intermediate class. Having mastered basic skills with rope and rock, I figured that was sufficient preparation to enlist in a Himalayan mountaineering expedition.

Admittedly, I had no experience with actual mountaineering. I met a few climbers on the Base Camp Trail, but I had not even seen a video about Himalayan mountaineering. I was naively ignorant of the fact that rock climbing is only a miniscule piece of Himalayan mountaineering. Pictures of mountain climbers usually depict them roped up and lunging to dig their fingers or toes into a crack on a sheer rock face. So that's what I imagined I needed to learn to become a climber. In reality Himalayan mountaineering is mostly slogging up and down high mountain passes and across glaciers. The best preparation for a flatlander is to find a hill and run up and down it with a full pack until you're exhausted; then do it again.

On the upside, rock climbing in West Virginia gave me an excuse for motorcycling through the scenic Appalachian hills and mountains. The campground at Seneca Rocks was in a pretty little dale within the Monongahela National Forest. Some of the skills I learned were transferable to mountaineering. Several of the mountains I later climbed had one or more rock faces to deal with on the way to the summit. Unfortunately, I tore the medial meniscus in my left knee trying to stick a twisting lunging-move on the last day of training on Seneca Rocks in July, 1997.

The injury occurred three weeks before the date of my scheduled departure flight to New Delhi, India. I'd signed up for a mountaineering expedition and already paid $4,000 (equivalent to about $6,060 in 2019 dollars) to join. Damned if a knee injury was going to ruin my dream of climbing a Himalayan peak! The same knee was injured playing college football. I played through the pain then, I could do it again. The orthopedic doc at Methodist Sports Medical Clinic accepted my emphatic statement that surgery was not an option and that I was not backing out of the mountaineering expedition I'd been planning for two years and already paid for! He prescribed pain and anti-inflammatory meds, a flexible brace, and an inflatable ice pack that could be filled with ice or cold water.

I packed those items in my newly purchased expedition backpack, along with an ice axe, crampons, climbing harness, figure eight, carabiners, ascender, sling, gaiters, and borrowed (that proved to be a mistake) plastic climbing boots. Snow Lion sent a "gear list", including all that stuff, to the members of the expedition. The Base Camp trek was such a great experience, I signed up with the same company for the mountaineering expedition in 1997. Snow Lion sent two additional pages listing the rest of the stuff we needed to bring for camping equipment, cold weather clothing, personal effects, etc.

I had no idea how to use an ice axe. Trying to walk in the heavy-clunky plastic-climbing boots I'd borrowed was as difficult and clumsy as trying to walk in ski boots. I didn't understand how these damnably uncomfortable boots could help me get up the side of a mountain. Rock climbing shoes fit tightly, but were light weight and very flexible. Climbing boots took up a lot of space in my pack and were the heaviest of all the required items on the gear list. I did not look forward to adding a couple pounds to each of my feet along with all the weight I'd be carrying in a backpack climbing over 20,000 feet above sea level. But, so it goes.

On August 10, 1997 I arrived in New Delhi anxious to meet the members of the mountaineering team I expected to spend the next three weeks with. The leader of the expedition was one of America's most famous living mountaineers, John Roskelley.

One of the reasons I chose this particular expedition was because John was the leader. He'd led many expeditions in the Himalayas, Andes, and Alps. John had scaled some of the most challenging peaks in the Himalayas, including K2, Dhaulagiri, and Nanda Devi. John authored several books about his mountaineering adventures. My favorite was *Nanda Devi: The Tragic Expedition*, which I read just before departing for India. Roskelley had lived through incredibly harsh, and some tragic, experiences on mountains. He once spent more than 60 days on the side of K2 without changing clothes, waiting for the weather to allow a summit attempt. At 49-years old, John had given up extreme climbing. He was a county commissioner in Spokane, Washington and raised mules. John's primary motive for leading this particular expedition was to introduce his fifteen year-old son, Jess, to Himalayan mountaineering.

Getting to New Delhi was excruciatingly tedious; 30 hours of flying and layovers. A visa had to be obtained from the India Consulate in Chicago prior to departure. That required mailing the completed application with my passport (yikes!) and a $42 fee to the consulate. (In 1997 you couldn't apply for a visa over the Internet.) To get to New Delhi, I flew to Boston, then to Frankfurt, Germany, and then Delhi. Enduring a dull ache and occasional sharp pain in the injured knee increased the discomfort of those 30 hours of travel.

At the Imperial Hotel in New Delhi I was surprised to be met by, not John Roskelley, but the fellow who was to be my room and tent mate for the next three weeks. Dax (not his actual name) excitedly informed me he'd arrived two days earlier and had upgraded our room to an executive suite at no additional cost by making various complaints to management. He talked a mile a minute reeling off his bio. I learned he was a New Yorker, but also had a place in California, owned two Porches and a Bugatti motorcycle, height: 5 ft. 10 in., weight: 230 lbs., weight lifter, Jewish, made hundreds of thousands of dollars per year as a sales rep, and this was his first Himalayan expedition, but he'd learned to climb in the Rockies. He finally asked me a question, which was about him, "You know what I am, don't you?" I correctly guessed that he was gay.

I grew up in Goshen, Indiana, which had no black people, Muslims, or gays (so far as we knew). But I'd lived in London a couple months and Chicago for four years. One of my closest friends in Chicago was gay. I was not a country rube horrified at the prospect of sharing a hotel room or tent with a gay guy. Dax seemed a little disappointed that I didn't register any shock at his gayness revelation. We hit it off immediately. Dax's next revelation was that the banana lassis in the Imperial Hotel's café were marvelous. (Lassi is a popular drink in Southeast Asia made with yogurt, water, spices and sometimes fruit.) He absolutely insisted on buying me one.

Ladakh

We flew from New Delhi up to the highest airport in the world – altitude over 11,000 feet – just outside of Leh, which is a city of 30,000 in the Ladakh region of India. Ladakh is at the very northern tip of India with Pakistan immediately west and Tibet (because of the brutality of the invasion and subjugation of the Tibetan people and culture, I will not refer to Tibet as a province of China) to the north. As a political entity Ladakh is divided into two administrative districts (like two counties) within the Indian state of Jammu and Kashmir. Leh is the center of the northern district and the smaller town of Kargil is the center of the southern district of Ladakh.

The mountains we planned to trek through in Ladakh are a section of the Greater Himalaya. Some geographical maps call this section of the Himalayas the Karakorum Range. Others refer to them as the Zanskar Range. To add to the confusion, maps produced in India designate the portion of the range inside the borders of Ladakh as the Stok Range. Geographical maps identify the particular mountain we aimed to climb as Stok Kangri, but the local people call it Kanglachan (which is the name used in this book).

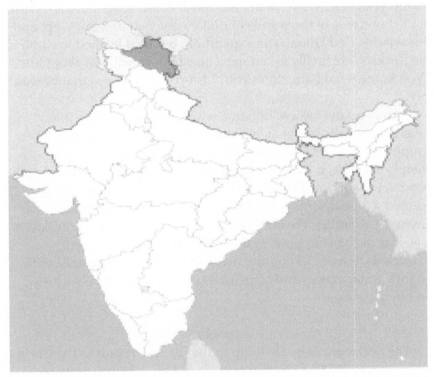

Ladakh is highlighted (map image from Wikipedia Talk)

The Greater Himalayan Range began to arise over 45 million years ago through the geologic process of plate tectonics. The Indian Plate crashed into the Eurasian Plate and started folding over it. The landscape created by this folding process was not rolling hills. It was a messy and smashed-up looking landscape. Thousands of mountains in different shapes and sizes were created as the Indian Plate smashed and broke apart to create the Himalayas. The Greater

14

Himalayan Range spans the borders of Tibet, Bhutan, Nepal, India, Pakistan, Afghanistan, and the other "Stan countries.

For several hundred years Ladakh was a small but independent Buddhist kingdom on the Silk Road. Ladakhis fought wars with the neighboring Buddhist kingdoms of Tibet and Sikkim (Sikkim has an interesting history. It managed to maintain independent rule until 1975, when India revoked its status as a "protectorate state" and incorporated it as a province.) Ladakh was invaded and temporarily conquered in the 16th Century by Muslim Baltistan. (Baltistan is a territory within modern Pakistan). A significant percentage of the population of Ladakh has been Muslim since the 16th Century invasion. Native Ladakhis eventually ousted the Balti invaders, but the kingdom's independence ended in 1801 when Ladakh was forcibly incorporated into the Sikh Empire. Large swaths of what is modern India and Pakistan were dominated by Sikh rulers until the British rule over the Indian Subcontinent, which lasted from 1858 until 1947. The line of separation the Brits drew between India and Pakistan placed Ladakh on the Indian side. The territory all around Ladakh has been disputed ever since 1947 by Pakistan, China, and India. Ladakhis have suffered through border wars fought between India and Pakistan and India and China.

Photographs of the Dalai Lama were framed and hung or taped to a wall in every Ladakhi-Buddhist home I entered in 1997. Ladakhis, Sherpas, and Tibetans are religious, cultural, and ethnic "cousins". Most of them recognize the Dalai Lama as the highest and most respected religious and cultural leader, although he is "a man without a country" (or a man for all countries). As tourism began to develop in Ladakh in the 1970s, a trickle of Kashmiri Muslims started to flow north into Ladakh. By 1997 many of the shops in Leh selling traditional Ladakhi goods, like yak-hair blankets, prayer wheels, jewelry, pottery, and thangka paintings to tourists were owned by Kashmiri Muslims. Conflicts flared up between Buddhist Ladakhis and recent Muslim immigrants. Buddhist Ladakhis complained that newly arrived Kashmiri Muslims were taking over marketplaces and pushing traditional Ladakhi traders out of business. Violence from the Kashmiri independence struggle against India spilled over into Ladakh. In 1995 the Kashmiri-separatist terrorist organization, Al-Faran, captured six Western trekkers just south of Ladakh and killed five of them.

Before beginning the trek to Kanglachan, our eight-member group spent four days acclimating to the 11,000-foot elevation of Leh. We toured the countryside in 4-wheel drive vehicles. Most of the adult Ladakhi-Buddhist women we saw wore traditional clothing as in this picture. Clothing of men was more diverse. Some tended to dress like Westerners and others wore hats similar to that of the woman in the picture, knee-length robes, and flannel pants.

We encountered many Indian soldiers on our drives outside of Leh. Our guide arranged a visit to an outpost near the Pakistan border manned with light artillery. The elite forces stationed there proudly called themselves mountain tigers. Each of the "tigers" looked extremely fit. Most were over six feet tall, which is unusual for Southeast Asians. The commanding officer bragged that they occasionally lobbed shells across the border into Pakistan. He said his men regularly laid ambushes for Kashmiri guerilla fighters attempting to cross the border into Ladakh. We were not allowed to take pictures.

On a more tranquil note, we visited several Buddhist gompas (a gompa is a teaching monastery) during our drives around the country. Resident monks at each monastery graciously served tea, gave a tour, and answered our questions about the history of the gompa and life as a monk. The most interesting monastery we visited is Hemis Gompa. It was built into the inner elbow of a mountainside and looks as much like an impregnable fortress as a place of worship and spiritual retreat. The monks told us Hemis was originally built in the 10th Century, but eventually fell into disrepair and was little used. It was renovated in the 17th Century. It's been in continual use since then. Our hosts boasted that Hemis holds the largest festival in Ladakh.

Hemis Gompa

We lucked into witnessing a Buddhist festival at Lamayura Gompa. Lamayura was also originally built in the 10th Century. The purpose of the festival was to celebrate and represent the magical feats of Padmasambhava. He is a mythic-legendary figure bearing the titles of The Lotus-born, Guru Rinpoche, and The Second Buddha. The myth of Padmasambhava begins with his incarnation as a child born in a lotus blossom. After attaining Buddha consciousness he flew over the Himalayas landing in Tibet, where he founded the first Buddhist monastery in the 8th Century. There, legend and history intersect, because historical records establish that a person bearing the name Padmasambhava did establish a Buddhist monastery at that time in Tibet. Padmasambhava supposedly practiced an esoteric form of Tantric Buddhism involving magical rites, asceticism, and sexual abandon. (Whoa Nelly!) Padmasambhava supposedly subdued the evil spirits in Tibet while spreading the Dharma (rule or way) of Buddhism. On of the ways he subdued evil spirits was through the oppression of worshipers of Bon, the more ancient animistic religion of the Himalayan region. The historical Padmasambhava was a popular leader who gained many followers and was a key figure in establishing Buddhism as the dominant religion in Tibet, Bhutan, Sikkim, Ladakh, and the Khumbu region of Nepal.

The festive ceremonies we observed at Lamayura involved very stylized dancing in colorful costumes. The local people seemed happy to have our group of eight Americans in attendance. They gave us apricots and slices of cooked mutton. It was a lovely experience and a nice send off to begin our trek through the mountains to Kanglachan.

The itinerary for our expedition was to drive west from Leh to Lamayura Gompa and then trek back east to the center of Ladakh, where Kanglachan is located. The mountain could be reached in one long day hike from Leh, but the purpose of the trek was to experience the country and local culture on foot, strengthen our endurance for the climb, build team spirit, and acclimate to higher and higher altitudes.

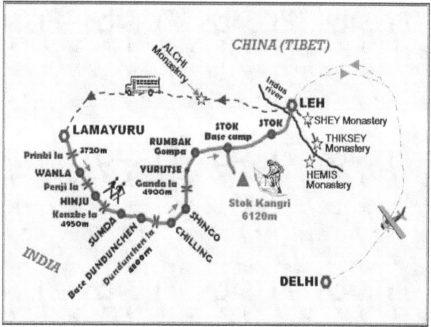

Map provided by Dare2Venture, an India-based trekking company. The trekking route sketched is similar to the route Snow Lion planned. The driving tour is also similar to the route we followed when we visited Hemis, Lamayura, and the other gompas before we began trekking.

The Group and the Trek

Our group for the driving tour included two members who booked with Snow Lion to visit Leh and tool around Ladakh with us. A newlywed couple I'll call George and Rachel were young, fit, and beautiful, except for Rachel's smoking addiction. They were spending their weird and wonderful honeymoon traveling around India. George and Rachel waved a parting good-bye as we hoofed it out of Lamayura.

In 1997 Molly was a 40-year-old medical doctor and former Outward Bound instructor. She was a small but mighty ball of energy. She had lots of experience in the Rockies, but this was her first Himalayan expedition. Judy was a tall, strong 40-something Montana tree-farmer who'd been on a previous trekking expedition in the Himalayas with Roskelley and was a friend of the family. She took a motherly interest in 15-year-old Jess. My new friend and tent-mate, Dax, was a couple years younger than me, and, as he informed me at our initial meeting at the Imperial Hotel, a New York Jew, weight-lifter, Porsche and Bugatti owner, and millionaire.

We were all Americans aged 15 to 49. We were strangers in a strange land, theoretically led by a world-renowned mountaineer. "Theoretically", because John had never set foot in Ladakh before our arrival. We were totally dependent for directions and food on our guide and cook and on a mule team for carrying the tents, cooking equipment, our gear and clothing.

This team of mules served as our porters. The mules were exchanged for human porters after we crossed the Indus River.

During the next seven days we trekked through deep gorges.

Crossed glacier-fed streams and passed by stupas
(local Buddhist shrines).

We hiked through yak pastures (called kharkas) and looked into the dark eyes of the great shaggy beasts.

Passed dead animals

Played with baby yaks

The Ladakhis we met were either subsistence
farmers or yak herders.

We bathed in streams.

Washed our clothes in the same streams

We crossed over the roaring Indus River in a metal bucket pulled hand-over-hand with a rope. The last member of our party to cross was our sirdar (chief guide), Tsering Phunchok, alone in the gondola. The lower rope -- the one pulled to move the gondola -- broke just as Tsering reached the safety of our side of the river. Good thing we didn't have to cross back.

We marveled at the mountain vistas during rest breaks.

Posed for photos on high passes

Our cook, Dorge, prepared amazingly tasty meals each day using a kerosene-fueled stove and water fetched from the nearest stream or river. He boiled the water in steel pans.

We slept two-to-a-tent. Most of the campsites were yak kharkas.

Team member lost, crappy weather, and dangerous conditions on the mountain

This is a description of the trekking route to Kanglachan from Dare2Venture's website: "Join us for the trek to Stok Kangri. Stok Kangri Peak trek is considered one of the most challenging treks in this region of Himalayas. The final altitude that is achieved in the trek is 20,080 ft, which is almost 70% height of the Mount Everest. You must be mentally and physically fit to complete this trek. Most people return from the base camp of Stok Kangri without even completing the last leg."

Literature from Snow Lion in 1997 listed the mountain's summit as 20,315 feet. It claimed that Kanglachan's elevation is five feet higher than Denali (Mt. McKinley), the highest peak in North

America. Recently googling Kanglachan and Stok Kangri, I found various heights ascribed to the mountain. Most sources list the altitude at the summit at around 20,200 feet, but some set it as high as 20,500. The name "Kanglachan" means "view of all the mountains" in the Ladakhi language. It is the highest peak in Ladakh.

In retrospect, the approach taken by five inexperienced climbers to our first Himalayan peak was downright cavalier. But you don't know what you don't know. This is a warning about attempting to climb Kanglachan posted on the website of IndiaHikes by author-owner Arjun Majumdar on March 29, 2011.

The Stok Kangri trek requires proper acclimatization... Here are some real stories: In 2008, a close friend of mine had to return half way from the trek, hit by AMS (acute mountain sickness, aka, altitude sickness), despite spending two days at Leh acclimatizing. Only one member from her team of 15 made it to the Stok summit. In 2009, a team of 6 trekkers made it 70% of the way to the summit in July and had to return, hit by a snow storm. The same team attempted Stok once again last year and all of them had to turn back, some with bleeding noses, hit by acclimatization issues – few of them were only meters away from the summit.

Most itineraries of trek operators are rather questionable. They have two days of acclimatization at Leh, as if acclimatization at 11,500 feet would help overcome a summit at 20,500 feet. The two days of acclimatization at Leh is required not for the Stok summit, but to get adjusted to the mountains after a sudden flight from Delhi, which is almost at sea level.

Do not attempt Stok Kangri if you cannot spend at least 10 days in the mountains of Ladakh. And do not attempt Stok Kangri if you do not have the physical fitness to endure a trek that climbs nearly 5,000 meters prior to the Stok Kangri trek. What it means is you are going to do two very high altitude treks back to back. This requires a high order of physical fitness, for which preparation needs to start couple of months in advance.

... [M]ost first time trekkers throw caution to the wind about some things that happen frequently at extreme high altitudes. The first of these is the weather. It changes colour like a chameleon. A bright sunny day turns into a blizzard in a couple of minutes. Caught unawares, a trekker without enough experience can panic. On a trek like the Stok Kangri you can hardly afford to do that. You need to keep your wits about you to get out of these situations. To do this, you need to prepare well.

AMS is another issue. The Stok Kangri trail gains altitude rapidly. Here, a person normal at 16,000 feet can suddenly start developing symptoms of AMS gaining only another 500 feet in altitude. This can be a potentially fatal situation if timely action isn't taken.

I do not recommend the Stok Kangri trek for someone who has never done a high altitude trek before. Attempt Stok Kangri only if you have done treks above 14,000 feet. If you are new to trekking, do not attempt the Stok Kangri trek.

Only John and Judy had previously trekked or climbed above 14,000 feet. The highest altitude I reached on the trek part way up the Everest Base Camp Trail was 14,300 feet at the Pheriche Medical Clinic. But I was only there a short while before hiking back to our campsite at Tengboche Gompa at 12,700 feet. That was the highest "sleeping altitude" I'd previously achieved. Only John was qualified for the climb, according to Arjun Majumdar's requirements.

After six days on the trail Dax confided to John and me that whenever he tried to pee all he got was a few drops of blood. Dax was having a rough time. He was sunburned on his face, neck and arms. For the last two days of the trek he had bouts of blurry and unfocused vision.

Dax was tremendously strong. He was a competitive weightlifter. On the second or third day of the trek Dax picked up a small boulder, which must have weighed around 200 pounds. He carried it a few yards and then dropped it in a stream near our campsite. It created a little pool for clothes washing. But the excess muscle Dax carried made him the slowest hiker in the group. He really struggled pushing 230 pounds up steep mountain trails.

Dr. Molly decreed that Dax needed medical attention and had to bail out of the trek. She was convinced he'd developed a kidney infection.

We were resting at the top of Kanga La, a 16,000 foot high pass. The views were fantastic. We could see the entire Zanskar Range to the south, the great peaks of the Karakorum to the north, and the spiny tip of K2 to the west. ("La" is the Tibetan word for "high". "La" is included in most of the names of the high passes in the Himalayas.)

Dax refused to quit. He argued that it was his right to continue. He'd paid to do the whole expedition. Dax desperately wanted to climb Kanglachan.

A group of Israeli students hiked up the Kanga La. They were taking photographs of the mountains and themselves. The young Israelis danced and cavorting around exulting in the accomplishment of reaching the summit of the high pass. After they calmed down we learned they'd driven two Land Rovers out from Leh. The vehicles were a four-hour hike down the trail from the Kanga La. The Israelis offered to give Dax a lift back to Leh. Dax vehemently refused.

He got mad. Damn it, he had a right to finish the trek -- he'd paid for it! Molly and John listened patiently while Dax blew off steam arguing his point. Finally, in a quiet but firm voice John told Dax that Dax had to quit for his own good. As our leader John had the authority to make the call. He told Dax that none of us were leaving Kanga La until we saw Dax's backside going downhill with the Israelis. I hugged Dax and told him I'd take his new ice axe to the top. He finally relented and we watched him reluctantly trudge downhill with the group of Israeli students.

(Ten years later Dax returned to the Himalayas with a group I organized to trek the Langtang Trail in Nepal. He had remade his body. His weight was down to 185 pounds, and he'd trained as a climber in the Rockies. Dax had no problem hiking up the high passes of the Langtang trek in 2007.)

The weather turned crappy in the late afternoon and early evening during the hike from Kanga La to the base camp at Kanglachan. We'd had a week of hot, rainless days and cool nights – fine for trekking. But now, cumulus clouds enveloped us, the temperature dropped, and it began to rain. For the first time on the trek we unpacked and put on raincoats or ponchos and strapped rain covers over our backpacks.

Below Kanga La the trail disappeared into what looked like a river of rocks about seventy yards wide with sheer limestone cliffs rising on our left and low dirt and lichen-covered hills on the right. I had never seen a moraine before, let alone hiked over one. There was no solid ground, only rocks, millions in all shapes and sizes. It was clumsy, slippery hiking in rain. My boots got soaked from crossing and re-crossing a shallow glacier-fed stream trickling down the middle of the moraine.

Judy is a tough Montana forester and was a veteran of previous Himalayan and Andean expeditions, but she was beginning to wear out. I hung back with her. I didn't mind slowing my pace. I was tired too. The dull and constant ache in my knee was wearing on me. I'd lost at least 10 pounds of body weight and my shoulders ached where the backpack straps dug in.

The rain turned to sleet and the temperature dropped further. We were getting colder and wetter. I wanted to hurry on to camp and the warmth and comfort of hot Sherpa tea and my sleeping bag. But I humped along in step with Judy's slower pace. The rest of our party disappeared out of sight somewhere ahead of us. There was no trail to follow within the moraine. We were forced to cross and re-cross the confounded stream to stay on the lowest and flattest line. The sun began to set behind the mountains.

One of our porters came into view hurrying back toward us. John began to worry about how long it was taking Judy and me to reach camp, so he sent Stanzin out to find us. Stanzin pointed straight ahead indicating we needed to continue hiking up the moraine to base camp. I asked Judy if she minded whether I hiked on ahead. She laughed and shook her head. She joked that she was walking so slowly because she so much enjoyed walking in the rain. I took off hiking as fast as I could, but careful not to turn an ankle on slippery rocks. I made it to base camp around 7:00 p.m. Stanzin and Judy arrived about fifteen minutes later.

Our Kanglachan base camp, August, 1997

We were a sorry bunch in camp that night. Judy, Jess, and I were beat. Jess had a cut on his hand from a fall on the rocks. Molly had altitude sickness, couldn't eat, and spent the evening retching behind her tent. Even John seemed a little weary.

Before med school Molly spent ten years as an Outward Bound counselor. At 40, she still ran competitive marathons. We kidded her about being part mountain goat, because she was so quick up the highest passes and never seemed tired at the end of the day. Instead of hiking boots Molly wore sandals several days on the trek. Lots of local people wore sandals hiking in the Himalayas, but it was quite extraordinary for a Westerner. For a couple nights Molly slept outside her tent with the pack animals to star gaze. She ended that practice when a couple yaks decided to inspect the strange bundle in their pasture and nuzzled her with their snouts.

Molly had a miserable night in base camp. She was weak and wasted the next day. After a day of rest, she reported that she was fully recovered and ready to climb.

Other than tired and a little cut and bruised from a fall in the moraine, Jess seemed fine at base camp. Jess later became an outstanding high school wrestler, football player, track and field star, white water kayaker, and the first certified ski-patrol snowboarder in Washington State. He worked as a guide on Mt. Rainier.

Jess Roskelley also became the youngest American to summit Mt. Everest at age 20 in 2003. He and John climbed Everest as a father-son team. Even at 15, Jess was an extraordinary athlete, and he was a delightful trekking companion. He was already as tall as his dad, at around five foot nine. No doubt he would soon be adding more inches of height and pounds of muscle to his skinny 15-year-old body.

For John, our expedition was a great way to introduce Jess to Himalayan mountaineering. At 49 he was past his peak years as an elite climber. But John was still tough as nails, had a full head of light brown hair, and didn't have an ounce of fat on his compact muscular frame. Several times during the trek, John raced Molly up a pass or to the campsite when it was within sight. He was 49, but our trek was "a walk in the park" compared to many of the extreme expeditions John had led. It was a special treat for father and son to share a tent on Jess's first experience of trekking and climbing at high altitudes.

Kanglachan's summit is well below the "death zone" of 25,000 feet, where human brain cells begin dying due to insufficient oxygen. But no matter the elevation of the mountain, climbing is a risky enterprise, especially in bad weather. Unfortunately, we had a schedule to keep. We needed to be back in Leh by August 28th to catch our flight hack to Delhi.

For two days sleet, snow, and high winds were our constant companions in base camp. There was no let up on the third day. We were running out of time for a summit attempt on Kanglachan.

Being stuck in base camp had one advantage. It gave us plenty of time to practice mountaineering skills. John demonstrated and tested each of us on the use of ice axe and crampons. He made sure we knew how to step into our harnesses and tie a climber's knot with perlon rope on the harness.

During lunch in the meal tent on the third day, John asked if we wanted to go for the summit despite the rough weather. The wind howled and lashed at the sides of the tent. The vote was unanimous. We wanted to go for it.

John talked us through the plan. We'd rest until 1:00 a.m., then eat a carb-heavy breakfast and be ready to leave base camp at 2:00 a.m. We'd climb at night to avoid the heat and glare of the sun. John explained that climbing during the day can be dangerous, because the body can over-heat from the extraordinary physical exertion demanded. Bright sunlight can fry your retinas from the reflective glare off the ice and snow. And the most significant reason is that warm sunlight might cause an avalanche. Melting ice and snow can start the process that will bring down the whole side of a mountain. You don't want to be up there, if that starts to happen.

My inexperienced-based reasoning led me to think that sunshine seemed like it would be a lesser concern than the crappy weather that had been pummeling our tents for over two days. And the prospect of climbing in darkness was a bit terrifying. As a humble novice, I kept my mouth shut about my concerns.

John also decided that our Sherpa guides should carry everyone's boots, crampons, gaiters, harnesses, carabiners, and the ropes up to a high camp at 18,000 feet. Without specifically saying so, the implication was that our group was in no condition to carry all the gear we'd need for the final push to the summit. But the major change of plans from Snow Lion's published itinerary was that we would not spend a night at a high camp. We'd stop and rest at high camp, eat a snack, don our climbing gear, and push upward for the summit.

Early in the day that we hiked to base camp we'd met a climbing group on the trail coming down from Kanglachan. The group was led by the famous English mountaineer Adrian Burgess. Adrian and his twin brother, Alan, were well known to John. He had climbed pioneering routes with the brothers on 8,000 meter peaks. It was fun to see these veteran mountaineers engage in friendly and competitive story-telling during our first rest stop that day. We learned that Adrian's team was blown off the mountain at high camp. Some of their tents were shredded by gale-force winds.

Adrian was tall, lanky-muscular, with a weather-beaten and sharp featured face. He had floppy blond hair, and the appearance of a British rock star from the 60s melded with a California surfer dude. He was full of piss and vinegar and determined to outdo John with tales of mountain bravado. The looks on the faces of Adrian's clients were in stark contrast to Adrian's bravura. Each of the members of his group looked ragged, beat up, and downcast. They had little to say, except, "Be careful up there."

The reason John changed the plan to attempt to summit in one day was based on what he'd learned about the conditions of high

40

camp from Adrian. He reasoned that we'd have a better chance of summiting if we tried to do the climb in one push rather than spending the extra time and effort to set up another camp on an even higher and more dangerous place on the mountain. John also snidely remarked that he was going to take great pleasure the next time they met in letting Adrian know that we summitted. That little victory would be more evidence to support his side in their running argument over whether Americans or Brits were superior climbers.

Epiphany

Awaiting the 1:00 a.m. breakfast call, I lay in the North Face tent by myself. I'd lost my tent mate when Dax lumbered down Kanga La with the Israelis. Wind riffled and sleet crackled against the nylon cocoon. I was excited and frightened, my senses too heightened for sleep. In a few hours at the age of 44 I would be attempting to climb my first Himalayan peak. Thoughts of family, home, and random memories clicked through my consciousness like an out-of-control slide show. My oxygen depleted brain tried to make sense of why I was lying in a sleeping bag over 15,000 feet high on a snow-covered mountainside in Ladakh.

When I was six weeks old, my father was discharged from the US Army and my family moved from Fort Leonard Wood, Missouri to Indiana in a little trailer. Perhaps the experience of riding in a dresser drawer across the Midwest imprinted a love of travel on my infant psyche. I grew up in the same small town my mom's family had lived in for five generations. Life in that town was very stabile and secure. Stability and security are important for the healthy development of a child, but by the time I was a teenager I wanted adventure, not stability or security. I thought I had experienced all the adventures Goshen, Indiana had to offer.

Before I graduated from high school I began hitchhiking around the Midwest and eventually as far as New York, Florida, and California. I spent a summer studying and bumming around Europe at 19 and motorcycled across the US and down through Mexico when I was 20. I returned from Mexico with a steel pin in my shoulder, a cast on my right arm, and considerably less money after buying my way out of jail for being a Gringo who got broadsided by a Mexican driver. My motorcycle was totaled, so a combination of train, bus, and hitchhiking were the means of transport my pal, Tim, and I utilized to get home.

During college and law school I regularly escaped the rigors of the academy for motorcycle, scuba diving, skiing, and canoe trips throughout the Western Hemisphere. Even in my early 30s, after marriage, passing the Bar, a mortgage and two kids, I occasionally found time for what was being called "adventure travel".

In my late 30s I had become a partner in a small law firm. I was an involved dad. I loved being with my little boys. We had "we sing" every Thursday night, when Alicia had a late class. I read or told bedtime stories to JJ and Andy every night. When they were old enough to play recreational sports, I volunteered to coach their teams in basketball, football, soccer, swimming, and one season of baseball. Alicia was active in the Parent Teacher Organizations at their schools. I took the lead in Andy and JJ's religious upbringing. I taught Sunday school and served as a deacon and elder in our Presbyterian church.

All those activities and responsibilities squeezed the opportunity to hit the road and go adventuring out of my life. It was a great life. I loved my family and we were involved in many worthy activities. When I turned 40, a subconscious reaction to all the time consuming obligations to family, clients, church, and boards I served on, combined with a feeling of loss of that younger adventurous self, began to manifest as a mid-life crisis. A sports car and Harley didn't cure it. The joyful satisfaction I'd felt with my family, friends, and business was constricting while a whiney discontent was expanding in my psyche and behavior.

When she reached her limit of toleration, that's when Alicia told me to go take a hike on the other side of the world. The simple pleasure of putting one foot in front of the other hiking the highest trail on planet Earth released the pressures that had built up in my psyche. My wife's prescribed therapy worked, but it required repetition. With Alicia's loving understanding, and a handshake agreement that she should travel to England and wherever else that suited her fancy at least once every year, I resumed making adventure travel a regular part of my life.

During that first trek in Nepal, and then exploring Jakarta and diving on Bali with Long John, I experienced an interesting duality. I dug the adventures we were having and I missed my family and office. I realized that being grounded at home and in a career with all the responsibilities that attached did not mean that an adventurous approach to life must be put away like childish things. Not everyone feels the pull to go where the pavement ends, but for those that do, it need not end because you're a grownup with grownup responsibilities and obligations.

Trepidation

After reflecting on the epiphany I'd received about how to cope with the terrible burden of a loving wife, two beautiful boys, a growing law business, and leadership roles in worthy organizations, I turned my attention to the more immediate issue. I was supposed to get some sleep by order of our fearless leader. But sleep did not come. It was comfy in my synthetic-down sleeping bag. Leaving my little yellow cocoon to be assaulted by wind and sleet while pushing myself up a 20,000-foot-high mountain was not an appealing prospect.

Trekking through Ladakh was both exhausting and uplifting. But that last day of hiking --slogging over that vast slippery moraine in the rain -- and then enduring blizzard-like weather huddled alone in a tent the better part of two days -- was cause for questioning the wisdom of my great revelation about living adventurously. Before I left for India, when I was imagining what it would be like to climb a 20,000-foot-Himalayan peak, I saw a beautiful vista after ruggedly meeting the challenge of boldly summiting the peak. It would be a glorious "peak experience". I knew it would be tough, but I'd be prepared. I would take photographs that would bring wonder to the eyes of the folks back in Indiana.

I had not imagined feeling so physically whipped and mentally spent as I was that night awaiting the 1:00 a.m. breakfast call. We had not seen the summit of Kanglachan from base camp, because it was hidden by clouds every day. It rained, sleeted, or snowed every minute of the two and a half days we'd been in base camp. Fog made it impossible to photograph the peak we intended to climb. What little I could see of the mountain looked dark, angry, and hard.

Given my torpid state, it seemed absurd that the guys in our crew were singing and laughing in the kitchen tent. The joyful-musical sounds of their voices slipped through the tent flaps between harsh gusts of wind. While Dorge prepared breakfast, Tsering and three other climbing guides, who had joined the staff after we crossed the Indus River, packed ropes and all the gear for the climb. The expedition and the crew's work were nearly over. The guys were happy in anticipation of tips, a final paycheck, and release from work. The rotten weather was of little concern to them.

I was much less sanguine than our crew. There had been plenty of pain during the trek -- foot blisters, tired legs, the dull ache of the torn meniscus in my left knee, sunburn, wheezing to catch my breath after humping up a high pass -- but the ratio of pleasure to pain was mostly positive. The majestic vistas of the Karakorum, an eagle riding the wind currents at eye level at the top of a 15,000-foot pass, hearty fellowship at the end of a day in the meal tent, and surprisingly delicious dinners cooked by Dorge over a single gas burner – those experiences tilted the balance toward pleasure on the pleasure/pain scale. The climb, on the other hand, with near-blizzard conditions and a dark and cloudy night … the ratio of pain to pleasure was going to take a turn for the worse, I feared.

The Climb

John led our group, along with Tsering and the three additional Sherpa climbing guides, out of base camp at 2:00 a.m. The rotten weather calmed. Was the cessation of sleet and high winds an invitation from the mountain gods?

It felt good to be on my feet, out of the tent, and hiking up the mountainside. No more wallowing in dark ruminations. The climb was on whether the mountain welcomed our attentions or not.

We were a string of pearls, a line of headlamps moving upward in complete darkness. Thick clouds blanketed the sky. Neither starlight nor moonlight pierced the blackness that surrounded the mountain. There was no trail to be seen through several inches of fresh snow, but the Sherpa guides hiked determinably as if they were led by a sixth sense. After a couple hours of steady hiking, we halted on a level expanse. John asked in a low voice whether this was the usual place high camp was set up. Tsering nodded. He said the elevation here was about 18,000 feet. John said it was time to change out of our trekking boots into hard-plastic climbing boots and gaiters.

Other than one practice session under John's instruction, I'd never worn climbing boots before. The boots I'd borrowed from a friend back in Indy were not broken in. With the first step the toes on my right foot were painfully pinched.

I'd never been this high in my life, except in an airplane. I felt fine on the hike up to high camp from base camp. As soon as we stopped to gear up and eat a snack, I began to feel sick. The wind picked up. Light snow turned into dense snow alternating with sleet. My stomach began to churn and then seize up. I had to evacuate my bowels. It felt like a spike was being driven into the middle of my forehead. I was dizzy and couldn't stay in file with the other climbers. I fell behind. I had to crap again. When I pulled my pants up and looked for the string of headlamps to follow, it had disappeared in the darkness. I didn't know where the route was that I was supposed to follow.

Visibility by headlamp had degraded to ten feet. It was a little after 4:00 a.m. Blizzard-like conditions resumed. I tried to find tracks in the snow to follow, but my vision was too blurred to make sense of much of anything. Still, I struggled onward and upward. Periodically I thought I saw the glimmer of headlamps up ahead. I knew I was falling further behind and felt worse with each step up and gain in altitude. Any tracks that might have been left by my teammates were quickly covered with blowing snow.

The team was leaving me behind and I couldn't catch up! A feeling of panic started to creep up the back of my neck. It might have been worse, but altitude-induced nausea reduced the intensity of any feeling. I barely noticed the pain in my pinched toes. Suddenly, out of the screen of blowing snow and darkness appeared Dawa Sherpa, one of the three climbing guides added to our staff. He motioned to follow him.

After struggling for half an hour to follow Dawa's pink down-parka, I knew I was finished. The altitude was probably around 19,000 feet. The nausea was too much. My legs were too tired, and my head and the toes on my right foot hurt too much. We had no hope of catching the main party and would just fall further behind as the weather worsened. I told Dawa to go on, catch the others. I had to go down to get well. He shrugged, raised a hand in salute, and then began to vanish into the blowing snow and blackness above.

I was alone again and exhausted. This was definitely not how I had imagined my first mountain climb. There was no glory in this. I wouldn't even have any photos to show off. The pleasure/pain principle clearly dictated descent.

Meanwhile, unbeknown to me, Judy was 1,000 feet below having fallen behind as soon as we left base camp. I don't know how we missed each other, but we did. She later reported that right after leaving base camp she was short of breath and leg-tired. Pemba, the climbing guide John assigned to Judy (the guide with John, Jess, and Molly was also named Ang Pemba Sherpa) did not have a rope and Judy's crampons were in the other Pemba's pack. The batteries in her headlamp died (too many hours of late-night reading in her tent) and she didn't have spares. When she reached the first crevasse above high camp, Judy knew she was done. It was only about a five-foot jump, but with no rope, headlamp, or crampons, leg-tired and struggling to breathe, Judy made the right decision to descend with Pemba.

After Dawa left, I leaned against an exposed boulder taking the weight of my gear-laden backpack off my shoulders. After resting for a few minutes my head began to clear. The wind and snow backed off a little. Tears started welling out of my eyes and froze on my cheeks. I thought of my boys, and I thought of failure. I did not want to come home to tell my nine and eleven-year-old sons that I had not reached the summit.

Then, Jesus! It dawned on me – I had no idea how to go down. I couldn't see our tracks and didn't know the route down any better than the route up. I could step off a precipice or fall into a crevasse. No one would know. Shit! I had to try to find the others.

So I didn't quit – partly out of shame and partly due to fear. The best choice was up, not down. I had so little leg strength left, I had to plunge the point of my ice axe into the snow and ice above and pull myself up with both hands relying on arm strength. I plunged the axe down and pulled myself up, again and again.

I gained a hundred feet of altitude. Tears continued to leak out of my eyes and turn to icy crust on my cheeks. I couldn't be sure whether I was going up the correct route or not, but I was determined to keep up this painfully slow progress until I reached the summit or collapsed trying. I don't know how long this three-legged sort of upward movement lasted, but eventually two figures appeared through the blowing snow in the illumination of my headlamp. Sitting contemplatively on a rock ledge like two gargoyles were Tsering and Dawa serenely watching my progress.

John sent Tsering back to look for Dawa and me. When Tsering and Dawa met up, they decided to relax and watch my headlamp to see what I would do. Like Olympian gods, they watched my struggles from above. They seemed unsurprised to see me when I finally staggered up to the ledge they were sitting on. I hoped the tear-stains weren't noticeable.

With Dawa leading, Tsering bringing up the rear, and me sandwiched in between, our little train chugged upwards. Twice I fell from exhaustion and dizziness. Tsering pulled me up both times. He stayed close enough to grab hold of me and to make sure I didn't begin to tumble and create an avalanche. Dawa grasped my wrist, and I held onto his, whenever he sensed I was faltering. Six or seven times we stopped for Dawa to cut steps with his axe into seracs, which were ten to fifteen feet high, that we had to climb over.

We traversed two narrow ridges with sheer drops of what I assumed were hundreds of feet on both sides. It was still too dark to see anything below. We crossed ice fields and moraines and climbed up steep and craggy rock formations. I had to stop and rest every ten minutes. I wanted to quit every time we rested. What drove me now was that I did not want to disappoint Dawa and Tsering. They were working so hard to help me reach the summit.

It seemed like the mountain rose up into infinity. The summit remained elusively out of sight. Every time we briefly stopped to rest I strained to see the end point to this Sisyphean torture. Finally, it was there!

The rock face leveled off onto a twenty yard by six-foot platform. Damn! It was a false summit; just a hump below the true summit. Dawa patted my shoulder, smiled winsomely, and urged me on. He said the true summit was only about 30 feet above.

I had to stop and rest three more times before reaching the actual summit. It was marked by an arch of old, ripped Buddhist prayer flags. My breath came in aching rasps, my lips were chapped all over, I was nauseous and dizzy, and my legs felt so weak I didn't think they would support me any longer. I managed to snap a photo of Dawa and Tsering.

47

Tsering is on the left, Dawa is to his right.

I felt no joy or triumph, just mild relief that part of the trial was over. I could tell my boys I'd made it.

We needed to put on crampons to descend. In the confusion of gear distribution at high camp I'd picked up the extra pair of crampons that were fitted for Dax's boots instead of mine. Tsering worked for fifteen minutes without gloves trying to fit Dax's crampons onto my boots. It amazed me that his fingers worked at all in the sub-zero temperature. I'm sure the wind chill was well below zero with wind gusts up to 30 mph.

With crampons finally secured we began the descent down a different side of the mountain than the one we came up. Not far down from the summit we were confronted with a steep, glacial ice field. I expected to rope up, but without explanation Dawa led on and Tsering followed me. (I wasn't sure whether Dawa didn't bother to rope up because he was so confident I wouldn't fall, or because he was sure I would fall and didn't want to be tied to me when I did.) We jumped over a couple small crevasses. At each one, Dawa jumped across first, followed by me. Tsering gave me a helpful shove and Dawa grabbed my arm as I landed on the other side. Then Tsering jumped across.

After jumping across the last crevasse the next challenge was a large messy rock fall, called a supraglacial moraine. After all the work to get the crampons on, we had to take them off to pick our way down through the rocks and boulders. At the end of the moraine was another long glacial ice field. It was about 700 yards long and 50 yards wide. The slope of the glacier was steep enough to get my nerves jangling again.

Dawa and Tsering started to pull their crampons out of their backpacks. I knew that Tsering would work with stoic determination to re-attach mine. But I didn't want Tsering to risk frostbite to his fingers. I suggested that we just slide down the glacier's surface on our butts. The two Sherpas huddled and conferred in their local language. Tsering flashed me a smile, let out a whoop, jumped on his ice axe and shot down the glacier on his butt. Dawa showed me how to sit on the blade of the axe with the handle in between my legs as a steering mechanism. I took off and rocketed down the ice faster than any sled ride in Indiana. The makeshift sled started to veer out of control perilously close to a rock pile on the right side of the ice field. I rolled off the axe and tried to brake using the self-arrest technique John taught us during our training sessions. The axe was ripped out of my hands as soon as the blade struck ice. I rolled onto my stomach, splayed my legs out and braked by putting pressure on my gloved-hands, elbows,

knees, and sides of my boots. It worked! Just before crashing into the rocks, my momentum slowed and I skidded to a stop.

(I later learned that glacier butt-sliding has a high-faluting name, "glissading".)

Photo from *Wikipedia* entry for "glissade"

"I'll never do that again!"

At base camp I collapsed into my tent. Before I fell asleep I looked at my watch. It was 12:15 p.m. My trial on the mountain lasted only ten hours and 15 minutes. It seemed much longer. I stayed in my tent until dinner-time around 6:00 p.m., sleeping intermittently, groaning, and nursing sore muscles.

The pinched toes in my borrowed climbing boots hurt every step on the way up to the summit. On the way down most of my toes felt numb. On inspection, the right little toe, the next two toes, and the left little toe were purple with frostbite. It took over three months for the four toes to regain their natural color and feel normal again. When I finally yielded to Tsering's entreaties to come to the meal tent for dinner, 18 hours had passed since I'd eaten anything other than a Power Bar. But I felt too nauseous to eat. I couldn't even swallow soup broth Dorge made for me. I was too sick to participate in the conversation with the other members of the team. All I had to say was that I would never do that again.

I learned that John, Molly, Jess, and Pemba had summitted with little difficulty. But on the descent Jess fainted three times from acute mountain sickness. Luckily, he was roped to John and Molly when he passed out and only suffered a few more bumps and bruises, along with nausea and dizziness. Jess made a quick recovery at the lower altitude of base camp and felt fine by dinner-time.

Back in Leh, I repeated my pledge to Dax. Never again! When we returned to Delhi I told Snow Lion's agent, and anyone else who asked, that the trek was wonderful, but I was finished with mountain climbing.

Spending a few days touring India and visiting the most beautiful building ever built restored my strength and sense of well being. It did not lessen my resolve to be a one-time-only mountain climber.

The most beautiful building I've ever seen in person or pictures, the Taj Mahal, 1997

About the first thing out of my mouth to Alicia back home in Indiana, after hugs and kisses, was to implore her not to let me forget that one mountain was enough. No way would I do that again! Glad I made it to the summit for the sake of ego, and it was a hell of an adventure, but it would be a once-in-a-lifetime experience. Kanglachan would be the only mountain I ever climbed in the Himalayas.

I know there is a tendency to forget the intensity of the pain in painful experiences that have happy endings. Hence, the so-called "halo effect", which supposedly explains why women are willing to endure labor more than once. I would not let my guard down and give in to the halo effect through the passage of time. The memory of climbing Kanglachan was not going to fade into a rosy glow of a triumphant conquest of a Himalayan peak.

I told anyone who asked during the first few months after my return from India, that the trek was great and the climb was hell; and I'd never try Himalayan mountaineering again. I gave Tsering a generous tip and Dawa a substantial one too. I'm not sure what would have happened to me on Kanglachan without their help. I

51

regularly thanked the God I believed in back then for my safe return home. It felt so good to be back on the flat land of Indiana.

I did feel some pride telling my sons about the adventure. I knew I didn't have to endure the pain and suffering to reach the summit in order to prove to my children that I was worthy to be their father. At the ages of nine and eleven they were more impressed with pictures of weird-looking tropical fish from dive trips than mountains. I knew it for the immature egoistic feeling that it was. But I wanted to be able to look into the eyes of my boys and tell them I did my best, and that I succeeded.

"Dear Dad, I want to be with you ..." A note from 9-year-old Andrew that I carried in my pack during the expedition.

Pride is one of the seven deadly sins condemned by Christian tradition. I knew my family would've preferred that I behaved cautiously rather than recklessly. So it's kind of irrational that ego/pride, wanting to live up to fictional expectations of family, and sheer determination to achieve a fairly frivolous goal drove me onward and upward. Of course, these motivations are not unique to me and have been the source of many far worthier accomplishments than standing on top of a mountain. But it worked.

Chapter Postscript

Jess Roskelley died on April 16, 2019, while I was writing this book, but after this chapter was drafted. Jess was in Canada on the east face of Howse Peak in Banff National Park with two other world-class climbers from Austria, David Lama and Hansjorg Auer. The route the three climbers were attempting is nicknamed "M16", because of its unique dangers. It had only been climbed once before, back in 1999. An avalanche struck and the three teammates were lost. Jess's wife, Allison, was quoted in press accounts describing her husband as a man "who loved with all of his heart." Jess's younger sister, Jordan, was quoted, "My brother died doing what he loved, what he lived for."

Acute Mountain Sickness
Teamwork on Pokalde Peak, Nepal 1998

In 1998, a year after returning from India, I climbed Pokalde Peak in Nepal for the first time. Its summit is 19,050 feet high. The final 50 of the 19,050 feet are the most exciting. Not only because that's the top of the mountain, but because the final 50 feet to the summit are up a steep rock wall that can only be surmounted using rock-climbing skills. Rock climbing at 19,000 feet wearing heavy climbing boots is a lot more thrilling than climbing the granite walls of Seneca Rocks in West Virginia. Pokalde is situated just south of Mt. Everest in the Khumbu region of Nepal. The views from its summit of the Everest Massif to the north, the Himalayan Range as far as the eye can see from east to west, and the singular white peaks and river valleys of the Khumbu to the south are spectacular.

Pokalde Peak, 1998

Within a few months after my return from India the halo effect began to revise my memories of the pain and suffering experienced on Kanglachan. It wasn't really that bad. Hey, no harm no foul! It was actually a pretty cool experience. My sincere commitment not to climb another Himalayan peak eroded and then collapsed.

The membership roster of the American Alpine Club listed one other person in Indiana as a member, Tom Proctor. I contacted Tom and invited him to meet me for dinner. We immediately bonded. Tom told me that, despite growing up in the flatland of Indiana, he wanted to climb mountains all his life. A family story was that before baby Tom could walk his favorite thing to do was to crawl up the stairs in the Proctor house.

Tom's home was in Terre Haute, where he owned and operated a carpet-laying business. He was also trying to develop a mountain guiding company in Nepal. He had a loose partnership arrangement with a Kathmandu-based company called Himalaya Wonderland Treks, which was owned by a Nepali named Keshav Prasad (KP) Kafle. For the last two years Tom had spent half the year in Nepal climbing and working as a mountain guide and the other half laying carpet in Terre Haute, Indiana.

By the end of our dinner meeting winter of 1998 Tom and I were planning a two-mountain expedition for October, 1998. The plan had three major goals. First, trek to Everest Base Camp; second, hike south to climb Pokalde Peak; and third, hike east to climb 20,305-foot-high Imja Tse aka Island Peak. Tom's job was to hire the crew and lead the expedition. Mine was to pay for it.

Mt. Everest Base Camp and dealing with altitude sickness
As we neared Mt. Everest Base Camp I developed a severe case of Acute Mountain Sickness. The first symptom was a headache, which felt like a nail being driven into my forehead. The headache lasted all night at Lobuche. The headache was painful, but I could deal with it. Lobuche is two trekking days shy of Base Camp, our first goal. A bad headache was not going to deter us from achieving goal number one.

The headache subsided while we were hiking up the trail from Lobuche to Gorak Shep the following day. The last and northern most campsite on the Base Camp Trail below Everest Base Camp is at Gorak Shep (meaning dead crows or ravens). Gorak Shep is a yak kharka at 16,900 feet. It was used as the base camp for the Swiss climbing team, which nearly succeeded in achieving the first summit of Mt. Everest in 1952, a year before the first successful summit by Edmund Hillary and Tenzing Norgay. The Brits established their base camp for the attempt to climb Everest in 1953 on a moraine immediately adjacent to the mountain. That location has been Everest Base Camp since then.

In 1998 Gorak Shep was an austere place; a dead and frozen lake bed covered with sand and rocks. There are four lodges in Gorak Shep now. But in 1998 the only structure was a low, wood shed barely fit for temporary human habitation. It was a shelter for porters, who worked independent of any expedition companies and didn't have tents to sleep in. At night, these ruggedly tough men gathered inside the shed around a lone iron stove for warmth. They picked up clods of yak dung and tossed it in the stove for fuel. The porters huddled together on the dirt floor sharing body heat, while they slept. Piles of their shit and piss accumulated around the outside of the shed. Gorak Shep was a very unpleasant place before the lodges were built, but it was the last campsite on the trail to Base Camp and provided the only shelter for porters without tents between Lobuche and Base Camp.

Nausea struck the night we camped at Gorak Shep. I didn't barf, but my roiling stomach sent me dashing out of the tent to rip my pants down as fast as I could to spray the ground with diarrhea. In the morning when we started the last stage of the trek to Base Camp, I was experiencing ataxia (a terrible feeling of fatigue, dizziness, and loss of muscle control). Ataxia is the last symptom of altitude sickness before death. But I was absolutely determined to make it to Everest Base Camp.

I had great views of Mt. Everest during the last stages of the 1995 trek, but the terminus of the trek was several hiking-days south of Base Camp. I badly wanted to see Base Camp. And, if we failed to achieve the first of our three goals for the expedition, because I couldn't handle trekking to Base Camp, how could Tom and I possibly accomplish our second and third goals, which were actual mountain climbs!? No matter how bad and how weak I felt, I couldn't spoil the expedition for Tom, or for me.

I took this photo of Mt. Everest during the 1995 trek. I think the shot was taken near the medical clinic at Pheriche. Mt. Everest is called Sagarmatha in Nepal and Chomolungma in Tibet. Its summit is the highest elevation on our planet at 29,029 feet.

Our sirdar, Krishna, argued that we should hire a strong porter to carry me back to the medical clinic on the Base Camp Trail in Pheriche. Earlier that day, we'd seen a big, red-headed German climber, who was suffering from AMS, being carried down the Base Camp Trail in a doko basket by a Nepalese porter half the big redhead's size. (People in Nepal are referred interchangeably as either "Nepalese" or "Nepali". The national language is also called "Nepali".) I stubbornly refused Krishna's advice. I was going to finish the trek to Everest Base Camp if I had to crawl there.

So I staggered on up the rugged trail behind Tom and Krishna. We parked our butts on a ridge over looking Base Camp. I did not have the strength to walk down onto the moraine where the colorful tents of climbing teams were pitched. No matter, our first goal was accomplished, sort of. I didn't quite get there, but I got to see Base Camp.

The scene was kind of disappointing. By the third week of October, which is late in the climbing season, most of the mountaineering teams had already torn down their tents and evacuated Base Camp.

Bleak-looking Everest Base Camp in 1998 on the huge moraine adjacent to the mountain; elevation 17,600 feet

When it was time to start back down the Base Camp Trail, I had difficulty standing up because of dizziness and ataxia. Krishna and Tom were convinced that I needed immediate medical assistance. They wanted to call for a helicopter evacuation. A benefit of the American Alpine Club was mountain rescue insurance. Since I was a member, the club's insurance would cover a helicopter rescue. But pride (that insidious sin) did not allow me to accept any form of help to extricate myself from the predicament. I got myself into the mess. I needed to hike my way out of it.

The American pioneer ethic of self-reliance was passed down through generations of my family. My ancestors were early settlers in what became Elkhart County, Indiana. Whether it is small-town Midwestern cultural upbringing (nurture) or a strain of genetic stubbornness (nature), prideful stubbornness is one of my character traits. My parents chided me from the time I was a small child for being stubborn, "like a Missouri mule". We considered ourselves Indiana Hoosiers, but the first six weeks of my life were at Ft.

Leonard Wood in Missouri.

It took us two and one-half days to hike up the trail from Pheriche to Everest Base Camp. It takes less time to hike back, because the trail going south from Base Camp is mostly downhill. It was going to be a long, painful day with Tom walking in front of me and Krishna at my side.

Tom is built similar to John Roskelley, around five-feet-nine-inches tall but slimmer than John. Like John, Tom didn't carry an ounce of fat on his muscular frame. He also had John's tough as nails approach to life. I thought of myself as fairly athletic and disciplined, having played varsity sports in high school and college. The toughness of serious mountain climbers is on a completely different level.

Nepali mountain guides also have a uniquely high level of gritty toughness. Krishna was around five foot four; about average height for a Nepali in the 1990s. But he was more powerfully built with more muscle than the typically slight build of Nepalese men. One day on the trek his foot broke through a rotten board on a footbridge. He scraped the entire length of his shin from the top of his hiking boot to his knee. Blood ran down his leg and pooled around the sock. He just shrugged and kept hiking.

My consciousness was fuzzy, like an analog TV set not quite tuned on to a station. My focus and determination was singular, as we hiked hour after hour down the trail to Pheriche – don't fall and put one foot in front of the other. We arrived well after sunset with our headlamps lighting the trail the last few hours. It took over 12 hours to hike from Gorak Shep up to Base Camp and then down to the medical clinic in Pheriche. Pride and stubbornness prevailed once again over caution and good sense. But it worked.

Treatment at the highest medical clinic in the world

In 1998 Pheriche (altitude 14,340 feet) was a dry, dusty-wind-swept plateau. It was nothing more than a yak herding station, until the Himalayan Rescue Association (HRA) built a medical clinic there in 1975. A couple of the Sherpa families, who were yak herders and potato farmers in the area, saw an economic opportunity and built primitive lodges near the HRA clinic. Their customers were outpatients of the medical clinic and trekkers who wanted a break from sleeping in tents.

We spent the next two days in Pheriche while I recovered my strength. Tom was not disappointed in this turn of events. A former climbing partner of his was one of the volunteer doctors at the HRA clinic. Sandra (false name) was about six feet tall with dark hair, a light complexion, and beautiful strong-features. She looked like a superb athlete, and Tom said she was. Dr. Sandra was a delightful conversationalist and an experienced Himalayan climber. The best part of my therapy for AMS was sitting outside the clinic at night under the gigantic star-lit sky listening to Sandra and Tom trade tales of their climbing adventures. The stories got better the more chang (beer) and rakshi (moonshine) they drank.

Left to right: Krishna, Sandra, and Tom

Sandra explained that the key to relief from the symptoms of AMS is sleeping at a lower altitude. She agreed with Tom that it would also be helpful to stay in a lodge for a couple nights instead of a tent. I'm not sure how sleeping in an unheated room with plywood walls was any more therapeutic than sleeping in a tent, but I acquiesced. Sandra also prescribed diomox, drinking lots of water, rest, and light exercise. All symptoms of AMS vanished after two days and two nights at the lower altitude in Pheriche.

I was not ready to acknowledge it in 1998, but after a couple more experiences with AMS, it became clear that I am very susceptible to altitude sickness. Research indicates that there is a genetic component which gives rise to a predisposition to AMS. That may explain why all my known ancestors dating back to 16th Century England lived in lowlands. My love of the Himalayas was at war with my genes.

My lodge room in Pheriche was typical of lodges on the Everest Base Camp Trail in the 1990s. The toilet was an outhouse (*charpe* in Nepali) with a bucket of water beside a hole in the ground; no shower facilities. Lodges along the Base Camp Trail are much improved since then. Most have private bathroom facilities, heat and air conditioning.

Finding Pokalde Peak, glacier melt, and sheep without a shepherd
We had a little excitement and frustration trying to establish a base camp at Pokalde Peak. Neither Krishna nor Tom had climbed

or scoped out Pokalde prior to our expedition. Our trek from Pheriche to Pokalde came to a halt when we discovered that a section of the trail Krishna thought led to the base camp was covered with a mass of rocks and boulders from a landslide. Tom and Krishna scouted ahead picking their way over and around boulders and rocks strewn across the narrow mountain trail. While our cook, Ram, three porters, and I sat on boulders off the trail awaiting Tom and Krishna's scouting report, a few small rocks came whistling down off the mountain. Two bowling-ball-sized rocks bounced down the mountainside and rolled across the trail just ahead of us. When they returned, Krishna looked embarrassed and downcast. Tom was annoyed. He announced that it was too risky, especially for the porters with their heavy loads, for us to try to scurry across this dangerous section of the trail. We had to turn around and spend the rest of the day retracing our steps to find another trail to Pokalde base camp. This "lost" day put us three days behind schedule. The other two were my recovery days at the HRA clinic.

In 1998 Pokalde Peak was a great introductory peak for a novice climber. There was enough ice and snow that climbing boots, crampons, and ice axe were required for the climb. It was steep enough that climbers needed to rope up for a portion of the ascent. The summit was reached with an exciting wall climb at 19,000 feet in the shadow of Mt. Everest. The entire climb from base camp to summit and back could be accomplished in six to eight hours. That description still holds today, except that almost all of the ice and snow on the mountain have melted due to the warming climate throughout the Himalayan region.

The world's glaciers are currently losing 369 billion tons of snow and ice each year and are shrinking five times faster now than they were in the 1960s, according to a 2019 study by the World Glacier Monitoring Service at the University of Zurich. And, the melting rate is increasing. I've witnessed close up the impact of global warming on two peaks in Nepal, Pokalde and Yala Peak (elevation 18,700 feet). When I returned to Pokalde in 2006 it was completely barren of ice and had just a bit of snow on one side near the summit. I was on Yala Peak for the first time in 2004 and it had a glacier covering two-thirds of one side of the mountain. On a return expedition in 2007, there was no glacier on the mountain.

What's especially worrisome about glacier and permafrost melt in the Himalayas is that glacier run-off and ice and snow melt are the water sources for the Himalayan region. All the rivers and streams across the Himalayas from Bhutan, Tibet, Nepal, Northern India, Pakistan, to Afghanistan and beyond are created by runoff from the mountains. Many millions of human, animal, insect, and plant lives depend on the reliability of that water source.

When Krishna, Tom, and I arrived at the base of the 50 foot wall immediately below Pokalde's summit we discovered six European climbers looking distraught. They were shuffling around and arguing about what to do. It wasn't clear whether they were together in one group or were a bunch of individual climbers trying to figure out how to get over this last barrier to the summit. They didn't have a sirdar or climbing guide. They looked like a small herd of sheep with no shepherd to lead them.

Our three-man team sprang into action. Krishna hauled a 60-meter coiled nylon rope out of his pack. Tom looped one end of the rope around a boulder at the base of the rock face. He deftly tied a double-figure-eight knot and tested the rope to make sure it was securely anchored by the boulder. Krishna shouldered the rope and began free-climbing the rock wall playing out the rope as he ascended. Krishna powered his way up the rock face with quick strong moves like he was climbing a ladder. He disappeared for a few minutes beyond the crest of the summit. I knew Krishna was tying the other end of the rope around a boulder at the summit. He reappeared, leaning out from the summit waving his hand to signal the rope was secure.

While the other "climbers" watched, Tom stepped into his harness, pulled it up so the leg loops fit snug around his thighs, and then buckled the belt firmly around his waist. I did the same. Tom clipped two interlocked carabiners onto the loop at the front of his harness. He clipped a third carabiner onto the rope, then clipped and locked it onto the other two. I did the same. Tom began ascending, climbing with more graceful and careful moves than Krishna. When he was about twenty feet up the rock face, he signaled me to start climbing.

It occurred to me that we were violating many of the rules of safe rock climbing I'd learned at Seneca Rocks. We weren't belaying each other. Krishna had not set any protection into the wall. The purpose of securing a rope to the rock face every ten feet or so with nuts or cams is that, if a climber slips off the wall, she won't fall all the way down. The device securing the rope to the wall will break the fall, so the climber will fall no farther than back to the last fixed point plus the number of feet he was above the fixed point. Since we weren't belaying each other and the only fixed points of the rope were at the base and summit of the rock face, if Tom lost his grip and fell, he'd come crashing down on top of me. Our bodies would be smashed on the boulders at the base of the rock face.

A picture of our mangled bodies lying there where my boots were as I reached up to find a hold and begin the climb did not enter my mind. Instead, the thrill of climbing that wall infused my body with an excited energy. It was an adrenaline rush to put my climbing skills to the test at 19,000 feet. The climb was essentially free climbing the wall. A carbineer clipped to a rope offered no protection other than the possibility that, if I lost my hold on the rock and started to fall, I might be able to grab hold of the rope. Not sure how I could have gotten a grip back on the wall while hanging on a rope, but that was a theoretical issue. After I clipped on to the rope and began climbing, my attention was focused laser-like on finding the next crack to jam my fingers into and the next bump for a foothold.

Tom Proctor climbing the final pitch toward the summit of Pokalde Peak, 1998

As soon as I pulled myself up over the last impediment to stand on the summit, Krishna and Tom grasped me in a group bear hug. We whooped and hollered for a few seconds, then looked down. A grizzled old German fellow (he looked over 50; 10-15 years younger than the author is now) wearing a brown deer-stalker hat with its earflaps down was climbing up the rock face clipped onto our rope. When he reached the top, we slapped him on the back and congratulated him. He didn't speak English, so we communicated with sign language. Tom and Krishna pointed at and named all the high peaks we could see. Then, we took turns taking pictures with each other's cameras. None of the other climbers followed.

Left to right: Tom, Krishna, and the author on Pokalde Peak summit with Mt. Everest in the background, 1998

Why didn't any of the other Europeans, who were milling around at the base of the rock face, follow us up to the summit? I can't speak for the grizzly German in the silly hat, but I had confidence in the two professional guides, who selected the route up to the summit. Tom, Krishna, and I practiced rock climbing on a hillside by Pheriche. They'd observed my technique during our practice sessions. We knew how to work as a team, to anchor the rope, tie on, and climb securely. Although we didn't set protection on the rock wall, I trusted Tom and Krishna's judgment that my free-climbing skill was sufficient to handle the challenge.

Some people might assume that the old German and I were risk-taking adrenaline junkies. I don't see it that way. On each of the fourteen Himalayan expeditions I did, there was a professional guide. If a mountain climb was planned, professional climbing guide(s) were added to the crew. One of the criteria for a "good" adventure is to know your own limitations. Another is to make use of professional help, when needed. I became a trek organizer and expedition leader, but not a professional guide. I am not and never intended to become an elite climber or a guide. I always relied on the real professionals on Himalayan expeditions to make the hard decisions, like whether to cross an avalanched trail or climb without protection. (Except for the "getting lost" experience described in the last chapter of the book.)

As an aside, Nepalese people in the tourist industry resent Westerners who try to trek or climb without using a local guide and porters. Tourism is the second biggest industry in Nepal after agriculture. Spending money to utilize the services of Nepal-based expedition companies is very important to the local economy. Had the European climbers we encountered on Pokalde hired a local guide, they would not have looked like lost sheep without a shepherd.

Survivor's Guilt
Mera Peak, Nepal 1999

Due to the time lost for my recovery from altitude sickness, Tom, Krishna, and I were unable to attempt climbing Imja Tse (Island Peak). But hey, achieving two out of three goals ain't bad. The next Himalayan peak Tom and I set our sights on was Mera Peak the following year, 1999.

We planned the expedition to Mera in October. Two friends, Judy (same Judy as in the Ladakh expedition) and Heather, who we met during the Pokalde expedition, signed up for the expedition. The elevation of Mera Peak is a 21,247 feet. The mountain is in the south-eastern corner of the Khumbu region in Nepal. Most of the trekking and mountaineering expeditions in the Khumbu commence at the airstrip in Lukla Village. After landing in Lukla, the vast majority of trekkers and climbers head north up the Everest Base Camp Trail. The trek to Mera goes south from Lukla and then east. If the lower right corner of the map of Sagarmatha National Park (previous page) was extended to cover more territory, Mera Peak would be located below the Legend.

The expedition was staffed by Tom's friend, KP Kafle, through his company, Himalaya Wonderland Treks. Our sirdar and climbing guide for Mera was Seth Chettri. We had the same cook for Mera, Ram, as for the Pokalde expedition. A kitchen boy, Suk, and four porters, Jid Baldoo, Mon Baldoo, Pal Mansung, and Chandra completed the roster of our team. The eleven-day trek to Mera base camp was surrealistic, over high mountain passes, across rushing glacier-fed streams, slipping and sliding through a muddy bamboo forest, and past the remains of a Sherpa village that was wiped out by an avalanche. It rained every day the first week of the trek. The next four days we hiked above the snow line, which was 14,000 feet. Hiking at the higher elevations we were no longer getting soaked from rainfall, instead, we hiked through blowing snow the last few days to base camp. The snow was knee-deep on the high trails. Drifts were thigh high. At base camp, we endured four days of harsh weather; high winds, blowing snow, and sleet.

Every attempt to summit Mera was stymied by blizzard conditions. We did manage to set up a high camp between 19,000 and 20,000 feet. But each push for the summit was cut short by dangerous conditions on the mountain. No one in the fifteen different climbing teams we shared Mera's base camp with in October 1999 managed to summit the mountain.

I spent the last day on the mountain in a tent by myself, retching and wretched once again with altitude sickness.

Mera Peak high camp

Snow continued falling when our defeated and bedraggled team finally gave up and hiked out of base camp. At sunrise on the second day of the hike out, my tent sagged with five inches of snow which accumulated over night. Flakes the size of cat paws continued falling as we ate breakfast, packed gear, and then trudged 2,000 feet up the backside of a 15,000-foot high pass, called Zatrwa La. This was the last high pass we had to cross before the trail dropped down to lower elevations and leveled off the last few miles to Lukla Village. Once we were over and down the Zatrwa La the end of the misery of daily rain, snow, and high winds would be close. We'd be in Lukla Village by dinner time. A restful night in a lodge awaited; we'd fly out of Lukla the following day in a Twin Otter back to civilization in Kathmandu.

By the time we post-holed up to the crest of the pass, the fresh snow on Zatrwa La was over two feet deep.

Barely visible through the falling snow on a ridge above and behind us were splotches of red and yellow. I could just make out the figures of three Nepalese porters from another climbing team in their colorful parkas. The three Nepalese guys were inching their way across the ridge, slowed by the blowing snow and the heavy loads they were carrying.

Deep-unconsolidated-fresh snow on a mountainside creates the potential for avalanches. The snow all the way across the Himalayan Mountains in October, 1999 was extraordinarily deep due to unusually extreme precipitation. The rain that fell on us every day the first week of the trek was snowfall on mountains at the higher elevations. Whenever the sun was able to peak through the clouds and raise the ground temperature on the mountains, ice melted beneath the deep-unconsolidated snow and avalanches roared down the mountainsides. We saw several avalanches on the trek to Mera base camp. In base camp, while we hunkered down in our tents hoping the weather would clear, we heard the distant roar of avalanches every day. They were not close enough to be dangerous.

When Seth, Tom, Heather, Judy, and I crested the Zatrwa La, the altitude was around 15,000 feet. We paused to look down the 4,000-foot descent into the valley below. We were tired from post-holing through deep snow for several hours to reach the top of this high pass. I was still weak from a lingering case of AMS. The trail down from the high pass is very difficult. It is steep with multiple switchbacks. We could not see any evidence of the trail. The mountainside was covered in a blanket of snow.

I think all five of us had a sense of foreboding as we looked down the steep ridge breathing hard from the struggle up the backside of the pass. There was more to that sense of foreboding than contemplating the challenge of descending the steep and slippery slope. It was eerily quiet.

Heather suggested we spread out for the descent. She feared one person might slip and knock others down in the fall. Or worse, a tumbling body could cause an avalanche. Tom argued that we should stay close to each other. If one of us started to fall, the others could grab and support their teammate. Judy and I glanced nervously around. Although we hadn't roped up when we hiked up the Zatrwa La on the trek to Mera base camp, I wondered whether we ought to do so for the descent. Seth was carrying rope in his pack, so we could... Heather yelped and took off running. Tom cursed. Seth bellowed, "Go!" There was a low rumbling sound behind us.

We started running after Heather. Judy fell and cried out. Tom and Seth grabbed her arms, pulled her up yelling in her face, "Run! Run!"

I saw them out of the corner of my eye as I pounded down the rocky, snow-covered slope, stumbling into and over boulders hidden by snow. My consciousness narrowed to a pin hole. The only thought was run! Run, keep going down to survive. The roar of the avalanche was deafening. Spindrift enveloped everything in an opaque whiteness. I could barely see my gloves and boots. I couldn't see my teammates. I ran, slammed a boot into a snow-covered rock, stumbled, ran, scraped a shin on a boulder, ran...

At the bottom of the pass I fell to my knees gasping. All five of us made it. We stared at each other mutely. I turned to look back up the mountain. There was nothing to see except a vast whiteness. There was no sky, no mountain, white dust filled the air. The avalanche petered out before it reached us in its cold fury. Only spindrift thrown up by the crashing wave of rock, snow, and ice blew up around and over the five of us as we ran down the mountainside.

The three Nepalese porters from the other expedition had disappeared -- vanished in the gigantic white wave. We later learned they were killed. Four other men died in a series of avalanches across the Nepal-Tibetan Himalaya within a couple days. We also learned that the three men who died above us were taking a more dangerous shortcut to avoid the Zatrwa La in an effort to get their sahibs' gear back to Lukla before the sahibs arrived. (During British rule over the Indian Subcontinent "sahib" was a term applied by Indians to Brits. It was used to refer to the boss man and/or white colonialists in general. In the 1990s some Nepalese still used the term to refer to white men, especially customers or clients on trekking/climbing expeditions.)

One of the seven men who died in that series of avalanches merited international news coverage. The famous American mountaineer, Alex Lowe, was killed by an avalanche on Shishapangma in Tibet. The deaths of the six Nepalese porters in avalanches were mentioned in news reports as footnotes to the loss of a great American mountain climber.

Aftermath of the avalanche and Didi's loss

Seth, Tom, Judy, Heather and I sheltered behind a low rock wall at the bottom of the Zatrwa La. After we brushed and shook the spindrift off our packs and parkas, Seth instructed the four of us to hike on to Lukla. He planned to climb back up to the top of the pass to find our four porters and kitchen boy. The five of them were carrying the tents, cooking equipment, and the duffel bags containing most of our clothing, sleeping bags, and climbing gear. Ram and the five of us left camp that morning ahead of the porters. Seth instructed Ram to take the lead in order to mark a path through the snow we could follow. Seth wanted the porters to follow us, because six pairs of boots breaking a path through the deep snow would make easier work for the porters to get through. So we left camp while the guys in our crew were still packing tents and cramming gear and bags into their doko baskets. Post-holing through drifts of thigh deep snow was difficult enough for us carrying our expedition packs. It would be murderously hard for a porter carrying 70 or more pounds of gear in a wicker basket by a cord looped over his forehead.

We didn't know whether our porters had been injured in the avalanche or were trapped on the other side of the Zatrwa La. They were a couple hundred yards behind us the last time I'd seen them before the avalanche struck. Ram must have been speed-hiking well ahead, because we didn't see him on the Zatrwa La. He probably didn't even know we'd just avoided catastrophe.

We followed Seth's instructions. We slung our expedition packs onto our shoulders and watched Seth disappear up into the blowing snow. We turned our backs on the Zatrwa La and resumed the trek to Lukla.

You already know Tom and Judy from previous chapters. Sorry for delaying a longer introduction to Heather. Tom and I met Heather at Pokalde base camp the year before the Mera expedition. It was a surprise meeting. Recall that we'd been stymied by an avalanched trail in our initial attempt to find the base of Pokalde Peak. We established a base camp near the mountain in a lovely secluded meadow. The standard base camp for Pokalde climbers was closer to the mountain. But we liked our camp, because there were no other humans in sight. It was a little surprising to see a petite, light-brown-haired woman walking toward our camp the afternoon before we climbed Pokalde. We invited her to join us for a pot of tea Ram had just brewed. Heather said she was Canadian. She was with a trekking group camped back at Pheriche. She'd wandered off by herself to enjoy some solitude and to do some photography on her own.

There was an immediate attraction between Heather and Tom. Before they parted that day, contact information was exchanged. I wasn't too surprised when Tom informed me a few months later that Heather was joining our Mera Peak group. They became "a thing" during the Mera expedition. They shared a tent when we were near a water source and they could wash up enough "not to smell like homeless people", as Tom put it.

It took ten hours to hike to Lukla Village, after splitting with Seth. I was still weak from AMS, so my task once again was to focus on not falling and to put one foot in front of the other. We had to wade across three knee-deep glacier-fed streams. The water was freezing and running fast as the massive snowfall melted and ran off the sides of the surrounding mountains. We were bone tired, wet, and emotionally drained when we arrived at our lodge (coincidentally named, Mera Lodge) in Lukla Village. Ram was already there and on his third glass of rakshi.

We pulled off soaked-through hiking boots and socks and huddled up to the wood-burning stove in the Mera Lodge trying to warm up cold, wet feet. Ram, Heather, Judy, Tom, and I were safe, but as the night wore on we became increasingly worried about Seth and the other five guys. Hours ticked by. No sign of them.

Around midnight, Tom and Ram hiked back to the nearest stream. It was the last of the three streams we'd crossed to get to Lukla. They returned with a disturbing report. The knee-deep stream we crossed around 6:00 p.m. had become a raging river, neck high. It was impossible to cross. They ended their hunt for our missing guys and returned to the lodge.

Ram and Tom's report dramatically increased our shared anxiety about the fate of our friends. Did the porters survive the avalanche? If they did, how could they possibly cross a swollen stream five feet deep?

Fearful ignorance about where our guys were was bad enough, but another concern arose. The son of the owners of the Mera Lodge was supposed to arrive that evening in Lukla by helicopter from Kathmandu. The helicopter had not arrived. Fear was spreading through the lodge that the chopper might have gone down. It left Kathmandu on schedule. Didi was growing increasingly distraught with worry. ("Didi" means "older sister" in Nepali. Women who own or run lodges in the Khumbu are commonly called Didi. The term is used like it is the woman's name but also her title as owner-operator.) Didi's husband was away on business. She had to bear the dread of what might have happened to her son without her husband. Didi had two younger daughters to try to comfort.

Before exhaustion drove the guests at the Mera Lodge into our respective sleeping bags on cots in the lodge's common room, over twenty of us gathered in the dining room to pray. Buddhists, Hindus, Christians, atheists, and agnostics all united in the fervent hope for the safe arrival of Didi's son and for Seth and our porters. Sick, wet, and exhausted, as most of us were, we tried to fight off with prayers the dread that was melting away confidence in the safe return of our friends and Didi's son. People sang, chanted, spoke quietly, and meditated silently, each in their own way.

Heather, Didi and her two daughters; the photo was taken before we learned of the helicopter crash.

We had to wait another day-and-a-half to learn what happened

74

to Seth and our crew. Seth found the five guys huddled together near the crest of the Zatrwa La. The two youngest, Suk, our kitchen boy, and Chandra, were hypothermic and too weak to make it down the 4,000-foot descent under their own power. Seth and Jid Baldoo, the senior porter, carried Suk and Chandra down to the bottom of the pass. Seth and Jid climbed back up to the top of the pass and brought Suk and Chandra's doko baskets down.

The ethics of Nepalese guides and senior porters do not allow them to abandon their sahibs' gear. They will risk their lives to preserve their company's tents and their clients' personal belongings. I once saw a sirdar dive off of a ridge with a 1,000-foot drop to save a daypack carelessly dropped by a client. He caught the pack and slid to a stop about twelve feet down the side of the ridge with torn clothes, scratches, and bruises from the tumble. With a grin on his face, the sirdar handed the pack back to his client.

Seth Chettri is large for a Nepalese guy. The Chettri are the warrior caste in Nepal. In 1999 he stood about five-foot nine-inches tall and I guessed about 160 pounds. Seth was in his early twenties with a mop of straight black hair typical of all Nepalese regardless of caste. He spoke English well, and he told me his dream was to win a scholarship to the National Outdoor Leadership School in the US. He loved to practice English telling and hearing dirty jokes.

Jid Baldoo was also tall for a Nepali at about five-foot eight-inches. He probably weighed 140 pounds. Most Nepalese porters are small and slight standing five-foot-two to five-foot-six inches and weighing between 120 and 140 pounds with virtually no body-fat. Jid is Tamang, which is one of the many tribal-ethnic groups in Nepal. The Tamang have lived for centuries on the slopes of the Himalayas as subsistence farmers and herders, neighbors of the Sherpas.

After the government of Nepal opened the country to tourism subsequent to the first summit of Mt. Everest in 1953, Tamang men, like their Sherpa neighbors, sought employment with expedition companies as porters. Over time, Sherpas moved up the economic ladder in mountain tourism becoming cooks, guides, lodge owners, and owners of expedition companies. Most of the Tamang working for trekking companies remained on the lower rung, employed as porters. Ram had worked his way up to cook, but his English was too rudimentary to become a guide.

Left to right: Seth, Pal Mansung, Suk, Mon Baldoo, Jid Baldoo, and Chandra
playing cards in the meal tent at Mera base camp

Jid Baldoo was a trusted senior porter with Himalayan
Wonderland Treks. He recruited the rest of our crew of porters from
his village. Although he spoke no English, I got to know Jid during
the 1998 Pokalde expedition. We developed a friendship, because he
carried the duffel with my clothes and gear on the 1998 and 1999
expeditions. I gave him my rain jacket on the second day of the
week of rain we endured hiking to Mera base camp. I had a rain
poncho to wear in place of the raincoat. Jid was the envy of other
porters on the trail, because, back then, expedition companies were
not required to supply porters with rain gear or cold weather gear.
Most of the porters wore cloth coats which soaked through in rain
and weren't sufficient protection to ward off the cold at high
altitudes and at night.

In the 1990s most Himalayan expedition-porters wore flip flops
or cheaply-made Chinese tennis shoes. Some even went barefoot on
snow-covered-icy trails. They were paid $4 to $8 per day and had to
provide their own food. They were treated abysmally by Western
standards. But for subsistence farmers, working as a porter on an

expedition was a plum job. The average income in Nepal back then was about $1 per day. Making four to eight times that amount, plus the expectation of a tip and receiving a share of the food, clothing, and gear left over at the end of the expedition, was a bonanza for those lucky enough to get hired.

After Seth and Jid carried the two loaded dokos to the bottom of the Zatrwa La, they divided all of the gear and equipment between themselves, Pal Mansung, and Mon Baldoo, the two other porters strong enough to carry a heavily laden doko basket. Pushing Suk and Chandra along, the six of them set off in the dark for Lukla.

When they reached the first stream, it was waist high. Seth tied a rope to a boulder, waded across and tied the other end to a boulder on the other side. He helped Suk and Chandra cross the river. Jid, Pal, and Mon passed the dokos filled with gear across. They repeated the process at the second stream. The third stream was up to Seth's shoulders and running too fast to cross. The six of them spent the rest of the night in a tent soaking wet beside the river. The temperature that night was below freezing.

Around 9:00 a.m., after waiting two nights and a day, I heard whistling coming up the lane outside the Mera Lodge. Suk and Chandra were barely walking, still suffering from hypothermia. Seth was whistling a jaunty tune as he walked up the steps into the lodge. Seth proudly announced that none of the gear was lost. He and Jid each carried about 120 pounds from the bottom of the Zatrwa La to the Mera Lodge. They hiked around twenty miles on mountain trails and across three swollen, fast-running streams, part of the time in the dark, while caring for Suk and Chandra. Seth climbed down the Zatrwa La three times and back up twice before starting the hike to Lukla.

The vigil for Didi's son did not have a happy outcome. The aged Sikorsky transport-chopper crashed. A messenger informed Didi in the early morning after our prayer service. Didi joined a search party later that morning to find the downed helicopter and hunt for survivors. We learned that evening that there were none. Didi's son died with all the others on board.

The bad news spread quickly and quietly among the guests at the Mera Lodge. It left each of the members of our team with a terribly empty feeling. We couldn't even express our sorrow for her loss to Didi. She didn't return to the lodge that day. Seth, Judy, and I flew out of Lukla before she returned. Tom and Heather left to do some easy trekking on their own.

When Tom and I stayed at the Mera Lodge at the beginning and end of our Pokalde expedition the prior year, it was so different. After we returned as "conquerors" of Pokalde Peak, Didi invited us to a private party she was hosting of local dignitaries. We sang, danced, drank booze, and stuffed ourselves with food. Didi and her friends taught us a style of Nepali folk dancing. Tom and I demonstrated how to fast dance to rock 'n' roll. It was a blast.

Planning the Mera Peak expedition, Tom and I looked forward to staying at the Mera Lodge again. I imagined we'd have another great time at the lodge, when we returned after summiting Mera Peak.

There was no celebration to commemorate "conquering" a mountain after our return from the Mera Peak expedition. There was a brief moment of joy at the lodge, when Seth and the crew returned. But then, we had to tell the guys about Didi's son. The joy over our crew's safe return flickered and died.

PTSD?

About six months after returning to Indiana from the Mera Peak expedition, I was driving home on College Avenue from my office in downtown Indianapolis. Tears started streaming down my face. I pulled the car over into a parking space on the side of the street. I sat in the car crying and shuddering for several minutes. I felt overwhelmed with grief and guilt. I had a few sleepless nights after returning from Nepal, but nothing like the incident on College Avenue. The picture was seared in my mind of the three porters just before they disappeared in the white tsunami. That vision often appeared unbidden while I lay in bed awaiting sleep. It started showing up during the day when my consciousness was not fully engaged with work.

I did nothing to help those three men. Rationally, I knew there was nothing I could do for them. I did nothing to help Seth and Jid care for Suk and Chandra. Rationally, I knew I would have just gotten in the way had I tried to help. I was weak from AMS. As strong and experienced a climber as Tom is, he knew that only Seth was physically capable of climbing back up the Zatrwa La to aid our guys. I knew there was nothing I could have done to save Didi's son. But it was so unfair, so terrible, that this kind and generous woman lost her eldest child that way.

It didn't matter that my inability to help was just the way it was. I was a lawyer and a father. It was my job to solve problems, help people in need, and care for weaker and smaller people. I knew it was irrational, but I was carrying a deep feeling of guilt. It broke to the surface that day I was driving home from the office.

When I regained control of my emotions and later pondered on the meaning of that momentary breakdown in the car, I self-diagnosed the incident as symptomatic of a minor case of PTSD. More importantly, what really hit home was the realization that there was something terribly wrong with Nepalese porters risking their lives to carry sahibs' gear through an area where avalanches were occurring. It wasn't right that the tough, small, strong, and sweet-tempered men, who worked so hard as expedition porters, were dying in order to give First World climbers and trekkers an exciting adventure in the Himalayas. How utterly, selfishly ridiculous! So we could gratify our egos by standing on top of a peak and claim to have "conquered" a mountain, these lovely people were risking their lives for a few dollars a day. It wasn't right. It was wrong.

I called Tom in southern Indiana and Judy in Montana a few days later. I told them about the emotional turmoil I was experiencing. Both of them said they too were having trouble dealing with what happened. Whether it was a form of survivor's guilt or mild post traumatic stress disorder, we agreed that porters should not have to risk their lives on mountaineering expeditions to please their "masters". It was not justifiable.

I was well aware of the material benefits to the men the expedition companies employed, but I no longer wanted to take part in an enterprise that could be responsible for the injury or death of Nepalese farm boys trying to make extra money for their families by portering for mountaineering expeditions.

I had participated in four Himalayan expeditions in five years. I swore off mountaineering after the 1999 Mera expedition.

I did not return to Nepal for four years. It was no longer safe to visit Nepal, anyway. A violent Maoist revolution against the King had broken out. Pitched battles were fought between the Maoists and the Monarchists. There were shootings and bombs going off in Kathmandu. A significant portion of the population supported the Maoist guerillas. President George W. Bush declared the Maoists a terrorist organization. The US State Department declared Nepal unsafe for American travelers. The number of tourists visiting Nepal drastically declined.

To slake my need for adventure I began doing solo and group sea-kayaking expeditions. The risks were all on me or on the group members. No poor natives in need of cash involved.

Golden Jubilee and Hillary's inspiration to philanthro-trek

May 29, 2003 was the golden Jubilee, 50th Anniversary, of the first summit of Mt. Everest. Nepal beckoned. The country desperately needed tourists to return. The Maoist rebels and the government declared a truce in the civil war. The Hillary family put its considerable resources to work at bringing tourists back to Nepal. Sir Edmund was going to co-host with the King of Nepal a black-tie affair in Kathmandu, and Hilary's son, Peter, would co-host with the High Lama of Tengboche Gompa the highest party in the world on the grounds of the monastery at 12,700 feet.

I decided to heed the call and return to Nepal. I didn't plan to climb any mountains. Instead, I would trek through the Khumbu to Everest Base Camp at 17,600 feet and then to Tengboche Monastery for the big party. I wanted to interview Sherpas who lived in the Khumbu, old-time mountaineers, and novice trekkers along the Base Camp Trail and at the highest party in the world. I wanted to learn what people thought about how 50 years of tourism had affected the local culture and environment. I wanted to know whether the risks porters were taking were worth it. I needed closure. The way I would get it would be to research and write about the whole damn enterprise that started with Hillary and Tenzing's "conquest" of Mt. Everest.

What I received from my journalistic trek in 2003 was not exactly what I wanted. But, as Mick Jagger put it, "You can't always get what you want, but if you try sometimes you just might find, you get what you need." I wanted to do one last trek in Nepal and write about what I discovered as to how 50 years of exposure to tourism had affected Sherpa culture. An editor at *The Atlantic* responded positively to my query about publishing what I wrote, so my ultimate goal was to write a piece worthy of publication in the magazine.

My supposition was that tourism had irreparably damaged the local culture. I would prove that point, and pin the blame squarely on the shoulders of the Western mountaineers who first invaded the Khumbu and spread the infection of materialistic consumerism, which had contaminated Sherpa culture. Sir Edmund Hillary, the first and foremost violator of the purity of Sherpa culture, would be an easy target to blame.

Instead, I came away from Nepal in 2003 with the inspiration to emulate what Hillary had done in partnership with the Sherpa people. I could do it on a much smaller scale!

I didn't meet Hillary. He was too infirm at age 83 to do any mountain trekking. I did meet his older sister, June, his son, Peter, and many members of the extended Hillary family on the Base Camp Trail. Instead of wallowing in guilt about men who suffered or died helping him and his climbing partner, Tenzing Norgay Sherpa, to become the first men to summit Everest, Hillary devoted much of the rest of his life to working with Sherpa communities to improve the standard of living of the Sherpa people through Hillary's family foundation. Hillary's primary function with the foundation was to raise money. The Hillary Foundation capitalized on Sir Edmund's popularity as one of the 20th Century's most famous people. He became a great fundraiser, and the money he raised was spent on building schools, medical clinics, water systems, and hydroelectric plants in the Khumbu.

I returned to Nepal many times after participating in the Golden Jubilee celebrations in 2003. Instead of focusing on the adventure and personal challenge of climbing a mountain, I started a foundation, organized "philanthro-treks", and developed a special relationship with the Rai people of Basa Village. In partnership with the people of Basa and a sister foundation in Nepal, the Basa Village Foundation USA ("BVF") has funded two school buildings, a water system, a hydroelectric plant, and sponsored many other culturally sensitive projects to improve the standard of living in the Basa area. The foundation became a major part of my life.

I thought up the term "philanthro-trek" one evening at the North Face Café in Kathmandu after completing the Base Camp trek. A bunch of veteran mountaineers and trekkers gathered there for food, drink, and conversation after the Jubilee celebration was over. We were talking about how much we loved coming to Nepal to hike and climb and that we wanted to give back to the people of Nepal. We each felt a deep indebtedness to the country which had given us such wonderful experiences. One member of the group supported a shelter in Kathmandu for unwed mothers and their children. Another raised funds for several village schools. A third worked with a technical school on the edge of the Kathmandu Valley. Two others had each spent a year as teachers in village schools, and another helped staff one of the few medical schools in Nepal.

Having studied the Ancient Greek language in college and seminary, the made-up word "philanthro-trekking" came to mind. *Philanthropos* means love of humanity in Ancient Greek. Attach the English word, trekking, and you've got philanthro-trekking.

My comrades liked it. We agreed that "philanthro-trekking" expressed what we were talking about in combining trekking with giving back to the people of Nepal. Organizing treks to introduce other Americans to the beauty of the Himalayan region and doing culturally sensitive development projects through the BVF became the primary way I've engaged in philanthro-trekking.

1999 was the last time I trekked or climbed with Tom. By 2004 he had given up on trying to develop a guiding business and was focused on developing his carpet-laying company and a real estate business in Terre Haute. It's been fifteen years since our last communication. I lost touch with Heather soon after returning home from the 1999 Mera expedition. Although Judy and I have not seen each other since our shared experiences in the Himalayas in 1995 and 1999, we are still in contact by email and Facebook. After more trouble at high altitude, Judy figured out that she had "altitude induced asthma". She tells me that she has since restricted her climbing adventures to 14,000 feet or lower.

On philanthro-treks I led since 2003, I sometimes stopped at a trail bend looking out at a magnificent Himalayan vista and remembered without tears. I remembered and honored the heroic strength and goodness of Seth Chettri. Seth fulfilled his dream to come to the US and train as a mountain guide in the Rockies. Tom related to me a couple years after the Mera expedition that Seth had married an American woman, was living in Seattle, and working as a house painter. I also remember and honor Jid Baldoo, an illiterate subsistence-farmer and porter, whose strength and heart were as great as anyone I've ever known. And, I remember the three porters I saw disappear in the avalanche. I honor them too.

I have not felt guilt or shame about what happened on the Mera expedition of 1999, since I received the gift of inspiration from Sir Edmund Hillary and his family in 2003.

Desecration of Mother Goddess, Hiking with Hillarys, Threats to Sherpa Culture, Speed Climbing Everest, and Lama Tenzing's Koan at the Highest Party in the World
Everest Base Camp and Tengboche Gompa 2003

The Golden Jubilee of the first summit of Mt. Everest was celebrated in May 2003. Among the festivities was "the highest party in the world" at Tengboche Monastery. I spent over three weeks from mid May into early June trekking around the Khumbu region of Nepal. The primary purpose of this trek was to interview Sherpas and veteran Himalayan mountaineers about the effects on Sherpa culture of 50 years of exposure to Westerners. I planned to write an article about the Jubilee celebrations and what I learned from the interviews and additional research.

Three treks in the Khumbu during the 1990s led me to conclude that traditional Sherpa culture was at war with modernity, and tradition was losing most of the battles. Research supported that conclusion. The following quotes from a September 1983 article by Mathew Kapstein, titled "Sherpas: Religion and the Printed Word" in *Cultural Survival Quarterly Magazine* summarizes the concerns expressed by many of the experts on the subject.

During the sixties and seventies, an appallingly rapid cultural deterioration occurred in some communities. Villages that a generation ago could boast at least rudimentary skills in written Tibetan among the entire male population now had only one or two old men who could read the language of their religion. Monasteries, temples, and libraries fell into disrepair. Precious collections of printing-blocks began to rot. With little support for the exercise of traditional artistry, skilled craftsmen now had to earn their livelihood by producing tourist art, e.g., woodblock prints of Spiderman for the Kathmandu marketplace.

The author did, however, see "signs of improvement", because of the diligent efforts of the abbot of Tengboche Gompa, Lama Tenzing, who you will meet in this chapter.

In Khumbu, the most heavily-touristed of the Sherpa districts, the situation has recently shown signs of improvement. Tengboche monastery, on the trail to Mount Everest, has, through the efforts of its industrious abbot and many local and foreign friends, reasserted its position as a living center of Sherpa Buddhism.

Kapstein ends his piece with the unremarkable conclusion that the ultimate fate of traditional Sherpa culture will be determined by the local people themselves.

It is to be hoped that once the present period of intense cultural change has passed the Sherpas will find a balance between their old traditions and their current national and international roles; for, in the final analysis, the survival of Sherpa culture depends on the Sherpas themselves. Some foreign support can be beneficial, however, if applied to locally designed projects and institutions which stand in real need of immediate assistance. Negligence in these cases will only leave the next generation with a poorer legacy, and all too little from which to rebuild.

The major challenge of the 2003 Jubilee trek was to determine whether the decline of traditional Sherpa culture had reached an irreversible tipping point. A secondary challenge was to do a trek carrying all my own stuff. The only one of the 14 Himalayan treks I did in which I carried my own gear and food was in 2003. All the others were staffed expeditions with porters carrying most of the clients' personal kit, tents, food, and kitchen. All the stuff needed for a 24-day trek was split between Hari Pudasaini and me. Hari served as my guide and interpreter for the interviews I conducted. Hari is a big, gregarious Nepali of high caste, Brahmin birth. Hari was from a "suburb" of Kathmandu. He is a city-slicker, unlike most Nepalese sirdars, who come from mountain villages. Hari has the fine-textured black hair of high caste Nepalis and a robust figure rather than the small, slight frame of most of his countrymen. He stands about five-feet-nine inches tall and probably weighed around 160 pounds in 2003.

Carrying a significant portion of our supplies for three weeks reinforced my admiration for Nepalese porters. My burden was only about 45 pounds, and I carried it in a North Face expedition backpack. I typically carried around 15 pounds in a backpack on treks. The only exceptions were on climbs when carrying the extra weight of climbing gear was necessary. It was tough hiking up and down Himalayan trails from 7,000 to 18,000-feet high carrying 30 more pounds than I was used to. Before that experience I was amazed at the ability of porters to carry loads of 60 to 120 pounds in their doko baskets. After the experience of carrying 45 pounds for three weeks, I was even more amazed.

The first article I wrote after returning from Nepal in 2003 was entitled, *Rape of the Mother Goddess*. As the title indicates, the tone of the article was angry. It expressed my disgust at how Mt. Everest had been desecrated with pollution. When I visited the Khumbu in 1995 its austere beauty, both the mountains and Sherpa Buddhism, deeply touched me. When I returned after the grievous experiences of 1999, my eyes and pen were more critical. It was clear to me that trekking and mountaineering had polluted the local environment and culture of the Sherpas. I understood the desire of Sherpas to benefit materially from the economic development of tourism. And I understood that environmental pollution was one of the unfortunate consequences of economic development. What I wanted to better understand was why Sherpas had cooperated in the rape of the environment and seemed willing to trade their austerely beautiful culture for lucre.

In retrospect, I have to admit that my anger and guilt over what happened to the porters on Zatrwa La and Didi's son influenced the tone of that article. *Rape of the Mother Goddess* was a release through writing. It was also true.

I did not attack Sir Edmund Hillary. The article expressed tremendous admiration for him and his family. Hillary spent much of his life introducing "white people" to the beauty of the Himalayas through his travel company, World Expeditions. He combined that with his philanthropic efforts through his family's foundation, the Himalayan Trust. By encouraging trekkers and climbers to visit the Himalayas, Hillary was inevitably contributing to the pollution I was so incensed about. What differentiated World Expeditions from some of the other expedition companies was that it was an early exponent of "green trekking". Its leadership and staff were diligent in practicing the green ethic of "take nothing, leave nothing". I learned from Hillary's family about "Big Ed's" gratitude to the Sherpas who helped him become rich and famous. The approach Hillary took to working on development projects in the Khumbu was first to listen to the local people. He wanted to learn what help they wanted from him rather than telling them

86

what they needed and how they should change. Hillary was a great admirer of the   Buddhist traditions of the Sherpas.

Researching and writing *Rape of the Mother Goddess* was the beginning of my study of the issue of whether development led by "first world" philanthropists and governments, which is intended to improve the quality of life in "third world" villages, ultimately helps or harms the local community. After writing a few more articles and a book (**Bringing Progress to Paradise**), which addressed that issue, I developed a college course on the topic. I taught the course at Marian University for one semester and Butler University for two semesters. I wanted to help open the eyes of young people to consider how "we" should try to help "them", or whether they should just be left alone. Hillary's approach to development in the Khumbu was the inspiration for my ideas of "philanthro-trekking" and "culturally sensitive development".

Economic development can improve the quality of life of under-developed communities in certain measurable respects, such as reduced infant mortality, increased life expectancy, better equipped schools, better trained teachers, more sanitary drinking water, greater crop yields, etc. But the values of materialism, commercialism, and consumerism, prevalent within developed capitalist-nations, are probably in conflict with the traditional values of the local culture to some extent. So, can people from the developed countries in which materialistic values are the norm work with communities in under-developed countries, like Nepal, to offer the benefits of improved infrastructure, while respecting the traditional values of the local communities? Will communal-cooperative values and a more spiritual approach to life necessarily be "polluted" by commercialistic-consumerism by the cross-cultural contact of tourism? (One can question the accuracy of my assumptions that the indigenous cultures of the Himalayan region are more cooperative than competitive and more spiritual than materialistic. Fair enough; but that view is shared by academics who have studied the local cultures and by everyone I know who has direct experience with the traditional cultures of the Himalayan region.)

The tentative conclusion that I reached in 2003 was that "culturally sensitive development" requires leadership and ownership at the local level. Outside help should be limited to financial aid and advice, when asked for. If that delicate balance could be maintained, then it might be possible to improve the material aspects of life in indigenous communities and have a minimal impact on the local culture. Hillary family members didn't express their approach to development in the Khumbu exactly that way. But that is the conclusion I drew from my research in 2003.

During the Jubilee celebrations I encountered well-intentioned people from developed nations and well-intentioned indigenous people dealing consciously and unconsciously with the conflicts in values that inevitably occur when an under-developed community seeks outside help to raise its standard of living. There are many examples of Western materialistic values overwhelming traditional communal values in less developed nations. But how to do development within traditional-indigenous communities the right way requires more sensitivity than just recognizing the danger in trying to impose "outsider values" on a community.

The first example of this issue that I tried to analyze was the relationship which developed between Sherpas and commercial mountaineering. Mountaineering brought tremendous economic benefits to the Khumbu Sherpas. It also brought tremendous amounts of garbage into the Khumbu and changed the traditional way of life of many Sherpas. Did it have to go that way?

Brief history of the rape and efforts to rescue Chomolungma
Sherpas and Tibetans call Mt. Everest "Chomolungma", which means Mother Goddess in their indigenous languages. Sherpas know through their folklore that their ancestors migrated from the Tibet-side of Chomolungma to settle below her southern flanks. Ethnologists agree that the Sherpas did, indeed, cross over the Everest Massif into what is now the Khumbu district of northeastern Nepal around 600 years ago. For many generations Sherpas lived around Chomolungma and the other great peaks in the Khumbu without any desire to try to summit the high peaks. The oral histories of the Sherpas do not relate any stories about climbing mountains for sport. But the Sherpas' relationship with Chomolungma and the other high peaks in the Khumbu began to change in 1921.

In 1852 the Great Trigonometric Survey of British India determined that Peak XV is the highest mountain in the world. An

Indian mathematician employed by the Brits, Radhanath Sikdar, calculated that the peak was over 29,000 feet high. His boss, Surveyor General Andrew Waugh, recommended the mountain be named after the previous Surveyor General, Sir George Everest. In 1865 the Royal Geographical Society accepted Waugh's suggestion (over Everest's protest). There was no serious attempt to map and climb the mountain until after World War I ended. In 1921 the first British expedition to attempt to climb Everest approached the mountain from the Tibetan side. Nepal prohibited European explorers from entering the Khumbu region until after World War II. Tibet, on the other hand, after a military invasion by the UK and threat of further violence, allowed a few European cartography and climbing expeditions to enter the country during the 1920s and '30s. It closed its borders again after World War II.

The 1921 British Everest Expedition approached the mountain up through India and then across Tibet. Some Sherpas were employed, along with many Tibetans, as porters, cooks, and guides by the British. Members of that first team of cartographers and climbers extolled the virtues of their Sherpa "coolies". Word began to spread among European alpinists about these tough and loyal people called Sherpas.

The reaction of Tibetans and Sherpas to the European efforts to climb the high peaks was quite different. Tibetans were taught by their high lamas that Everest and the other 8,000 meter peaks were inhabited by demons and yetis. Dzatrul Rimpoche, the abbot of the Rongbuk Monastery, who was worshipped by Tibetans as a living Buddha and incarnation of Padma Sambhava, warned the second British Everest exploration team and its "coolies" in 1922 of the dark and dangerous forces awaiting them on the mountain. As to mountain climbing, the Rimpoche wrote in his autobiography: "I heard … with great effort they use magical skills with iron nails, iron chains and iron claws, with great agony, hands and feet frozen … to have limbs cut off, the others stubbornly continue to climb … I felt great compassion for them to suffer so much for such meaningless work." (Quoted from *Into the Silence*, pg. 406.) Before the 1922 expedition reached its base camp at the foot of Everest it's no wonder that all the Tibetan porters and yak herders threw down their loads and refused to get any closer to the demon-infested mountain. After a near riot during which stones were thrown by

Tibetans at the British sahibs, the Tibetans were paid off and released from their duties.

The Sherpa porters did not desert their paymasters. They did not consider employment by "white people" on a mountaineering expedition "meaningless work". They took to it, like they were born to it. Even fatal accidents which befell fellow Sherpas on climbing expeditions didn't deter other Sherpas from working for the sahibs. 9 of the 11 deaths which occurred on Mt. Everest during the attempts by the British to "conquer" the mountain in 1922 and 1924 were Sherpas. The other two were Englishmen. The Brits began to call their most valued Sherpa porters "Tigers", because of their strength and fearlessness at high altitudes.

Many of the high peaks in the Himalayas were summitted by Europeans with Sherpa assistance during the 1920s from the Tibetan side. The highest, Everest, eluded them. The most famous mountain climber of the era, George Leigh Mallory, died in the attempt along with his climbing partner, 22-year-old Andrew Irvine. Mallory and Irvine died in a summit bid on June 9, 1924. The monsoon had just begun, which brings even stronger winds and more snow and sleet to the mountain. Except for one observer in high camp the rest of the climbers and support staff had retreated down the mountain due to illness and the increasingly dangerous weather conditions. The best evidence is that neither Mallory nor Irvine made it to the summit.

Irvine's body has not been found. Mallory's was found 75 years later in 1999 by a team with the specific mission of trying to locate the two climbers' remains and to try to determine whether they reached Everest's summit or not. Mallory is best remembered for his oft quoted response to the query, why try to climb Everest? "Because it's there." The statement was made in response to an American journalist's question the year before Mallory died on Everest. He went on to explain in the interview that he thought it was part of human nature to try to conquer the whole universe. Mallory was very much a man raised in the traditions of British public schools and imperialism.

When the King of Nepal finally agreed to let Western explorers, cartographers, and mountaineers into the Khumbu region after World War II ended, the next generation of Sherpas happily joined the assault on the Mother Goddess. They welcomed the economic opportunities created by the "white people" who wanted to "conquer" the Mother Goddess. There might be yetis up there, but Sherpas were not afraid of the demons that frightened their Tibetan cousins. Sherpas proved their mettle to Western mountaineers in the 1920s and were ready to prove they were still the Tigers of the Himalayas when attempts to climb Everest from the Nepal side began in the 1950s.

In the early 20th Century the Sherpas were the poorest tribal-ethnic group in Nepal. "Sherpa" simply means "the people in the east". They were the hillbillies, who eked out a subsistence living herding yaks and growing potatoes. Sherpas were looked down on by the dominant castes of Hindus in Nepal. Sherpas are less than 1% of Nepal's population. Yet, by the end of the 20th Century they were internationally famous and admired, because of their mountaineering skills. They were no longer the hillbillies of Nepal. Mountain tourism in the Khumbu made the Sherpas the richest tribal-ethnic group in the entire Himalayan region.

The imperialistic expeditionary-style of mountain climbing in the 20th Century employed armies of porters in siege-like assaults. The 1953 British expedition to Everest, under the military-style leadership of Sir John Hunt, employed 350 porters and used 20 local guides. The vast majority of the support staff were Sherpas. To feed and supply the expedition, tons of food and material supplies were carried into the Khumbu on the backs of porters, yaks, and mules.

How many members would you guess were in the actual climbing team? The correct answer is 10. Of those 10, it was expected that only two would be able to summit. The small army of almost 400 members left behind mountainous piles of trash on the way to and at the besieged mountain. All that pollution of the land was collateral damage so that two men could stand on the summit for a few minutes. But at least none of the Sherpas or climbers died on Everest during the 1953 expedition. Each of the many massive expeditions that sought to "conquer" Mt. Everest and her sisters through the 1950s and well into the 1960s trashed the mountains and trails in the Khumbu. (That's why I used the term "rape" in the title of my ranting article.)

During the 1970s the style of mountaineering began to change. Advocates for more of an alpine style of climbing, like Reinhold Messner and Peter Habeler, influenced the change. Messner and

Habeler were the first climbers to summit Everest without oxygen in 1978. In 1980 Messner was the first to solo climb Everest. Sherpas were still needed by most Everest climbers, but in smaller numbers. The economic loss to the Khumbu Sherpas from the reduction in scale of mountaineering expeditions was offset by increasing numbers of climbers on mountains other than Everest and the increasing popularity of trekking.

Sherpas who worked on the mountaineering expeditions in the 1950s and '60s as porters, cooks, and guides learned how to make money from the Western expeditions. In 1964 the government of Nepal opened the Khumbu to trekking tourism. Many people from wealthy countries wanted to hike through, gaze at, and photograph the High Himalayas. Sherpas leaped at the opportunity to increase their financial take from hard-earned wages as porters and guides to profits from campsite rentals, teahouses, lodges, restaurants, and eventually airlines.

Litter along the trails and on the mountainsides was a small price to pay for the economic benefits mountain climbers and trekkers brought to the Khumbu. It's also important to understand that yak herders and mountain villagers had no familiarity with trash on the scale brought into the Khumbu by Westerners. Virtually everything people in the Himalayan region used was biodegradable. Houses were made of stone, wood, and hardened mud. Clothes were made from wool and yak or other animal skin and pelts. Containers were mud-baked pottery. Fuel was dung and sticks. Himalayan villagers did not understand that metal and aluminum containers, plastic bottles, rubber boots, and the many other items made from synthetic materials brought into the Himalayas by climbers, trekkers, and tourists, would not go back to the earth. Even during the 1990s I witnessed local people just dropping candy-bar wrappers, plastic bags, and foil tobacco-pouches on the trails. My sirdar in 1995, Nyima, explained, "The local people, they don't know any better. We are just learning about environment."

To Sherpas, trashing trails and mountainsides was an unfortunate consequence of their new economy. A more enlightened understanding of how to deal with trash began to evolve through a long, slow process beginning in the 1970s. The ethics of mountaineering began to change as the approach to mountain climbing transitioned from the militaristic assault on the mountain to more of an alpine style of climbing. A greater concern for the environment, and a sense of responsibility, began to develop among climbers, trekkers, and local communities. The "take nothing, leave nothing" ethic has spread throughout the Himalayan region.

The government of Nepal issued regulations in 1979 which required trekking and climbing expedition companies to burn or bring their garbage out of Sagarmatha National Park. The regulations were largely ignored and not enforced. In the 1990s various organizations and expedition companies led voluntary cleanup projects in the Khumbu. Locals were enlisted to help. The first expedition devoted to removing trash from Mount Everest occurred in 1994. 3,200 kg (704 lbs) of trash and two-hundred discarded oxygen tanks were carried out of Sagarmatha National Park. In 2014 the government issued a new regulation as a condition for receiving a climbing permit for Everest. Each member of an expedition is required to bring out of the park at least 8 kg (17.6 lbs) of garbage in addition to the trash they generate themselves. Each expedition team has to deposit $4,000 with the Sagarmatha Pollution Control Committee. The deposit is refunded when the required amount of trash is delivered to rangers at the park entrance as the climbers exit the park. In the spring of 1999 a cleanup campaign led by Sherpa climbers brought down 7 tons of garbage from Mt. Everest and 4 tons along the Base Camp Trail.

(We'll return to the topic of green ethics in a later chapter. You'll learn why the Rai people of Basa Village deserve to be called super-environmentalists.)

Something else Sherpas gained from working with "white people" on the early mountaineering expeditions were the techniques of mountain climbing. Some of the Tigers of the early expeditions were taught rope skills and how to use crampons and an ice axe. High altitude porters needed mountaineering skills to transport supplies from base camp up the mountain to the high camps. The inherent racism and pride of British and European expedition leaders excluded the possibility of considering a Nepali or Tibetan worthy of being an actual member of a climbing team. The "coolies" could do the hard work to give climbers the chance of conquering a peak, but, "Harrumph and dear me old chap! We certainly couldn't consider one of them worthy of standing with one of our lads on a summit."

That attitude changed when Himalayan climbing resumed after World War II in the 1950s. A Tiger, Tenzing Norgay Sherpa, was elevated from high-altitude porter to membership on the 1952 Mt. Everest Swiss Team. Tenzing came very close to summiting Everest with the Swiss in 1952. In 1953 he was co-star of the British team with Ed Hillary.

Fifty years prior to my 2003 trek, on May 29, 1953, Tenzing Norgay Sherpa and a lanky Kiwi, Edmund Hillary, were the first known human beings to stand upon the pinnacle of Chomolungma. The mountain was measured at 29,035 feet above sea level. (The accepted elevation measurement was later reduced to 29,029 feet, based on the highest point of solid rock, as opposed to ice and snow.) In the early 1950s the Brits, Swiss, and other European teams devoted tremendous resources to putting the first man on the summit of Mt. Everest. It seems kind of funny that the two men who achieved the goal were from Nepal and New Zealand. A generation later, Sherpa climbers have equaled, broken, or set every significant sport-climbing record on Mt. Everest, including speed of ascent and number of ascents. Sherpa climbing guides set ladders and ropes for the other climbers on Mt. Everest and serve as the lead guides for most of the commercial climbing expeditions.

Hillary and Tenzing ascending Mt. Everest (photo by Flickr user agirregabiria, Smithsonian.com, May 22, 2013)

The "conquest" of Everest in 1953 did not stem the tide of climbers wanting to try to "stand on top of the world". Instead, the demand for permission of mountaineering teams to attempt Everest increased. The Nepalese government gave in to the demands and began to issue more permits each year after 1953. When the government began issuing trekking permits in 1964, the flow of "outsiders" into the Khumbu increased almost every year for the next four decades. The government and the Sherpas realized that mountain tourism was a revenue source unlike any previously known in Nepal. So many people from wealthier nations wanted to hike among, gaze at, and photograph the highest mountains on Planet Earth. The number of trekking permits issued to enter Sagarmatha Park reached 25,000 by the end of the 1990's. The vast majority of trekking permits issued were for hiking the Base Camp Trail during the months of May and October. (Snow drifts block the high passes of trails in the Khumbu during the winter. Hiking is very unpleasant during the rains of the summer monsoon. So, spring and fall are the most desirable times to trek and climb.)

Within a few decades tourism became Nepal's second-largest industry after agriculture. The foundation of the Sherpas' economy was transformed from yak herding and potato farming to seasonal tourism.

So it was that the attraction of the Mother Goddess brought the wealth of the West to the Sherpas. The Sherpas learned how to porter, cook, and guide for mountaineers. They were happy to put those skills to work when trekkers began flowing into the Khumbu. Some Sherpas realized more money could be made by owning their own mountaineering and trekking companies, rather than working for foreign-owned companies. Others were inspired by the capitalist spirit to try entrepreneurial ventures, like campsites, teahouses, restaurants, lodges, and even domestic airlines.

How did the Sherpas repay the Mother Goddess for what she did for them? Initially they contributed to the desecration of the mountain with human waste, rubbish, O2 canisters, and the dead bodies of failed climbers. Many Sherpas have come to regret the rape of the Mother Goddess, and some are now at the forefront of her rescue.

Satellite phone station at Everest Base Camp, 2003

Whores and hypocrites or the strongest and kindest people in the world?
A friend, who is the leader of a Buddhist community in Sikkim, told me in 2003 that he thought the Sherpas had become "whores" for tourist dollars and "sold off their sacred places." He claimed that Buddhist communities in Sikkim, Bhutan, and Ladakh have done a better job of protecting their sacred places than the Sherpas.

Yet, most Westerners, who encounter the Sherpas on treks in the Khumbu, leave extolling the virtues of these amazing people. Their characteristic super-human toughness and gentle Tibetan-Buddhism inspires effusive praise. "They are the strongest, toughest, yet kind, friendly and most gentle people I've ever met." That is the sort of description I've heard numerous first-time trekkers exclaim about the Sherpas. Old Himalayan hands gush about them just as enthusiastically. "It has been my privilege to work with and get to know these kind, generous, extraordinarily gifted people." (Quoting Jim Whittaker, the first American to summit Mt. Everest, in a letter to *Outside Magazine*, July 2003.)

Are Sherpas whores and hypocrites, or the most amazing and wonderful people in the world? I became well-acquainted with a number of Sherpas during my treks through the Khumbu prior to 2003. Despite the rancor I felt about the business of mountaineering, my view in 2003 was that calling Sherpas whores or hypocrites was far too harsh. It seemed to me that most Sherpas are, like most of us, economic opportunists. They saw the opportunity to do better financially through tourism, so they seized it. Sherpas who owned land along the trekking trails developed campgrounds, teahouses, lodges, and restaurants. By the beginning of the 21st Century Sherpas owned one of the most profitable domestic airlines in Nepal, Yeti Air. Wouldn't it be more than a little hypocritical for well-off citizens of developed nations to look down on these folks for seizing the economic opportunities "we" helped to create?

By 2003, most of the porters, kitchen boys, and cooks employed by expedition companies were not Sherpas. They were Tamang, Rai, and Gurung, the tribal-ethnic groups that are neighbors of the Sherpas. Most of the climbing guides and sirdars were still Sherpas. But so many Sherpas found easier ways to make a living through tourism than working the manual-labor jobs for expedition companies, the companies had to look outside of the Khumbu to find employees.

During my fourth visit to the Khumbu I intended to discover to what extent the successful development of tourism had changed the character and culture of the Sherpas. Did my Sikkimese friend's charge that they'd become whores to capitalism and Buddhist hypocrites have merit? Or, had Sherpa culture managed to accommodate entrepreneurial capitalism, and its fruits, i.e., material wealth, without losing its traditional values and way of life?

Unfortunately for the Khumbu Sherpas, and all of Nepal, tourism began to decline in the 21st Century because of the Maoist insurrection and the political instability that followed the June 2001 slaughter of the royal family by the Crown Prince. After 9/11 and the paranoia in the US about international terrorism, the Maoist rebels in Nepal were classified as a terrorist organization by the State Department. Travel to Nepal was discouraged. The outbreak of SARS in 2003 in Southeast Asia further fueled fear of travel to Nepal. (We return to these destabilizing historical developments in a later chapter.)

When the number of tourists visiting Nepal dropped to half the average number it had been in the 1990s, increasingly desperate economic conditions dictated that something had to be done. So the government devised a plan. Use the May 29, 2003 golden Jubilee of the first summit of Mt. Everest to entice tourists to come back to

Nepal.

The family of Sir Edmund Hillary joined forces with the government to promote tours, treks, mountaineering expeditions, and even a marathon run starting in Base Camp. Sir Edmund would co-host with the King of Nepal a black-tie affair in Kathmandu, and Hilary's son, Peter, would co-host with the Incarnate Lama of Tengboche Monastery the highest party in the world. The government negotiated a temporary truce with the Maoists, so there would be no disruption of Jubilee events. I responded to the plea to return to Nepal by planning to trek around the Khumbu during the celebrations, and to drill down on the question of how 50 years of exposure to Western values had actually affected the Sherpa people.

Jubilee Trek and the Hillary Clan

The first day on the trail to Base Camp, I was surprised by the number of new lodges and lodges under construction since my last visit to Nepal in 1999. If tourism had declined over the last four years, why were so many new lodges being built? I asked this question of local people as I hiked through Sherpa villages on the way to Base Camp. The responses I received expressed optimism about the future of tourism in the Khumbu. Most of the local people I spoke with were certain that trekkers would return in even greater numbers in the future. Several Sherpas I interviewed, who made their living off tourism, expressed the view that the problems of the world, and even the national problems of Nepal, were irrelevant in the Khumbu. They argued that trekking in the Himalayas was an escape from the problems their customers had back home. So it just made sense that tourism would increase again when Americans, Europeans, Australians, Japanese, etc. were reminded by the Jubilee Celebration that Himalayan trekking is the greatest escape of all.

Sherap Jangbu Sherpa, owner of the Panorama Lodge in Namche Bazaar, put it this way: "Chomolungma and all her princesses are still here, unchanged and beckoning to the adventurous spirit of the Western trekkers and climbers. And the Sherpa people will await the return of the visitors. We will be here to provide the food and lodging and guiding, when it is needed again."

Sherap's response is a lyrical expression of Sherpa optimism. Neither he nor anyone knew in May 2003 that the Jubilee was but a brief respite in the civil war between the Maoists and the Monarchists. The war resumed when the celebrations ended and the fighting continued for three-and-a-half years.

In Phakding on the second day of the trek, I asked the young manager of the Himalayan Chain Resort Lodge, Chimi Tsering Sherpa, whether tourism had changed the essential character of the Sherpa people. He assured me that the character of Sherpas had not changed, but supplied contradictory information to support his assertion. "Tourism brings us much more money, and so is good for Sherpa people," Chimi insisted. "Khumbu is not good place for agriculture. It is too hard to grow food here," he explained. He went on, "Sherpas copy foreigners, but the character of Sherpas has not changed. We are strong. We can carry 40 kilos (88 lbs.) to 5,000 meters (16,404 ft.)." But Chimi followed up that proud assertion about Sherpa strength with contradictory statements. "Because of tourism, some are rich and fat, but the tourism money is all good." He also said, "Sherpa people are shy. They don't like to see girls in shorts and pee by trail. Sherpas hide. Sexy dresses still bother Sherpas. Thirty percent of Sherpa children copy foreigners and learn Bob Marley and Ricky Martin songs. The ones that go to school in Kathmandu change the most."

The contradictions in Chimi's responses reflect a cultural conflict. Sherpas are still strong. But some Sherpas are fat and rich, because of tourism. Sherpas still have conservative-traditional values, so they are offended by revealing clothing. But 30% of young Sherpas prefer contemporary-foreign culture to their own. On the surface Chimi's contradictory statements may seem confused. In truth, I think they well represent the conflicts Sherpas have been dealing with since their economy began to transition from barter-trading, herding, and subsistence farming to be dominated by tourism.

My guide and interpreter, Hari, and I camped on the grounds of The Himalayan Chain Resort, where Chimi worked. When we sat down to dinner in the lodge's meal room, seated to my left was an elderly white-haired woman who turned out to be June Carlyle (age 86), Sir Edmund Hillary's older sister. Around the table were 15 Hillary family members, including Sir Edmund's nieces, nephews, cousins, and in-laws. The Hillary Clan, led by their matriarch, June, was making a pilgrimage trek up the Base Camp Trail. June planned to hike to Khumjung Village, where the first school for Sherpa children was funded by the Himalayan Trust. She also planned to visit the nearby Kunde Village Hospital, the first medical clinic established by the Himalayan Trust.

June Carlyle was very excited about making one last visit to the school and hospital. She spoke excitedly over dinner about honoring her brother's work with the Sherpa people by participating in the Jubilee celebrations. But, she said, the main reason she was doing the trek was to personally check out how the school and hospital were doing.

Hillary's older sister, June Carlyle, and members of the Hillary Clan at the dining table in Phakding, 2003

Just before everyone left the dining room to retire to their rooms or tents, June became wistful reminiscing about her brother's love of the Sherpa community. Hillary is revered by people all over the world as the "conqueror of Everest". The Sherpas call him "King of the Khumbu", and several local people told me that Hillary was far more popular than the King of Nepal. June told me that her brother was actually shy by nature and had never been comfortable with all the accolades he received. He'd always been more comfortable doing anything physical than speaking to an audience. June said, "Ed would rather be trekking with his family and visiting his Sherpa friends than giving speeches and interviews in Kathmandu. When Ed was young, he loved to personally work on laying brick and stone to help build schools and medical clinics in Sherpa villages. He had so much fun!"

The hike from Phakding to Namche Bazaar is the first real test of whether you have what it takes to make it to Base Camp. Hari and I walked and talked with Hillary family members as we hiked out of Phakding. Like all trekking groups, Hillarys began to string out based on trekking speed and strength during the long, steep hike up Namche Hill. It takes a fit trekker hiking at moderate speed about four hours to hike up Namche Hill, which is the last of several uphill sections of the trail from Phakding to Namche Bazaar. Hiking with a 45 pound pack required a perverse commitment to self-infliction of pain and suffering. The feeling that my legs might wear out before I set foot in the village was not mitigated when much smaller porters passed by carrying much heavier loads than mine. (It would have been truly ego-crushing had 86-year-old June Carlyle passed me.) When a trekker tops out on Namche Hill the reward is a scenic view of Namche Bazaar tucked into an elbow of mountains.

Namche Bazaar is the administrative center and has the largest open-air market in the Khumbu. Stone dwellings, teahouses, and shops with brightly painted red, green, or blue tin roofs are built on terraces forming a horseshoe around a steep, convex hill. At the opening of the horseshoe is a large whitewashed stupa, which has the all-seeing eyes of Buddha painted on each side. Namche's elevation is around 11,300 feet. It is guarded by the mystic-looking spires of Kusum Kangri and Thamserku, two white-capped Himalayan giants.

Over breakfast at the Panorama Lodge, I talked with the lodge owner, Sherap Jangbu Sherpa. Sherap was in his early 50's and wore neatly pressed Levis and a light blue cotton shirt with a collar. As noted above, I interviewed him about the changes in the Khumbu over the last fifty years. "Changes are always good and bad. Tourism gives better jobs and money. Fifty years ago we could only be porters and guides to the expeditions. Now we have doctors, pilots, and we can go to Kathmandu."

In Sherap's view, tourism is the foundation of all improvements in the Khumbu. "People visit the Khumbu and they like the Sherpas." When I asked him whether there is a downside to the changes, he admitted there was some, but not much. "Men only wear traditional clothes for ceremonies now. Modern clothes are easier to wear and warmer. Young people like modern ways. They're not as interested in singing and dancing. Kids in Kathmandu don't even speak Sherpa. About one-half don't come back."

Sherap's estimate of 50% of young Sherpas being seduced by pop culture and urban life in Kathmandu was higher than Chimi's 30%. Sherap was also more cognizant of the conflicts within the Sherpa community about the effects of tourism. He wisely recognized that there is always an upside and a downside to economic and social change. Cultural traditions in clothing, singing, dancing, and language were giving way to modernity. While Sherap argued that the economic benefits were worth those changes, his tone was wistful when he spoke of traditions that were fading away.

Sherap gave Hari and me directions to the home of Namche's most honored resident, Gheylsan Sherpa. Gheylsan's worn and gentle face was the cover image of the April 2003 issue of *Outside Magazine*. The featured article was a story about the three surviving high altitude porters from the 1953 expedition.

With Hari interpreting Gheylsan told me "the best thing" he's done in his life was to go up to the South Col on Everest with Hillary and Tenzing in 1953. He said he was very happy Hillary had come back to Nepal for the 50th Anniversary. He talked about how the people from Namche followed "the white people" all the way to Base Camp. "We were so curious about these people who drank water from bottles. We thought these people were very special and had special things. Some of our people followed the tourists just to look at them."

Gheylsan was adamant that, "No bad things have come from the 1953 summit and the tourism since then. The Sherpa people are still very strong, still very friendly." Out of respect, I didn't press him on the issue.

I gave Gheylsan a copy of the issue of *Outside Magazine* with his picture on the cover. His wife and two daughters served Hari and me rock candy and Tibetan yak-butter-tea, called po cha. It actually tastes quite horrible to me. It is made with salt and churned yak butter. It is heavily creamy in consistency with a very strong taste of salt and butter. I pretended to enjoy the tea, and declined a second cup only on the grounds that I was too full.

Khumjung Village

The following day Hari and I hiked to Khumjung to visit the first school built in the Khumbu by the Hillary family foundation. According to Mahendra Kathet, the headmaster at the school, "Without tourism, we couldn't survive here." He flatly stated that no one in Khumjung thinks the changes brought about by tourism have been bad for the village. "Even the old people who maintain traditional dress think changes are good, because they have better food, like salt. Life is much easier."

He related that before the Himalayan Trust built the school in 1961 people in Khumjung lived at a subsistence level. "There was no difference between the Khumbu and Tibet. All food and clothes were traditional. The food was porridge. All the houses were just stone. There was no education. Tourism had the effect of Sherpas seeing the outside world and to value education."

Khumjung Village, 2003: Note the modern running shoes and jacket worn by the Sherpa woman over her traditional dress. One plentiful resource in the Himalayan region is rocks. The villagers in Khumjung built rock walls along all the paths through the village.

At 6:00 a.m. the following morning, while drinking milk tea and eating muesli, I watched porters carrying stacks of stones in wooden dokos. (The doko baskets used by porters for carrying cargo over long distances are made from woven bamboo strips. Stone masons and carpenters use dokos made of wood, which are heavier but stronger, to move stone and lumber around a building project. Both types of dokos are strapped to the forehead and hang from the back of the head down to the lower back. Cargo is often piled up in the doko higher than the porter's head.) A statue of Sir Edmund Hillary was being erected at the Khumjung School.

East of Khumjung Village, the sun summitted the massive white shoulders of Ama Dablam, the most beautiful mountain in the Khumbu, and lit up her alabaster majesty. Hari and I shouldered our packs and hiked north toward Tengboche Gompa.

Tengboche Gompa

The final stage of the trail to the monastery grounds zigzags up 100 meters through a forest of scrub firs, birches, and rhododendrons. The trail ends on the plateau of Tengboche. The weary trekker is able to drop his pack, rest beside a gray-stone stupa with a golden spire, and take in one of the most impressive sites in the world. The monastery is a traditional Tibetan-style complex of stone and whitewashed buildings with brightly colored red and green sheet-metal roofs. A four-story temple is the largest building within the complex. Giant white-capped mountains surround the plateau.

Hari and I dropped our packs and rested by the stupa on the edge of the monastery grounds. Tents dotted the soccer-field size grounds. It was springtime and the rhododendron trees covering the hillsides of the plateau were in bloom festooning Tengboche Plateau in pink, white, and violet. I could just make out the sound of the glacial-fed Imja Khola River rushing through the steep gorge cut below the west side of the plateau. Directly north beyond Ama Dablam, was the high relief of the Everest Massif.

The entrance into the monastery's temple is through eight-foot high double wooden doors. Across the room is a fifteen-foot tall statue of Shakyamuni Buddha. (The Shakyamuni is one of several manifestations of Buddha. It is his human form after achieving enlightenment at Bodh Gaya.) Each wall of the inner temple is completely covered in colorful Buddhist paintings. Visitors remove their shoes and sit on mats against the sidewalls during puja (worship service). Burning yak oil candles create a heavy milky quality to the air. Morning and afternoon services are open to the public. The monks arrange themselves on rows of low benches. They are seated in a hierarchical order with a senior monk sitting in front facing the others. He leads the novice monks in chanting their lessons. A young monk serves tea to the older monks. During certain chants, some of the monks blow on trumpet-like instruments while others beat on drums or cymbals. The music is atonal and sounds to the Western ear like an out-of-tune kindergarten band. But the steady chanting occasionally interrupted by the blowing, bleating, banging, and clanging of instruments is hypnotically restful.

A koan from Lama Tenzing?

Tengboche is the highest major gompa in Nepal at 12,700 feet, and is presided over by the Incarnate Lama (or Rimpoche), Nawag Tenzing Sherpa. Lama Tenzing is the most revered of all Sherpa lamas. He enjoys having tea with visitors. There is a ritual and cost involved. Before you enter the Lama's study an attending monk will give you a kata (yellow silk scarf). You place a money offering for the monastery in the folded kata. Then, you enter the room where Lama Tenzing is seated behind a table. You hold the folded kata out, spread across both extended arms with the offering hidden in the folds. You bow before the Lama. He takes the kata and deftly removes the Rupees from it before draping the scarf around your neck. Lama Tenzing gestures for you to take a seat on a floor pillow in front of his table.

In the course of my rambles around the Khumbu I've visited Tengboche Gompa and had tea with Lama Tenzing four times, in 1995, 1998, 2003, and 2006. So I know the drill well.

When I visited Tengboche in 2003 it had been five years since I last saw the Rimpoche and nine years since I first met him. He looked little changed. He is a small, slight man with white hair. His skin is soft looking and mahogany colored. He wears a mango colored cloak. As abbot of the monastery, he regularly receives visitors and considers welcoming trekkers from other countries one of his most important duties. He sits placidly on his divan looking at his guests with kindly interested eyes. His facial expression rarely changes. Brightly colored thangka paintings (sacred Buddhist paintings draped with lengths of red silk) decorate the wall behind him.

In 2003, after the little welcoming ceremony with the katas was completed Hari and I sat on the floor in front of the Rimpoche. An assistant monk brought out a tray with delicate white and pink china teacups, a pot of black tea with milk already mixed in, a container of sugar cubes, and several pieces of rock candy. He filled two cups and indicated Hari and I should each take one. The monk carefully set the tray down in front of us, gestured toward the sugar cubes and rock candy on the tray, politely bowed to Hari and me, then to Lama Tenzing, and exited.

Through Hari, I asked Lama Tenzing his thoughts on the 50th Anniversary Celebration. The Rimpoche replied, "The Jubilee is good for Sherpa culture, but climbing mountains has nothing to do with Buddhism." He went on to explain that he had invited all of the Sherpas from as far away as Lukla to come to Tengboche for the celebration on May 29 to say thank you to Hillary's son, Peter. When I asked him what he thought of the effect of tourism on Sherpa culture, he said that he was "Not happy and not upset about Western influence on Sherpas. People should do what they want."

After about 20 minutes a monk entered and signaled that our time with Lama Tenzing should conclude. The Rimpoche smiled slightly and gestured for Hari and me to come forward. He handed each of us a mandala. It was an image of the Buddha with Tibetan calligraphy and auspicious symbols in red ink on post-card-size delicate yellow paper. We thanked Lama Tenzing, placed our hands together below our chins and bowed slightly toward the Rimpoche, as is customary. He returned the gesture.

As we walked across the grounds of the Gompa to the lodge where Hari and I had stashed our packs, clouds that partially blocked the view north cleared. A theater curtain was drawn open revealing the Everest Massif on stage. A wispy cirrus cloud trailed like a kite tail from the pinnacle of Chomolungma. This is the scene that pilgrims from all over the world come to Tengboche to see. Peace and harmony emanated from the temple outward to the surrounding mountains and was returned.

On a solitary stroll around the monastery grounds after we supped, my own peace and harmony was disturbed by a niggling thought. Wasn't Lama Tenzing being disingenuous in his separation of religion and economics? By saying mountain climbing has nothing to do with Buddhism, and then indicating an indifference to the influence of Westerners on Sherpas, how did that square with his role as the chief representative of traditional Tibetan-Buddhism for the Sherpa people? For sport and ego mountain climbers had trashed and brought needless death into Sherpa lands. Sherpas had aided and abetted these desecrations for money. Wasn't there some contradiction, or violation, of the Dharma (the Buddhist way) in polluting the land and seducing Sherpas away from their traditional way of life? Or, did the Rimpoche see all that as a manifestation of "maya", the ever-changing but superficial reality we live through in our daily lives? Maybe that explained his indifference to the issues I raised.

People want to climb mountains and that pollutes the mountains. Other people want to clean up the mountains, and so they do that too. Humanity lives with many conflicting desires. It can be good and it can be bad to free the ego, let loose, live adventurously and have fun. It can also be good and bad to be carefully responsible. It's good to take care of yourself and treat others and the environment responsibly. But one can be so careful and repressed life is no fun, there's no juice in it. We all know people who live on either extreme of this polarity. There's the narcissic rake leaving destruction in his wake. And there's the tightly wound prude, so Victorian she never let's her true feelings out. Ancient Greek philosophers advocated finding a balance in life, the "golden mean". Taoism has the concept of yin and yang.

Lama Tenzing's statement, "People should do what they want," sounded utterly narcissic. But perhaps it was a koan; a paradoxical statement given by a Buddhist teacher for the student to contemplate. Meditating on a koan is supposed to help open the mind to a higher state of consciousness on the way toward enlightenment. It is a gateway from the material reality of phenomena to the spiritual reality of noumena. Did the Rimpoche give me a koan, along with milk tea and rock candy? Did he mean that the desires to stand on the top of mountains and to achieve material wealth meant nothing on the level of Buddha consciousness? But what about damage to the environment and to an ancient culture; was that irrelevant from the perspective of a higher state of consciousness? I would have to meditate on that as Hari and I hiked on to Base Camp.

Hanging out in Pheriche and then on to Base Camp
Hiking through the rhododendron forest beyond Tengboche, Hari and I crossed over the rapids of the Imja Khola on a new suspension bridge made of steel. It replaced an old suspension bridge made of rope and wood slats, which was typical of bridges throughout the Himalayas before 2003. We passed intricately carved mani stones (stone slates with Tibetan prayers carved on them) and then a series of chortens (conical stone memorials with a spire). Hiking higher and higher above the river gorge we made it to the windswept plateau of Pheriche at 14,340 feet before the end of the day.

Hari and I stowed our packs at the Panorama Lodge and had some bracing black tea with the owner, Ang Rita Sherpa. I became acquainted with Ang Rita when I stayed at the Panorama during my recovery from AMS in 1998 after hiking down from Base Camp with Tom and Krishna. Many trekkers go no further up the Base Camp Trail than Namche or Tengboche, so Ang Rita's business is more precarious than the lodges in the lower villages.

Ang Rita was as thin and weathered-looking as an old fence post. His brow furrowed with worry while we chatted and sipped tea. He told me that he was disappointed in the number of customers that came to his lodge for the anniversary celebrations. "Not enough customers come back. Business is a little better, but not as good as it was in the 1990's," Ang Rita declared. He went on to say that, if business didn't improve, his family would have to go back to yak herding and growing potatoes. "Before tourism, Sherpa people very poor. Traded with Tibetans and took crops to Namche to trade. Now we can buy things with money. I don't know if business will get better. Just wait and see. If we have to return to farming, we have land here. This is Sherpa home. Can't go anywhere else."

Near Ang Rita's lodge is a shiny steel monument to climbers who died on Mt. Everest. It was erected in 2002 on the grounds of the Himalayan Rescue Association ("HRA") clinic. There were 178 names on the monument in 2003. That number was consistent with an oft-cited statistic that for every ten climbers who summit Everest there is one death on the mountain. 1,659 had summitted by the end of 2002. There was space left for many more names. (By 2019 around 4,000 people had summitted Everest since 1922. Around 300 had died on the mountain.)

I looked in at the HRA later that evening and asked the v volunteer physicians whether they would agree to be interviewed. The HRA doctors in 2003 were Dr. Martin Wilcox, a retired U.S. Navy surgeon, and Dr. Kirsten Moller, a Dane from Copenhagen. Both docs accepted, and invited me join to them for a Coke from Dr. Wilcox's private stash.

We talked about their personal experiences at the HRA and what they'd learned about the local Sherpa community. Dr. Moller described how lung problems had been endemic among Sherpas in the past. Sherpas traditionally cooked over open fires and inhaled a lot of smoke. By 2003 most Sherpa homes had iron stoves with smoke stacks to vent the smoke outside the house. Although yak dung and sticks remained the primary fuel sources used by Sherpas, pulmonary disease had significantly declined and life expectancy had increased, because they were inhaling so much less smoke on a daily basis.

I asked the doctors whether they thought there is a tipping point, when Sherpa culture has changed so much it is no longer Sherpa. Neither had a definitive answer to the question, but agreed traditions were eroding at an increasing rate in the villages along the Base Camp Trail. Dr. Moller still described Sherpas as "the most helpful, thoughtful, friendly people I've ever known." Yet, she worried that Sherpa culture might reach a tipping point such that the character of the people she so admired changed. "But when so many changes in Nepal improve the quality of life, how can we criticize?" she asked. (More conversations with the doctors are reported in the next chapter.)

The hike from Pheriche to Lobuche is only about four hours, but the gain in altitude is 2,000 feet. At the top of the 16,000 foot-high Lobuche pass, prayer flags whip in the wind and chortens, cairns, and stacks of mani stones stand in testament to climbers killed on Everest. Hari and I drank water and rested by the memorials and watched shaggy yaks trudge by. Their bells tinkled as herders "shooed" and threw stones at the yak's hulking backsides to keep the beasts moving. Above and beyond the pass rise the massive white and gray Chomolungma and her giant maidens, Lhotse at 28,000 feet, Nuptse 26,000 feet, and Pumori 23,000 feet.

Hari on the Base Camp Trail hiking across Lobuche Pass toward the Everest Massif, 2003

We had dinner at the Eco Lodge in Lobuche with Andy and Johannes, German journalists covering the Jubilee. This was their fifth trek in the Khumbu sine 1996. They related that, in their experience the attitude of some lodge owners towards guests had changed for the worse. Johannes complained about a lodge owner in Dingboche who wouldn't deign to speak with his customers. "Before, lodge owners treated customers like guests in their home. Now, they are only interested in money," Johannes said.

An English trekker sharing the dining table with us chimed in. He claimed that the lodge owner at a different lodge in Lobuche told him to "go back to Gorak Shep," when he complained that food prices were higher at the lodge than in Gorak Shep.

The consensus around the dinner table was that some Sherpa lodge owners had lost the traditional value of hospitality. My companions that evening in the Lobuche Eco Lodge -- all from wealthy nations -- condemned many Sherpas for becoming too materialistic and letting go of traditional values.

I questioned my companion's analysis by countering that success in a service business depends on satisfied customers. To be an inhospitable lodge owner was to shoot your self in the foot. Surely these Sherpa businessman weren't that stupid. My experiences with Sherpa lodge owners were that they were quite hospitable and not stupid. But I had to admit that I had not heard such complaints from trekkers in the 1990s. Still, wasn't there a bit of hypocrisy in visitors to the Khumbu from the wealthiest nations complaining about local people being too materialistic?

Speed Climbing Everest

On the final stage of the trek to Base Camp Hari and I dodged several yak trains lumbering down the trail. Everest climbing expeditions were decamping and sending their gear out tied on to the backs of yaks. The trail skirts the gigantic Khumbu glacier, which is pock-marked with little lakes, vast moraines, and rock falls. Base Camp looked like a crazy quilt city of multi-colored tents strewn all over a ridiculously rocky moraine below the forbidding Khumbu Icefall.

Hari and I searched out the Nepal Mountain Madness campsite. One of the climbing Sherpas with that expedition, Lakhpa Tsering, was a friend. He was the lead climbing guide on the ill-fated expedition to Mera Peak in 1999. We found the campsite, but learned that Lakhpa was still on the mountain with an American client. By sheer serendipity we discovered that Lakhpa Gelu Sherpa, another member of the Mountain Madness team, had just broken the record for the quickest ascent and return from the summit. He arrived at the Mountain Madness campsite just after we found it.

Lakhpa climbed from Base Camp to the summit by "the standard route", pioneered by Hillary and Norgay, in ten hours and 56 minutes. He completed the descent to Base Camp in a total time of 18 hours and 20 minutes.

What to compare this with in terms of amazing physical feats? Assuming no delays for bad weather or acclimatization problems, it takes most elite climbers at least seven days to summit and return to Base Camp. Lakhpa Gelu completed it in just over 18 hours. That has to be one of the most difficult feats performed by any human being. Less than 1,700 people had successfully summitted Everest in the history of the world by 2003. The vast majority of those climbers spent a total of two months on the expedition and they paid up to $65,000 to make the attempt. Only about one of ten climbers who attempt it successfully summits. And, for about every one hundred climbers who attempt the climb one person (mostly Sherpas) dies on the mountain. It usually takes 2-3 weeks to acclimate and trek to Base Camp. Then, with the help of climbing guides and high altitude porters, 5 camps are set up along the route to the summit, which usually takes about two weeks. The climbers gradually adjust to the increasing altitude and use oxygen masks above 25,000 feet. The descent is the most dangerous part of the climb. Climbers coming off the mountain usually look like raccoons, because of the sun burn/tan lines which form around glacier glasses and oxygen masks.

Immediately after completing his incredible feat, Lakhpa sat with me outside the Mountain Madness tent and patiently answered my interview questions. There were no other journalists there, so mine was the first exclusive interview of the new record-holder.

In 2003 Lakhpa was 35 years-old. He didn't look like Super Man. He was just a little taller than average for a Nepali man. He said that he summitted Everest the first time in 1993. He told me he didn't do anything special to train for his record attempt. "Just climb mountains." I asked him what the record meant to him and why it was important. "Record is important because set on Golden Jubilee. I wanted to set record for several years, and wanted to do it this year. It is important that Sherpa set record. Sherpa are strong." When asked how he was feeling, he said his upper legs and throat hurt a little.

Lakhpa Gelu Sherpa and the author just after Lakhpa set the speed record on Mt. Everest in May 2003.

I ducked into the Mountain Madness meal tent to escape the blazing sun. It felt awfully close at almost 18,000 feet and reflecting off the glaciated flanks of Nupste and Everest. In the tent were three Brown University students winding up a research project for NASA on the effects of hypoxia on climbers. They'd spent two months working with the Mountain Madness team and were preparing to leave in the morning.

About Lakhpa Gelu's record, one of the students said, "You know, the whole record thing is Western inspired, it's not really Sherpa." In her view, the attitude of Sherpas toward Chomolungma had changed for the worse. "They used to worship the mountain, but now they are the leaders of assaults against the mountain." She went on, "It's brought them fame as climbers, which means higher fees as climbing guides." Despite her criticisms, she and her fellow researchers were enthusiastic in complimenting their Sherpa hosts for their gracious help. One of the other students exclaimed, "They're great guys!"

Modern conveniences, traditions, and global warming

Three days later, Hari and I walked stiff-legged back into Tengboche on the afternoon of the Golden Jubilee date, May 29, 2003. Given the number of people arriving in Tengboche for the celebration of "the highest party in the world", we felt lucky to secure a room at the Tashi Delek Lodge. ("Tashi delek" is the Tibetan greeting, equivalent to "Namaste" in Nepali.) The Tashi Delek has fantastic views from the second floor of the Everest Massif. While unrolling my sleeping bag onto the cot in our room, I saw Peter Hillary through the window being interviewed by a small crowd of reporters in front of the Gompa. I grabbed my camera and notebook and hurried out to join the crowd of journalists.

Peter Hillary's responses to questions from other reporters and me:

Climbing Everest has offered much to Nepal. It has brought badly needed wealth to the country, which is the fifth poorest in the world. ...There is so much enthusiasm among local people about the celebration of the 50th anniversary. It's a dream come true for the Hillary family. ...Westerners sometimes look at a culture like the Sherpas and their first impression is that it is idyllic, because these people are so amazing. But would you want to carry your own water everyday and have no schools to send you children to?

I think the people have retained their culture to a much higher degree than most people in the West. Nepalese and Sherpas have changed, yes, in 50 years, but the traits of character we admire are still there. ...This is a great day, because it reflects the cooperation of the Nepalese people and my family. Ed Hillary and Tenzing Norgay climbed Everest, Sagarmatha, together. Cooperation was the key to their success. Cooperation between the local people and my dad is why the Foundation has been successful. Dad didn't come in and tell the people what they needed. They told him what would be of help to them."

After the interview ended I told Peter that I met his Aunt June hiking in Phakding. He lit up at the mention of Aunt June. We both marveled at the strength and determination of an 86-year-old to trek to Kunde for a last visit to the hospital she helped to establish. Peter shook his head sadly when I said it was a shame his father was unable to see all the great work his foundation had done for the Sherpas. Peter replied that his father never wanted to take any credit, because his relationship with the Sherpas "was a partnership, just like climbing with Tenzing."

I thanked Peter for his time and then walked around the monastery grounds with his friend, Ang Temba Sherpa, who is a sirdar employed by World Expeditions, the Hillary's trekking company. Ang Temba was handsome and tall for a Sherpa, about the same height as Peter Hillary, around five-foot ten. He wore a white cowboy hat, a grey vest over a white shirt with fringe at the bottom, and grey pants.

Ang Temba told me he attended the Hillary school in Khumjung for ten years. After graduation, he began working as a trekking guide for World Expeditions. When I asked for his thoughts on how Sherpa culture had changed in 50 years, at first he insisted that the culture had changed little. "People want to save the culture. I tell my children about the culture and want them to keep it."

But when I pressed him, he shared a memorable anecdote. "When I was a child we walked downhill every morning to fill our water buckets. It took half hour to walk down to river and longer to walk back with full buckets. At river, women talked and children played. Then white men came to village and said a wonderful thing. They could bring water to our house. We would have water by turning a handle. And we were very happy." Then he sighed and looked away. He responded wistfully, "Women and children do not go to river to talk and play anymore. People in my village are not so close now." I asked if he thought his village was better off with running water at their houses. He looked me in the eye, and then answered in a firm voice with a question. "If you had to walk down hill and carry all water you need for day, or turn handle and have water at house, which would you choose?"

Indeed, which would you choose? Ang Temba's question succinctly explains why people are willing to change or give up cultural traditions for the benefits, comfort, and convenience of modern life. To the students in the classes I taught at Marian University and Butler University, and during programs I've given about philanthropic development in Nepal, I've posed Ang Temba's question. If you were in his shoes, how would you choose? The answer is always the same. We'd choose comfort and convenience. So, if a traditional culture is worth preserving, the trick is to figure out how to do development in the least harmful way.

Ang Temba's "water story" is relevant anecdotal evidence about another important issue. It helps to explain why reversing global warming and reducing pollution is so difficult. The human desire for convenience is a major driver of global warming. Much of the pollution of air, water, and soil is due to our desire for convenience For many people it's more convenient to drive a car than walk, bicycle, or take public transportation. It's more convenient and less expensive to package goods in plastic than more bulky bio-degradable materials. Coal, oil, and gas have been easier to deliver and cost less than cleaner energy sources. The desire for less hassle and less expense will not cease. Climate crusaders need to recognize that few people are willing to sacrifice much in the way of convenience and cost. The crusaders who are making real progress are the ones devoting their own energy to developing cheaper and more convenient energy sources and alternatives to plastics. Those who self-righteously harangue the public to give up comfort and convenience to save the planet are prophets crying in the wilderness.

Ang Temba's family chose tap water because it was much more convenient that walking down and up a hill with a bucket. I know many Americans who profess to be on the right side of environmental issues, but who choose the comfort and convenience of fossil fuel and plastics every day over less polluting but more expensive and less convenient alternatives. Do you use the most fuel-efficient and least-polluting way to get where you need to go? Do you avoid purchasing items that are in non-recyclable or non-degradable containers, and reject the use of plastic bags and straws, whenever possible? Do you turn off lights, computers, and all your electronic devices at all times they are not in use? Are you also vigilant about turning off tap water, showering instead of filling a bathtub, and not watering your lawn? Or, are you like me and most Americans, who do some of those things, but less than we could?

My heart tells me to be hopeful that we humans will reverse the dangerous trajectory we are on to permanent, irreversible warming of Mother Earth. My head is pessimistic, because of Ang Temba's water story and my own inclination toward comfort and convenience. My hope is with the scientists and engineers more than the politicians.

Green Mountaineering

I continued strolling around Tengboche with Ang Temba and asked him whether the Sherpas had changed their attitude toward Chomolungma in the last 50 years. Ang Temba became quite animated. "Mountain can't change, but the records change every year. Westerners want to make records and they care a lot about

118

records. Sherpas need to show they are the strongest climbers, so they keep trying to break records."

Ang Temba was critical of the West's influence on Sherpa attitudes, yet justified Sherpa participation in the desecration of Chomolungma because Sherpas need to prove they are the best climbers. But he claimed the Goddess could be pacified "by doing puja (praying)." I asked if that was not trying to have it both ways, participate in assaults on the mountain, but pray for forgiveness? Ang Temba argued that the Sherpa attitude wasn't hypocritical; rather, it is a more enlightened understanding of mountaineering.

"Before the 90's, people died every year, and again in 1996. Goddess was unhappy. But government made rule that people must bring trash off mountain. She's happy if people bring rubbish off mountain. Goddess is happy if people climb in way that is clean. In our culture it is bad to burn rubbish, because of smell. Should burn it someplace else. In 1996 people burned rubbish in Base Camp and Goddess was unhappy. People are better now, so Goddess is happy." (1996 was the year 8 climbers died within 24 hours on Mt. Everest, which was made infamous by Jon Krakauer's book and the subsequent film with the same title, *Into Thin Air*.)

Ang Temba explained that the government had passed regulations that required mountaineering expeditions to bring their trash back to Namche and have it burned there. Or, he claimed, the company could bring the trash back to Kathmandu and get back a $10,000 deposit. (Better sources list the deposit/refund in 2003 at $4,000.) Ang Temba said guiding companies were now required to bring all oxygen canisters and batteries out of Sagarmatha National Park. He thought the government finally understood the problem of the pollution and desecration of the mountain. Ang Temba was optimistic that the problem was "getting under control."

Ang Temba's description of the right way to do mountaineering is consistent with the enlightened "green ethic" of "take nothing, leave nothing." Do puja and keep the mountain and the air clean, and the gods will be happy.

Sir Edmund Hillary was not as sanguine as Ang Temba. In speeches and interviews during the anniversary celebrations, Hillary called for a moratorium on climbing Everest and for all trash to be cleared from the mountain before climbing resumed. Government officials made public statements in support of Hillary plea. They were just paying lip service to a living legend. His call for a moratorium on climbing was ignored. In 2003 the government was charging a $10,000 fee for every climber on Everest. It increased the fee to $11,000 in 2015. Every wannabe Everest climber adds thousands of dollars beyond the permit fee to Nepal's economy. The country and Sherpas would have lost a lot of dough had the government acceded to Hillary's request.

(On August 14, 2019 the Nepal Ministry of Tourism announced that it was planning to raise the fee for an Everest climbing permit to $35,000. This followed outcries about the record number of 381 permits issued for the spring climbing season and 11 deaths on the mountain.)

As Lama Tenzing said, mountain climbing has nothing to do with Buddhism, but it has a lot to do with money. Nepal was struggling in 2003, and continues to struggle, with finding the right balance for its tourism industry. Tourism supports worthy government programs and provides employment opportunities. But Nepal needs to protect its natural environment and traditional cultures from irreparable damage. Finding the right balance is a work in progress. We'll return to how much progress has been made since 2003 in subsequent chapters.

The highest party in the world

The official Jubilee Celebration at Tengboche commenced at 4:00 p.m. on May 29, 2003. It was held in a big blue tent pitched beside the monastery. There were many speeches and a fine dinner of yak steak and champagne. Black bowties were handed out to male attendees and ladies wore long evening dresses over hiking boots. The master of ceremonies, Peter Hillary, wore knickers with his suit coat and bow tie. I know this, not because I attended the black-tie affair inside the big blue tent, but because I, like about 100 other peons who had not paid the $400 admission fee (most of which was go to the Himalayan Trust) stood outside of the tent. We people-watched the permitees enter the tent and peeked inside as the tent flaps opened. World Expeditions porters wearing blue company shirts and multi-colored topis (traditional Nepalese brimless caps) were stationed around the tent to keep out the undesirables. A particularly burly porter stood at the main entrance with a lethal-looking two foot-long club in his hand.

When the tent flaps were Velcroed shut and Peter Hillary's welcoming remarks leaked out of the tent, a bunch of us peons decamped to begin our own Jubilee celebration in a nearby teahouse. A bottle of Everest Whiskey was passed around as a chaser to the glasses of chang and rakshi ordered from the barkeep. After a couple hours of rowdy drinking word reached the teahouse that the big blue tent was open to the public. Peter ordered the guards to let anyone in after the official event ended. The tent flaps were thrown open and the unwashed rabble of trekkers, climbers, porters, and locals poured in.

Tengboche grounds on May 29, 2003, the 50th Anniversary of the summit of Mt. Everest by Ed Hillary and Tenzing Norgay. The big blue tent in the middle was the venue for "the highest party in the world" hosted by Peter Hillary and Lama Tenzing.

Two of the topi-wearing porters began to pound out a beat on gourd-drums and started singing a Nepali folk song all the locals knew. The crowd of about 300 began to clap and sway with the beat. The volume of the drumming increased and the singing turned into rhythmic chanting. Women were hoisted up onto the shoulders of the bigger guys in the crowd. Nepalis of different ethnic groups and castes and trekkers and climbers from all over the world shouted and clapped to the pounding beat. Lithe-limbed Nepali porters danced with graceful snake-like movements of their hands. Long-haired trekker girls and scruffy sun-burnt mountain climbers stomped and shook their booties. Moon-eyed trekkers high on hash bobbed their heads and swayed around the tent. The dancing became more frenetic as the drummers pounded away with wild abandon.

is group of revelers couldn't afford the $400 admission fee to the official party. We are waiting for the big blue tent to open. Hari is on the far right leaning against the author.

At 10:30 the lights in the tent were extinguished. But the spirit of revelry propelled the crowd into a snake dance out of the tent and across the monastery grounds to the porter dormitory. A couple of guys staying in the dorm piled up wood planks, logs, and sticks and started a huge bonfire. Flames rose ten-feet high and burning ashes shot up into the night sky. Dancing, drumming, and singing around the fire lasted well past midnight. Many bottles of chang and rakshi passed from hand-to-hand, until they were emptied.

In the wee hours of morning 50 hardcore-party-animals snake danced once more across the monastery grounds. We ended up behind the monastery on the edge of a 500-foot drop-off. We danced and sang for another hour shining our headlamps in a communal beacon up at the stars.

Holding each other up wheezing and laughing, Hari and I finally staggered back to the Tashi Delek Lodge with a few other revelers staying at the lodge. I was bone tired hiking from Pheriche that morning and partying all night. But I didn't want to let go of that magical, joyful night.

Hari stumped into the lodge and up the stairs to our second-floor room. I leaned against the stone wall of the lodge and gazed up at the huge starlit night. The silhouette of Ama Dablam glimmered in the starlight way off across the valley past Deboche and Pangboche. Ang Dawa Sherpa, a fellow party-animal staying at the Tashi Delek, ended my reverie. He slapped me on the back and gasped, "It is funny, man! So much drinking and dancing at Tengboche Gompa, this place of sacred meditation and prayer." With arms around each others' shoulders for support, we each put one foot in front of the other, struggled up the stairs and then down the hall to our rooms.

Everyone who had not already passed out or fallen asleep by the campfire finally drifted away to their lodge rooms or tents to dream and sleep. No human voices disturbed the quiet of the monastery grounds. Occasional snuffling of yaks was the only sound that broke the silence.

Tantric practices encourage the loss of self consciousness. Padmasambhava, founder of Buddhist Tantraism, supposedly engaged in ecstatic practices and encouraged his followers to reac a higher state of consciousness through orgy. The Nyingma scho of Buddhism practiced by the monks at Tengboche Gompa evolv from Tibetan Tantric traditions. The legendary founder of Tengboche, Lama Sange Dorje, flew from Rongbuk Gompa in Tibet over the Everest Massif and left his footprint at Tengboche. The monastery was built on the site of the mythical footprint in 1916.

Sherpa culture retains some pre-Buddhist influences of the ancient animistic religion of Bon, according to anthropologists with expertise in the study of Sherpa culture. Observing the orderly operation and practices of the Tengboche monastery, Tantric and Bon influences are very well hidden. But when the common folk took over the Jubilee celebration at Tengboche, those influences ruled the night. The meticulous orderliness of the monastery gave way to the more ancient and earthy ecstasies of Tantraism and Bon.

Lama Tenzing advised, "People should do what they want." And so we did that magical night at Tengboche, even though we didn't pay the $400 entrance fee or have black bowties around our sweaty necks. Through the ecstatic practices of song, dance, and drink we revelers were uplifted to a higher state of communal consciousness.

In the morning, trekkers, climbers, porters, and guides quietly packed their gear and resolutely set out on the trail. The monks blew their horns to call the members of their order to their disciplines in the temple. It was another beautiful day at Tengboche. A cirrus cloud waved like a pennant from the spire of the Mother Goddess. Her regal face reflected the morning sunlight.

Three days later, I sat beside Lydia, a college student from Maine, on a Twin-Otter to fly out of Lukla Village. Lydia had cently completed an international studies program in Kathmandu. ᐁ trekked up the Base Camp Trail to join in the Jubilee bration at Tengboche. She spent most of her time in Nepal in verished villages in the interior.

pretty young flight attendant in formal Sherpa dress with reen and blue-striped apron walked down the narrow aisle g out cotton swabs and rock candies. Lydia and I each stuck swabs into our ears and sucked on rock candy as the airplane lown the runway. It dropped off the end of the runway, he lift it needed and then swooped up into the blue sky. a Airstrip is cut into a cleft in the mountainside with a sheer on one end and a mountain face at the other. It's a harrowing adventure just to fly in and out of Lukla. But when you look out the window of the plane on a clear day, you can see the highest mountains in the world in all their spectacular beauty. Between turbulent bumps, when Lydia wasn't turning white and gripping my arm, she answered my questions about her experience in the Khumbu.

"Sherpas were more materialistic than I expected, and more wealthy. The poverty in Kathmandu and the villages in the interior is much greater than what I saw in the Khumbu. But I liked the Sherpas I encountered. They seem to have learned what Westerners want, haven't they?"

Yetis, Yaks, Nepal's Supermen, and the Highest Medical Clinic in the World
Pheriche, Nepal 1995, 1998, and 2003

The author visited the Himalayan Rescue Association Medical Clinic in Pheriche on his first Himalayan trek in 1995.

I was born in the spring of 1953, a month before Edmund Hillary and Tenzing Norgay stood on the summit of Mt. Everest. Traveling to Nepal to participate in the celebrations of the 50th Anniversary of the first summit of Mt. Everest was sort of a birthday present for turning 50. After experiencing the trauma in 1999 -- running from an avalanche, which killed three Nepalese porters and trapped members of our Nepalese crew, and then learning that Didi's son died in a helicopter crash – I thought I would never return to the Himalayan region. If I'd sworn off mountaineering, what was the point? Plus, Nepal was experiencing a national trauma.

A Maoist-led insurrection was cascading into a full-blown civil war. The nation was further traumatized on June 1, 2001, when Crown Prince Dipendra shot 13 members of the royal family, including his father the King, at a dinner party. 9 died immediately. Dipendra shot himself in the head. He died three days later. He was crowned King of Nepal while he was in a coma. Dipendra's uncle, Gyanendra, succeeded him as King.

News reports about Nepal described King Gyanendra as an unpopular authoritarian ruler. His older brother, Birendra, was regarded as a benevolent ruler. King Birendra helped transform Nepal into a constitutional monarchy with a parliament. Gyanendra tried to reverse the course of history by reclaiming the power of absolute the monarchy. He dismissed the duly elected Parliament. He declared a "shoot on sight" after-dark curfew in Kathmandu enforced by AK-47 toting soldiers.

(Walking back to our hotel in 2004 after a night out with Nepalese friends, two trekking mates and I had a very uncomfortable encounter with a group of soldiers. Our Nepalese friends shrunk into the shadows in an alley to hide from the soldiers. They probably wouldn't have been shot, but our friends would certainly been arrested or beaten. Most of the army recruits during the civil war between the government and Maoists were poorly-trained-young-uneducated village boys. Three very young, nervous-looking soldiers pointed their guns at the three of us, but seemed at a loss about what to do next. We began trying to talk our way out of the situation, but the soldiers didn't understand English. Luckily, their sergeant arrived a couple minutes later and told them to let us go. He chided us in English to get back to our hotel. He told us to confine our movements to restaurants, bars, or hotels that catered to tourists.)

Gangs of loyal royalist-ruffians beat up dissidents. My friend Raaj was severely beaten and his arm broken, just because he had long hair and looked like an anti-royalist. King Gyanendra temporarily shut down Internet and telephone service and closed the country off from international flights. The people responded with massive demonstrations, worker strikes, and riots. Maoist guerillas responded by ambushing army patrols and the rebels began to take control of large parts of western Nepal, including the popular Annapurna Circuit trekking trail.

The country was sliding into chaos within the first two years of Gyanendra's rule. But then, Sir Edmund Hillary stepped in to help broker a truce between the government and Maoist rebels for the Jubilee Celebration. Kathmandu and the Khumbu would be safe harbors during the festivities. So, just after celebrating my own 50th anniversary on earth, I boarded a flight for Kathmandu.

King Gyanendra facing Hillary, who is stooped with age and using a cane; the famous Italian climber Reinhold Messner (with the beard) is just behind Hillary (photo from gettyimages by Paula Bronstein).

Yeti Skulls, magic, and a painful hike in 1995

One of the places I intended to visit and learn more about during the Jubilee trek was the Himalayan Rescue Association Medical Clinic in Pheriche ("HRA Clinic"). The first time I was there was in 1995. Our Snow Lion trekking group's northern terminus was Tengboche Gompa. The itinerary called for the group to spend three days in Tengboche. After visiting the gompa, seeing the monks perform puja, and meeting Lama Tenzing, I wanted to experience more of the mountains. I'd heard of the HRA Clinic, which was another hiking stage further north. I thought it would be interesting to see what the highest medical clinic in the world was like. I asked our guides if it could be arranged that those of us in the group who wanted to could hike up there, rather than spend another day in Tengboche. Three other group members, Long John, Steve, and Harris said they wanted to go for it. Our sirdar, Nyima Sherpa, agreed so long as Mike went with us.

Mike was our American guide. He was a recent college

graduate; a tall, handsome, and rangy young man with brown hair and blue eyes. Our 1995 group was only his second trek with Snow Lion. His first ended just before ours started. He was a cool young guy; always wore a baseball cap, sometimes with the bill in front and sometimes in back. He worked in Colorado as a rafting guide in the summer and a ski patrolman in the winter. His knowledge of Nepal and the local culture was very limited. Nyima was clearly in charge of our crew of porters and kitchen staff. Mike's role was mainly to joke around with the clients. He did not speak Nepali. Near the end of the trek, Mike sheepishly confided to me that he was paid more than Nyima. Mike also admitted that he received the largest share of the tips given by our group members to the crew at the end of the trek. It was customary for the Western guides with Western-based expedition companies to receive a higher salary and a larger share of the tips than the Nepalese sirdar, and every other member of the crew, even though it was the sirdar who did the bulk of the work. (When I began organizing trekking and mountaineering groups in 2004, I made sure that my groups would not follow that custom. An American or European guide is completely unnecessary when the group employs a competent local sirdar.)

Nyima was not a joker. His demeanor was business-like. He took his role as sirdar very seriously. He dressed neatly with creased trekking pants and a collar shirt. He carried a briefcase with a steel exterior. I don't know what all was in Nyima's briefcase, but he always kept it close at hand.

After he agreed that four of us could hike up to Pheriche with Mike, Nyima explained that so long as we stayed on the main trail we would not have a problem finding the HRA Clinic. We understood that it would be a long, hard hike, because the hike from Tengboche to Pheriche is considered a one-day hiking stage on the Base Camp Trail. We would have to hike back to Tengboche that day. Nyima said, if we hiked at a reasonable pace, we should be able to complete the hike in 8 hours, including rest stops and a break for lunch.

Our cook prepared an early breakfast and gave each of us a pack lunch of roti (Indian flat bread), a potato, 2 boiled eggs, and a banana in a little brown paper-sack. Nyima urged us to take an extra water bottle in our packs.

Our first rest stop and diversion off the main trail was a visit to Pangboche Monastery, elevation over 13,000 feet. Mike told us that we had to visit the Monastery, because it contained a yeti scalp and hand. Neither the hand nor the scalp looked authentic to my skeptical eyes, but the aged monk who guarded the glass box containing the yeti relics assured us they were the real thing. Over the years, all the Sherpas I've asked about the yeti told me they hadn't seen one personally, but they all knew someone, a cousin, sister-in-law, somebody, who had seen a yeti. Well, whatever... the yeti has been good for tourism. Sadly, the yeti hand was later stolen from the monastery.

The yeti or abominable snowman continues to fascinate the public and scientific community. As recent as April 30, 2019 I saw news reports of yeti footprints discovered in Nepal. This one is from *NBC World News* online:

The Indian army says it has discovered footprints in the Himalayas that appear to belong to a yeti, known in the U.S. as bigfoot or the abominable snowman. Measuring 32 inches by 15 inches, they were found near Mount Makalu base camp on April 9... (however) Some noticed that the photos appeared to show the footprints in a straight line, one behind the other, similar to what might be expected from a model... (and) Research carried out by Barnett and fellow ancient genetics expert Ceiridwen Edwards found that re-analysis of DNA samples taken from reported yeti sightings matched brown bears local to the Himalayan region... (but) "You can't kill a legend with anything as mundane as facts," he said.

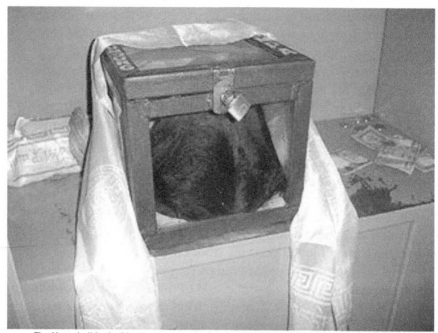
The Yeti skull looked better groomed when I saw it at the Khumjung Gompa in 2003.

After the steep climb up to Pangboche, my buddy, Dr. John, decided he preferred to just hang out, drink tea, and smoke a cigarette at a nearby teahouse, rather than hike all day to see the HRA Clinic. John is about six-foot three-inches tall and routinely whacked his forehead on the lintel of doors designed for the much shorter Nepalese people. He did it again at the gompa. Rest and a cigarette was what John prescribed for his headache. The other three trekkers slung our packs and followed Mike up the trail.

We arrived in Pheriche in the middle of the afternoon. To my dismay, we discovered that the clinic was closed. As shown in the photo at the beginning of this chapter, the HRA Clinic's sign was leaning up against the outside wall of the building. I held it up and Mike took a picture of me with my camera. The medical clinic is only open seasonally, because, although local people are treated, it was funded by the HRA primarily to treat trekkers and climbers who got sick or injured on the upper Base Camp Trail. Nyima later explained to me that tourists can afford to pay the HRA for medical treatment, whereas yak herders and subsistence farmers who need medical treatment probably couldn't afford to pay for it. Nyima was generally positive and upbeat, but was quite critical and cynical about the materialistic motives of the HRA. He thought the clinic should be kept open year-round to serve local people.

Mike decided we should hike on up to Dingboche, since there were no open teahouse in Pheriche. It would add a couple more hours to the hike, because Dingboche is further north and then east off of the main trail. Our 8-hour hike would take at least 10 hours. But no worries; we all felt fine.

We found an open teahouse in the Dingboche Village. Mike ordered a round of dudh chiyaa (black tea with milk, pronounced *dude chee-yah*) for Harris, Steve, himself, and me. We learned from the Didi who ran the teahouse that the clinic in Pheriche had closed early that year. She'd heard that the clinic ran out of supplies and money, so the staff just locked the door and left.

I was feeling pretty beat after about six hours of hard, mostly uphill hiking. Leaning against the side of the teahouse was what looked like a solid wood wheel with dried mud covering one side of it. It was tilted at an angle that made an attractive backrest. I set my pack aside, sat down on the ground, rested my back against the dried mud, and pulled my cap down over my eyes for a nap. Before I could fall asleep I heard a couple Nepalese voices chuckling and giggling. A few minutes later, Mike nudged me and told me I was resting against yak dung. He explained that the Didi who owned the teahouse went out each day collecting yak dung off the trail and slapped it on the boards I was using for a backrest. After the dung dried in the sunshine Didi would use it for cooking and heating fuel in the teahouse.

Not sure if my embarrassment had anything to do with it, but Mike obtained an invitation for the four of us to have dinner with Didi and her family. The teahouse was also the family's home. What a cool experience! We got to share a home-cooked meal with a Sherpa family of four, mother-Didi, her two daughters, a little one and a 12 year-old, and Didi's mother-in-law. Didi's husband was away from home working as a guide on a mountaineering expedition. Didi's English was pretty rudimentary, but the elder daughter attended the Hillary School in Khumjung and was delighted with the opportunity to practice her English. She spoke English much better than her mother, who was self-taught.

Didi and her two daughters outside their teahouse, Dingboche, 1995

Didi and her daughter served out dal bhat, which Didi prepared fresh in the kitchen. Dal (lentils) bhat (rice) is the most popular dish in Nepal. Didi added little chunks of yak steak and boiled potatoes. After six hours of hiking a dusty mountain trail, dal bhat with a bottle of Orange Fanta made a marvelous meal.

The grandmother looked 90, but Mike whispered that she was probably in her 60s. The old lady sat at the far end of the table away from us. She muttered sullenly to herself during the meal, and did not seem happy about the sahibs' presence in her house.

Bajai (Nepali for grandmother) was dressed in traditional Sherpa clothing, a long striped robe with a head scarf. I asked if I could take her photo, but she shook her head indicating she didn't want me to. Didi chuckled, and her daughter explained that old people think a camera can steal their soul when it takes their picture. When I thought she wasn't looking, I held the camera down at my side and snapped a photo in the direction of the grandmother. It was wrong, and unfortunately the flash went off. Bajai jabbed her finger in the direction of the camera and made a hissing sound like she was zapping the camera. Didi laughed, and her daughter explained that Grandma put a curse on the camera. When I had the pictures developed (remember, this was 1995, before digital photography) there was no photo, not even a negative, of the old Sherpa woman.

The day was slipping away. We needed to get back to Tengboche. Mike said not to worry; it was mostly downhill. Steve, Harris, and I were the strongest hikers in the Snow Lion trekking group. I was the oldest at 42. Harris was a couple years younger and Steve was in his early thirties. But Mike, in his mid-twenties, could leave us behind if he chose to. And he did.

Mike took off from Dingboche at a brisk pace. The three of us kept up, but my legs were really starting to feel sore, and I could tell that Harris was struggling too. Steve seemed to be doing okay. Before we found the main trail south of Pheriche, Mike took off jogging. He didn't say anything; he just started loping down the trail. The sun was beginning to set, so I guessed he wanted to make it back to Tengboche before it got dark.

Steve took off after Mike. Harris and I looked at each other, shook our heads and kept walking at a steady clip. It didn't take long before Mike's and Steve's backsides were out of sight. A half hour later we saw Steve standing alone at a trail intersection. He said he'd fallen behind Mike, and didn't know which trail was the main one back to Tengboche. The evening sky had gone grey. It was too early for any stars or moonlight. Neither Harris nor I were sure which way to go. While we were debating the issue, three Tibetan traders carrying huge rolls of yak-fur rugs tied to their backs camp humping down the trail to our right. We got their attention by waving, pointing in different directions, and loudly pronouncing "Tengboche" in a questioning voice. The leader seemed to understand our predicament, and nodded his head in the direction they were walking. We followed with fingers crossed that they were, indeed, going to Tengboche.

By the time we arrived at a little settlement called Deboche the moon and stars speckled the night sky. But, yeehaa! We knew we were on the right trail, because we'd walked through Deboche not long after we left Tengboche in the morning. Deboche is surrounded by a rhododendron forest, which is gorgeous in the spring with multi-colored flowers. But that night in late October the moonlight created an eerie glow around the naked-spidery-looking branches of the rhododendron trees. I remember the scene as both spooky and beautiful because of the weird shadows the gnarly tree branches cast all around us.

We made an odd-looking line of six silhouetted-figures trudging along, three burdened with six-foot-long rolls of carpet and three with light packs. The Tibetans had probably walked as far, or farther, than us that day with much heavier loads. Yet, it took all of our strength to keep up with them.

While we were plodding through the forest, a curtain of clouds turned off the light from the moon and stars above. Steve, Harris, and I stopped to fumble in our packs for our headlamps. The Tibetans marched on. By the time we were squared away with our headlamps fixed on our foreheads and packs strapped back on our shoulders the three Tibetan traders were out of sight. The trail turned abruptly uphill. The steeper the trail got the darker the night became. I could no longer see any sign of a trail. Steve, Harris, and I got separated struggling up a damnably steep hillside through the forest. I heard other voices on the hillside and above shouting, whistling, and singing. I surmised that this hill must be the Northside of the Tengboche plateau. My legs felt like they were dead. The last hundred yards up I had to use both hands to grasp a leg behind the knee and lift, one leg at a time, to finally reach the crest.

I stumped my way to my tent, hoping Steve and Harris had also made it back to our campsite on the monastery grounds. But I was too weak to give it much thought or look for them. I unzipped the fly and fell onto my sleeping bag, way too beat to remove any clothes or say anything to John other than groan.

I refused to get out of the tent for breakfast. I just lay on my sleeping bag nursing my sore legs and a grudge against Mike for abandoning his three clients.

The 1995 trek group and some of the crew; the author is front row far left; Dr. John is back row far right. Nyima took group photos on each of our cameras, so he is not pictured.

Super human ability of Nepalese porters

Before Hari, my guide and interpreter, and I arrived at the HRA Clinic in May, 2003, I'd learned that the most serious medical issues were not treated at the clinic. While we were camping at Phakding, where we met June Carlyle and the extended Hillary family, a porter suffered a severe stroke. Rather than transport him to the Hillary hospital in Kunde or to the HRA Clinic, the porter was evacuated by helicopter to Kathmandu. In three previous treks through the Khumbu I had seen only one helicopter rescue. By 2003 helicopter evacuations were a thriving business in Nepal. Several private firms competed for the business. In 2003 it cost up to $3,000 for a heli-evacuation.

The partially-paralyzed porter was carried to the lodge in Phakding to await the rescue chopper. He was quite old for a porter. He looked like he was around 50. (To Western eyes, young Nepalese always look younger than their actual age. But when they reach middle age at 40 or so, they always look older than they are.) Lucky for this particular porter, his employer, a trekking/mission group from Northland College, Wisconsin, had rescue insurance which covered their porters. The students, instructors, and guides "passed the hat" to collect donations for the porter's family. That, I thought, was the right way to treat porters – as fellow human beings, not beasts of burden.

The author is trying to hoist a load with the help of two porters half his size; Man Bahadur to the left and Ratinbir to the right, employees of Adventure GeoTreks; Kangel-Basa-Khumjung Trek 2009. Expedition porters typically carry loads like this one, which weighed around 80 lbs.

Most of the injuries suffered on trekking trails in Nepal are to porters. I have seen porters on Himalayan trails carrying unbelievably heavy loads. But despite appearing to have super-human strength, men and women working as porters are just as susceptible to injury as anyone doing heavy manual labor in dangerous circumstances. Porters not only work for trekking and mountaineering expeditions, they also work carrying tremendously heavy loads of lumber and rock. Carrying huge loads day after day for years is going to break the body down no matter how strong the frame.

As noted earlier, most Nepalese porters are between five foot two and five foot six in height and weigh 120 to 140 pounds. A study of porters in the Namche Bazaar area, reported in the Journal of Experimental Biology in 2016, found that, "On average, the men carried nearly 90 percent of their body weight. A quarter of them carried more than 125 percent of their own weight. ... The women carried an average of 70 percent of their weight." In 1998, I saw a porter literally running down the trail, carrying in his doko basket a six-foot-four 200 pound German climber who got sick at Everest Base Camp. The 2016 study found that "the porters' muscles were slightly more efficient at turning oxygen into work than the Western grad student test subjects," but the porters' ability seemed to depend mostly on the sheer determination to endure, rather than some physiological trait radically different from the rest of us. Their metabolism does work more efficiently at high altitudes. Porters typically maintain a steady pace, but take regular rest breaks when carrying heavy loads. The research indicates that what is truly different about Nepalese porters is the way they live and where they live.

It seems that the Nepalese porters are optimized for walking slowly with heavy loads. At that speed–load combination, their muscular efficiency is higher than that of the control subjects because they perform approximately the same mechanical work but at a lower net metabolic cost. One of the remaining explanations is that Nepalese porters have developed a skill in minimizing co-contractions to reduce the metabolic cost, without mentioning their high metabolic capacity, thanks to their training, anatomy and adaptation to high altitude. Moreover, the strategy of short intense exercise periods followed by frequent rest periods allows them to work at a high intensity level, spread out over many hours each day. "The mechanics of head-supported load carriage by Nepalese porters," G. J. Bastien, P. A. Willems, B. Schepens, N. C. Heglund, *Journal of Experimental Biology*, 2016.

Nowhere else in the world do people carry heavy loads exactly the same way as porters in the Himalayan region. The doko has a cloth strap or "tumpline" that fits over the porter's forehead and is long enough that the doko rides on the porter's back. The load weight is distributed down the porter's spine from the forehead. Some dokos have strings attached to the sides of the basket so the porter can shift the weight from side to side without stopping. Dokos do not have shoulder straps, like Western backpacks. Many porters carry a staff, called a "tokma", which is used for support and balance on steep trails. When stopping to rest, a porter might place his tokma under the bottom of the doko to take the weight of the load off the porter's forehead. The resting porter will just stand there on the trail breathing hard for a couple of minutes, then pull the tokma out from under the doko and start walking up the trail. For longer rests, they set down the doko and squat or lie down by the side of the trail.

Porters are the tractor-trailers of the Himalayan region, moving the supplies and materials for expeditions and construction projects. At lower altitudes their competition is mules; at higher altitudes it is the yak. Novice trekkers often assume that yaks are more economical to use, because they carry more gear than a porter. Not true. Yaks weigh up to 1,500 pounds, and can reach almost six feet at the shoulder. But they typically carry only 120-150 pounds of cargo. Current rental cost is around $40 per day. A porter can be hired for $12 to $20 per day and carry 60-120 pounds. The common belief in Nepal is that high-end expedition companies prefer hiring yaks to haul gear in blue 50-pound drums, because it makes a more aesthetically pleasing picture than a small human in shabby clothes burdened with a huge load.

Porters preparing their meal in a cave where they slept; Phakding, 2003

So, why are Nepalese porters able to carry so much weight at high altitudes? There is evidence that nature or nurture has endowed these folks with a higher red blood-cell count than sea-level dwellers. But Western trekkers whose red blood-cell count shows they are acclimated to high altitude cannot perform similar feats of strength and endurance. (The study cited above bears that out, and so does my experience. We had a pulse oximeter – it measures the oxygen saturation level in blood -- on our 2009 trek. Several members of the group had oxygen levels comparable to those of our staff, but there is no way any of us could carry the loads our porters were carrying. These small people can carry loads equal to their own body weight on steep rocky trails wearing cheap Chinese-made sneakers or flip-flops, or even barefoot. Only the most elite and well-trained Western climbers can handle comparable challenges, and they do it wearing high-tech boots, trekking poles, and the best backpacks and clothing that money can buy.

Not long ago porters hired by expedition companies typically wore handmade clothes or clothes given to them by members of expeditions they worked for. If there was no lodge by an expedition campsite, porters slept in caves or huddled together in the corner of a mountainside. They might get to sleep in the meal or kitchen tent on some expeditions, but tents specifically for porters were rarely provided on expeditions. If they slept in a lodge, it was on the floor in the dining room, not in sleeping rooms. For food, porters carried cloth bags of rice tucked into their shirts or pants. They cooked the rice in tins over an open fire and ate rice every meal. Porters were typically paid $4 to $8 per day.

The higher the elevation reached during a trek, the higher the pay scale. That rule is still followed, and pay has more than doubled in the last 10 years. Treatment of porters began to improve after the civil war ended in 2006. The government of Nepal has passed regulations requiring expedition companies to provide proper footwear, gloves, and sunglasses, if porters work above the snow line. Adventure GeoTreks, the expedition company I've used since 2006, provides complete outfits of yellow and red wind pants and hooded windbreakers for its porters regardless of the anticipated elevation of an expedition. But they still carry huge loads.

More about AMS at the HRA Clinic and a famously arrogant climber
While I didn't see the inside of the HRA Clinic in 1995, you'll recall that I was treated there for AMS on the way to Pokalde Peak in 1998. The Jubilee Celebration trek of 2003 was my first

opportunity as a non-patient to observe the operations of the highest medical clinic in the world.

To reach the HRA Clinic in 2003 Hari and I hiked through the rhododendron forest beyond Tengboche, where my legs gave out on the hike back from Pheriche in 1995. In 2003 Hari and I were able to enjoy the beauty of the flowering trees, since it was springtime and I wasn't dead-tired hiking after dark. When the rhododendron forests are in bloom, the Himalayan Mountains below the tree-line are speckled with colors ranging from white, pink, red, and purple. In the fall the mountains look more rocky and austere. In all seasons the great white peaks rise up to the clouds sparkling in the sunlight.

Hari and I criss-crossed over the glacier-fed rapids of the Imja Khola River, passed intricately carved mani stones and a series of chortens high above the river gorge. We always kept to the left of the mani stones and chortens, as is customary when passing sacred places in Buddhist areas in Nepal. After about five hours of pleasant and scenic hiking we arrived at the windswept plateau of Pheriche at 14,340 feet altitude.

Hari's nephew, Bhuwan, a good-looking 20 year-old with the clear coffee-complexion and fine-straight-black hair typical of high caste Hindus, was working for the HRA Clinic as a physician's assistant. After hugging Hari and greeting me with the customary "Namaste" and head bow with palms together below the chin, Bhuwan ushered us into the clinic's small office and offered us tea. According to Bhuwan, the HRA had originally intended the clinic to have at least a skeleton staff year round. But volunteer medical doctors from developed countries were only willing to staff the clinic in the spring and fall during the trekking-climbing seasons.

I was skeptical that the HRA intended to provide year-round medical services to local people. I remembered Nyima's cynical criticism about the financial motives of the HRA. Very few Sherpas live year-round as far north as Pheriche. The few lodges in Pheriche, Lobuche, and Gorak Shep, the last three stops before Base Camp, all close during the winter and summer. There would only be a few yak herders in the area during the monsoon and winter season. The Hillary-funded hospital in Kunde does operate year-round and its purpose was to provide medical services to the local people, not trekkers.

141

I had no complaints about my treatment as a patient in 1998. I thought the care provided by Dr. Sandra and the staff was right on. AMS treatment was obviously the primary focus of the clinic. There were only a few local people being seen for sickness or injuries unrelated to trekking or mountaineering expeditions. Most of the AMS patients were trekkers, but some were Nepalese porters.

When Hari and I arrived at the clinic in 2003, a gaggle of porters were standing inside the door waiting to see a doctor for minor problems ranging from AMS-related issues to contusions and abrasions, strains and sprains, sunburn, and vision problems. In the treatment room a 60ish German woman was being given oxygen. Bhuwan told us that she was in Reinhold Messner's trekking party, and she'd gotten altitude sickness on the way to Base Camp. Messner is a living legend. He was leading a trek to commemorate the Golden Jubilee of Hillary and Tenzing's summit of Everest and to celebrate the 25th anniversary of the first ascent of Everest without supplemental oxygen. That ascent was accomplished by Messner and his climbing partner, Peter Habler.

Bhuwan shook his head in disgust and said, "Messner is famous climber, but is arrogant man." Bhuwan explained that Messner showed no sympathy for the ailing woman and seemed very annoyed that he had to waste some of his time dealing with her medical situation. We gathered from others we met along the trail that Messner was not at all popular in the Khumbu. Unlike Hillary, who was beloved and admired by local people and climbers, Messner had offended many people with his arrogance. He had become world famous for climbing Himalayan peaks, like Hillary. Unlike Hillary, Messner had not endeared himself to the Nepalese people.

Hari and I stowed our packs at the Panorama Lodge and then hung around the grounds of the clinic waiting for the volunteer doctors to finish with their patients for the day, so that I could interview them. Bhuwan joined us outside the clinic during a break from his duties. He excitedly told us the latest news he'd heard through the Everest Base Camp Trail grapevine. 32 climbers had summitted Everest the day before, May 22, 2003, including an Indian team, Nepalese Army team, and a Japanese team. Two weeks of bad weather had prevented any summit attempts prior to this, and there was worry throughout the Khumbu that there might be no summits during the Jubilee. Wow, 32 in one day! (That seems ridiculous, but according to *Wikipedia* the most summits in one day was on May 19, 2012, "when 179-234 reached the top." It's not clearly explained, but I think the figure indicates that 179 summitted on the Tibet side and 234 on the Nepal side.)

By 2003 I was with Sir Edmund Hillary; leave the mountain alone for awhile! I didn't share that sentiment with the local people whose livelihoods depend on mountain tourism.

People in the Khumbu reacted to news of activity on Everest much like fans of local sports teams in developed nations. Word-of-mouth and the one radio station that could occasionally be heard at night were the only means of transmission of information up and down the Base Camp Trail. The only news anyone seemed interested in on the Trail in May 2003 was about activity on Mt. Everest and the Jubilee celebrations.

As described in the previous chapter, in 2002, a monument to climbers who had died on Mt. Everest was erected on the grounds of the Pheriche clinic. While we waited for the doctors, Hari and I counted 178 names on the plinth. The official count of summits was 1,659 by the end of 2002. By the end of the 2018 climbing season around 4,000 climbers had summitted and 296 people (119 Sherpas and 177 other climbers) were known to have died on Everest since 1921.

To my dismay, Bhuwan reported that the doctors would not be able to sit down for an interview that day. Bhuwan looked even more disappointed than I felt. He wanted to impress Uncle Hari with his importance at the clinic. Bhuwan assured us I'd be able to conduct the interview tomorrow. Then he brightened and said we could attend a lecture, which would be starting very soon, about Acute Mountain Sickness. Bhuwan proudly announced that one of the volunteer docs, Dr. Kirsten Moller, would be giving the lecture and he would be assisting her.

Bhuwan explained that the clinic offered twice-daily programs to trekkers about AMS and other common health problems developed from hiking the high altitudes of the Khumbu. There was nothing else to do, so Hari and I attended the lecture presented by Dr. Moller, a slight, athletic-looking, blond, Danish internist.

Dr. Moller informed the 20+ in attendance that ignorance and carelessness were contributing causes of many trekkers and climbers getting sick. She said that about 35,000 people hike through the Khumbu each year, but only 1,500 stop at the clinic to hear the lecture on AMS. "Ninety percent of our patients wouldn't need treatment, if they just stayed on a schedule of three hundred meters maximum altitude gain per night. But not enough people get this information. And too many think they are strong climbers and can ignore it." I raised my hand and offered testimony about my experience in 1998 as an example of one of the ignorant and careless ones.

Some climbers and physicians are convinced that taking Diamox will prevent AMS. Others, like Dr. Moller, are not opposed to using it profilactically, but think the best approach is to gain no more than 300 meters (1,000 feet) sleeping altitude per night on a trek or climb. How much altitude a trekker/climber gains during the day isn't critical. Climb or hike as high as you want to during the day. What may cause altitude sickness is camping/sleeping at an elevation more than 1,000 feet higher than the previous night. If that rule was followed, Dr. Moller thought Diamox would only be needed if the trekker/climber still got AMS.

On the other hand, **WebMD**, a site I've consulted for various medical issues, recommends: "To *PREVENT ALTITUDE SICKNESS*, start taking ACETAZOLAMIDE (Diamox) 1 to 2 days before you start to climb. Continue taking it while you are climbing and for at least 48 hours after you have reached your final altitude. You may need to continue taking this medication while staying at the high altitude to control your symptoms."

The problem I have with taking Diamox profilactically is that it is a diuretic. When we're hiking at high altitudes, we are already consuming, as we should be, more liquids than normal. If it's a warm day, you're sweating, so you should be drinking enough water to avoid dehydration. And, another recommendation to avoid AMS is to drink even more water than you normally would during vigorous physical exercise. So, you're already peeing more often than usual, because you're drinking much more water than normal. When you also take a diuretic, your pee stops dramatically increase.

The first time I took Diamox, prescribed by Dr. Sandra, I had to pee every ten minutes. Krishna and the guys in our crew started calling me "Pee-Pee Man". (Tom was "Sexy Man".) The only time I took Diamox profilactically was on the 1999 Mera Peak expedition. I started experiencing symptoms of AMS the first night of the trek. It was weird; almost like taking Diamox caused altitude sickness. That experience convinced me to take Diomox only in the event that I definitely had AMS and not profilactically. It was also evidence that I have a genetic predisposition for AMS. The only way I can try to ward off altitude sickness is to drink a lot of water, pee a lot, but be vigilant in not gaining more than 1,000 feet per night.

A problem with the 300 meters/1,000 foot rule is that on some trails there are no campsites or lodges within 1,000 feet of each other. It's not feasible to follow the 1,000 foot rule on some Himalayan trails. For example, the elevation difference between Phakding at 2,640 meters and Namche Bazaar at 3,438 meters is over 800 meters, which is a gain of over 2,600 feet! So, the rule is grievously violated by most trekkers and climbers on the second night of the standard Base Camp trek.

It also struck me that, while listening to Dr. Moller's lecture, providing the information about the 300 meter rule at Pheriche has a serious drawback. We were already over 14,000 feet elevation. If you were going to get altitude sickness on the Base Camp Trail, you might already have it by the time you heard the lecture.

The doctors and Bhuwan worked late that evening. A Russian climber arrived during the lecture. He was helped down from Base Camp with symptoms of pulmonary edema. In the morning they were occupied with treating a Sherpa climbing guide suffering from appendicitis. The Russian could be treated at the clinic, but the Sherpa guide had to be evacuated by helicopter.

Dr. Martin Wilcox, one of the two volunteer docs, told me the Army helicopter, which transported the Sherpa guide, was the same chopper which performed the highest altitude rescue on record. It picked up a Taiwanese climber and Dr. Beck Wethers off Mt. Everest at 20,000 feet. Wethers was a member of Jon Krakauer's *Into Thin Air* climbing team. He lost his nose and part of his hands to frostbite, but he survived.

Dr. Wilcox was a tall, hearty, white-haired retired U.S. Navy general surgeon. He'd lived a full and active life, but called his three months at the HRA Clinic "the most rewarding of my life." He spoke with delight about the opportunity to practice medicine using "rudimentary equipment without a lab, but focused simply on helping people get better."

Doctor Wilcox invited Hari, Bhuwan, and me to join him in "the sun room", which was an odd square-shaped structure of glass with a Plexiglas roof. It got unbearably hot during the day, but when the sun began to set behind the western peaks it offered the medical staff a respite from the small, cramped, windowless clinic. Dr. Wilcox brought out and passed around bottles of Coca-Cola from his private stash.

After Dr. Wilcox enthused about his experience at the clinic, his tone changed to angry frustration about corruption he'd experienced with the government in Nepal and the HRA Board. One example he gave was that the clinic was required to use a particular helicopter-rescue company whenever a heli-evac was needed for a private-paying patient, such as the German woman in Messner's party. Dr. Wilcox was sure there were kickbacks involved with the helicopter company and the HRA Board, because the patients had to pay $3,000, which was a huge sum in Nepal in 2003. In the case of the German woman, Dr. Wilcox related that she waited over 24 hours for the helicopter to arrive. He was sure another company could have flown a chopper in sooner, if clinic staff were allowed to check availability of other companies. Dr. Wilcox was also upset that the clinic had taken in over $30,000 in patient fees, yet, because of inadequate equipment, the clinic had fifteen power failures and twice run out of oxygen in the three months he'd worked there.

Dr. Wilcox became visibly upset describing how a porter had needlessly died. "No one knew what to do for first aid. He needed an emergency evacuation, but there was no way to call one in, so they just brought him here." He shook his head sadly, "But it was too late."

A major health problem in the Khumbu, according to Dr. Wilcox, was the lack of means of communication. In 2003 there were very few satellite phones in the Khumbu. The primary means of communication was foot-messenger. The good doctor planned to present a proposal to the Motorola Company to develop a communications system among the villages, so that first-responders could communicate with physicians at the HRA or Kunde Hospital. (I imagine Dr. Wilcox knows, and is gratified, that cell phone service finally reached most of the remote areas of Solu-Khumbu

Province by 2016. I don't know whether he ever made any progress with his idea for a first-responder communications system.)

Dr. Moller joined us in the sun room for a Coke and conversation. I reported in the previous chapter her explanation of improvements in the health of Sherpas on account of the switch from open fire cooking and heating to iron stoves with smoke stacks. Another example Dr. Moller gave of how life was changing for the Sherpas involved childbirth. She said that "Sherpas believe it is a bad omen for a child to be born outside of the home." However, she and Dr. Wilcox, and volunteer docs who preceded them at the clinic, were urging Sherpa mothers to go to the Kunde Hospital to give birth. I asked whether she thought giving that advice was being culturally sensitive. Dr Moller admitted to worrying that there may be a downside to the way better healthcare and infrastructure improvements were introduced into Sherpa communities. She said she was glad the world recognized the Sherpas for their climbing achievements, but predicted that in the not too distant future the adaptations of Sherpa culture to Western ways would push it over the tipping point. "But so many changes improve the quality of life, how can we criticize?"

The volunteer doctors' three-month stint was up at the end of May. Dr. Moller planned to fly to Kathmandu by helicopter when her last patient was evacuated. Dr. Wilcox wanted to make the trek back to Lukla with Bhuwan. They'd have to fly standby from there to Kathmandu. Volunteer doctors at the HRA Clinic had to pay their own travel expenses and were paid no stipend for their service.

What porters think

Hari and I left the clinic in Pheriche to hike on up to Everest Base Camp, where we met Lakhpa Gelu after he broke the Everest-summit speed record. Then we trekked back down to Tengboche for "the highest party in the world".

We paid for our late night of revelry with rubbery legs on the trail south of Tengboche. Thank god the trail back to Lukla is mostly downhill.

It pissed off Hari, but on the last day of the trek, I hired a personal porter to carry my pack from Namche to Lukla. It was so liberating to be free of that burden. I felt light as a feather and started skipping down the trail between Namche Bazaar and Phakding. After the joy of losing 45 pounds began to wear off, I waited for Hari to catch up. I listened meekly to his grumping at me for running off and leaving him behind. "That is not being a good client, Jeff dhai," Hari scolded. ("Dhai" means "older brother" in Nepali, but is also used as a term of affection by a younger man of lesser status for an older friend of higher status.) I was tempted to reply as Don Quixote would have responded to an upbraiding from Sancho Panza, but thought better of it. Anyway, Hari forgave me after I explained our next task. I wanted to interview several porters along the trail back to Lukla.

Hari was delighted with the plan, and knew he would be invaluable as my interpreter. In 2003 it was very unlikely we'd find a porter that spoke much English. It would be bad form to try to interview a porter while he was carrying, so we stopped at a couple different teahouses where porters were resting.

The first interview was with the porter I hired to carry my pack for the day. Tham Bahadur Rai was 43 years old, ancient for a porter. But he leaped at the chance to earn a day's pay, when I walked into a low-end teahouse, whose clientele was locals and porters rather than trekkers, and asked whether anyone was looking for work. Tham easily hefted my backpack and strode sprightly down Namche Hill as if he wasn't carrying a thing.

At the bottom of the hill we stopped to rest and I conducted my interview of Tham through Hari. Tham said he was "very happy" about the 50th Anniversary celebrations. In 2002 he worked on an Island Peak and Base Camp expedition, but he "had more business this year," so that made him happy. He told us that a landslide near his home village killed around 40 people. He hoped the area where he lived "would get more attention, because of Anniversary."

Hari approached six other porters we met along the trail, but only two were willing to be interviewed. Man Bahadur and Suk Aram worked for the same expedition company and came from the same village. Man said, "I don't care about 50th Anniversary or 100 or 150th anniversary, but, if more tourists come, that's good for us." Suk agreed and added, "If tourists don't come, not good, no work." They both said they didn't care about Tenzing or Hillary or climbing Everest. Although both men were willing to talk, they certainly did not share the upbeat and friendly attitude I'd experienced with most of the people I'd met in the High Himalayas. They weren't impolite or hostile, but definitely not friendly.

The attitude of the two porters surprised me. They were Tamang. Hari reminded me that people from other parts of Nepal were coming to resent the wealth and fame Sherpas had acquired. Other tribesmen were glad for the money they made as porters, but it didn't go unnoticed that fewer and fewer Sherpas had to take the low-end job of portering. Instead, Sherpas were making the big bucks as teahouse and lodge owners or they got the high-paying jobs as sirdars and climbing guides.

While we hiked on toward Lukla, I asked Hari whether he thought the unwillingness of porters to be interviewed and the unfriendly attitude of the two porters we interviewed had something to do with the trekking season being nearly over. I speculated that the porters returning home might not have made as much money as they'd hoped to. Hari chuckled and said, "Porters like those guys spend all the money they make on rakshi (booze) and food on the walk back to their village." He remarked indifferently that they'd be dirt farmers again when they got home.

Imagining Suk and Man returning to their village empty-handed after working so hard filled me with pity for them. When I expressed that to Hari, he shook his head, shrugged his shoulders, and said, "That's the life of a porter."

Hari was the son of a Brahmin priest, but had secretly converted to Christianity. Yet, he retained the Hindu understanding that humans were born into a certain status or caste. It was very unlikely that fate would pluck one out of "the wheel of life". So, you should expect to live and die in the caste you were born. That's just how it is. That fatalistic attitude is contrary to the American spirit. "Anyone can grow up to be President!" Americans like to think we are masters of our own fate. The attitude is quite different in Nepal.

We asked a few other porters what they thought about while they were humping heavy loads down the trail. I wasn't quite sure if the answers we got were accurately translated by Hari or they were his own ruminations. Hari said all porters think about the same things, their family, their village, their girlfriend if they're not married. I asked if they chanted mantras while they carried to help keep their minds off the pain of carrying such heavy loads. He laughed and said, "Porters are like truck drivers. Some like to listen to a transistor radio, but most can't afford that. They might hear a song in their head, but it's not to be religious. They just want to get the job done so they can eat their rice and rest."

While I stood in line to check in for my departure flight from Nepal at Tribhuvan International Airport in Kathmandu, I spotted Dr. Wilcox. He was leaning against the ticket counter for Thai Airways, the major carrier for international flights back then. He had a tired but patient look on his tanned face. He told me he was flying standby and his prospects were not good. With the Jubilee festivities over, many people were leaving the country. When my flight was called, it made me feel guilty to board. Dr. Wilcox had given three months of volunteer medical service in Nepal and he was flying standby. I glanced back at the good doctor as I entered the curtained area to go through security. He gave me a wane smile and waved goodbye.

The People's War and an Inauspicious First Philanthro-Trek
Langtang and Yala Peak 2004

I left Nepal in 2003 with tremendous admiration for how Sir Edmund Hillary combined his love of mountaineering with philanthropic development projects in the Khumbu. I was fired up to emulate Hillary's efforts; on a comparatively minuscule scale, of course. My first attempt to organize a philanthro-trek was the following year in the fall of 2004.

The effort yielded pretty meager results. I raised $1,820 and collected 65 pounds of school and medical supplies. Most of the donations were made by friends at the church I belonged to back then, First Meridian Heights Presbyterian. I delivered the money and supplies to an organization called SEEDS; an acronym for Social Economic Environmental Development Services. My understanding was that SEEDS would deliver the supplies to a school for deaf children in Pokhara, Nepal's second-largest city, northwest of Kathmandu. The cash would be used to help fund a water project for a village in the remote and very poor Dolpa District of Nepal, which is also northwest of Kathmandu.

I was confident the money and supplies would be put to good use by SEEDS. The nonprofit was founded and run by KP Kafle, who owned Himalayan Wonderland Treks, the outfitter company Tom Proctor hired for our 1998 Pokalde and 1999 Mera expeditions. It was also the company Hari worked for, and Hari was the supervisor of the water project. I didn't actually see the funds put to use or the educational materials and medical supplies delivered. The lack of personal involvement tinged the effort with a feeling of unfulfillment. But it was a start.

KP is a successful businessman, high caste Brahmin, and philanthropist. He is small, even for a Nepali, with fine-boned sharp features. His English is excellent. He's a licensed massage therapist, and takes a massage chair on treks he leads. I never trekked with KP, but imagined it must have bewildered or amused local people to see a massage chair carried up Himalayan trails and then white people being rubbed and thumped in it by KP. But what a treat for tired legs and a sore back at the end of a long hiking day!

KP did a fine job outfitting the Pokalde and Mera expeditions and helping to plan the 2003 trek with Hari. KP stayed at my house for a weekend in 1999 during a fundraising trip for SEEDS in the US. I arranged for him to give a talk about trekking in Nepal, and a pitch for donations to SEEDS, at First Meridian Heights Presbyterian Church. We've been out of touch since 2006. That's the year I began working with Niru Rai to organize treks through Adventure GeoTreks (AGT).

I checked out SEEDS' current website for this chapter. The organization is still very active with multiple projects in the works. I also did an online search for KP and learned that he changed the name of his trekking company from Himalayan Wonderland Treks to Heart of the Himalaya Treks. When I last talked with KP in 2005, he had negotiated a deal with the American outdoor-recreation company, REI, to staff treks REI sponsored. In KP's bio on Heart of the Himalaya Treks website it states that KP was "recognized as one of REI Adventure's Top Guides of the Year" in 2008.

It was also interesting to learn from the Heart of the Himalaya Treks website that Hari Pudasaini still works for KP as the company's senior guide. It was really delightful to learn from the SEEDS website that Seth Acharya, sirdar and savior of our porters after the avalanche on the 1999 Mera Peak expedition, is on the SEEDS Board of Directors. When I last spoke with Tom Proctor, a couple years after the ill-fated 1999 Mera expedition, Tom told me that he'd heard Seth had married an American woman and was living and working in Seattle as a house painter. The SEEDS website bio for Seth states that, "He is the co-owner of Everest Waterproofing and Restoration in San Francisco, California. Seth is married and lives in San Francisco, CA with his wife (who is also from Nepal) and two beautiful children ..." I don't know if the dream Seth told me he had -- to become a licensed guide in the US Rocky Mountains -- ever came true. But it seems he had another dream -- to become a successful US businessman and marry a Nepali woman. And it did come true.

As fond as I was of Seth, Hari, and KP, the expedition I organized in 2004 to trek and climb in the Langtang region of Nepal was my last association with them. I tried unsuccessfully to connect with KP in 2005 to plan a philanthro-trek for 2006. I later learned that during the month I tried to contact him KP was on a fundraising trip in the US. He did not receive or didn't respond to several emails I sent requesting help to plan a 2006 expedition to climb Lobuche East, a mountain just southwest of Mt. Everest. So, I conducted an online search for an alternative outfitter company. That's when I discovered AGT and began my email relationship with Niru Rai.

The relationship with Niru blossomed into the special relationships I developed with AGT and with Niru's home village, Basa. I had no complaints about services provided by KP's company, and I was sure the money and provisions donated to SEEDS were put to good use. But getting directly involved with the Basa area of Nepal and working intimately with Niru to organize and plan trekking expeditions for other groups, as well as my own, created a more fulfilling relationship than what I'd developed with KP and SEEDS.

President W's and the Commies' damage to Nepal's tourist trade
The results of my efforts to recruit members to a trekking-climbing expedition in 2004 were even less auspicious than the fundraising. Six people initially planned to join the group, but five chickened out due to US State Department warnings that it was dangerous for Americans to travel in Nepal. Only one friend, Elliot Schwartz, came through.

Elliot was a college buddy and University of Chicago Rugby Club teammate. Elliot is just under six feet tall and his playing weight on the rugby team was around 200 pounds. He's a big strong guy, who still runs marathons. In college Elliot was well known for his acerbic wit, streaking through Regenstein Library, and changing from a long-haired hippie to a balding acolyte of Milton Friedman. He moved to South Africa a few years after receiving his MBA from Chicago. The experience Elliot and I shared in 2004 was so cool, Elliot joined another expedition with me back to Langtang in 2007. Since then, he's organized and led expeditions with AGT almost every year. I became AGT's liaison in the US and Elliot took on a similar role for AGT in South Africa. But in 2004, it was just going to be the two of us on a Langtang-Yala Peak expedition.

As soon as the 2003 Jubilee celebrations ended, the civil war in Nepal resumed. The country had experienced the material benefits of the boom in tourism during the 1980s and 90s. It experienced a significant loss of those benefits when tourism declined over fears about the Maoist insurrection in the late 90s and early 2000s. Nepalis in the tourist industry hoped the 2003 Jubilee truce would hold and the flow of tourists would continue after the celebrations ended. Those hopes were dashed. Tourist dollars were not a sufficient incentive for the two sides to negotiate a permanent truce. The more important issue of who should govern Nepal was at stake. The fighting resumed in 2004 and the State Department's warning to Americans remained in effect.

It was galling to me that the US government discouraged travel to Nepal, because it threw a wrench into my plans for organizing that first philanthro-trek. What was more distressing was the change I'd witnessed in Nepal with respect to violence. Just before my first visit to Nepal in 1995, a Nepalese guy killed a European tourist in a bar fight in Kathmandu. The entire nation was in mourning when Long John and I arrived. There was a feeling of national disgrace and sorrow over a guest of Nepal being killed by a Nepali. A year later the ten-year-long civil war broke out. According to the *BBC*, the official body count of Nepalese killed during the war was 16,278. About two-thirds of the deaths are attributed to government forces. The Maoists were responsible for the other third. What changed in the soul of a nation that considered the death of one foreign guest a national disgrace, and then killed over 16,000 of its own people in a civil war?

The simplest answer to that question, given by most of my Nepali friends, is that King Gyanendra was an asshole and a terrible ruler. Had he continued the trajectory his older brother, King Birendra, started – parliamentary democracy based on the rule of law which protected civil rights – the Maoist insurrection would not have escalated into a civil war.

Explaining the causes of the civil war and downplaying the risks to foreign guests did not relieve the fear my American friends had about traveling to Nepal. Anyone traveling to an unfamiliar area should consider the risks involved. And, different people have different levels of risk tolerance. Elliot's reaction, for example, in learning that the five Americans had bailed on the expedition, was amusement. He thought Nepal would be safer during a civil war than Johannesburg. South Africa's capitol had one of the highest rates of street crime in the world. Given the high rate of violent crime in the US, as compared to Western Europe, one might have expected the decline in US visitors to Nepal would have been less than the decline of tourists from Western Europe. That was not the case. European tourists were less risk averse about visiting Nepal than Americans. There was a drop-off, but substantial numbers of tourists from Western Europe, Japan, Taiwan, Australia, and New Zealand continued to visit Nepal during the civil war. The flow of American visitors was reduced to a trickle.

The drastic decline in Americans visiting Nepal was especially disappointing to Nepalis in the tourist industry. Americans are well-liked in Nepal. A major reason is the difference in our custom of tipping from that of most other nations. Nepalese sirdars and European and British expedition leaders I've discussed this topic with are in agreement that Americans are the biggest tippers, on average, of any nationality. The conventional theory is that Europeans, Brits, and Asians are used to having service charges included in their bills. Americans are accustomed to giving a tip to wait staff, bell hops, valet parking attendants, etc. So, Americans are generally happy to generously tip their trekking crew and other service workers in Nepal. Tourists from other nations, who are not habituated to giving tips, might be unaware of the custom of tipping at the end of a trek or they might resent the expectation.

Whether it's true or not that Americans are the biggest tippers, Nepalis working at hotels, restaurants, and for outfitter companies have told me that, "We like Americans!" And yet, the US State Department under George W. Bush seriously damaged Nepal's second largest industry by scaring off American tourists.

It's a disturbing fact that over 16,000 Nepalese died in their civil war (called "The Peoples' War" by the Maoist-Communist Party of Nepal) between 1996 and 2006. Yet, no trekker, climber, or visitor to Nepal I met during the war experienced an actual physical act of violence directed against a visitor to Nepal by fighters on either side of the war. One of the few indirect experiences I had of the violence of the civil war occurred in October 2004. While I was mucking around in Tribhuvan International Airport trying to find lost baggage (more on that below), I heard sirens wailing outside. When I exited the terminal, Elliot, who'd been waiting for me, pointed to a smoke cloud rising in the distance. He said an explosion just went off in downtown Kathmandu. We learned from news reports at our hotel that Maoist guerrillas rolled three hand grenades into a government office building. Several people inside the building were injured.

The US State Department had a legitimate concern about the potential for American tourists being injured as collateral damage of the war. Declaring all of Nepal unsafe to visit was an over-reaction. The Bush Administration ratcheted up unhelpful pressure by declaring the Communist Party of Nepal a terrorist organization. The Maoists did use terror tactics, but government forces killed far more Nepalis than the Maoists. Many Nepalis considered the Maoists freedom fighters. The country was divided into three major camps, similar to the American revolution against the British monarchy. Like American Tories, some Nepalese were loyal to the monarchy, some supported the revolutionaries, and some were neutral. Post-war developments in Nepal indicate most Nepalis want the country to evolve into a democratic republic.

The war ended when the communists and the "democrats" were able to align, oust King Gyanendra, and hold parliamentary elections. The Communist Party won the largest number of seats in Parliament after the first election. Those who actually understood the socio-political-economic situation in Nepal knew it was too simplistic to label the Maoists as evil terrorists. Their tactics could be criticized but their goals of forcing an unpopular king to abdicate and to create a parliamentary system were ultimately accepted by the Nepalese people; just like the result of the American Revolution.

[As an aside, if you think Americans go for crazy conspiracy theories, get a load of this one. During the war period, a couple Nepalese friends told me that many Nepalis believed there was a conspiracy involving the King, the Maoists, and the Bush Administration. The theory was that these forces were actually working together for the malign purpose of preventing parliamentary democracy taking hold in Nepal. Suspicions that have more credence are that the Chinese government was aiding the Maoists and the Indian government and CIA backed the King. There were also many wild conspiracy theories circulating around the country about who was actually behind the slaughter of the royal family and suicide (or was it murder?) of Prince Dipendra. Given the circumstances, it's not surprising that the official report would generate skepticism and wild speculation. The heir to the throne shot his parents and siblings at the dinner table and then turned the gun on himself!?]

The one tactic of the communist revolutionaries that directly impacted trekkers was claiming territorial rights over certain trekking trails. Trekkers hiking those trails became revenue sources for the Maoists. Armed bands blocked the trails and ordered any foreigner stopped by the roadblock to pay a fee to use the trail. The leader of the band would give the trekkers a lecture about politics in Nepal and then issue each trekker a certificate confirming the fee had been paid so other Maoist war bands would not collect a second fee from the trekker. If a trekker didn't have enough money to pay the fee, the Maoists would take a camera, climbing gear, a down jacket, or some other valuable possession.

An Irish trekker I met in Kathmandu told me that when he was stopped by Maoists on the Annapurna Trail he complained, pointing out that he'd already paid the government to purchase his trekking permit and it was unfair of the Maoists to charge more money. The leader of the Maoist patrol replied, "They are the government in Kathmandu. We are the government here. If it's fair that you pay the government in Kathmandu, it's fair you pay the government here."

The amount charged by the Maoists was usually around $100. After the US added the Maoists to its list of international terrorist organizations, the Maoists declared that any Americans stopped by a Maoist patrol had to pay double the amount they charged all other nationals. I wrote "Canada" on my trekking duffel with a Sharpie, just in case. But I never encountered a Maoist checkpoint in the many miles I hiked in Nepal during the war years of 1996 through 2006.

The Maoists were unsuccessful in penetrating Sherpa communities in the Khumbu, where I did most of my trekking and climbing. The unpopularity of communist doctrine among Sherpas is not surprising, since the Sherpas benefited more than any other tribal-ethnic group from tourism. However, every Westerner I met in Nepal who hiked the Annapurna Circuit in the late 1990s through 2006 got hit up for money by Maoists. Gurungs are the dominant ethno-tribal group along the Annapurna Trail (more on Gurung culture in a later chapter). In the Khumbu, what we encountered was an ever-increasing military presence. Each year, more government soldiers manned an increasing number of military checkpoints. It did not make me feel safer to be stopped by farm-boy soldiers with loaded guns on the trekking trails. But, at least they didn't shake us down for money.

Things always work out, sort of, in Nepal

Not only did the first philanthro-trek get off to an inauspicious start in recruiting members and fundraising, neither of my checked-in bags arrived at the airport in Kathmandu when I did. I went back and forth between the Kathmandu Guest House (KGH), where Elliot and I were staying, and the airport for three days checking with Royal Thai Airlines, the carrier I'd flown from LA to Bangkok and then to Kathmandu. On the second day, I was directed to go down into a huge room under the terminal. An elderly attendant gestured at hundreds of suitcases, duffel bags, and backpacks randomly spread out across the vast room. Without much hope, I began looking through the sea of bags. To my amazement, within a few minutes of looking I found my five-foot-long Army Surplus duffel with my name and "Canada" written in large black letters on the side. I'd packed the 65 pounds of donated items for the deaf school in the big duffel. Great! But I didn't find my expedition backpack with all my climbing gear, down parka, and most of my clothing.

Damn it! Frustration over the loss of my pack and mountaineering gear overwhelmed the joy of finding the duffel with the donated supplies. Yet fate has a way of patching things together in Nepal. Nothing ever goes strictly according to plans, but things always seem to work out one way or another.

A Swiss member of an earlier mountaineering expedition with Himalayan Wonderland Treks left his expedition pack and all his gear with KP. The client planned to return in 2005 to do another Himalayan expedition. KP loaned me the pack and gear. To my delight, the climbing boots fit as well as my own; much better than the borrowed pair I used on Kanglachan. KP also loaned me a down parka, long underwear, glacier glasses, and a balaclava. I was ready for the mountains with a patched-together kit. (KP received notice from the airport while we were up in the mountains that my pack was found. So I had clean clothes for the flight home.)

More good luck through a chance encounter in the hotel's internet café! Two days before we were scheduled to drive up into the mountains, Elliot and I were hanging out in the KGH's internet café sending emails home, drinking tea, and chatting. Elliot heard a South African accent behind us. We turned and Elliot nodded in the direction of a tall, beautiful, blond young woman, who was purchasing time on a computer from the café's clerk. We struck up a conversation and learned that "Briggie" (her real nickname) was traveling around the world for a belated gap year. She wanted to do a Himalayan trek in Nepal and was looking for a group to join. We told her about our plan to trek up Langtang Valley and climb Yala Peak. I was pretty sure KP would be able to accommodate her. In truth, with the downturn in tourism, I knew KP would be delighted to have another paying client.

Briggie admitted she had no climbing experience, but neither did Elliot, and I was by no means an expert climber. We assured her she'd fit in just fine. Briggie's common nationality with Elliot's adopted country was probably reassuring. She was young, having a great adventure traveling around the world, so why not join an expedition with these older gentlemen? And so she did.

Amazing Abilities of Nepali Sirdars

Hari Pudasaini, my guide and interpreter for the Jubilee, served as the sirdar for the Langtang-Yala Peak expedition in 2004. Hari was a delightful trekking companion. Like Seth, I think he could have made a living as a stand-up comedian on the club circuit in the United States. Hari loved telling and hearing dirty jokes. Any stick-like item, trekking poles, an ice axe, firewood, etc., provoked a phallic reference. Elliot's and my forte was more scatological and fart oriented. But Hari enjoyed humor of any genre, so he was happy to increase his repertoire by learning scatological jokes in English.

Hari was also dedicated to his work as a sirdar. So he was properly decorous around Briggie. There was clear gender discrimination within our group the first few days of the trek. The guys were careful to stifle the urge to make stick and fart references when Briggie was within earshot. She was no prude, but she wasn't a guy. Hari, Elliot, and I were brought up to act like "gentlemen" around a "lady". After a few days on the trail, however, certain niceties, along with bathroom customs, tend to break down. Briggie was fully integrated into our little team within a few days on the

Langtang Trail. Language was probably a little cleaner in the meal tent with Briggie on the team, but not much. A guy's crotch might get a gentle poke with a trekking pole under the table. A backside sticking out, when bent over stuffing a pack, might merit a poke with an ice axe, followed by an appropriate piggy-squeal. Briggie joined in the laughter at the butt of the joke, but was never the victim.

Hari's fun-loving personality was somewhat at odds with his role as sirdar. The first two sirdars I had were both Sherpas, Nyima on the 1995 Base Camp Trail trek and Tsering on the Ladakh-Kanglachan expedition. Their personalities were stoically serious. They weren't into joking around. They were natural leaders whose reserved bearing and efficient command of any situation inspired respect in their judgment. Krishna put on a serious face whenever he was acting in his official role as sirdar, but was happy to loosen up when his duties were done for the day. Seth and Hari, on the other hand, handled their responsibilities as well as the other sirdars, but did so whistling and cracking jokes. No matter how physically whipped and drained we were, they managed to find something to laugh about.

All of these guys, and sirdars you will encounter in later chapters, are some of the finest examples of human beings I know. Most Himalayan mountain guides grow up in mountain villages, learn the expedition business, and rise up through the ranks to the highest position in an expedition crew. Because they've carried the heaviest loads themselves, they have the strength of porters. And because they've worked as kitchen boys and cooks, they've learned what appeals to their clients' palate. Sirdars must command the respect and loyalty of their crew. And, because they deal with clients from many different nations and cultures, they must be able to adapt themselves and their crews to different expectations of different nationalities. Most sirdars have a basic command of English, several European languages, Chinese, Japanese, and many of the local tribal-languages of Nepal. Nepalese sirdars combine the skills of an army platoon leader, logistics officer, and are multi-lingual to an amazing degree.

Langtang Trek
The drive from Kathmandu up into the mountains was the first

test of endurance for our little team. It took over twelve hours. We endured inspections by grumpy, sneering soldiers at six military checkpoints and stops to repair two flat tires. The mode of transportation was a local bus. Most of the passengers were local people, who lived in villages outside of the Kathmandu Valley, but worked in Kathmandu. One young man I spoke with told me that he worked and attended a business school in Kathmandu. He stayed with relatives in Kathmandu during the week. He rode the bus home to his village in Langtang every weekend and then back to Kathmandu every Monday. His dream was to get a job in a bank, marry his hometown girl, and then raise a family in Kathmandu.

This photograph of some of our fellow passengers climbing over the landslide-blocked road to Dunche was awarded 2d place in the Indianapolis Star's travel photo contest in 2005.

That young man was another example of the Nepalese character

I found to be so winsome. He endured a horrendous commute every week, and he did it in good spirits. My respect doubled when the bus stopped a couple hours before we were supposed to arrive in Dunche Village, where the road ended.

Looking through the front window of the bus I was dismayed to see a huge mass of boulders and rubble piled higher than the roof of the bus. The road was blocked by debris from a landslide. I assumed we would have to walk the rest of the way to Dunche. The locals knew better. With grim determination my young friend and the other passengers picked up their luggage and exited the bus. Briggie, Elliot, Hari, and I followed. We picked our way through the rocky mess over the landslide. Lo and behold, another bus was parked there waiting for us. We loaded up and drove on to Dunche.

One of my most treasured hiking experiences in the Himalayas was on the sixth day of our Langtang trek. It was a 10-hour-long hike from Kyanjin Village to Langshisa Ri. The sky was overcast all day and the temperature dropped below freezing mid-afternoon. Fluffy snow flakes were falling throughout most of the afternoon. We had to don our down parkas and mush through the gathering snow on the way back from Langshisa Ri to Kyanjin Village. But the mountain vistas along the border with Tibet, dominated by the 26,289-foot-high Shishapangma, were heavenly. We sheltered in a cave to eat our pack lunch. South of the cave was a lone horse grazing in a kharka (open pasture). Snow was collecting in the horse's mane.

Hari had excused himself from the hike to Langshisa Ri, claiming he needed to deal with the logistics of preparing for the climb of Yala Peak. I poked his tummy, which had grown outward a bit since our trek the previous year, and joked that he seemed especially interested in overseeing food preparation this year. He laughed good-naturedly and shooed us on the way. The previous five days on the Langtang Trail to Kyanjin Village were not particularly challenging. We had gorgeous views of mountains, crossed two rivers, and camped near lovely Tamang villages as we trekked up the Langtang Valley. (Photos at the end of the chapter provide a taste of what Langtang offers trekkers.) Kyanjin Village was supposed to be the end point of the trek before gearing up to climb Yala Peak. But my *Lonely Planet* guide book described the hike from Kyanjin Village to Langshisa as a tough but very beautiful one. So, instead of taking the scheduled rest day before the climb, Elliot, Briggie, and I opted to use the day to test our conditioning and experience the beauty of the hike to Langshisa Ri.

The 10-hour hike gave Briggie, Elliot, and me the chance to get better acquainted with Lakhpa Sherpa, our climbing guide. Lakhpa led the hike to Langshisa and back, while Hari prepped and probably sampled the food supplies for base camp.

Yala Base Camp

Elliot and Briggie proved on the Langshisa hike that they were physically fit for their first Himalayan climb. Briggie was a triathlete and Elliot ran marathons. I did neither and, despite appreciating the beauty of the long day-hike, by the end of it my nose was running like a waterfall, my eyes were red, and I thought I might have developed a sinus infection. So naturally, the next day turned out to be another very long and tough day of hiking to Yala base camp.

To make matters worse, damn it, Elliot! He hiked out ahead of our crew with Ram, our cook, hurrying after him. We lost sight of them and Lakhpa and Hari thought Ram and Elliot must be lost. We searched for awhile, gave up, and hiked on up to the standard base camp. Hari said we could hunt our lost teammates down after we dropped our loads at the base camp. Surprise! Ram knew the area and he and Elliot were already there awaiting our arrival. In the meantime, our porters had fallen behind and now we didn't know where they were. After a couple hours of confused searching, whistling, and shouting, we found the porters. They had set up camp at a different, and arguably better, site for a base camp. There were two goths (yak herding shelters) with stone walls, which provided the campsite with some shelter from the cold, biting wind. The downside was that the camp chosen by the porters was a much greater distance from the base of Yala Peak. The hike to the mountain before the climb was going to be more time-consuming than we'd anticipated.

Ram prepared a hot Sherpa stew on his kerosene-fueled camp stove for dinner. There are variations of Sherpa stew, but it usually has corn, potatoes, some veggies, and spices, such as cumin or turmeric, and some bits of meat. Like every dish in Nepal, it's usually accompanied with rice. Ram added chunks of (this is not a joke) ram meat. Ram added ram to many of the dishes he prepared for us. The first day of the trek Hari purchased and Ram butchered a whole ram. So, ram meat was on the menu every day.

The stew was very tasty, but I was pretty beat from two long hiking days. My cold was getting worse, and I feared I was also getting AMS. Elevation of our base camp was estimated to be around 14,500 feet. The dreaded spike-in-the-forehead headache hit that night. It was a cold, windy and mostly sleepless night at Yala base camp for me. Everyone else seemed fine. In the morning – praise Vishnu, Buddha, Jesus, or whoever – the symptoms had moderated and I felt strong enough to give Yala Peak a try.

Seeing with hands and feet on Yala Peak

We started hiking toward the mountain at sunrise. Lakhpa realized that after two days of 10 and 12 hours of hiking we needed as much rest as possible before we started humping our gear to the base of the peak. So, instead of scheduling the start of the climb in the dead of night, we were allowed to sleep through the night. I tried.

Yala Peak, 2003

As the sun rose and heat and light reflected off the snow and ice, we began to sweat profusely on the hike from base camp to Yala. The hike to the mountain took about three hours. The first challenge was a slippery moraine. Moraines are difficult to hike, because of the uneven rocky-surface. This one was also slippery due to melting snow and sleet. We had a couple more hours of sweaty trudging through snow fields to reach the base of the peak. Blindingly bright sunlight reflected harshly off a long white glacier covering the near side of the mountain.

We'd met a group of Dutch climbers in Kyanjin Village. They told us that the glacier on Yala was melting. That report was affirmed by a British group we also talked with in Kyanjin. The leader of the Brits told us they decided Yala was too dangerous to climb, because the glacier was breaking up. "It's slippery and dangerous, a bloody mess!" he exclaimed. But we also met a more intrepid group of German climbers before leaving Kyanjin. They were jazzed with excitement over their successful summit of the peak.

Lakhpa Sherpa, climbing guide, followed by the author on Yala Peak, 2004

During the hike to base camp, Lakhpa told us the Dutch and Brits were correct. The glacier was receding. But when we arrived at the base of the mountain, it looked like a great white beast. Snow and ice covered the near side of the mountain. We unstrapped our ice axes from our packs, put on our climbing boots and crampons, and tied on to a single line. Lakhpa was leading; I was second, then Briggie with Elliot in the rear. We dumped everything we didn't need to climb beside the glacier. Hari and Rajaman, one of our porters, hiked with us from base camp to the mountain. They guarded the discarded packs and waited at the bottom for our return.

Struggling up the Yala glacier was more difficult than crossing any other glacier I'd experienced in the Himalayas or in Alaska. I was used to a relatively hard, icy surface. This glacier was soft with deep snow; because, as the Dutch and English had warned, it was melting.

During the hike to Yala I was worried that I wouldn't be able to handle the climb. The symptoms of AMS returned. My ass was dragging, and I was slowing the rest of the team down. Struggling up the glacier drained all my reserves of energy. I was completely gassed when we arrived at the upper edge of the glacier. Just beyond the end of the glacier was a 15-foot rock wall. Crampons came off and up the wall we climbed. Something about the thrill of rock climbing -- the challenge of finding the right holds for fingers and placement of boots -- I love that feeling of combining strength, balance, and coordination. The heaviness and weakness I felt slipped away.

The top of the rock face turned out to be a false summit. The actual high point on the mountain, the true summit, was on the other side of a sheer rocky ridge which ran about 40 yards across and 70 feet higher than where we stood.

Lakhpa decided it would be too risky to cross, and told us to enjoy the view, take photos, and relax. Briggie would have none of it. She was determined to stand at the pinnacle of 18,110-foot- high Yala Peak. She got down on her hands and knees and started crawling across the rocky ridge. Lakhpa frantically hustled after her and coaxed her back to the safety of the false summit. We debated what to do. Briggie was adamant that we had to reach the true summit. I agreed. The issue was resolved by Lakhpa anchoring the rope on a boulder and then scampering across the knife-edge ridge. He tied the rope off on the granite summit and signaled we could cross. Elliot had begun to feel dizzy, so he elected not to cross. Briggie and I carefully worked our way across the ridge with our harnesses clipped to the rope by locking carabiners.

Lakhpa, the author, and Briggie on Yala Peak summit, 2004

I was amazed at Lakhpa's ability to skip across the narrow, rocky ridge. Yet, his skill was typical of Sherpa climbing guides. I asked him how he did it. "Sherpas have eyes in their feet," he laughingly explained. I have seen elite Western climbers move with a careful grace on mountainsides. They are equal to Sherpas in the ability to climb the most challenging peaks. But it seems like there is a subtle difference. Elite Western climbers use their eyes to see the holds and place their feet, and they do it with incredible skill, strength, balance, and coordination. Sherpa climbers do it with such natural ease it seems like they don't have to look for the holds -- as Lakhpa said, like they have eyes in their hands and feet.

Back on the false summit, we rappelled down the rock wall, which was even more fun than climbing it. I don't know whether she had caught Elliot's dizzy spell or it was a "Freudian slip", but on the rappel down, Briggie managed to kick a stream of rocks off the ledge, which almost brained Elliot and me. I had to slap one away from my face with my heavily padded glove-hand. Briggie did the same thing on the ascent, so Elliot had to twice duck away from a mini landslide. The irony was that Briggie was the only one wearing a helmet. She should have been the one under the rock shower instead of causing it. But so it goes.

Yala was an 11-hour-long tiring, beautiful, and exhilarating experience. We slipped and clambered and sunk into deep snow up and back down a 1,000-foot-long glacier. We jumped across a five-foot-wide crevasse, climbed up, and rappelled down a 15-foot rock wall, and then picked our way across a 40-yard knife-edge ridge. And we ducked and jumped to avoid getting smacked by loose rocks kicked down by our own teammate. What more would you want in a day of adventure in the Himalayas?

Even now, remembering the magnificent views 15 years later, I drift into reverie. The day was beautiful. It was warm and sunny with a lovely cerulean sky. A couple fluffy cumulus-clouds floated just above the glinting white peaks lining the border between Nepal and Tibet. It was a true peak experience.

By the time we finished the long hike back to Kyanjin Village, I was so tired and physically drained, I was sure I'd never want to do that again.

Briggie, Elliot, and Hari hiking back to Kyanjin Village from Yala Peak

Celebrating Dasain Festival with Tamang People in Kyanjin Gompa

I was not ready to admit it yet, but my enjoyment of the Himalayan region was beginning to shift away from the thrill and grueling work of mountaineering to the cultural and aesthetic experiences of trekking and spending time in the villages with local people.

The dominant tribal-ethnic group of the Langtang region is the Tamang people. Like their Sherpa neighbors to the east, most Tamang are Buddhist. They are more numerous than Sherpas, but are a small percentage of the population of Nepal, about 5.6% and around 1.5 million, according to a 2011 census. (The Sherpa population is around 160,000.) Like the other ethno-tribal groups in Nepal, the Tamang have their own language, which has multiple dialects. The ancient oral-traditions of the Tamang claim that they, like the Sherpas, came over the Himalayas from Tibet to settle on the south side of the great mountains.

[Sources differ on the exact number, but there are between 40 and 50 different tribal groups in Nepal. There are around 100 different castes. Every traditional occupation is considered a caste. For example, carpenter and potter are different castes. Sources also differ on how many indigenous languages there are in Nepal. Some of the disagreement is over whether a particular tribe has a unique language or it is a dialect within a language. But most sources agree there are well over 100 distinct indigenous languages spoken in Nepal.]

Tamang involvement in mountain tourism developed later than it did for the Sherpas as a consequence of location. They didn't live as close as the Sherpas did to the big fish the Europeans were obsessed with catching, Mt. Everest. As the Sherpas prospered through tourism in the Khumbu and no longer wanted to work as porters, the Tamang and Rai people, the closest neighbors to the Sherpas (Tamang to the west, Rai to the southeast) took up those jobs. Eventually, trekkers and climbers expanded their interest in Nepal beyond the Kathmandu Valley and the Khumbu. Langtang Valley offers a gorgeous alternative.

However, local people initially resisted government efforts to develop tourism in Langtang. They did not want their beautiful valley inundated by trekkers. The Tamang were aware of how tourism changed the Sherpas way of life, and many of them were not thrilled with the idea of following suit. The government, however, realized that opening another tourist-trekking trail would bring in more revenue. In 2001 the Nepal Tourism Board sent representatives into Langtang to teach local people how to deal with tourists and to encourage the development of campsites, teahouses, and lodges. In 2007, the main trail through Langtang Valley was rechristened by the Tourism Board as the Tamang Heritage Trail.

It's understandable why there was reluctance to follow the example of the Sherpas in transforming the local economy into tourism. The traditions of the Tamang in clothing, religious practices, the arts, and communal relations run very deep. Community leaders realized their traditions would be at risk, when young Tamang had daily exposure to Western ways and styles. The local economy in Langtang was more diverse than the Khumbu's. Unlike the Sherpas, whose economy before tourism was little more than yak herding and potato farming, Tamang were weavers, potters, artisans, and builders.

Briggie, Elliot, and I were fortunate to experience the richness of Tamang culture at Kyanjin Gompa. The 15-day festival of Dasain was being celebrated while we trekked through Langtang. Dasain was originally a Hindu holy festival. But it is celebrated all over Nepal as a national holiday and has taken on a secular dimension. For non-Hindus, and many Hindus, the primary purpose of the holiday season is to visit one's home village and party with extended family. It's a celebration of family and community.

Note the prayer beads in the women's hands; Dasain celebration at Kyanjin Gompa, 2004

I've been in Nepal several times during Dasain, but the most interesting Dasain celebration I experienced was at the 600-year-old gompa in Kyanjin in 2004. Hari arranged an invitation for Elliot, Briggie, and me from the caretaker monk to participate in the monastery's festivities. First, the monks performed a chanting ceremony and played gongs and wind instruments, led by an aged monk with a long, wispy white beard. The village women bustled around serving everyone who came to the ceremony hot chang from large iron kettles. They dipped a ladle into the kettle and poured chang into porcelain cups.

Monks enjoying some hot chang during a break from chanting at Kyanjin Gompa during Dasain celebration, 2004

The monks drank glass after glass of chang. I felt a buzz after just two cups. The monks' ability to maintain sufficient focus to keep up the chanting and play their instruments while drinking all that chang was truly impressive. The chang inspired Briggie, Elliot, Hari, and me to join in the chants.

What a wonderful religious ceremony! Buddhist monks invited a Brahmin Hindu turned Christian (Hari), a white South African of Boer descent (Briggie), a Jewish-American expat living in South Africa (Elliot), and a Presbyterian soon to become an agnostic animist attending a Quaker Meeting (me) to participate in a Hindu festival celebrated in a Buddhist temple with Tamang villagers. Everybody got drunk and happy while the monks chanted and played atonal music.

Experiencing Langtang

There are many other incidents I could describe about the experience of trekking through Langtang in October 2004. The following is a rapid-fire synopsis.

The first day we hiked through a pretty little terraced settlement called Dimsa, which is surrounded by pine forests. We passed by a magnificent waterfall and camped in a village called Thulo Syabro. A friendly horse hung around our campsite. We met Dr. Pierre and his 14 year-old son, Thomas. They were from Zurich, Switzerland. We met them again in Kyanjin Village, where Dr. Pierre gave me antibiotics to fight the sinus infection I'd developed.

In Langtang Village we bathed in the Langtang Khola and pumped and filtered water for our water bottles out of the same river. We crossed that river and another, the Bhote Koshi, on suspension bridges. We drank tea and played cards at teahouses, with names like Lama Hotel and Landslide Lodge. Elliot and I taught Briggie how to play poker, and she took on Dr. Pierre in chess. A shop owner proudly displayed an array of cheese balls strung across the shop on a rope.

We saw a number of horses along the trail, which surprised me. You rarely see a horse in the Khumbu. We learned that the Tamang are horse riders, wranglers, and breeders. Sherpas are not; they breed and herd yaks.

We saw a 50-something American hanging on to a pony for dear life riding into Kyanjin Village. He was the only American we met on the trail. Kim told us he was a lawyer who represented banks. He said he became so disgusted with practicing law and bankers that he decided to take a year off to travel around the world. He'd planned to hike from Dunche to Kyanjin, but "got pootered out, so I had to rent a horse."

We saw snow leopard tracks on Yala Peak.

On the hike back down the Langtang Trail we camped by an army post in Ghora Tabela. Elliot and I played volleyball with a group of soldiers and villagers. We were the tallest players. The Nepalis were very impressed the first few times Elliot and I blocked or spiked a ball above the net. The smaller Nepalese players were quicker at running down and digging balls. They seemed unaffected by the fact that we were playing at an elevation over 12,000 feet.

Flying back to Kathmandu by helicopter I noticed the pilot was hugging the west side of Langtang Valley. I asked why. He said that Maoist guerillas occasionally took pot-shots at helicopters from the east side of the valley.

Back in Kathmandu we were hosted by my friends, Raaj and Mingma, for a family celebration of Dasain in their home. Several of Raaj's musician friends came over and we had a wonderful time singing, dancing, eating dal bhat and momos (dumplings stuffed with veggies or meat) and drinking rakshi and chang. The family was sheltering a Tibetan, who was a follower of the Dalai Lama and a refugee from Chinese oppression.

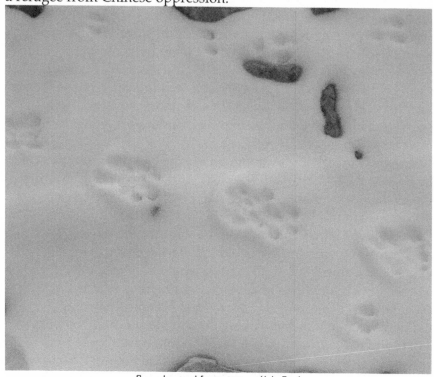

Snow leopard footprints on Yala Peak

Sadhus, Sirdars, Yaks, British Aristocrats, and Rai Animism
Gokyo, Lobuche, and Pokalde Peak 2006

As explained in the last chapter, communications broke down between KP and me after the 2004 expedition. I felt deeply attached to Hari, Seth, and Jid Baldoo, the brave porter who helped Seth bring the rest of the crew safely back from Mera, and Ram, who was our camp cook on the Pokalde, Mera, and Yala expeditions. But I needed to move on, when I couldn't get a response from KP about planning a 2006 expedition. I'd looked up at the mountain I wanted to climb from its base in 1998 and 2003. The summit of Lobuche East is just over 20,000 feet. It's a formidable-looking peak, but similar to the others I'd climbed. So long as the weather cooperated, the technical challenges would be minimal. Endurance would be more important than mountaineering skills.

I wanted to trek to the mountain via the Gokyo Trail rather than the Everest Base Camp Trail. The Gokyo Trail parallels the northern (upper) half of the Base Camp Trail. I'd never been on it. Far fewer trekkers use the Gokyo Trail than the Everest Base Camp Trail. I wanted to hike a trail and visit Sherpa villages that were not yet transformed by tourism. We could trek back down from Lobuche on the Base Camp Trail, so the group would still have the experience of hiking the most famous of all Himalayan trails. My last emails to KP expressed frustration at his failure to reply. I finally gave up and began looking for another outfitter company.

I found Adventure GeoTreks (AGT) online and began corresponding with Niru Rai by email. I learned that AGT had very little experience with Americans. Most of Niru's clients came from Germany and France. He'd organized a few treks for French Canadians. He sent me copies of glowing reviews AGT received from European and Canadian clients. I contacted three of AGT's clients and received replies from all three praising AGT's guides and crews to the heavens. I sent Niru a description of the expedition I wanted to do. He replied with a proposed programme, which was priced very reasonably. (English spellings are used in Nepal. "Programme" is the term used by AGT and other outfitters for a trek itinerary.) The decision was made. It was disappointing to know I wouldn't be seeing my friends in KP's company in 2006, but I was excited to make contact with this company that was so highly praised by its clients.

Preparing an expedition programme is a big job in itself for the outfitter company. All in-country services for the group must be determined, a total cost calculated, and then a price per member figured. The costs will vary depending on the number of group members. It costs more to buy food for ten than for five, and the more members, the more porters needed. But economies of scale can reduce the per member cost of food and supplies

Determining the cost is just the beginning of the outfitter's work. Hotel reservations in Kathmandu and transportation from the airport must be arranged for each group member. Most outfitter companies only keep senior guides employed year-round. Porters, cooks, kitchen boys, and some guides are seasonal workers. So, for each expedition the outfitter must find and contract with the guys (some women do work on expedition crews, but they are rare) to staff the trek. All food and fuel that won't be purchased or scavenged along the trail must be purchased, stored, and then transported to the trailhead. Same with the camp stove(s), cooking supplies, tents, ropes and climbing equipment; everything that's needed for the expedition that can't be obtained up in the mountains must be provisioned in Kathmandu. Trekking and climbing permits must be purchased in advance for each group member.

All the planning, calculating, and provisioning must be done to create a daily programme that the organizer-leader, me, can show on paper to potential group members. The work product Niru delivered to me for our "Gokyo-Lobuche-Base Camp Expedition" was a daily itinerary and a sliding scale price list. The cost went down by $50 for each additional member over four, not counting me. I could email a copy of the programme to anyone interested in a detailed description of what the group would be doing and what it would cost to participate.

The outfitter company's office staff must be very detail-oriented and careful in their calculations. But it's the trekking crew that has the hard manual-labor of executing the programme. Everything the expedition needs to get from point A to point B must be handled by the crew, led by a sirdar. A successful outfitter company's crew will work extremely hard to make sure the clients have a (relatively) safe and enjoyable (on some level) experience. Although it never goes exactly according to plan, almost everyone who does a Himalayan trek considers it a wonderfully transformative experience. Most clients go home with a desire to give back and come back to Nepal.

The responsibilities of the organizer and so-called leader (as will be seen, a title mostly in name only) are much simpler. You come up with an idea for an expedition. "Sell" it to a few people who can afford the time and cost. Make sure all members pay by the time the outfitter company needs the cash. And then leave everything else up to the Nepalese guys actually doing the work. My deal with KP was that, if I recruited four members, then he wouldn't charge me for the trek. For every member I recruited over four, he would pay me $100, which, in theory, I would use to reduce the cost of my airfare to/from Kathmandu. Those dollars remained theoretical, because I never put together a group with KP which had four or more paying clients.

When I began corresponding with Niru Rai about a spring 2006 expedition, I told him about the deal I had with KP. He said that AGT, in addition to a "free" trek for me, would pay me $100 for each member of the group no matter how many members I recruited. That surprised me, but, yeah! I was okay with it. I knew I would still be paying a significant amount out of my own pocket for airfare, expenses in-country, and a generous tip for the crew.

The possibility of spending less money to participate in an expedition was attractive, but my primary motive was to introduce Americans to the mountains, cultures, and people I had come to value so much. I could offer to help make that happen at a lower cost than what American-based expedition companies charged. Working directly with a Nepal-based company removed the cost of an American guide's salary and tip from the equation. And, the profit margin expected by local companies was less than what American-based companies expected. I compared the cost AGT charged for the programme Niru prepared to what several US and UK-based expedition companies charged. AGT's price was 30 to 50 percent less. That would make it a lot easier to recruit members. And, it should make it a lot easier for the group members to tip the trekking staff generously.

To put a finer point on it; AGT's charge for the 2006 expedition was about $2,000. Snow Lion's charge for the 1996 Ladakh expedition was around $4,000. Both programmes were about three

178

weeks long. Snow Lion's charge for the 10-day introductory trek part-way up the Base Camp Trail in 1995 was almost $2,000. Snow Lion's charges were similar to those of other Western-based companies. The additional cost of an American-based guide and larger profit margin tend to just about double the price of a Himalayan trek.

Two days before the scheduled arrival of our 2006 trekking group in Kathmandu, King Gyanendra suspended martial law and agreed to give up his dictatorial hold on executive power. Parliament was recalled.

In the preceding weeks hundreds of thousands of demonstrators had taken over the streets in Kathmandu and other cities to protest the King's abuse of power. The King's initial response was to order the military to shoot demonstrators. 17 pro-democracy demonstrators were killed by soldiers. The response of the Nepalese people was to engage in even more massive street demonstrations against King Gyanendra's anti-democratic practices. Even anti-communist Nepalis were disgusted with the King, because of his inability to defeat the Maoist rebels. Hostility toward King Gyanendra among the Nepalese people had reached a boiling point. Many citizens would not be satisfied with reforms which limited the King's power; they wanted an end to the monarchy.

Our group consisted of five middle-aged men, Bill, Vitto, Mac (false name), Greg, and me. Two women initially signed up, but cancelled out of fear generated by news reports of the violent response of the Army to the demonstrations. We had anticipated arriving in a country at war. But the day our flights left the US, April 24, 2006 was the date King Gyanendra agreed to relinquish autocratic rule and reconvene Parliament. The Maoists declared a 90-day truce with the understanding that power-sharing negotiations with the major democratic parties would occur. Street demonstrations ceased. Instead of violence and mayhem, when we landed in Kathmandu we found a country in party mode. Nepalis were thrilled that there was finally a real prospect of lasting peace, the restoration of parliamentary democracy, and possibly an end to the monarchy.

Unfortunately for Nepalis working in tourism, it would take awhile before the good news of the commencement of a peace process resulted in an up tick of visitors. The US State Department's warning against travel in Nepal was still in effect. The mass demonstrations and the Army's brutal response even scared away many European, Australian, and New Zealand trekkers and climbers. We learned from Niru and Uttam, the manager of Kathmandu Guest House who had become a friend of mine, that tourism was down by 75% in 2006. 50% of booked expeditions were cancelled after the Army's brutal attacks against peaceful demonstrators. Of the 13 times I spent time in Kathmandu, I saw far fewer Westerners in the narrow, winding streets of Thamel in 2006 than any other year.

Thamel, the hippie and tourist Mecca of Kathmandu

Thamel is the "old town" section of Kathmandu. The Kathmandu Guest House and most of the hotels, restaurants, and shops frequented by tourists are in Thamel. It's a fascinating destination in itself. Street vendors selling trinkets, prayer wheels, musical instruments, tiger balm, and hash share the streets with rickshaws, sun-burnt trekkers, and saddhus in loin cloths. There are tiny shops with a single seamstress selling handmade purses and embroidered shirts. Just up the street you'll notice a modern bank next to an outlet store for a major Western retailer, like REI. Down that same street there may be an open bazaar with handmade icons, rugs, and jewelry from Tibet. A beggar with a crippled child sits on the corner with her hand held out to each passer-by. Thamel is an incredible potpourri of humanity and a moving feast of things to buy and sell.

Pop culture in the 1960s and '70s was fixated on India and Nepal. If you're old enough, recall Transcendental Meditation, Ravi Shankar, the Hari Krishnas, and the Beatles emulation of all that. If you're not that old, you've surely heard as a golden oldie, Bob Seeger's 1975 hit *Kathmandu*; "Goin' to Kathmandu, that's what I'm gonna do!" Back then, a lax attitude toward hash and pot smoking, along with the custom of hospitality and tolerance by the Hindu-Buddhist culture, encouraged hippies and spiritual seekers to come to Kathmandu. Thamel is where they landed. For a couple decades a section of Thamel was known as "Freak Street", because a number of Westerners partnered with locals to open a bunch of head shops, vegan restaurants, yoga parlors, and meditation centers. By 2000 most of the Western hippies had left, but many of the businesses started by the hippies remained and were owned by local people.

But in the spring of 2006 the streets of Thamel were nearly empty of the tall-blond-haired climbers, hearty trekker gals, glassy-eyed dope fiends, and spiritual seekers (the "white people") I was accustomed to seeing in Thamel. There were even fewer of "us" on the mountain trails. We met a few intrepid Israelis up in the mountains, but they were about the only non-locals we encountered on the trek.

Street corner in Thamel that was crowded with Western tourists in previous years, but in the spring of 2006 the cabbie and rickshaw driver have no customers.

I felt bad for people in Kathmandu and the Khumbu dependent on tourism. But the tiny number of other trekkers made it easier for our group to have more personal experiences with local people. On the trails, there were no human traffic jams at narrow bridge crossings. There were fewer yak trains to dodge. Finding a private place to pee along the trail was less challenging. Fewer customers in the teahouses and campsites gave us more options to choose from. With no other campers around, our all-male group was able to engage in less restrained farting and belching, which is always enhanced by altitude and unfamiliar foods.

Uttam and the Kathmandu Guest House

Before we flew up to Lukla to begin the trek, I enjoyed catching up with my friend Uttam at the Kathmandu Guest House. Every day I have been in Kathmandu since meeting Uttam in 2003, we have met for a pot of tea and conversation. I met Uttam by chance, because the driver KP sent to pick me up at the airport for my 2003 trek with Hari did not find me.

I was standing outside the terminal looking jet-lagged and bewildered, when a big, handsome Nepali in a neatly-cut dark blue suit approached and introduced himself as Raaj, the Tour Director for the Kathmandu Guest House. He offered to drive me to the hotel. I thanked him, but explained I was supposed to be picked up by someone from Himalayan Wonderland Treks and that I wasn't staying at the KGH. After looking around for another ten minutes and not finding KP's druver, I accepted Raaj's offer.

A wise and friendly-looking little guy in a white shirt and dark tie with a bald pate and glasses, named Uttam, was the night manager at the hotel. I explained that KP Kafle's company had a reservation elsewhere for me, but I needed a room for the night and would sort out matters with KP tomorrow. When I mentioned KP's name, Uttam clapped his hands with delight and asked who my sirdar was. It turned out that Hari and Uttam had worked as interior painters together at the KGH, when they were teenagers. They'd been friends ever since then. He assured me there would be no problem changing the hotel booking KP had made.

The next morning Uttam invited me to share a pot of tea with him in the placid green space of the open courtyard at the KGH. The KGH became my favorite hotel in Kathmandu and where I recommended the other members of groups I organized stay. Uttam and I made it our practice to meet for tea and conversation each time I was in Kathmandu. We maintained that tradition as Uttam moved up the ranks within KGH management. In 2015, with some partners, Uttam bought the Moonlight Hotel near the KGH. So the last time I visited Nepal in November 2017 I stayed in Uttam's very own hotel, the Moonlight. Over the years, Uttam and I have consumed many pots of tea and engaged in lively conversations about everything from local and international politics to philosophy, religion, and our families.

I was surprised to learn from him that Uttam and his family were moving to the US in 2019. That gives me one less reason to return to Nepal.

Milk Baba and Sadhus

Before our group left Kathmandu in 2006, Sanga, a guide supplied by AGT, led our group on tours around the Kathmandu Valley. We witnessed Hindu cremations by the Pashupatinath temple complex on the bank of the Baghmati River, ate lunch overlooking the giant sparkling-white stupa of Bouddhanath, and took photos of the frisky monkeys running around the temples of Swayambhunath high above Kathmandu. Having done all that several times, I most enjoyed meeting a holy man I'd heard of but had not met.

Sanga arranged an audience with the Milk Baba (his name is Dudh Dhari, but everyone refers to him as Milk Baba) at his home across the river from Pashupatinath. Milk Baba had consumed no food or drink, other than milk, for over 25 years. He was slim, healthy in appearance, and an engaging conversationalist (through his attendant and interpreter). He prepared bowls of dal bhat and a pot of tea for Sanga and our group. The Milk Baba did not partake in the meal he offered us. He explained that he had chosen to engage in this discipline as a way of doing penance for the sins of all humanity. He didn't claim to be a savior, but did think of himself as a teacher by example. He wasn't trying to recruit or develop a following, and didn't ask for a money offering. (We left some Rupees with his attendant, anyway.) Milk Baba told us that to Hindus milk is a pure substance, so he was taking in purity while giving up what was impure in his personal effort for purification. He hoped others might be encouraged to avoid impurities in their lives.

The Milk Baba in his home in 2006. Note the TV and VCR.

Wikipedia defines "sadhu" as "a religious ascetic, mendicant or any holy person in Hinduism and Jainism who has renounced the worldly life... It literally means one who practices a *sadhana* or keenly follows a path of spiritual discipline." There are what I call "commercial sadhus" hanging around Pashupatinath and other temple areas in Kathmandu. They have elaborately painted faces, wear loin cloths or colorful robes, and will gladly let you take their photo in exchange for 100 Rupees (around one US Dollar).

The author with two "commercial sadhus" by Pashupatinath, 2006

The most pathetic effort at being a sadhu I've seen was in 1998. A young Englishman with long-ginger-colored hair tied back in a pony tail, and a scraggly little beard, dressed in a white robe carrying a traditional beggar's pot was followed by his pretty little blond girlfriend. Both were barefoot when I saw them start up the Base Camp Trail. After a day of walking they were filthy, limping badly, and sunburned. I hope they were rescued.

The concept of sadhu explained to me by Hindu friends is that, when a man has fulfilled all his familial obligations, he may go on a spiritual quest. He is not to work or earn money. But he may beg and receive gifts of food or money to survive. If he has children, he may not leave on his spiritual quest until they are grown. If he has a living wife, he may leave her only if he has provided for her for the rest of her life or as long as the spiritual quest lasts. It is a blessing to a fellow Hindu to give sustenance to a true sadhu.

Assaulting mountains; camping vs. teahouse trekking

For the fifth time since 1995 I flew from Kathmandu up to the airstrip in the Sherpa village of Lukla. The first time, in 1995, was in an aging Russian military helicopter. The passengers tossed their backpacks, duffel bags, cartons of food, boxes with live chickens, whatever, into the middle of the floor. Rope mesh was thrown over the cargo and securely tied down. The human cargo sat in a circle around the baggage and held on for dear life as the big chopper roared upward. There were no seats or seat belts. That same helicopter crashed in 1999 taking the life of the Mera Lodge Didi's son.

By 2006 all the old military transport-helicopters had crashed or were taken out of service. A couple of their hulking carcasses still squatted near a hanger at Tribhuvan Airport in Kathmandu. The old choppers were replaced by Twin Otter prop planes used by the three domestic airlines that flew up to Lukla. The planes were an improvement in safety and you could actually enjoy the spectacular views sitting in a seat, which had a seat belt, by a window. The landing was still a big thrill as the runway begins above a sheer drop-off of hundreds of feet and ends at a cliff-face, leaving no room for pilot error. I was delighted to see that the fence made of busted props, wings, tails, and a rusted fuselage remained on the north side of the runway in 2006; evidence that not every pilot made the landing error free.

In Lukla we met up with our crew of porters, cook and kitchen boys, and climbing guide, 17 in all. Our sirdar, Ganesh Rai, flew with us from Kathmandu. The other 16 guys Adventure GeoTreks hired to staff our expedition walked to Lukla from their home villages. It seemed kind of ridiculous that it took 17 Nepalis to tend

185

to the needs of five sahibs for 15 days of hiking, camping, and climbing. I learned from Ganesh on that first AGT trek that Niru over-staffs expeditions to provide employment for men from the Basa area, if they are in need of work.

Himalayan expedition companies run treks and mountaineering expeditions in the British tradition established in the 1920s. Those early mountaineering expeditions were organized and led by British military officers who'd served in World War I. The approach was to assault the mountains with an army. So they hired hundreds of Tibetans and Sherpas to do the grunt work. They brought in or purchased tons of supplies for the battle with the mountains. The "commanders" of the expeditions being British aristocrats, the supplies included, for example, "sixty tins of quail in foie gras and forty-eight bottles of champagne, Montebello 1915, the general's favorite vintage." (*Into the Silence* by Wade Davis, pg. 483)

Into the Silence includes journal entries and letters written by the early British Himalayan mountaineers, such as George Mallory, as well as press accounts describing the expeditions of the 1920s. It's clear from the materials Davis assembled that the British public looked upon the challenge of being the first to summit Mt. Everest similar to the way Americans wanted one of our own to be the first to stand on the Moon. It was a national effort as worthy as going to war against an enemy. The enemy for the Brits between the two great wars was Mt. Everest. There was an ugly jingoistic aspect to the way the Brits treated people native to the Himalayan region in the war waged against the mountain that straddles the border of Nepal and Tibet. But those were less sensitive times. The goal of summiting Everest was regarded as a heroic quest which was not intended to kill people. There were unfortunate casualties among the porters and climbers to be sure; George Mallory being the most famous. But that was collateral damage, not the purpose of the battle. Unfortunate deaths by avalanche and loss of body parts due to frost bite were acceptable casualties in the quest to conquer the greatest peak on Earth.

Davis describes coverage by the *London Times* about anticipation for the 1924 expedition to Everest (which ultimately claimed Mallory's life):

> ... the *Times* heralded the upcoming expedition as not just an inspiration to the nation but as the very embodiment of

British values and spirit, the essence of the race. "Whether the result be victory or defeat," the piece noted, "the third attempt to conquer Everest will mean like the two before it an inspiring display of the resolution and endurance and indifference to discomfort and danger that all through the ages and to the uttermost ends of the earth, have made the people of these islands, above all a race of pioneers. When General Bruce (leader of the expedition) says that the great adventure of Everest has now become almost a pilgrimage, he touches upon a profound truth."

After the mountain was finally "subdued" by Tenzing and Hillary in 1953 and the military purpose of mountaineering had run its course, some aspects of that style of mountaineering hung on for the tourist trekking and climbing that followed. The tradition of staffing expeditions with a small army of porters, cooks, kitchen boys, and guides continued. Like the early British mountaineers, clients are able to engage in challenging hiking or climbing but will be well fed and have others tend to the logistics of preparing and tearing down campsites and waste disposal. Either porters or animals carry all needed supplies up steep Himalayan trails, while the clients shoulder light packs to carry only what is needed for the day's hike.

In 2006 one of our members even had our sirdar, Ganesh, carry his day pack each day due to a flare up of low back pain. It's not that uncommon for a group member to be relieved of the burden of carrying her own pack due to sickness, tiredness, or an aching back. To a critical observer, few vestiges of a heroic quest appear to remain in tourist trekking. To the one hiking up and over a 10,000-foot-high pass, it still seems, if not heroic, a hell of a challenge.

Around 2000 the Nepal Tourism Board began to discourage camping treks and to promote teahouse treks. Clients sleep and eat in lodges on teahouse treks. The Tourism Board encouraged locals to build lodges and restaurants along the trekking trails. The Board's thinking (dubious in my view) was that the environmental footprint of a teahouse trek is smaller than a camping trek, because land is not cleared for campsites and human waste and garbage is not left behind at the campsites. But land has to be cleared to build lodges and restaurants and waste disposal remained a problem because there was no sanitary-waste-disposal infrastructure in

187

mountain villages. The obvious consequence of eliminating camping treks is a reduction in employment for local people. Fewer porters are needed and the positions of camp cook and kitchen boy are eliminated, because meals are prepared in lodges or restaurants.

Back on the Base Camp Trail; another visit with Gheylsan Sherpa
Our 2006 group spent the first two days trekking the Everest Base Camp Trail through the lower Khumbu region. We spent the first night of the trek at the Sherpa village of Phakding and the second in Namche Bazaar. Namche is called Bazaar, because it is the traditional trading center of Sherpa and Tibetan commerce. Its elevation is over 11,000 feet and its resident population is less than 2,000. Hiking up Namche Hill is a grueling half-day hike and the elevation gain from Phakding to Namche is around 2,500 feet. That's way over the AMS-avoidance rule of gaining no more than 1,000 feet of sleeping altitude per night. Namche became the typical place for the first "rest day" on a Base Camp trek. Business with trekkers and climbers became even more important to Namche's economy than trade with Tibetans.

Instead of resting, since we were a mountaineering team and expected to be in top condition, Ganesh led us on a four-hour day hike up to the Everest View Hotel for lunch, then through the village of Khumjung, where we viewed the famous/infamous Yeti skull and toured the first Hillary school for Sherpa children.

We gave pens, colored pencils, magic markers, and writing tablets to children we met along the trail. As payback for the interview Headmaster Mahendra Kathet gave me in 2003, and to maintain my commitment that each time I returned to Nepal it would be in some sense a philanthro-trek, I delivered a cache of school supplies to the Khumjung School and first-aid kits to the nearby Kunde Hospital.

After the group finished the excursions up country and returned to Namche, we visited the village's most eminent resident that evening. Ganesh called Gheylsan Sherpa "monjo", which Ganesh said meant "big man". Ganesh described Gheylsan as "the unofficial mayor of Namche". You'll recall that I first met and interviewed Gheylsan in 2003. He was one of the three Sherpa porters, who carried gear and helped establish the highest camp on Mt. Everest from which Tenzing and Hillary launched their

188

successful bid for the summit on May 31, 1953.

Gheylsan had no mountaineering training. Through sheer physical strength, determination, and his Buddhist faith, he was able to carry critical supplies up to the "Death Zone" on Everest. The last camp was almost 28,000 feet high, just a little more than 1,000 feet below the 29,029-foot summit. Most of the elite climbers who had attempted to reach the summit prior to Tenzing and Hillary did not get as high up the mountain as the high camp of the 1953 British team. The untrained Gheylsan Sherpa climbed that high carrying a heavy load of supplies, helped set up the camp, and then spent the night there before descending out of the Death Zone.

Gheylsan thanked me again for bringing him a copy of the April 2003 edition of *Outside Magazine* with his picture on the cover. One of the first things he did after inviting our group into his home was to show off the worn and tattered magazine he kept on a shelf by his side at the family dinner table. The magazine's condition indicated Gheylsan had proudly shown it to many visitors in the three years since I delivered it to him.

Right to left: Gheylsan, his wife, Pemba Lagi Sherpa, and daughter Diki in 2006

189

His family was delighted I'd returned with a group of friends. Gheylsan's daughter, Diki, served us salted yak butter tea. Yuck! I politely choked it down, and was grateful for the cookies offered to ameliorate the awful taste of the tea.

Gheylsan and his wife were quite old for Sherpas. They were both in their late 80s. Gheylsan cheerfully told us that most Sherpas didn't live to 50. Gheylsan's hearing had deteriorated somewhat since our meeting in 2003, but otherwise he was still vigorous and sociable.

As we were preparing to leave, Mac and Vitto asked me whether we should offer the family a gift of money. I summarily dismissed the suggestion as inappropriate. Outside the house, we conferred as a group and Ganesh said a gift of money would be well received. When it comes to local customs, the sirdar knows best. We each pulled some Rupees out of our wallets. Ganesh and I knocked, went back inside, and presented Gheylsan a gift of 2,000 Rupees (just under $30 in 2006). We explained it was from our group and was a token of our appreciation for the family's hospitality and in honor of Gheylsan's great deeds on Mt. Everest. Gheylsan was so touched he leaped from his seat and presented Ganesh and me with katas (traditional silk scarves). We bowed our heads and Gheylsan draped and then tied the katas under our chins.

The great pee bottle debate and yaks on the Gokyo Trail

The next day we hiked out of Namche and branched off the Base Camp Trail onto the Gokyo Trail. Our programme was to hike it up to our target mountain, Lobuche East, then hike back down the Base Camp Trail. Gokyo would be a new experience for me, and the other four guys on the team would still get to experience the entire Everest Base Camp Trail on the way back from Lobuche. Niru designed a programme that exactly fit the parameters I'd given him.

But remember, nothing goes exactly according to plan in the Himalayas. Before we arrived in Namche Mac developed low back pain. Mac was a proud US Marine and a colonel in the USMC Reserves. To show off how fit he was after the first day of hiking, he dropped and did 30 push-ups in our campsite at Phakding. Hiking up the Namche Hill next day he was struck down with crippling back pain. Mac refused to drop out of the trek, but handed his pack over to Ganesh to carry. With his own pack on his back and Mac's

190

in front, Ganesh looked like a pregnant camel walking upright. An even more ridiculous-looking picture was Mac taking a drink. His backpack had a built-in CamelBak hydration system. Whenever he needed a drink, Mac had to suck water out of his pack strapped to Ganesh's chest. It looked like Mac was suckling from Ganesh's breast. That was not exactly the optics US Marines like to portray of themselves; but, so it goes.

Mac's humbled position is a point to consider in the raging debate within the mountaineering community: CamelBak or water bottles, which is superior? CamelBaks were becoming increasingly popular by 2006, because of the ease of hydrating on the move. Just turn your chin and suck on the tube. A CamelBak fits in your pack or you can strap it on your back. It's easy to carry. I still clung to the old ways in 2006 and preferred water bottles for two reasons. 1. A water bottle could be converted to a pee bottle. During severely cold nights, when you dread leaving your tent to freeze your weenie off for a pee, it is such a relief to pee into a bottle without leaving the comfort of your tent. (That argument might not fly with the fairer sex. And, if you planned to drink out of the water bottle the next day on the trail, better remember to wash it out first.) 2. I'd seen trekkers drop their packs and the CamelBak tube -- the end you suck -- flop into dirt where a yak might have pissed or worse. Did they notice? Better clean the end off before you take the next sip. Mac's situation added another point in favor of the old water bottle. He could have carried one and not had to suckle at Ganesh's breast. (My son James gave me a CamelBak for Christmas in 2012. Love it! But I still took a water bottle to use as a pee bottle.)

The next problem was with Greg. He developed severe cold-like symptoms and migraines the first day on the Gokyo Trail. That afternoon, I started suffering altitude-related headaches and a runny nose. Ganesh and I decided that Greg and I should spend a recovery day in the stream-side village of Machermo, while the others trekked on to Gokyo Village. The following morning, Ganesh, our climbing guide Norbu, Bill, Mac, and Vitto hiked and scramble-climbed to the top of Gokyo Ri (5,360 me; 17,581 ft). Greg and I caught up with the group at lunchtime in Gokyo Village. Beautiful little blue lakes surround the village.

The following night we camped in a yak pasture, called Dragnag Kharka. Vitto confessed over breakfast he'd acquired a severe case of yak-phobia. He spent the night armed with a trekking pole in hand convinced that a giant yak was going to charge through his tent and gore him.

We'd seen quite a few yaks grazing along the Gokyo Trail. On the Base Camp Trail most of the yaks have 50-gallon-blue-plastic-drums and bulging duffel-bags tied to their backs and sides.

Those yaks are employed by Everest climbing expeditions. But the yaks we saw along the Gokyo Trail were either grazing in pastures or were carrying loads for local enterprises.

The yak is shaggy-haired, long-horned, and male. Females are supposed to be called naks, but locals and tourists commonly refer to either sex as yak. Yaks live at high altitudes in the Himalayan region. They are rarely seen below 10,000 feet. Their thick, heavy coat of hair is well-adapted to the colder weather of high altitudes. Yak lungs are larger than any other bovine, so they can breathe air with less oxygen.

Yaks do not graze and are not used as pack animals in the middle ranges of the Himalayas. Trekkers often mistake a dzopkyo (usually called "dzo") for a yak. A dzo is a yak-cow hybrid. It looks a lot like a yak, but a little smaller with a less shaggy coat and shorter horns. In the middle and lower Himalayas trekkers will see other bovine species, including water buffalo and ordinary cows and steers.

If you trek the High Himalayas, sooner or later you'll encounter a yak on a narrow trail or crossing a suspension bridge. In those circumstances, the fear of being gored by a yak is justified. The first time a trekker encounters a 1,000-pound shaggy beast lumbering down a narrow trail, it is a bit frightening. An important lesson for novice trekkers is to move to the mountain side of the trail whenever crossing paths with a yak, other animals, or a heavily laden porter. If you move to the side of the trail which has a drop-off, you might be sent tumbling down the side of a canyon by an accidental, or intentional, bump. Some of the trails, and most of the bridges, are not wide enough for both a pack animal, with 50-gallon drums tied to its sides, and a trekker to pass each other. Best that the human scramble a little ways up the hillside, or quickly backtrack to a less narrow point, because a loaded yak is not going to give way. It's also customary to let porters pass when they are carrying heavy loads.

Vitto's reaction to yaks was unusual. In my experience most trekkers are fascinated, not frightened, by yaks. The "Yak and Yeti" is the name of one of the most popular and expensive hotels in Kathmandu. T-shirts with some form of "yaketty yak" or "yakety yak, don't talk back" and images of yaks on the shirt have been selling well in Kathmandu since my first visit in 1995. The yak and the yeti are informal mascots of Nepal.

Yak pasture by the Gokyo Trail, 2006

Scramble climbing; the team splits up

The next morning we faced the daunting challenge of the Cho La. It is one of the highest and steepest passes in the Khumbu (5,330 me; 17,482 ft). To my dismay, I felt like I had caught Greg's cold. My nose was running, eyes were watering, and my strength felt sapped as soon as I began the steep scramble hike up the Cho La. Our cook, Dorge, hiked beside or behind me all the way up to the top of the pass. He was very patient as my progress was at tortoise-like speed. He was also sensitive enough to stay near me but without humiliating me with offers of assistance to take my pack.

Members of our crew sheltering from the high winds at the top of Cho La, 2006

Scramble hiking up the Cho La was the first of three consecutive days of very long and difficult hiking and more scramble climbing at high altitudes. Everyone among the crew and clients was grateful for a rest day when we arrived at Lobuche East base camp. In the meal tent at lunch, Mac shook his head and grunted that the last few days were the most physically challenging of his life. He said he hated to admit it, but he was having more trouble with the trek than he'd had with Marine boot camp. The rest of us were too whipped to bother pointing out that he was thirty years older.

All five clients were feeling pretty ragged. It was apparent from the worn-looking faces and drooping shoulders in the meal tent that commencing a climb of Lobuche East the next day was going to be a very tough ask. Nevertheless, in a cheery voice Ganesh informed the group that the climb of Lobuche East would be "at least one-hundred and fifty percent harder than Cho La."

Weary and nervous looks were exchanged around the table. Mac and Vitto excused themselves and slipped outside the tent to confer. Greg and I raised an eyebrow at each other, shook our heads and continued sipping tea out of the tin cups provided by AGT. As he was wont to do, Bill began meditating silently. Ganesh bustled about helping kitchen boys clear the table and checking on Dorge's progress with dessert. I guessed that Ganesh's cheery attitude in announcing what his clients perceived as bad news was actually intended to help us reach the conclusion that we were not up to the challenge of climbing a 20,000-foot high mountain on the morrow.

Vitto untied the tent flap and ducked back inside followed by Mac. Vitto stepped aside, shuffled his feet and looked down uncomfortably. Mac cleared his throat and announced that their goal to experience the Himalayas had been met, and they'd decided to pass on attempting the climb. He said they wanted to trek down to Lukla and fly back to Kathmandu as soon as possible.

I tried to catch Vitto's eye, but he refused to make eye contact. Of our group of five, Vitto and Bill had not suffered any particular ailments. Everything Vitto said on the trek up to that moment indicated he was keen to try his first Himalayan climb. I wasn't surprised that Mac wanted to ditch the climb; his back had been bothering him since the second day on the trail. But Vitto's decision was surprising and disappointing. I figured we'd just take an extra rest day, and then try to do the climb.

Bill was unperturbed by Mac and Vitto's decision, because he never intended to attempt the climb of Lobuche East. He'd made it clear when he signed up for the trek that he was not and did not want to be a climber. Bill visited the Tibetan side of Everest a couple years before our trek. The intended goal for his return to the Himalayas was to experience the mountain up close on the Nepal side. Niru made special arrangements in the programme for Bill to trek to Everest Base Camp while the rest of us were supposed to be climbing Lobuche East. The plan was for Bill and Gopal, a sirdar in training, to leave camp in the morning and hike up to Everest Base Camp. Gopal would carry Bill's duffel in a doko basket. After checking out Base Camp they were to hike down the Base Camp Trail and stay in a lodge at Gorak Shep. The programme scheduled the rest of us to meet Bill and Gopal after the two-day climb down the trail in Dingboche Village.

Mac and Vitto's decision to bail out of the climb left Greg and me with a difficult decision of our own. We both wanted to climb, but neither of us felt like we were at the top of our game. We were the two members of the group who had suffered through the trek with cold-like symptoms and probable sinus infections. Greg also revealed to me, when we were resting at Machermo Village, that he took a special medication for migraine headaches by injection. He kept a supply of the meds in glass vials stored in a special leather case with hypodermic needles. Despite careful packing a few of the vials broke and Greg was low on his meds. Still, he'd come to Nepal to learn mountaineering and wanted to try a peak.

I asked Ganesh what he thought of climbing Pokalde Peak as an alternative plan to the 2-day climb of Lobuche East. We could hike over to Pokalde, do the half-day climb of the easier 19,000-foot peak, and then meet up with the rest of the group in Dingboche. Ganesh shook his head gravely and said that would be a problem because our climbing permit was for Lobuche East. His guiding license would be in jeopardy if we were caught "banditing" another peak. The other problem was we'd have to split our crew in two, because Vitto and Mac needed porters and a cook, and so would we.

Ganesh left the tent and I could hear him speaking with Norbu in Nepali, while we clients consumed the cupcakes Dorge made for dessert. When he returned, Ganesh's usual broad smile had returned. He announced, "Jeff and Greg came to Nepal to climb a Himalayan peak, so that's what we do."

There was little risk of the authorities finding out or caring whether we climbed a different peak; so few climbers were up in the mountains in 2006. As to a crew, Ganesh said he'd serve as climbing guide, sirdar, and cook. He would assign a couple of the porters to our little climbing party, and we'd be good to go.

After dinner that evening, Vitto took me aside and told me he really wanted to try climbing Pokalde with Greg, Ganesh, and me. But he felt constrained to stay with Mac, who was adamant about getting out of the mountains as soon as possible. Vitto and Mac were long-time friends, and Vitto joined the group at Mac's suggestion.

I met Mac when I was solo-kayaking through the Rock Islands of Palau. He was on vacation with his family and they were doing a daytrip paddling around the island where I happened to be camping. I knew their guide, so I hung out with them for a couple hours. Mac had a tough-guy Marine personality, but he was also thoughtful, intelligent, and well read. With his wife, son, and daughter, they seemed like the perfect all-American family. We hit it off well enough that we stayed in touch by email. I invited Mac to join the 2006 expedition. He agreed and brought Vitto into the group.

Some friction within our team developed early on during the trek. Bill let it be known that he was bisexual. That disgusted Mac. He made a point of regularly sniping at Bill in the meal tent and around the campfire. It was annoying to me, embarrassing to Vitto, but didn't seem to bother Bill. That might have been partly due to the fact that Bill proved to be a stronger hiker than Mac. After he showed off doing pushups the first night of the trek, and then had Ganesh carry his pack, Mac's tough-guy demeanor seemed less authentic and more like a mask for insecurity.

Hiking to Pokalde; Greg is in the near foreground, Ganesh is in front of him, and Kumar and Mon Bahadur are in the distance. Mt. Everest is in the upper left corner partially hidden by clouds.

I actually felt some relief in the morning when Bill and Gopal headed north, Mac and Vitto with most of the crew headed south, and Ganesh, Kumar and Mon Bahadur, two of our porters, Greg, and I headed east. Since we weren't doing Lobuche East, and Ganesh would not put another guide's license at risk, he placed Norbu, the other licensed climbing guide on staff, in charge of the Mac-Vitto group. If we didn't meet up in Dingboche, Norbu could lead their party back to Lukla to catch a flight out to Kathmandu.

Pokalde Peak, a shrinking glacier, blind hiking, and a surprise from Ganesh

To reach Pokalde base camp, Ganesh, Kumar, Mon Bahadur, Greg and I had to scramble up a pass even higher than Cho La, the Kongma La (5,535 me; 18,155 ft). But we made it to Pokalde base camp by late afternoon. Unfortunately, Greg's cold symptoms returned crossing the high pass. Since Greg was a novice climber, despite his running nose and headache, Ganesh took Greg out to a snow field on the flank of Pokalde for practice with his ice axe and crampons. After an hour or so, they called it quits. Ganesh and Mon Bahadur prepared a Sherpa stew for dinner.

Except to slurp down some stew, I spent the rest of that day and night huddled in my sleeping bag trying to rest and regain as much strength for the climb as possible. Ganesh woke everyone up at sunrise. To my surprise, Greg announced that he didn't feel well enough to chance it. I wondered if the training with Ganesh had not gone well, or Greg was just too beat. It seemed a shame after all he'd suffered through not to give the mountain climb a try. But, so it goes.

Ganesh and I packed climbing gear, pack lunches of peanut butter sandwiches, skinned potatoes, hard-boiled eggs, cookies, granola bars, and water bottles of boiled water in our backpacks. We left camp and started to pick our way through the boulders around the base of Pokalde. Kumar, Mon Bahadur, and Greg tore down the tents and started the hike down to Dingboche Village.

Ganesh and I were the only ones on the mountain. Something confusing was that the glacier Tom, Krishna, and I had to climb over in 1998 had shriveled into a diminutive heap of ice and snow off to the side of the mountain. It had not completely disappeared, but it no longer stretched across and up a side of the mountain. Patches of ice and snow dotted the mountain, but no glacier to climb over. We didn't need crampons to climb Pokalde in 2006; they were useless hunks of steel in our backpacks. We scrabbled and slogged our way toward the peak; Ganesh leading and me following.

It was partly cloudy, so our views of the Everest Massif and the other 8,000 meter peaks in the area were a bit disappointing. But once again, the final fifty feet of rock climbing at over 19,000 feet was one hell of an adrenaline rush. Ganesh strung rope and set protection as he climbed the wall ahead of me. But I felt confident enough to ignore the protection he set and free-climbed the summit as soon as Ganesh reached the top.

After the down-climb I collapsed into my tent totally exhausted. I wanted to lie in the warm cocoon-coziness of my down sleeping bag the rest of the day and night. Unfortunately, Ganesh noticed another team cresting the Kongma La just as we were completing the descent. Because our climbing permit was for Lobuche East, not Pokalde, Ganesh wanted us out of base camp before the other group set up camp and came over to make conversation. He didn't want to answer any questions that might implicate us in banditing the peak. So we hurried away from the base camp hiking south toward Dingboche.

My leg strength was pretty well shot and I was laboring at a terribly slow pace. To make our situation a bit desperate, a dense fog settled in. We couldn't see more than ten feet in any direction. We knew our route was south, but the only means of navigation was to listen for the roar of the rushing Imja Khola River, which is fed by the glacier runoff from Everest. If it was to our left, we were walking in the correct direction.

After stumbling over a moraine for a couple hours with my legs on the verge of giving out, I halted and demanded to know whether we were lost. I had observed Ganesh casting nervous glances in different directions as we pushed through the fog. In response to my grumpy demand, Ganesh smiled sweetly and in a calm voice said, "No, Jeff dhai (big brother), we are not lost, just taking different way." I could not help chuckling. We weren't on any trail, and I knew damn well that Ganesh was just using his instinctive sense of direction and occasionally catching the sound of the river to guide us.

What should have been a 3.5 hour hike to Dingboche turned into five hours of blindly picking our way down rocky mountainsides and across a long, long moraine. Although I was almost crawling by the time we were in sight of the village, Ganesh's smiling mug, words of encouragement, and jokes gave me enough power to keep putting one foot in front of the other.

When the village was about a half mile away, Ganesh let out a whoop and took off running. I would have been pissed off to be left in his dust, but just before sprinting off Ganesh said he'd have a surprise waiting for me in camp. And, indeed, he did. While I was stumping through Dingboche looking for our campsite, Ganesh was preparing the surprise. It was a shower tent with a ten gallon drum full of hot water, a ladle, and towel, as well as a pot of warm dudh chiyaa. Once again, the strength and sensitivity of my Nepalese guide turned a painfully sour experience into a sweet memory.

Ganesh on Pokalde Peak summit, 2006

Puja at Deboche Convent and tea with Lama Tenzing at Tengboche Monastery
The main party with Mac and Vitto left Dingboche in the morning, while Ganesh and I were climbing Pokalde. Mac was so hot to get out of Nepal and reunite with his family, he insisted that Norbu and the crew pack up and depart for Lukla without regard for the rest of the team. Bill, Gopal, Greg, Kumar, and Mon Bahadur were waiting in Dingboche for Ganesh and me. After a restful night in which I did get to spend about ten hours in my cozy down bag in a single North Face tent, our diminished party trekked out of

Dingboche. The vast rhododendron forest around the Buddhist convent at Deboche was in full bloom. After "stopping to smell the roses" (actually rhododendrons), we paid a visit to the convent.

Trekking through the rhododendron forest by Deboche Convent; left to right: Bill, Ganesh, Greg, Mon Bahadur, and Kumar.

The nuns were happy to show us their living quarters and how they spent their time. One showed us how they performed puja. Another let us watch her engraving a stone for a mani wall.

We learned that the convent was founded in 1913 by Ani Ngawang Pema, who was a famous Buddhist holy woman. She spent 50 years in solitary retreat. The Deboche Convent is the oldest Buddhist nunnery in Nepal, but most of the nuns at the convent were Tibetan. They fled the brutal Chinese-military occupation of Tibet. They hiked over the 22,000-foot Nangpa La for shelter and asylum in Deboche. The nuns of Deboche travel around the Khumbu to perform puja at religious ceremonies. One of the nuns told us that they "pray every day for the happiness of the world and that all beings will treat others with compassion and loving kindness." It was a lovely mission statement, because the convent was devoted to action as well as prayer.

After visiting Deboche Convent we hiked on to Tengboche Gompa. From our campsite on the monastery grounds we had fantastic views of the 8,000 meter peaks of the upper Khumbu, Everest, Lhotse, Lhotse Shar, Nuptse, Ama Dablam, and Pumo Ri. Pokalde looked like a dwarf among those great white giants.

Nun performing puja at Deboche Convent

In the morning Ganesh and I obtained a private audience with Lama Tenzing. You'll recall that he is the presiding abbot over Tengboche Monastery and is the most revered lama of the Sherpa people. I presented him with a copy of *The Chrysalis Reader*, a book of essays, short stories, and art published by the Swedenborg Foundation. It included the article I wrote about the Jubilee Celebration of 2003 at Tengboche Monastery. My photographs of Lama Tenzing and Peter Hillary were published with the article. Lama Tenzing smiled appreciatively as he paged through the article. He didn't read English, but he seemed pleased to receive the book and enjoyed the photos.

Ganesh and I spent an hour in conversation with Lama Tenzing

(Ganesh interpreting). When asked what message I might take from him to friends in the US, he replied, "Tell everyone to cultivate love in their hearts. Tell the truth. And promote love in the heart and truth telling through religious discipline."

Lama Tenzing with *The Chrysalis Reader* presented to him by the author, 2006.

Bazaar, Buddha's Birthday, and the joy of peeing outdoors

Our diminished team trekked down to Namche Bazaar the following day. The timing was propitious, because it was Saturday market day. The market was less lively than I expected based on previous visits. There were very few trekkers nosing around to inspect the wares of the local Sherpa merchants and Tibetan traders. The downturn in tourism was evident in the few customers with light complexions. I wondered why there were far fewer Tibetan traders than I'd seen in previous visits to the bazaar.

Tibetan peddlers hike all the way down from Tibet, crossing the Everest Massif, to trade with Sherpas and sell to Western tourists at the open market in Namche. Ganesh said one reason fewer Tibetans were coming to Namche to sell their goods was that the Nepal government had begun imposing a tax on Tibetan traders. For hundreds of years Tibetan traders brought yak hair rugs, jewelry, bowls made from human skulls, and flutes made from human thigh bones to Namche without being taxed. Understandably, they were not happy about demands by Nepalese officials to pay the new tax. Life was tough enough for Tibetans living under the oppressive rule of Chinese overlords.

On the hike out of Namche, just a little way down Namche Hill, we encountered a group of gaudily garbed revelers dancing and chanting. Several wore feathered headdresses and were waving flowery batons. Ganesh said they were celebrating Buddha's birthday. When I asked why this wasn't a bigger deal -- as much as Nepalis love to party wouldn't Buddha's birthday merit a big festival? Ganesh answered that he wasn't sure today was actually Buddha's birth date.

Since the Buddhist calendar is lunar, the birth date would vary from year to year. A Google search when writing this chapter revealed that April 8 was Buddha's birthday in 2006. We didn't arrive in Nepal until April 26. But, so it goes.

Buddha "Birthday" revelers on Namche Hill, 2006

The revelers beckoned us to join the dance. They sprinkled flowers in our hair. They also offered to smear tikas on our foreheads. A tilaka, as it's called in India, but tika in Nepal, is a splotch of paste or powder normally applied to the middle of the forehead on Hindu holidays. The red spot "sported" by married Hindu women in India and Nepal is called a bindi. On special occasions in Nepal, even people who aren't Hindu will apply tikas to their foreheads made from a mixture of abir, a red powder, yoghurt, and grains of rice. So it wasn't totally weird that Buddhist celebrants had tikas.

Greg and Ganesh welcomed the revelers to smear a tika on their foreheads, but I declined. Given my propensity to get sick in the Himalayas, I became quite anal about germ avoidance. I always carried a bottle of anti-biotic soap in my pocket and turned down more offers of the application of tikas than I can count.

As a consequence of my experiences in Nepal, I developed some odd (for an American) habits. For example, to the embarrassment of my wife when we have guests, I don't flush a toilet until I've peed in it three times. (Since we have three in our house, one is designated "mine".) After dark before I go to bed, I usually pee outside in the yard. Clean water is a valuable resource and often hard to come by on a trek. The kitchen boys have to find a water source and then carry water in buckets to the campsite. The camp cook has to boil all the water he needs for cooking and to fill the clients' water bottles. If you run out of water on the trail, you'll need to use a sterile pump to hand-pump water from a stream or river into your water bottle or CamelBak. Tourists are advised not to drink water from any source in Kathmandu, unless you know it's been filtered. The electrical grid in Kathmandu regularly failed, and there was no electricity in the mountain villages the first several years I trekked in Nepal. So I became obsessive about not wasting water and about turning off lights, appliances, and electronics when not being used. The habit of husbanding scarce resources traveled home with me, even though there is no scarcity of clean water or electricity in Indianapolis. My habit of turning off taps and switches she might be planning to use a minute later annoys Alicia, but I'll bet our water and electric bills are lower than our neighbors.

Partying in Lukla and Kathmandu; cakes, silly singing, and stuffed at Niru's house

The hike to Lukla Village ended with the last hour in pouring rain; a good sign that it was time to go home. We located the rest of our crew at a lodge in the village. Norbu reported that Vitto and Mac had flown out the previous day. Bill, Greg, all the members of our original crew, and I spent our last night together in a lodge which had running water and hot showers.

Modernity was progressing through the Khumbu in a big way. In 1998 I got to use the first flush toilet installed in Lukla, and Tom and I witnessed the village-wide electrical system being turned on for the first time in Namche. By 2006 all the villages of any size had electricity and water systems.

The traditional end-of-trek party with the crew was terrific fun. We danced together, attempted to sing, and wolfed down huge pieces of the cakes Dorge prepared. The highlight was Norbu's rendition of 100 verses of RESHAM FIRIRI, which is a popular Nepali folk love-song and is sung at every party. The first verse, translated into English, is: "My heart is fluttering like silk in the wind." To an English speaker, the verse in Nepali sounds kind like, "I am a monkey; you are a donkey." So I created my own version of the song combining that and other English phrases mixed in with my pidgin Nepali.

Cutting one of the end-of-trek cakes prepared by Dorge with Bill

It always cracked up my Nepalese friends when I performed my version of RESHAM FIRIRI, and the AGT crew was no different. They were rolling on the floor when I serenaded them with my twisted version of the song. Doesn't really seem like it would be that funny? At the end of a trek, the most pathetic joke is hilarious. Ya' have to be there to understand.

Back in Kathmandu, Sanga, the AGT guide who led us around Kathmandu before we flew up to Lukla, acted as our local guide again for sightseeing in Pataan and Bhaktapur, temple cities in the Kathmandu Valley. When we weren't touring, Bill, Greg, and I explored Thamel and Durbar Square on foot. We shopped in Durbar Marg (market) for presents to take home. Our last dinner was at Niru Rai's house with his family, Ganesh, and Sanga. The feast consisted of too many courses to count and many glasses of Mrs. Niru's homemade rakshi.

It was a risk contracting with AGT to handle our expedition. No one in our group was disappointed with the service. I heard from both Mac and Vitto after we were all back home. They were both very complimentary about how Ganesh, Norbu, and the crew handled Mac's demand "to get out of Dodge". The AGT staff performed above my expectations, especially considering the difficulties we clients created by Greg and me needing an extra rest day in Machermo, Bill splitting off from the group to visit Base Camp, and Mac and Vitto bailing early, not to mention Ganesh's willingness to deviate from our permit to give Greg and me the chance to climb Pokalde. We were all amazed by the quality of the meals Dorge was able to produce from his makeshift kitchens. Ganesh's cheerful leadership and the crew's happy disposition eased the group through the challenges faced on the trek. I might have just lay down, curled up, and given up the ghost, I was so tired on the hike from Pokalde to Dingboche, were it not for Ganesh's prodding encouragement.

There were also surprising little treats Ganesh and the guys arranged, which I had not experienced on any of my previous expeditions. The shower tent in Dingboche was just one. Each night at the higher and colder campsites, Dorge boiled water for hot water bottles to stick in our sleeping bags. Ganesh gave each of us cotton-liners to add some extra warmth inside our sleeping bags. AGT provided pillows and thermo-rests to compliment our own, or to use in case we didn't bring them. At rest stops Dorge prepared hot Tang and Ganesh handed out cookies. If there was a teahouse nearby, Ganesh bought a couple pots of dudh chiyaa for the group. Instead of bringing our own duffel bags on the trek for the porters to carry in their doko baskets, AGT provided each client with a duffel bag to use on the trek for our personal kit, clothes, and gear. Niru made a gift of the duffels to each client at the end of the trek. Niru also gave each of us an AGT T-shirt when we ate dinner at his house. I did not regret my decision to hire AGT.

I did regret that none of the other guys were able to experience climbing a Himalayan peak, although no one expressed any disappointment over it. The night before our flight back to the US, Bill and I walked the darkened streets of Thamel one last time. We treated ourselves to a Guinness at Thamel's "authentic" Irish pub. We both mentioned in our conversation that night how much safer we felt on streets in Kathmandu, now that the civil war was over, than we would in American cities.

I left Nepal in May of 2006 with the reasonable hope that it would once again be such a peaceful country it would mourn the unfortunate death of a visitor, as it was in 1995.

Animistic Spirituality

I experienced something else walking the trail with Ganesh in 2006 that I treasure. Somewhere between Tengboche and Namche I started to kick a rock. It was a minor obstruction in the middle of the trail. Ganesh gently took hold of my arm and stepped in front of me. He moved the rock to the side of the trail. I asked why he did that. Ganesh explained that the Rai people believe everything in the world, even rocks, have spirit. So everything deserves some level of respect.

Ganesh is well educated. He has the equivalent of a Masters Degree in Business. He was aware that the spirituality of the Rai people is called "animism" in the West and the religion is considered "nature worship" by religious scholars. He used those generic terms when I asked him to explain why he didn't want me to thoughtlessly kick the rock out of the way. His explanation satisfied my curiosity at the time, but the incident stuck with me. It added another layer to my desire to continue a relationship with the guys who staffed Adventure GeoTreks.

Religious Studies was one of my three "majors" in college and I have a Masters in Divinity from Christian Theological Seminary. My academic experience with religion is primarily Christian theology, but I had a working knowledge of the other major world religions. I knew virtually nothing about the naturalistic religions of Native Americans and truly nothing about those of the Himalayan region. Ganesh's description of the animistic spirituality of the Basa Rai intrigued and impressed me. I had been uncomfortable with the theology of my Presbyterian heritage for some time, but loyalty and laziness kept me in the pew. Animism was a key to unlock the door that allowed my escape from traditional Christianity.

My theological and philosophical studies led me to conclude the most intellectually honest statement about the whole God question is: I don't know. Agnosticism is the most honest theological position. All the others are based on beliefs, which are as unsubstantiated as shifting sand. Yet, the Universe is; it lives. And a life lived respecting that fact and respecting, to some degree, all creation is a more meaningful life than atheistic nihilism.

Even if the "simulation theory" (that our Universe is a computer game and our reality is simulated via a computer program) is correct, then reality is animation and we are anime. So we might as well play our roles as well as possible. Treating all of nature with respect, as advocated by animistic spirituality, is a damn good start at playing our roles on this planet well.

Jenny Odell advocates this form of spirituality in *How to Do Nothing; Resisting the Attention Economy*.

> This version of the observational eros doesn't just recognize or appreciate the inhabitants of a place, but is willing to perceive the special agency of those beings and receive their attention in turn. Overcoming species loneliness is impossible if our subjects appear inert and lifeless to us, be they hummingbirds or rocks. In *Becoming Animal*, David Abram writes about what is lost when we speak and think about the rest of the world as less than animate:
>> If we speak of things as inert or inanimate objects, we deny their ability to actively engage and interact with us – we foreclose their capacity to reciprocate our attentions, to draw us into silent dialogue, to inform and instruct us.

These ruminations, which began when Ganesh treated that rock with respect, eventually led to my satisfaction with the label of "agnostic-animist". My 2014 book, ***Godless – Living a Valuable Life Beyond Beliefs,*** fully explicates this position and credits the Rai and Quakers for their assistance.

Chapter Postscript
    I see Bill every few years when our paths cross in Indianapolis. He returned to Nepal in 2008 to do the Base Camp trek with a young friend. AGT was their outfitter company. I have lost touch with Greg and Vitto. Emails to the addresses I have for them are not answered. Mac committed suicide a few years after our trek. I spoke with him a couple days before his death about a legal problem. His suicide came as a terrible shock, but I understood; if that makes any sense. May he rest in peace.

Mac is on the left with the author at the Everest View Hotel during a rest stop at Shyangboche on the 2006 trek. Ama Dablam is nearby in the center of the photo. Mt. Everest is further away in the upper left corner.

Dearly beloved friends, these things we do not lay upon you as a rule or form to walk by, but that all with the measure of light which is pure and holy may be guided, and so in the light walking and abiding these may be fulfilled in the spirit, not from the letter; for the letter killeth, but the spirit giveth life.

A "statement of faith and practice" issued by a gathering of Quaker Friends in Yorkshire, England in 1656 CE.

Appealing Spirit of Basa Guys and an Epiphany
Ganja La and Kyanjin Village, Helambu – Langtang Trek 2007

I realized in 2003 that on a very small scale I could do what the Hillarys were doing -- introduce others to the Himalayas and raise money to help improve the quality of life of mountain villagers in Nepal. By 2007 my effort to engage others in "philanthro-trekking" was beginning to bear fruit. In 2004, with the help of my church, just under $2,000 was donated for a water project in a remote village and 65 pounds of clothing, school and medical supplies were delivered for distribution at a school and medical clinic in a remote village. There were only three members in the trekking group, but it was a start.

The 2006 trekking group had five members. The "philanthro" side of that trek was all members brought writing utensils and tablets for distribution to school children we met on the trail. I delivered an additional twenty pounds of writing pads, notebooks, pens, pencils, and magic markers to the Hillary-Khumjung School. I also dropped off a batch of first-aid kits to Kunde Hospital. The school and medical supplies I took to Nepal in 2006 were donated by my law firm, a friend's firm, and a neighbor who worked for a medical device company.

The first two philanthro-treks were pretty limited in scope and scale. The most significant contribution to Nepal was probably the employment of about 35 people for the two treks, plus the money our group members spent in Kathmandu and at teahouses and villages along the trails.

In 2007 the trekking side of the philanthro-trek was ramped up through my membership in the Central Indiana Wilderness Club (CIWC). The Club helped promote the trek. Nine people joined the group, which included five CIWC members, plus Elliot and two of his friends, and my tent-mate from the Ladakh expedition, Dax. I asked all members to bring school and/or medical supplies to distribute in villages and to local people we met along the trails. The programme Niru designed was similar to the 2004 Langtang expedition with several days added to visit Gosainkunda, a spiritual retreat area in the Helambu District southeast of the Langtang Trail.

Elliot, Dax, and I were the only members who had been to Nepal before. The group did the usual sightseeing tours in and around Kathmandu. We visited many temples and palaces, including Bodnath, Swayambodh, Pashaputnah, Durbar Square, Pataan, and Bakhtapuhr. Niru assigned two guides, Sanga and Dilbal (called DB), to shepherd us around in a comfortable air-conditioned van. After two days of cultural and educational tourism, the group was pretty well "templed out".

But it was very gratifying to see the transformation of Kathmandu after a year of peace following the end of "The People's War". The warren-like streets of Thamel were once again teeming with life. Tourists shopped and bargained with local vendors. Messengers, hawkers, hash dealers, beggars, and businessmen swarmed the narrow streets, along with bleating animals, rickshaws, bikes, motorcycles, and cars.

The King's Way, a busy street in downtown Kathmandu, 2007

All of the novice trekkers in the group were fascinated by the strange and wonderful sights in Kathmandu. No one was turned off or frightened by the alien culture. Members of the 2007 group were curious to experience cultural differences and to take on a new challenge in Himalayan trekking and mountaineering.

One of the most fun experiences in Kathmandu was seeing my friend Wildman Raaj, "the Rock 'n Roll King of Kathmandu", and his band perform at a restaurant near Thamel. Raaj is the Nepali friend who was badly beaten by a monarchist gang because he looked like a hippie. He was actually a tea shop owner, entrepreneur, and musician, not a Maoist. Peace between the government and the Maoists ended his fear of being hassled by soldiers and beaten by monarchist thugs. After the war ended Raaj once again had the freedom to do what he loved. Rock out!

The road to Dunche is still blocked!
The Trek stalled before it got started. First, the bus Niru hired to transport clients and several crew members had a hell of a time maneuvering around the hotel's narrow parking lot. Baggage was stacked and tied down on top of the bus. A couple of the crew members rode up top with the baggage. To get out of the parking lot Ganesh and DB had to lift with trekking poles a bunch of low-hanging electrical and phone lines over the bus. Just down the street from the hotel entrance the bus bumped a motorcyclist who fell over. Negotiations occurred between the bus driver and the motorcyclist. When that matter was resolved, we were finally on the way out of Kathmandu.

There were far fewer military checkpoints on the road up to Langtang than in 2004. Our progress halted when we arrived at the site of the landslide that blocked the road in 2004. Rubble and scree still covered the road. Wouldn't it have made sense to put the military and Maoist fighters to work clearing roads after the fighting stopped? Guess not. The AGT guys riding with us lugged all the gear and duffels over the slippery mass, which was wet from a mild drizzle of rain. They loaded the baggage and hopped into another bus waiting on the other side of the landslide. Instead of jumping on the bus with the crew, Ganesh suggested we clients walk the two miles to Dunche Village. Thanks Ganesh! It felt damn good to stretch our legs and walk after ten hours in the bus.

2007 trekking group; last meal before leaving Kathmandu

Individual challenges on the trail; competition or cooperation?
The night we spent in a lodge at Dunche was the last time we slept under a roof until we were back in Kathmandu. Before we paired off into the tiny sleeping rooms at the lodge, we gathered for a group dinner in the dining room. Even before the trek actually commenced the group had begun to sort itself into cliques. The Wilderness Club members, Tim, Jim, Cathy (false name), and Nancy (false name) already knew each other, and Tim, Jim, and Cathy were friends. Elliot brought a buddy from South Africa, Hector. Dee (false name), who lived in Florida, was an old pal of Elliot's from summers spent as camp counselors when they were teenagers. My tent mate on the Ladakh expedition, Dax, was the floater. I was the only member of the group he knew. Some long and challenging days on the trail lay ahead. Some of the challenges would bring into sharp relief diverse interests, personalities, and styles of hiking

within the group.

I was delighted that Niru chose Ganesh to be the sirdar on my second trek with Adventure GeoTreks. Our nine-member group was supported by a crew of 25. A difference between the crew members from the Basa area and those hired locally in Langtang emerged when extreme conditions tested the team.

The first few days established the weather pattern we experienced most of the 16 days in the mountains; beautiful clear blue skies in the morning, cloudy afternoons with periodic showers, and then a huge sparkly star-lit sky at night. Instead of hiking north up the main trail in Langtang that Elliot, Briggie, and I trekked with Hari in 2004, Ganesh led us east on a much rougher trail into Helambu.

We camped above the two sacred lakes of Gosainkunda, called Gosainkunda and Bhairabkunda. These two alpine lakes are around 14,300 feet elevation and are both about 35 acres in size. The water color varied from a shimmering blue in the morning to dark blue, almost purple later in the day, and then grey in the evening.

We spent a day hiking around the lakes and checking out pilgrim shelters. I got mildly irritated with Elliot. Feeling fit after the first couple days of hiking, I decided to test my leg strength by sprinting up a steep 100-foot-high hillside. All of a sudden, Elliot was at my side turning it into a race. I didn't want to race, just wanted to test myself, but my own competitive instinct kicked in. And so we raced. It irritated me that a solitary run turned into a competition, but it inspired rumination about the dynamic of competition and cooperation for the human race.

Some people view the essence of life as a Darwinian competition. It is a struggle, not just to survive, but to win. Per, Vince Lombardi, "... winning is the only thing." An alternative understanding is that our world is an intricate web of cooperation. What appears to be competition for survival is systemic cooperation. The zebra that is eaten by the pride of lions is sacrificed, as was the grass eaten by the zebra. To the individual that "loses" the system may appear to be a struggle for survival -- a competition -- but as a system, all living creatures are participating in the cycle of life. From that perspective (a godlike view from above) individuals engaged in a competitive struggle to win are

216

playing roles in the complex web of life. By participating in the game of life we are all engaged in the cooperative effort to keep the wheel moving.

Putting aside philosophical ruminations, the dynamic of competition/cooperation became a theme within our 2007 group for several days of the trek.

Hiking out of Gosainkunda over the high Laurebina Pass we got drenched in a rain storm. The group gathered around the pot-belly stove in a teahouse at a yak-herding station called Gopte. A few other trekkers and local people were also trying to dry out and warm up in the teahouse. Our group was a bit more boisterous than the other people huddled around the stove. There was some stomping of feet and clapping of gloved hands. Voices were raised to lift up our soggy spirits. Our boisterousness was not so loud as to be out of line with customary behavior in Himalayan teahouses. So I was startled when a Korean trekker nudged me and spoke into my ear, "Your culture is too loud!"

Perhaps the gods agreed with her. I was the last of our group to leave the warmth of the teahouse. Outside, I looked around and didn't see anyone else on the three trails leading away from the isolated teahouse. It was misty and still drizzling. I picked what I hoped was the correct trail, which abruptly ended on a hillside behind the teahouse. Making a U-turn I slipped on the mud-slick path and fell bruising my right shoulder.

Several other uncomfortable experiences followed, some for the whole group and some unique to individual members. We discovered (or they discovered us) bloodsucking leeches at our next campsite, called Tarkeghyang. It was a miserable experience. To get there we hiked through what Ganesh called a "sky forest". It was a pretty alpine forest with streams running down the hillsides. What made it so awful were swollen black leeches which dropped out of trees onto our hats and rain jackets trying to find unprotected skin to lunch on. The bastards could even latch on to a hiking boot while you were walking. They'd work their way up over your sock to suck blood from your ankle before you noticed. Leeches even managed to sneak inside zippered tents and seek out sleeping victims for a nighttime meal. We used lighters and matches to burn them off, poured alcohol and liquid soap on them, and used tweezers and knives in battling the dastardly creatures. Everyone on our team left Tarkeghyang bloodied from leech encounters.

(So the reader can avoid, or enjoy an encounter with, the blood-sucking leeches of Tarkeghyang, it and the other sites mentioned in this chapter can be found on the Langtang map at the end of the earlier "Langtang and Yala Peak 2004" chapter.)

A few of our members coped with uniquely personal challenges. Cathy bet me 1,000 Rupees that she could fit inside her duffel bag and zip it up. She is six feet tall and the duffel was about three feet in length. She almost made it. After struggling for about twenty minutes, she gave up and forked over the Rupees. The next day on the trail she was plagued by over-stretched muscles and tendons. Being a nature girl, Cathy decided she would use leaves instead of TP on the trail. It was an unwise choice for someone unfamiliar with local flora. She developed an infection "down there". Cathy had chronic back pain from a car accident. The way she used trekking poles looked very unwieldy, because she set the height of the poles so her hands were as high as her head, instead of the recommended shoulder height. When I suggested she reduce the length of the poles, she waived away my advice. She said long poles worked better because of her back pain. I was skeptical, but she should no better than me.

Despite her queer style with trekking poles, Cathy was one of the most physically fit members of the group. Like Elliot, she also had a very competitive personality. The first few days of the trek, the two of them, without admitting to each other they were doing so, raced against each other every day. After about a week of this ridiculous competition, Cathy had a sort of breakdown. She'd run herself into the ground. She was exhausted and, I suspect, upset that Elliot usually beat her to the next lunch stop or campsite. Jim, Tim, and I consoled her, and after some tears, granola, and extra hydration she was back on the trail and hiking at a more moderate pace.

Before we left Kathmandu I gathered the group together and reiterated much of the advice I had previously shared by email. One of the points was: "It's not a race. Hike at your own speed. Stop to rest whenever you feel the need. One of the crew members will walk with the slowest trekker and a crew member will be out front. It's best not to get ahead of the lead crew member, because you might take a wrong turn at a trail crossing." Cathy and Elliot ignored the advice in their determination to win. Their competition affected some of the rest of us. Hector, Dax, and I admitted to each other that when either Elliot or Cathy came barreling up the trail it got our own competitive juices flowing and, at least for a stretch, we put it in gear and hiked faster trying not to let either of them pass.

When you're not used to high altitude, exerting yourself to the extent of your physical limits increases the chance you'll suffer the symptoms of AMS. Or, you might run yourself down to the point of becoming more susceptible to catching a cold. Elliot and Hector lived in Johannesburg at almost 6,000-feet elevation. So it was easier for them to acclimate to high altitudes than it was for the flatlanders in the group.

I mentioned in my talk before we left Kathmandu that there's nothing wrong with speed hiking or trail running when you're feeling strong and want to enjoy the muscular movement of your body. But the airiness of the mountain landscape and the communal culture of the mountain villages beckon the visitor to slow down and enjoy "being here now" (to quote Baba Ram Das). Why turn a Himalayan trek into a competition? Competition is well and good in its right place. Whenever I gave in to the competitive urge to "beat" someone else on the trail I lost touch with the beauty of my surroundings.

Ganesh's favorite phrase when he walks with a client is, "Bistari, bistari." It is Nepali for, "Slowly, slowly." I have to admit that, like Cathy and Elliot, I did not always heed that advice. One could interpret Lama Tenzing's statement, "People should do what they want," to encourage people with Type A personalities to engage in competitive practices whenever they felt like it. As an acolyte of Milton Friedman, I suppose Elliot viewed the world as an ever-changing opportunity for competition; and he enjoyed that. Competition in business and sports can be wonderfully inspirational pushing competitors to the limits of their creative abilities. But, in trekking a Himalayan trail? Come on, man.

Happily though, no one in the 2007 group suffered any injuries from hiking too fast or getting lost. Cathy recovered from the injury to her pride, soreness, and infection. And she proved to be one of the stronger climbers when the group was on Yala Peak.

Dee is a cancer survivor. She was a tough little trekker on the trail and a colorful figure in yellow or pink. But carrying a backpack for long hours was more than usually painful for her due to surgeries she'd had. Like Mac on the 2006 expedition, she turned her pack over to a crew member who walked with her along the trail. She used water bottles for hydrating, so she didn't have to suckle at the breast of Deepak (assistant sirdar) to hydrate. As a cancer survivor, Dee felt she had something more to prove than the rest of us. And she did. She was one of the four of our nine members who summitted Yala Peak.

Jim's unique challenge was hanging onto his camera. He was attending to business in a charpe (Nepali for outhouse) with his camera on his lap. When he stood up the camera slid off his lap down the charpe hole. As many village charpes are, this one was a little shack on the side of a ridge. Waste went down the hole and then down the hillside. When word got out in the village that a sahib's camera went down the mountainside, a bunch of villagers went bounding over the ridge to search for the camera. The lad who found it was rewarded by Jim with a couple hundred Rupees. Given the nasty business the camera had slid through, Jim indicated the smiling young man should keep the camera's case as an additional reward.

Jim was a great benefactor to the local economy. He was hiking alone one day and came to an intersection. Instead of waiting for a crew member to point him down the correct trail, Jim guessed, and he guessed wrong. We didn't miss him until everyone else had arrived at the campsite. Ganesh organized a search party of crew members, but Jim shortly arrived in camp led by a local farmer. Jim paid his temporary guide several hundred Rupees to guide him to the campsite.

Jim's beneficence wasn't just inspired by klutzy moves in charpes and bad choices on the trail. He was the most popular member of our group with children we met along the trail. He filled his daypack with stuffed animals, which he handed out to kids we met on the trek. The writing materials and school supplies the rest of the team passed out seemed pretty lame to village kids compared to Jim's stash of stuffed animals.

A few members of the group caught a bug, including yours truly. Nancy suffered the worst of it. She not only caught the infection, but managed to get pretty severely sunburned. Carrying a pack was painful for her. So one of the guys was assigned to walk with her and carry her pack. The two of them were the last into camp every day; sometimes more than an hour after the rest of us and often after sundown. Nancy was clearly suffering and had not trained sufficiently well for the trek. It was a little surprising, because, when she signed up, she told me she had trekked in Africa. But she pushed through it everyday, looking miserable but stoically uncomplaining.

The greatest challenge the team faced was getting ourselves and all our supplies and gear over the 19,500-foot-high Ganja La. We had to cross that incredibly high pass to get to the Langtang Trail to reach Kyanjin Village and Yala Peak. Niru's programme warned that the Ganja La would be difficult: "Very high and snow-covered, it would require ropes to cross." It turned out to be even more challenging than Niru predicted.

Crossing the Ganja La; a recalcitrant kitchen "boy" and a butt slide down
We arrived at the Ganja La after two afternoons of messy hiking in the rain. In the Himalayas, when it rains below the snow-line, which varies from 10,000 to 14,000 feet, it is snowing at the higher elevations. Above 14,000 feet the build-up of snow and ice can be massively deep. That was the case for the hike up the south side of the Ganja ridge; long, hard, and slow in knee-deep snow. But the real challenge was on the other side.

Peeking over the crest of the ridge, the Ganja La's north side looked impossible for porter's carrying loads to descend. It would be extremely difficult for clients with light daypacks, unless ropes were anchored and a line established from the top of the ridge to the bottom. The north face of Ganja was a sheer white drop-off. Exactly how deep was the snow on the north side? It would be deeper than on the south side, because the prevailing wind was from the north. Snow was being blown against and drifting on the north side of the mountain. It was about two feet deep on the south side.

While our group huddled behind a boulder trying to shelter from the biting wind, Ganesh took me aside and proposed a plan for getting down this dangerous-looking mountainside. Descending the La (mountain pass) at the usual crossing point was too risky, especially for the porters with the heaviest loads. The snow was too deep and the ridge line too slippery with ice. There was a trail with switch-backs under the snow, but it would be impossible to find and follow, because it was hidden under the thick blanket of snow. However, there was a narrow goat path just below the crest of the ridge. We could follow it over to the least-steep-line down the mountainside, which was about 50 yards to the left of where we were standing. Steps could be cut with an ice axe along the path and a rope could be secured to boulders along the path. Team members could hold onto the rope as a security line while traversing the top of the ridge. At the end of the security line ropes could be anchored for a rappel down to level ground.

Unfortunately, by Ganesh's calculation, if all the ropes he brought were tied together, the total length would be about 150 yards. But it would take more than 200 yards of rope to secure a line along the ridge and a rappel line down to the bottom of the pass. We would have to glissade the last 50 yards or so. (Remember how Tsering, Dawa, and I slid on our butts coming down Kanglachan? That's glissading.)

Ganesh shook his head sheepishly and confessed he thought he'd brought more rope than would be needed either here or on Yala. He had not anticipated the need to jerry rig a 50-yard safety line to traverse the narrow ridgeline plus string ropes together to create a 150-yard rappel to the bottom of the Ganja La.

Ganesh spent the better part of an hour surveying and working his way back and forth along the top of the ridge in blowing snow and below-freezing temperatures to work out his plan. He was convinced the scheme he'd developed was the safest way down. The porters and kitchen staff would have to ferry their loaded doko baskets, weighing from forty to ninety pounds, down the mountainside as they descended. The last 50 yards would be the most challenging for porters descending with baggage in their doko baskets, because there was nothing they could hang on to.

Ganja La, 2007

Prayer flags at the summit of the pass -- where we were standing -- were the guide posts indicating we were at the right place to descend down the north side of the mountain. But looking straight down from where we stood -- the descent would be down the steepest area on the mountainside. The drop-off was broken here and there by shoulder-high snow banks and boulders the size of automobiles. Off to our left was a concavity in the mountainside. Ganesh proposed to fix ropes down the near side of the bowl. He'd used his ice axe to carefully pick his way along the ridge and then down about thirty feet on the near side of the convex dip in the mountainside. From this scouting mission Ganesh determined that the snow was not as deep and the drop off not as steep where he proposed to fix a rappel line. The route was not pockmarked with scree, snow drifts, or boulders. His plan appeared to be the best option available.

Ganesh was our sirdar. He is twenty years my junior, but he was born and raised in the Himalayan Mountains. He is a licensed mountain guide. He had already proved himself to me on Pokalde. If I thought there was a flaw in his plan, as the titular leader of the group, I would have questioned it. He was clearly more capable than me of correctly assessing the situation and devising the best solution to the problem. My job was to support his decisions and to help explain the plan to the clients. While I did that, Ganesh informed the staff of his plan. After spending time in Kathmandu with Ganesh and observing his skill as sirdar on the trek, no one in our group questioned Ganesh's ability or his decisions. Everyone just wanted to get down off the ridge and out of the teeth of the biting wind and cold.

When Ganesh explained the plan to the crew, one member flatly said she wouldn't do it. She was too scared to descend the mountain. She didn't know how to rappel, didn't know how to climb, and wanted to go home. Her name was Kelsang Lama.

Ganesh hired three Tamang women as porters to join the crew in Dunche. You'll recall that the Tamang are the dominant ethnic-tribal group in Langtang.

Ganesh thought we were short-handed with the original crew Niru hired, so, with Niru's permission, Ganesh added the three extra porters to the crew at the commencement of the trek. The youngest of the three women, Kelsang Lama, was eighteen. To Western eyes she looked fourteen. She was small and slight even for a Nepali. Kelsang was shorter than five foot and probably weighed around 90 pounds. She carried a much lighter load in her doko basket than any of the other porters. She was still the slowest crew member on the trail. Kelsang also seemed to have trouble fitting in with the other porters. She either kept to herself or stayed close to her older sister, one of the other two women Ganesh hired in Dunche.

The day we hiked to Ganja, I felt compelled to order Kelsang to pick up her doko and get moving. She had dropped her load, sat down on a rock, and stubbornly refused to move on. Even Nancy struggling at the back of the pack, sunburned and sick, passed us. I was afraid Kelsang was either going to sit there until she froze to death or was waiting until no one was looking and would then light out for home. Neither option was safe. So I stood over her and shouted at her to pick up her basket and get moving. I walked along at her side chiding her for being foolishly stubborn. I think she got the message, although she never said more than a word or two in English. As we trudged along the snowy trail, Kelsang muttered to herself in her native language and occasionally shot caustic or defiant looks at me. She was probably bitching to herself about signing up for work this hard. I'm sure she wished she'd stayed in Dunche flirting with boys and hanging out at the local market. Who the hell did this crabby old sahib think he was ordering her around! We caught up with the rest of our party at the foot of the Ganja La. Kelsang made the steep hike up to the summit of the pass without any noticeable problems.

A couple days after she was hired on to the crew, I asked Ganesh why he'd hired someone so small and weak and did not share the hardy work ethic of the typical Nepali porter. Ganesh shook his head and said he regretted hiring Kelsang, but he was forced into it. He knew the older sister to be a good porter and excellent help in the kitchen. The older woman demanded that Ganesh hire both sisters because the family needed money. It would be Kelsang's first job as a porter. Ganesh gave in because there were no other porters looking for work in Dunche. The women would not have to carry full porter loads. Their job would be to carry some of the kitchen equipment and help with cooking, washing dishes, and camp clean up. Ganesh's expression changed from downcast and rueful to a confidential little smile. "The women, they will be Ram's kitchen boys." (Ram was our cook.) Ganesh walked away chuckling to himself about our crew having female kitchen boys. Ganesh's joke was not meant to be lewd or erotic. He just thought it was funny that women would be called "kitchen boys". A kitchen boy's job is to help the cook and carry the kitchen equipment on a Himalayan expedition. While it's a lowly position, the work is easier than that of a porter, because the load carried is much lighter.

The core members of our crew were men from the Basa area of Solukhumbu Province. Solukhumbu is the official name of the province in which most Sherpa and Rai live. It combines two districts, Khumbu in the north, inhabited mostly by Sherpa, and Solu to the south, inhabited mostly by Rai.

On top of the 19,000-foot La, the temperature was dropping toward zero Fahrenheit. If we didn't get off the mountain soon, some of our people would begin to suffer frostbite of fingers and toes. Clients and staff hunkered down behind boulders or just below the crest of the ridge trying to stay out of the wind. The south side of the ridgeline offered some shelter from the strongest blasts of wind. But we needed to get moving and Kelsang would have to overcome her fear or once again be forced to move. Ganesh assured Kelsang she'd be safe and he would personally help her down the slope.

Kelsang huddled up against her sister sniffling and whimpering. She didn't look consoled, but at least she shut up with her strident demands.

Ram watching Ganesh cutting steps and securing a rope for the traverse of the Ganja La, 2007

Ganesh and Ram worked for over an hour widening the goat path with their ice axes. The hour seemed to last a very long time as we squatted below the ridge line trying our best to stay out of the teeth of the biting wind. It took Ganesh and Ram another half hour to secure a line of rope to boulders just above the six-inch-wide path and then a rappel line down the mountainside.

Ganesh tested the ropes, and then signaled for the rest of us to begin the traverse across the ridgeline in single file. When the traverse was completed Ram helped anyone who needed assistance to grasp the ropes for the rappel down the slope. We weren't using any rappelling devices, just hanging on to rope to back down the mountainside. Ganesh waited at the end of the rope chain to assist anyone who needed help butt sliding down the rest of the way. The stronger porters hugged their dokos and whooped as they slid down as if they were on a carnival ride. Others rolled and pushed their loads down the hill. DB and Deepak helped each person up out of the snow and collected any baggage that broke loose.

Everyone and all the gear made it down the slope without injury or damage. The last fifty yards was actually quite fun sliding or rolling down the slope in three-foot-deep snow. Kelsang was the last to descend. She shrieked with laughter after she let go of the rope and slid and rolled through the snow down the slope. Ganesh clapped and cheered running and jumping along beside her like a crazy man. The descent got everyone's blood pumping. It was a lot more enjoyable than huddling like a pathetic group of refugees at the top of the La.

Regrouping after descending the Ganja La, 2007

Organizing camp with the enthusiastic spirit of Basa
After Kelsang was safely down the slope, Ganesh immediately began supervising crew members to retrieve the ropes off the mountainside and reorganize all the baggage. Ram and I volunteered to locate a campsite, while the rest of the team sorted itself out.

It was a relief to be over the high pass, but the sun was going down and we needed to find a site to get the tents up and everyone out of the cold. It was rough going for Ram and me, because the terrain beyond the base of Ganja was a moraine covered in snow with drifts thigh-deep. It was tricky post-holing across such a rocky snow-covered and icy surface. Holes and small crevices in the moraine were hidden by snow and ice. Ram and I both fell a couple times in those trip traps.

For reasons not apparent to me, every level spot we discovered Ram rejected as an acceptable campsite. My feet were so cold I was beginning to worry about frostbite, and I was running out of patience with Ram's finickyness. After an hour of frustrating searching it was dark enough that we had to use headlamps to see. Just before I was ready to brain Ram with a trekking pole to end the search for the perfect campsite, I heard Deepak yelling. He was bustling toward us through the darkness. Deepak announced that Ganesh already settled on one of the sites Ram had rejected. Hiking back, I broke through the icy snow once more and cracked my right shin on a rock. Jeez!

Back at the campsite, some members of the crew were organizing and assembling tents. The clients and less hearty staff members were stomping and hugging themselves for warmth. Some were huddled on a plastic tarp laid out to serve as an extra barrier between butts and the snow. Ram hopped to it ordering the kitchen boys to brew tea and boil soup.

Although he had worked all day in sub-freezing temperatures and icy winds, as soon as everyone was down the slope Ganesh threw himself into the next task of repacking dokos, finding a campsite, setting up the kitchen and meal tent and the other tents. Some crew members were shivering too badly to be of any help. The core guys from Basa, on the other hand, seemed impervious to the freezing cold and blowing snow. They cheerfully followed Ganesh's orders to organize a campsite and to get their clients and other staff members fed and out of the bitingly cold wind into tents as quickly as possible. As soon as it was ready, Ram, Kumar, and DB hustled around serving everyone hot tea and soup. The other guys set up the tents and distributed client duffels.

Breaking camp the morning after the descent of the Ganja La, 2007

When the tents were up, clients piled into their tents, wrapped themselves in multiple layers, and wriggled down into the warmth of their sleeping bags. The crew members rolled up in their blankets and sprawled against one another inside the meal tent.

Mon Bahadur made the rounds checking with each client and crew member for frostbite. He officiously rubbed the feet and fingers of anyone who feared frostbite. My hiking boots had turned into frozen concrete blocks. Mon Bahadur took them outside my tent and pounded the crap out of the boots for several minutes. When he returned the boots they were still pretty rigid but slightly more pliable from the beating Mon gave them.

Over the next few days, when we had time to reflect on the experience of the Ganja La, several of the clients and some of the younger crew members proclaimed it to be the coldest and hardest day of their lives. What impressed me, beyond the harshness of the conditions, was how well Ganesh and the crew of Basa guys handled the hardship. They smiled, laughed, and encouraged everybody else. These men seemed utterly unfazed by what others experienced as scary, miserable, and very cold. Their upbeat attitude in facing hardship called to mind Sir Edmund Hillary's admiration of the Sherpas as "the strongest and kindest people" he knew.

My reaction to the Basa guys was exactly the same as Hillary's to the Sherpas. Ganesh told me that "Basa" means "resting place". I was becoming quite curious to learn what it was about their home, their way of life, and resting place that gave these guys such physical and spiritual strength.

Bailing on Yala Peak; an epiphany

We had a second day in deep snow and another high pass to cross. Ganesh had to fix ropes again to get everyone down a mere 17,000-foot-high pass. Elliot, Ram, and I post-holed out front to break trail, while Ganesh made sure everyone made it over the second pass. Despite working much harder than anyone else, running up and down the sheer passes to fix rope and help the weaker crew members down, Ganesh never stopped smiling and laughing. His leadership by example was exemplary.

Descending the lesser pass after Ganja La, 2007

Ganesh's enthusiastic spirit was infectious, but by the time we staggered into Kyanjin Village most of the clients and crew were exhausted and needed rest. But we had a programme with a schedule to keep. Climbing Yala Peak was scheduled for the following day. Four of our members (three of whom were novice climbers) were determined to attempt the climb no matter how tired they were. And they did it!

On the summit of 18,110-foot Yala Peak; right to left: Dee, Cathy, Elliot, Hector, and Doma Sherpa, the climbing guide. Photo taken by Ganesh on Elliot's camera; photo provided by Elliot Schwartz.

While our more determined compatriots spent the day climbing Yala Peak, the other five clients, including me, spent a leisurely day exploring Kyanjin Village and its environs. Kyanjin is the first village south of the border with Tibet in Langtang. It is the northern terminus of what has come to be called the Tamang Heritage Trek.

We visited the Gompa, where Briggie, Elliot, and I participated in the Dasain celebration in 2004, and took photos of the elaborate thangka paintings. We checked out the goods brought across the mountains by a couple of Tibetan traders. Dax and Nancy stayed in the village to bargain with the tradesmen over gifts for home, while Jim, Tim, and I hiked out of the village and up onto Kyanjin Glacier.

I felt conflicted about bailing on the climb and ruminated as we hiked up toward the glacier. I was supposed to be the group leader, so shouldn't I at least attempt the climb? I'd had a wonderful but exhausting adventure with Elliot and Briggie just three years ago on Yala. It would undoubtedly be another great and exhausting experience to do Yala with my mates in the 2007 group. Remembering the long slog through deep snow and over the glacier just to get to the mountain was a very unappealing thought. Even imagining the fifteen-foot rock climb just below the summit didn't get my juices flowing. My batteries needed recharging, and an easy day of walking around the village and hiking up to the glacier was much more appealing than the challenge of Yala Peak. Hadn't Lama Tenzing said, "People should do what they want"? I wanted to take it easy and not push myself to my physical limits.

The decision not to attempt the climb added another layer to a growing realization that mountaineering was no longer my primary motivation for returning to Nepal. I had come to value the serendipity of cultural experiences and communing with nature more than meeting the challenge of an extreme adventure. And the philanthropic piece of philanthro-trekking was becoming increasingly important to me. In 2007 I helped to introduce another group of visitors to the country, culture, and mountains that I loved. We distributed school supplies to children and villages all along the trails we hiked. I did have a feeling of masculine-ego deflation for not climbing with the other four. However, had I climbed with them, I might not have had the epiphany that occurred outside Kyanjin Village with my friend, Tim Meyer.

Germination of the seed for the Basa School Project and a "Coke wedding"
After hiking up onto the Kyanjin Glacier, Jim returned to the village. Tim and I continued up the glacier. He was the first person I

talked to about something I'd been thinking about since we left Kathmandu. I'd spent some time with Ganesh and Niru separate from the clients in Kathmandu. They told me the village school in Basa only had three grades. The villagers wanted to add 4th and 5th grade classes to the school. There is a K-12 school in the largest village in the area, Sombare, which is a two-hour walk from Basa. The children who want to go on to 4th and 5th grade, to qualify for middle school, have to walk on their little legs all the way to Sombare and back. It's asking a lot of 10-year olds, even for children of the Himalayas, to walk four hours every school day. Niru and Ganesh assured me that amount of walking is no big deal for the older kids, but they thought it was expecting a little too much of 4th and 5th graders.

They went on to explain that $5,000 would pay for all the materials needed to add and outfit two classrooms plus two teachers' salaries for three years. A teacher's salary was $40 per month, so $80 for 36 months would be $2,880. The remaining balance of the $5,000 would be sufficient to purchase all the materials needed to add two classrooms to the school.

Niru and Ganesh explained that the government was supposed to take over paying teacher salaries for village schools after three years. But villages populated with subsistence farmers didn't have the means to pay teacher salaries. Subsistence farming really meant that the residents of Basa subsisted on what they grew. They didn't grow cash crops in Basa. Mountain villages like Basa had to find an outside funding source to pay the first three years of schoolteachers' salaries to establish a school. Niru and a French-Canadian NGO had paid the salaries of the original three teachers.

It seemed like a bizarre system, but that's what Niru and Ganesh told me. They asked if I would consider raising or donating $5,000 for the school. I told them I'd think about it. I'd been thinking about it during the trek, when my brain was warm enough for rational thought.

The 2007 expedition was Tim's first experience of the Himalayas. He was a past president of the Central Indiana Wilderness Club and an experienced outdoorsman. Nepal struck a chord in him. As we hiked across Kyanjin Glacier, I told Tim what Niru and Ganesh asked of me, and asked him what he thought. He immediately offered to be the first donor, if I decided to raise the requested $5,000 for the Basa School.

Tim was even more worn down than I was after Ganja La. He could have resented the hardships of the trek. Why give a damn about the village school of these men who herded him over those torturous mountains. Tim confided to me on the fifth day of the trek that it was, "Absolutely the hardest thing I've ever done!" And that was before Ganja La. But Nepal, the Himalayas, and Niru's crew had an opening-up rather than a closing-in effect on Tim. His immediate and enthusiastic willingness to join a campaign to improve the lives of children in Basa helped to open my own mind to start down a new path.

What a long path it has turned out to be. I didn't imagine that conversation with Tim on top of Kyanjin Glacier would begin a journey that still continues 13 years later. Tim was the first to contribute a check to the Basa School Project after we returned to the States. After the Project became a fully fledged nonprofit foundation, Tim joined the board of directors.

While Tim and I hiked back to Kyanjin Village we brainstormed how to promote a fundraising drive for the Basa School. I decided to call the effort the Basa School Project. We decided that we should start the fundraising effort with the Central Indiana Wilderness Club, since the CIWC helped to promote the trek. After our return, Tim, Jim, and Cathy created a slide-show program, and the Wilderness Club sponsored the first fundraising event for the Basa School Project.

Tim also offered to check with his church, First Friends Quaker Meeting of Indianapolis, to see if it could be of any help. I had become disenchanted with the Presbyterian denomination and dropped out of the church. So I was willing to check out the Quakers. I went to a meeting (Quakers call their worship services "meetings") and was introduced to the Clerk of First Friends, Beth Henricks. Beth was impressed with what Tim and I told her about the plan to assist this little village school in Nepal. She invited me to speak at a business meeting of the congregation. First Friends agreed to become the "fiscal agent" (IRS lingo for the funnelling source of tax-exempt contributions) for the school project. All donations to the Basa School Project were made to First Friends, and contributors were able to claim a charitable tax deduction.

Back in Kyanjin Village, Tim and I visited the couple shops of local weavers and traders. It was fascinating to watch a Tamang woman working the shuttle on her loom. Her hands and feet flew around the loom moving the shuttle device and pumping wooden treadles.

Tamang woman at work on her loom in Kyanjin Village, 2007

Three local Tamang women began to follow Tim and me as we strolled around the village. We tried making conversation. There was a lot of giggling and failed attempts to communicate through sign language and my rudimentary Nepali. The women spoke very little English, but they kept saying "Coke" and something about "wedding". We decided they were not trying to sell or buy drugs, but we couldn't figure out what they wanted. They kept pointing at us, then at themselves, and then nodding in a confidentially intimate way.

After lots of laughing, pointing back and forth and cagey nodding, we decided they wanted Tim and me to choose two of them to marry, and then we'd have a "Coke wedding". This request was a new one on me; not a Nepalese custom I'd encountered before. Tim and I were curious to find out what a Coke wedding was, but not willing to agree to a betrothal to find out. After more giggling and gesturing we figured out that they really just wanted us to buy Coca Colas for them. We guessed that they thought we'd be more willing to buy Cokes for them if they were willing to marry us. We declined the marriage proposals, but bought all three of the women bottles of Coca Colas at a local shop.

Trek tipping traditions and last chance shopping

The trek back down the Langtang Trail was a piece of cake. No rain and mostly easy downhill hiking. In Langtang Village we had a traditional end-of-trek party with our staff. Ram slaughtered a ram (again, no joke) and prepared a five course meal featuring mutton stew. He made several celebratory cakes. I think Dax ate half of them.

There is a tradition, presumably started by the British, for tipping at the end of a Himalayan expedition. The group leader collects tips from all the clients. The sirdar and group leader work out an agreeable formula for distribution of the tips among the crew members. The usual formula grants the sirdar the largest share of the tips, which Ganesh certainly deserved. The rest of the crew receive smaller shares in a descending order with the cook, climbing guide, and assistant sirdars on top, porters next, and kitchen boys at the bottom. The sirdar might suggest that one or more staff members receive a little more than the percentage allotted to the member's station, if some extra work was performed. Ram received a larger share, because he helped Ganesh cut steps and string ropes on Ganja. When the sirdar and group leader have agreed to the tip division, the sirdar takes the money and puts each crew member's tip in an envelope with the crew member's name on the envelope.

All the clients who have clothes, whether clean or filthy, along with any climbing or camping gear they are willing to leave behind, donate those items as extra tips for the staff. All that stuff is turned over to the sirdar for distribution to the crew members.

After the end-of-trek dinner is finished, the crew lines up and the clients line up opposite them with the group leader in front. The leader ritualistically hands the envelopes with the monetary tips to each crew member. The crew members go down the line of clients and thanks are exchanged between each crew member and each client. There is much bowing with hands under chin, handshaking, and hugging.

The way the non-monetary gifts are divided is by the sirdar devising an order -- Ganesh used a number-drawing system -- for the crew members to take turns picking items out of the pile of dirty clothes and gear the clients donated. It may seem gross to well-off Americans to give a soiled pair of socks or underwear as a tip, but believe me, Nepali porters are usually delighted to receive castoff clothing in any condition.

After the tipping rituals are completed the party ramps up into full swing with singing, dancing, drinking, and toasting.

The traditional tipping and partying is a delightful way to end a trek or mountaineering expedition. The two groups of people from very different cultures have shared difficult and beautiful experiences. The staff is grateful for the tips they receive in addition to their last paycheck. They are also happy because they will either be going home or have been hired for another expedition. The clients are usually very grateful for the amazing service they've received from the crew.

The 2007 party was very festive. Elliot, Cathy, Dee, and Hector were proud of successfully summiting Yala, which was a hell of a testament to their strength and endurance considering how taxing the experience of the Ganja La was. Dax, Jim, Tim, Nancy, and I felt good about making it over the high passes. We felt even better after the extra day of R and R and our interesting experiences in Kyanjin Village.

Rocking out during the end-of-trek party in the dining room of Lucky Guest House; our last campsite was on the grounds of that lodge in Langtang Village.

The day after the party we hiked down to Ghora Tabela, where Elliot and I played volleyball with the soldiers in 2004. The Army base and dirt volleyball court were still there, but there weren't any soldiers hanging out. We loaded gear into a helicopter and choppered back to Kathmandu. It took three flights to get the group and our baggage back to Kathmandu. This was not the big old hulking military transport chopper. We flew in style in a sleek modern helicopter, but it only carried the pilot and four passengers per flight.

The helicopter ride back to Kathmandu is a jolly good experience in itself with fantastic views of the magnificent Langtang Valley. Huge white-capped mountains line each side of the valley. In 2007 the pilot did not hug the right side of the valley as the pilot did in 2004. The Maoist rebels were no longer taking potshots at passing choppers.

We had a couple days of shopping and hanging out in Kathmandu before our flights home. In Nepal local merchants expect to bargain with customers, while prices are fixed in modern stores that sell imported products. On our first group-shopping excursion Dax demonstrated his technique of bargaining local shopkeepers down to the point they are in tears. Most of our members preferred to bargain just a little and to leave the poor shop owners with their dignity and a profit. Everyone bought presents for friends and family, such as kukri knives (traditional curved knife used in farming and combat by Nepalese hill tribes), prayer wheels (metal cylinder containing Buddhist mantras on parchment, which spins on a wood handle), embroidered T-shirts, jewelry, pashmina shawls (cashmere woven from mountain goat hair), and thangka paintings.

Niru hosted the group at his home for a 7-course feast the last night we were in Kathmandu. Many toasts were offered, especially to Ganesh. We also toasted Niru for being such a splendid host and for planning the programme.

Tim and I ended the adventure with a night in Bangkok at a 5-star hotel overlooking the Cho Prahya River. We swam some laps in the hotel pool and then had dinner at a recommended local restaurant. Nerdy Thai college students were getting hammered and singing American rock tunes, like "Born in the USA!" We were definitely back in "civilization".

[My journal and file of documents from the 2007 expedition disappeared. I don't know how or where. My photos were preserved digitally. Emails among group members and with Niru were also saved. Those two sources were helpful in recreating events. For this chapter especially, I had to rely on imaginative memory for some details. Other members of the trekking group will undoubtedly remember some of the events differently.]

A few more photos from the trek ...

241

The trek I did in 2008 was, for me, one of the least physically demanding of the 14 Himalayan expeditions I've done. It was also one of the most bizarre, had the most "casualties", and was the most consequential of the 14.

When our group arrived in 2006, just after a truce was signed by the government and Maoist rebels, the country was in a celebratory mood. Demonstrators and soldiers no longer occupied the streets of Kathmandu. Shoppers, vendors, beggars, and tourists returned. When I arrived in 2008 there was a growing confidence that the war was truly over and peace restored in Nepal. The despised King Gyanendra abdicated and left the country in exile. Maoist fighters laid down their arms under United Nations supervision. The political party of the Maoists participated in elections judged fair by neutral observers. The Communist Party of Nepal won more seats in the newly elected Parliament than any other party. A coalition government was formed, and a new constitution was a work in progress.

So much history had occurred in Nepal in just a few years. None of it, Niru and Ganesh told me, had any effect on Basa Village. According to them, Basa had changed very little in 500 years. There was no electricity or running water and nothing moved on wheels around Basa. While history roared through Kathmandu during the last decade, the only impact on Basa was word-of-mouth stories brought home by men who left the village for temporary work with expedition companies like Adventure GeoTreks.

There were two significant developments for the village within the last decade. A medical clinic opened in Sombare, the nearest major village, in the late 1990s. Infant mortality rates in the village fell dramatically and life expectancy increased dramatically due to the availability of some modern medicines and medical treatments. Ganesh told me that, "In the old days three of four babies died, but now three of four live." Niru related that older folks were living five to ten years longer, because of the medical care available through the Sombare clinic. The crop yields of the village farmers were not sufficient to handle the baby boom and increased life expectancy of the elderly. There was not enough arable land along the mountainside of Basa to feed so many more mouths living so much longer.

The second development was the village school. Niru explained that the villagers realized many of the children born in the baby boom of the current generation would have to leave Basa to find work in Kathmandu or another city. The kids would have no chance of finding employment without an education. Adventure GeoTreks was the only significant employer of Basa villagers, and the company had been struggling with the downturn in tourism during the civil war. While any hardy villager could work as a porter or kitchen boy, to move up through the ranks to become a cook or guide required skills and knowledge beyond the ability to carry a heavy load over mountain trails.

When Niru was old enough to go to school in Sombare, which was long before the school in Basa was established, he walked the four-hour roundtrip the first day of class. When he got home that evening, he decided that, if he was going to walk that far, he wanted to be paid for it. Niru left home and hired on with an outfitter company as a porter. He worked his way up to sirdar, and then left to start his own company. He had to learn English and other languages of European clients on his own. Niru had to learn bookkeeping and accounting on his own. He told me that one of the reasons he gave the land and helped pay the starting salaries of the teachers at the Basa Village School was to make sure all the kids in Basa got a basic education. It would launch the ones with ambition on their way to doing more than farming and portering. Niru knew through personal experience how difficult self-education is, and he wanted the current and future generations of Basa children to have a better education than he had.

Niru hoped most of the children of Basa would be happy to follow the life patterns of their parents and grow up to be farmers and to sustain the village as it was. But, because many in the current generation would have to leave, the brightest and most ambitious kids would have a better chance of making it in the outside world with a basic education.

"Yes" with reservations to the Basa School Project
When our group returned to Kathmandu after the helicopter

244

flight out of Langtang in 2007, I gave Niru and Ganesh the answer they hoped for to their question about raising $5,000 for the Basa School. I would do it. Niru immediately raised another subject. Instead of planning another mountaineering expedition, would I consider working with him to organize a trek to Basa?

Niru's idea was to tantalize donors to the School Project with the opportunity to do a trek like no other. Niru claimed that only one other group of "white people" had ever visited the village. A French-Canadian group came to Basa to work with the villagers to build the school in 2003. Another group from France associated with the NGO Sol Himal, which offered scholarships to village kids, was planning a visit to Basa in the spring of 2008. Niru hoped I would recruit an American group to visit Basa in the fall of 2008.

The idea of a trek off the tourist trails to a village which was nearly untouched by the modern world intrigued me. All the Sherpa villages in the Khumbu along the Base Camp Trail and the Tamang villages along the Tamang Heritage Trail had electricity and water systems by 2008. Most of their kids could attend school and there was a healthcare facility within walking distance. The Khumbu Sherpas even had heated lodges with hot water and their own domestic airline!

I imagined visiting Basa would be like going back in time to experience a Himalayan village similar to what the early British explorers discovered. But the experience would be even more meaningful than satisfying curiosity about an ancient indigenous culture. The philanthro aspect of a philanthro-trek to Basa would be the culmination of a fundraising drive to improve the educational opportunities for the children of Basa.

Before I left Nepal in 2007, Niru and I began to develop a plan for an October 2008 trek to Basa Village. Our assumption was that the trek would occur after a successful fundraising drive for the school.

I picked up bits and pieces about life in Basa from Ganesh and the guys in our crews over the course of the 2006 and 2007 treks. There were six small villages in the area called Basa. The largest, called Basa 6 by the government, was Niru and Ganesh's home village. It was called Basa Village by the local people. 63 families lived within the village proper for a total population of 357.

The village's water source was a fast-running stream twenty-minutes walk downhill from the village. Sticks were the main fuel source, burned in open fire pits for cooking, heating, and lighting in the homes. There were no stores in Basa. To purchase anything locally required a two-hour walk from Basa to Sombare, the market village which also had the nearest medical clinic and K-12 school. No vehicles could reach the village, because the nearest road ended a four-day walk from Basa. There was an airstrip a long day's walk from Basa in the large village of Phaplu, where there was also a hospital.

The day before I left Kathmandu in 2007, Niru, Ganesh, and I met over lunch for a final discussion about the Basa School Project. They shared an even more expansive vision for Basa Village. In addition to guarantying at least a 5th grade education for the village kids, they wanted to develop water and electrical systems for the village. They even dreamed about making Basa a tourist destination for trekkers. They viewed the development they'd seen in the Sherpa villages along the Base Camp Trail as totally positive.

My initial reaction to their enthusiasm about future development in Basa was ambivalence. I was reluctant to help Niru and Ganesh achieve their vision, because of the downside I'd seen to development in the Himalayan region. Sherpa villages along the Base Camp Trail had been transformed by tourist commercialization. In one generation those villages transmogrified from barter economies of yak herding and potato farming to monetary economies wholly dependent on tourism. In the early nineties there were no obese Sherpas. By 2006 many over-weight Sherpas sat behind desks counting the money they made in their restaurants and lodges. Ang Rita developed worry lines on his forehead as the number of customers for his lodge in Pheriche declined during the civil war. Did Niru and Ganesh really understand the implications of their dreams for Basa?

Because of my high regard for Ganesh, Niru, and the other guys from Basa I'd met through AGT, I didn't want to play an instrumental role in turning their rustic little Rai village into a tourist destination. I stewed over how the villagers would adapt to infrastructure changes like education, running water, and electricity. Wouldn't that change the character of the Basa guys, whose strength and kindness so impressed the members of the 2006 and 2007 expeditions?

I fell back on an ethical cop out. If I didn't do it, someone else would. So I returned to the US intending to raise the $5,000 for the school, visit Basa Village, and then decide whether I would have anymore involvement with Niru and his plan to bring progress to Basa.

Fundraising for the Basa School Project

In January 2008 I began emailing and calling friends, asking them to make a $25 to $500 donation-pledge to the Basa School Project. I also began recruiting members for an October 2008 trek. The expedition Niru and I planned would be an 11-day cultural trek. The group would fly from Kathmandu to the airstrip at Phaplu in the Solu region south-west of Basa. The trek would be a circuit around the area of Phaplu and Basa. The programme would include visits to various villages, gompas, and other cultural sites. After the return to Phaplu, we'd fly back to Kathmandu. The trip would conclude with a day tour of the Kathmandu Valley.

Our plan was to offer an introductory trek that would be easy enough for novice trekkers. We hoped the programme would attract clients who might not be experienced outdoorsmen, like the Wilderness Club members on the 2007 expedition, but who would enjoy a cultural trek and would want to help raise money for the Basa School Project. The highlight of the cultural trek would be two days and nights in Basa halfway through the trek.

Both campaigns, to recruit donors for the School Project and members for the trek, went well during the winter. Although I only asked for a pledge, most of the friends contacted sent in a check. As promised, Tim's was the first check received. But when the amount of donations hit $4,000, for some reason, the dollars stopped flowing in. As summer came and departure for Nepal in October loomed, I began to worry that I would have to make up the $1,000 shortfall. I was willing to do that, if need be. But I had hoped to make time and effort my major contributions rather than dollars.

My plan was to visit Basa in October, inspect the school, interview the teachers, and then, assuming I was satisfied, call in the pledges. Since $4,000 in cash donations were already made by friends who didn't care about waiting for my report from Nepal, I wanted to wrap the damn thing up and get on with life. It was frustrating that what started off so well had stalled. Then one day I saw a guy walking toward the fitness room at my YMCA branch wearing climbing boots and gaiters.

Bob Meyer (no relation to Tim) was training to climb the 8,000-meter peak, Cho Oyu, which is near Mt. Everest. On crummy weather days he ran treadmills and used elliptical machines at the Jordan Y to workout. I had never seen anyone in climbing boots at my Y. We struck up a conversation in the fitness room. The result of that conversation was a $1,000 donation from Bob's private foundation. The fundraising drive was complete. (Another $1,000 came in through pledges that were fulfilled after my return from Nepal, so the campaign generated $6,000.)

A group of 10 shrinks to 6, and a plane crash

Organizing the trekking group had its problems and surprises too. Ten members signed up for the trek to Basa. The philanthro-trek plan was working. Counting me, we had a one member increase over the nine-member 2007 trekking group.

It was going to be a fun and interesting group. Two high school teachers from the Indianapolis area planned to do a comparative study of education in Nepal. John, a physician friend from the Jordan YMCA, would be our expedition doc. (This Dr. John is a family practice M.D.; not the same Dr. John, aka Long John the chiropractor, who was my travel mate in 1995.) Dr. John planned to bring a load of medical supplies to donate to the medical clinic in Sombare. I had not seen my cousin David, who lived in the LA area, since he was a little kid. He'd heard of my Himalayan adventures through the family grapevine. We reconnected and Cousin David joined the Basa trek group. Two friends of friends, Karen and George from Biloxi, Mississippi signed up. Bill (false name), a friend from college living in San Diego joined. Carl (false name), a member of the Wilderness Club, who attended the program about the Langtang philanthro-trek, signed on. Once again, Dax joined to round out the group of ten, counting me.

By the time we arrived in Kathmandu, the group was down to six. The two teachers expected to receive a grant which would cover most of their costs. The grant fell through, so they canceled. Dr. John was in a serious car wreck just a month before the departure date. He cracked several ribs and was in no condition to trek and sleep in a tent. George from Biloxi informed me six months in advance of our planned departure that he planned to use the trek as motivation to lose fifty pounds. I had not met George in person. A couple weeks before the departure date, he called and told me he'd actually gained weight and was in no condition to attempt a Himalayan trek. He cancelled.

The remaining six did arrive safely in Kathmandu. Niru assigned Sanga, the guide for our tours around Kathmandu in 2006 and 2007, to be our sirdar. Sanga met with the group at the Kathmandu Guest House to review the programme with us. He distributed AGT duffels to the group and helped Karen and Bill whittle down the items they planned to take on the trek so that all their stuff fit into a duffel bag. Bill was required to unpack three of four pairs of blue jeans and two of three pillows (one had a sound system in it). Karen insisted that she had to take her sleep-inducing machine. Sanga relented. This was clearly not a hardcore mountaineering group.

Sanga and I reminded everyone we needed our passports for the domestic flight to Phaplu in the morning. We answered questions about how much water to carry, whether we'd need to keep rain coats in our daypacks or leave them in the duffels, and would the trail be dusty.

In the morning everyone was ready to go with their passports, at least two liters of water, raincoats or ponchos in their daypacks, and a bandana or surgical mask for dusty sections of the trail. But the weather was overcast and raining, so our flight to Phaplu was cancelled. We had another rest day in Kathmandu.

The next morning, we assembled again with our packed duffels and backpacks in the KGH lobby for the drive to the airport. We were watching the television in the hotel lobby waiting for Sanga and the transport van, when our attention was riveted by a breaking news report. The first flight of the day to Lukla had crashed. When Sanga arrived, he gave us the bad news that all flights into Phaplu, as well as Lukla, were cancelled due to the plane crash. He asked us to hang out while he checked with the airline and Niru. He'd meet us at lunchtime to let us know when our flight would depart.

More news came in about the plane crash. The pilot's approach was too low and he crashed into the mountain face below the Lukla airstrip. No survivors were expected. When Sanga returned he had more bad news. So many flights had been cancelled in the last two days that we wouldn't be able to get a flight for at least two more days. If we waited that long to fly to Phaplu, we would be unable to do the trek and be back to Kathmandu in time to catch our return flights to the US.

The group was sobered by the crash and, if I correctly read facial expressions and body language, there was some relief within the group when Sanga informed us we would not be flying to Phaplu. Sanga told us that Niru had prepared two alternative programmes and we needed to choose which one we preferred to do. One was an Annapurna trek; the other was taking a bus as close as we could get to Basa and then hike to Basa. The Annapurna trek would be a teahouse trek, meaning we would stay in lodges, because our tents, kitchen, cook, and porters were in Phaplu waiting to meet us. The other option was to take a private bus to Jiri Village, where the road ended, and then hike to Basa. We would spend the first two nights in lodges, but would then meet our crew on the trail. We'd tent-camp trek to Basa and then to Phaplu. Niru was confident regular flights from Phaplu to Kathmandu would be re-established by the time we finished the trek to Basa.

Sanga warned us that the trek to Basa would not be as leisurely as we'd planned. We were already two days behind the programme schedule. It would take a day to drive to Jiri, and then two days to hike to Phaplu. We would be five days behind schedule by the time we got to Phaplu. But, the plan was to spend a day in Phaplu before starting the actual trek, so we'd be four days behind schedule when we arrived in Phaplu on foot. The easy-introductory trek would be converted into a challenging trek in terms of the distance we would have to cover on the trail each day in order to get to Basa and then back to Phaplu in time to fly back to Kathmandu for our return flights home. We'd make up some of that time by skipping the two rest days planned in Basa Village, but Sanga estimated that the amount of time we'd need to spend hiking each day would increase from the planned four to six hours to eight to ten hours. Alternatively, the Annapurna trek would be a more leisurely trek with hiking distances similar to those of the original programme.

For me, the primary purpose of the expedition was to visit Basa Village, inspect the school, and bring back a report to donors about the school project. Of course, I hoped our group would have a great experience and I thought that visiting a village as untouched as Basa would be very cool. I told the group how I felt about the two options. I had not been to Annapurna, but I was sure it would be a beautiful trek. It is the second most popular trek in Nepal after the Base Camp Trail. But I hoped the group would vote for the Basa option. Experiencing Basa was why we'd come to Nepal.

There was little discussion. We had already lost two days and everyone was anxious to get on the trail. The vote was unanimous to go to Basa.

I shared with the group my strong desire to visit Basa and the school. I didn't share my reservations about how we might be the harbingers of a transformation of Basa as the first tourists to visit Basa. The French-Canadian and French groups who went to Basa before us had not come as tourists. They were secular missionaries there to work on the school building. We raised money for the school, but ours was a cultural-tourism trek, not a philanthropy mission. Our group was the first experiment with fulfilling Niru's dream to make Basa a tourist-trekking destination. The experiment was going awry.

On the road again; group dynamics and a gay surprise
Once we were out of the Kathmandu Valley on our little Tata bus, the road trip was typical of what I'd experienced driving through other areas in rural Nepal. The drive was long, slow, and hazardous up and down narrow, winding roads through many one-rooster villages. The road to Jiri in 2008 was dirt for stretches, but mostly paved. Signs indicated the road was constructed with funds provided by a Swiss organization.

You drive on the left side in Nepal, which is a result of the influence England had on India and India has had on Nepal. Pedestrians in the towns we drove through walked in front of our bus and other vehicles with impunity. Moving quickly out of the way of vehicular traffic was not a custom of the Nepalese living along the road to Jiri. Most of the villages we drove through were crappy-looking conglomerations of tin shanties thrown up around older stone and wooden structures. Each roadside village had a petrol station, tire repair shop, and a teahouse that served bhat (rice), chiyaa (tea), and chang (beer). We stopped about every two hours for the bus driver to fill his thermos with tea and to relieve himself of the tea he'd finished drinking.

Life in these roadside villages looked pretty miserable. The communities appeared to be a collection of poor people trying to eke out a living connected in some way with the commerce passing on the highway.  Presumably, most of the residents or their ancestors had left nearby farms. There was such a contrast between the roadside villages and the surrounding lush, green hills terraced with little farm plots of rice, millet, or barley. It was depressing to think about the life the town dwellers had given up to move from the aesthetically pleasing little farms on terraced hillsides to work in a tire-repair shop or teahouse. The farms outside of these villages were probably unable to support an increasing population, so, just like in Basa, people had to leave the family farm to find work somewhere.

The further from the Kathmandu Valley and the deeper into the Himalayan foothills we drove, the more engaging the scenery became. The road followed the Sun Kosi (River of Gold), which we

eventually crossed by a steel suspension bridge. Then the road wound through and out of a great valley created by the river. Our driver carefully negotiated switchbacks up the side of the valley until we were tracking along a ridgeline. Scenic photo ops became more frequent.

David had an impressive array of camera gear and lenses to use as we bumped along in our little bus. He did photography for the LA Galaxy soccer team, so he was clearly the most professional of the shutter bugs in the group.

One town we drove through, Dolkha, had the Communist hammer and sickle symbol painted in red on many of its buildings. Sanga nodded and said, "Maoists," in response to questioning looks from Karen and Bill.

Carl asked Sanga to tell us about the history of the Maoist rebellion. Sanga described the bloody revolt that ended with King Gyanendra being deposed. There were different reactions among the group members. Carl listened attentively. Karen asked whether there was a spiritual dimension to the civil war. David listened with a cocked ear but continued looking out the window for scenic shots. Bill wanted to argue a few points about the socioeconomic causes of the revolt. Dax butted in a few times, trying to bring the history lesson to a close.

Dax was impatient to bring the attention of the group back to what he thought should be our primary focus during the long bus ride, which was Dax. During the all-day drive, Dax blathered blithely away covering innumerable subjects, all intended to enlighten us less cultured rubes about good taste in music, art, cinema, automobiles and motorcycles, Asian cuisine, etc. Most of his disquisitions were more humorous than pedantic. Dax especially enjoyed declaring and defending intentionally inflammatory opinions. Because of my experience with Dax in 1996, 2007, and several visits in between our Himalayan adventures, I was well aware of the joy he took in surprising and offending those uninitiated in his brand of humor and conversation. Our 2008 group had a lot of easy targets for his malevolent jesting. Dax was a New Yorker splitting his time between NYC and LA. Carl, Bill, and I grew up in Indiana. David is a laidback Californian. Karen, with her languid Mississippi drawl, was Dax's favorite target for verbal pinpricks.

Whenever Dax senses homophobia in a person he is interacting with, he exaggerates his gayness. If someone makes an effort to show how liberal and accepting she is of gays, Dax makes derogatory jokes about queers. While he was holding forth on the bus, every now and then he would smile slyly at me and wink to let me know what he was up to. He was introducing the rest of the group to what they had to look forward to on the trail with Dax.

Dax was unable to do the climb of Kanglachan in 1996. He was so heavy with upper body muscle that he was very slow and unsteady on the trail. He got severely sunburned, dehydrated, and had altitude sickness before we reached base camp. Our leader, John Roskelley, ordered Dax, over Dax's strong objections, to hike out with a group of Israelis who had a four-wheel drive vehicle a couple hours away. Dax felt humiliated, although he knew John's decision was the correct one. Within a year, Dax shed 40 pounds of muscle, trimmed down to 185, and ramped up his aerobic training. He converted his body from that of a weightlifter to an outdoorsman. Like me, Dax elected not to climb Yala Peak in 2007, but he handled the Ganja La and the other high passes so much better than he'd performed on the trail in Ladakh. I figured his excess silliness on the bus ride was Dax's way to work off nervous energy in anticipation of a challenging trek.

Dax dominated the conversations, but Sanga's ebullient disposition set the emotional tone of the group during the day-long bus ride. We were all happy to be on the road to Jiri in our little white Tata bus, rather than spending another day in Kathmandu worrying about weather and plane crashes. So, for the most part we laughed with or at Dax as we rocked and rolled along the curvaceous mountain roads.

I noticed that when Dax made queer jokes or gay references Sanga looked confused. As a good sirdar, he laughed whenever the rest of us laughed. At the last road stop before Jiri, Sanga took me aside and asked me to explain why Dax made these jokes. He obviously did not understand that Dax was gay. When I told him that Dax was a homosexual, Sanga took in a sharp breath and whispered something to himself in Nepali. He confessed that he had never before had a gay member in any of the groups he led. I suspected that might not actually be true, but let it pass. I reminded him I'd shared a hotel room and tent with Dax on previous expeditions, and assured him Dax would not do anything untoward. Sanga was shocked and then intrigued by the prospect of getting to know a homosexual client. He assured me he would treat Dax no differently after our private talk. But then Sanga grasped my arm and said urgently, "Jeff dhai, we should not let the villagers in Basa know that Dax is homosexual. They would not understand it." I raised my eyebrows in surprise, but nodded agreement.

The group dynamics of expeditions can range from a closely bonded team to an interesting group to socialize with to volatile. By the time our Basa-trek group stepped off the bus in Jiri Village we had already spent the better part of three days together. Certain group dynamics were clearly emerging by the time we reached the end of the road in Jiri. Bill was enamored with Karen, calling her "sweetheart" and making a point of hanging out with her and then sitting by her for most of the bus ride. Karen was a very attractive thirty-five-year-old brunette. Bill's interest seemed more avuncular than romantic. Bill was 20 years older than Karen, a bit pudgy around the middle, and balding. I knew Bill to be a devoted husband and father, so I thought he was just enjoying a bit of flirting with a pretty, younger woman. Karen seemed to enjoy Bill's attention. Why not? He was clever, bright, a successful attorney in So Cal, and a gentleman. So far, their playful fondness seemed unlikely to boil over into passion. Karen made a point of mentioning and showing us pictures of her big, handsomely mustached, and muscular-looking boyfriend who was back home in Biloxi.

None of the other guys seemed interested in competing for Karen's attentions. Out of the question for Dax, and Cousin David is one of the most devoted hubbies I've ever known. His wife, Melissa, is blind, so his devotion stretches beyond the normal bonds of marriage. I did not know Carl well at all, but he seemed way too interested in maintaining a meditative attitude to get into a rooster competition for our one chick. He later confided to me that wounds from a divorce were not yet healed.

We arrived in Jiri well after dark. Sanga directed our driver to a lodge on the main street. We pulled our duffels off the bus as the lodge owner directed us to three rooms on the second floor. The rooms were typical for Himalayan mountain lodges; narrow plywood cubicles with one window.

Bill offered to share a room with Karen. When he discovered she intended to play her battery-powered sound machine all night to help her sleep, he immediately rescinded his offer and asked Carl to trade rooms. Carl placidly agreed to room with Karen for the night. Bill and Dax shared a room, as did David and I. In the morning we all made fun of Karen for bringing her sound machine. I pointed out that she might be the first trekker who slept in the Himalayan Mountains listening to the ocean. She accepted the ribbing with good humor.

The night in Jiri was good for male bonding with my cousin. David is 15 years my junior, and we'd not seen each other in 20 years. Through family reports I knew he was developing a very successful career as a techie in LA and he'd married Melissa, a pretty little Hispanic gal, who was losing her sight. David's twin brother, Vince, had gone off to work in advertising in London, England. The last time I'd seen the twins they were cute little boys serving as the ring bearers in their Aunt Barbara's wedding. Here we were in Nepal and David was thirty years old, was my height with muscular arms and broad shoulders. He still had the full head of thick, dark hair I remembered. To cap off our reunion and male bonding we peed together under the stars off the second floor of the lodge into the grass below. I was happy to learn that night that David did not snore.

The wonderful feeling of Himalayan trekking and an unplanned night hike

The next morning the sun rose bright and shining through the mountains east of Jiri. While we ate a hot breakfast of bacon, eggs, and toast at the lodge, Sanga reported that he'd made arrangements with the lodge Didi to secure our duffels. He instructed us to take everything out of the duffel bags we might need on a long day of hiking.

Remember, our programme plan was to fly to Phaplu and meet our crew there. And that's where they were with the tents and kitchen equipment, until Niru called Arjun, an assistant sirdar, by satellite phone and told him the plan changed. When we began the drive to Jiri, per Niru's instructions to Arjun, our porters started hiking from Phaplu toward Jiri. The kitchen staff began hiking to a village called Deorali, which is located in between Phaplu and Jiri.

Sanga informed us during breakfast that we would meet up with the entire crew that evening in Deorali.

What didn't make sense was how our duffels would get from Jiri to Deorali. We weren't carrying them, and our porters weren't here. I asked Sanga if he'd hired porters in Jiri to carry the duffel bags. "No," Sanga chuckled, "that is not the plan." Sanga explained that it was normally a two-day hike for local people to come from Phaplu to Jiri, and then back to Deorali would be a third day of walking. But our porters, he said, would manage it all in two days. The guys would've walked all day yesterday while we were on the road. "Today, while we will be hiking to Deorali, the porters will arrive in Jiri to pick up your duffel bags. They will walk fast enough to meet us in Deorali tonight," Sanga concluded complacently.

Dax and I smiled at each other while the novice members of our group looked bewildered and demanded to know how it was possible for the porters to hike fast enough to catch up with us tonight. Sanga laughed and waved away the questions. "The porters, they will hike through the night if necessary."

Bill insisted that the plan made no sense. "The porters can't possibly meet us tonight! They aren't even here yet to pick up our duffels. You said it's a long hike to Deorali. The porters have to get here, then carry the duffel bags -- while we're only carrying daypacks -- and meet us tonight. How is that possible?"

Sanga laughed again and replied, "The porters, they will take shortcuts."

So, we loaded up our daypacks, left our duffels at the lodge, and walked out of Jiri.

Children laughed and waved to us as we passed their plaster-walled and tin-roofed homes. A few local people hurried past us on the trail out of Jiri. The trail narrowed and became steeper and more difficult as the town receded behind us. The countryside was lush. The trail tracked in and out of an alpine forest with deciduous trees mixed in with conifers. The air felt fresh and there was a rich, earthy odor emanating from thick, green, bushy undergrowth along the edge of the trail. This unfamiliar terrain of the Middle Himalayas looked more like rain forests I'd hiked in Belize, Honduras, and Puerto Rico than the stark and rocky High Himalayas where I had spent most of my time in Nepal.

Jiri's elevation is just over 6,000 feet, so altitude was not yet an issue. The altitude in Kathmandu is just under 5,000 feet, so we were acclimated well enough to handle the first phase of the day's hike. Deorali, however, is at about 9,000 feet. The revised programme violated the "no more than 1,000-foot-gain per-night rule" the first day of the trek. Sanga assured me that would not be a problem, however, because we would lose altitude the next day. "And when we arrive in Basa we will be below 7,000 feet again."

Bill started to have trouble on the first significant uphill section of trail. His face turned red and he was sweating profusely. This was not good. If he was struggling this much on the first steep hill, how was he going to handle the higher passes which awaited us on the trek to Basa?

David seemed to be doing fine, but Karen's face was also flushed. She too was struggling much too hard for the first challenge of the day. Her gait was awkward, as though her hiking boots didn't fit well. They were unmarked and looked new. I wondered if she had properly broken in the boots. Carl was stronger, but somewhat unsteady. He is six-foot five-inches tall with size-17 shoes. He looked like a giant two-legged camel humping up the hill. Dax was clicking along with a wide grin on his face and his sleeves rolled up revealing well-developed biceps.

I took my shirt off and draped it over my shoulders to use as a sweat barrier between my back and daypack. In the 1990s, expedition companies instructed women to wear long skirts or long pants in Nepal, especially in the villages. Men were told not to go around bare-chested. By 2003 so many trekkers had ignored the "dress code" that many outfitter companies gave up on it. Westerners have always worn whatever they felt like in Kathmandu. In Thamel, female tourists wearing halter and tank tops and short shorts have been a common sight since the 1970s. Immodest Western dress may still offend some Nepalese, but Western women in shorts and men without shirts are no longer uncommon sights on the main trekking trails. Every year more young Nepalis adopt the clothing and grooming, or lack thereof, styles of tourists from developed countries.

After Rinpoche Tenzing of Tengboche told me that, "People should do what they want," I decided I would no longer wear a shirt on the trail when I didn't want to. In a village, if I felt like I was offending local sensibilities, I put my shirt back on. But for the most part, my experience is that going shirtless only offends self-righteous high-caste Hindus. It's unlikely you'll meet any of those types up in the mountains. Some villagers and mountain people find it curious and odd, but not particularly offensive, that a man would choose to go shirtless. The high country is populated mostly by Buddhists and animists. They are less uptight about personal dress than conservative Hindus. The only time I was actually confronted in Asia for going shirtless was when I was jogging in New Delhi. An orthodox Hindu lectured me in a haughty tone, accusing me of being "unhealthy" by exposing my chest in public. I pointed out that Gandhi went shirtless, as do Hindu sadhus. He stomped off muttering to himself.

It felt good to be hiking once again in the Himalayas. It was a warm day and it was getting hotter as the sun climbed higher. Sweat was trickling down my forehead, funneling along my eyebrows, and dripping off my face. My shirt was soaked through by mid morning and a sweat stain was growing on my backpack. So what! I felt so free and pure powering up and down the trails, arms swinging with a light pack on my back.

Despite the sweat, my soul sang. I looked forward to being enveloped by the gigantic night sky filled with stars so luminous they looked close enough to touch. We would soon hear the sound of a glacier-fed river rushing through a deep valley cut out of the great mountains. The distant peaks of the High Himalayas guarding the border with Tibet would be visible in their opalescent glory from the high passes. We would awaken to the gentle voice of a kitchen boy bringing tea or coffee to our tents along with a pan of warm water for washing the sleep from our eyes. The inviting aroma of brewed tea would begin to fill the tent as I washed my hands and face in the bowl of *taato pani* (warm water). We would hear the cook humming in the kitchen tent as the powerful scent of a hot breakfast wafted through the campsite letting us know it was time to roll up sleeping bags and come to breakfast. Around the meal table our little band of trekkers would share stories of other travel adventures and the crazy altitude-induced dreams we had last night, while our sirdar bustled around making sure everyone ate their fill and water bottles were full. Several days would be filled with the glorious feeling of my legs powering up and down steep rocky trails while my lungs and heart pumped life through my body. Those were the experiences I expected to have on the trek to Basa.

I hoped my comrades in 2008 would respond with the same delight I was feeling that first morning on the trail. But the way Bill and Karen were huffing and puffing painfully up every steep section we encountered made me wonder whether they could find any joy in the experience.

Trekking is not a normal or rational thing to do. Why pay money to hike for days up and down high mountain trails? Yet, away from your ordinary life you can experience nature more intimately and appreciate its aesthetics more consciously and deeply. You may notice and respond to minute or gigantic things you see as beautiful works of art. See that intricate articulated pattern in the bark of a tree! Look at the outrageous colors of those flowers beside the trail! How awesome is the sunshine reflected like a prism in multiple colors off that glaciated peak!

But it was increasingly apparent that Bill and Karen were not enjoying any of nature's beauty that we passed through that morning. The trail was mostly upward with only a few descending stretches. Sanga and I reminded everyone of the need to hydrate. Karen and Bill seemed to be drinking plenty of water, but they both had agonized expressions on their flushed faces. Bill draped a water-soaked bandana over his bald pate. Coping with the heat and loss of bodily fluids on a hot day can be as much of a challenge as dealing with altitude gain.

An old knee injury was beginning to bother Bill. A hitch developed in his gait. It was obvious that Karen had not properly broken in her hiking boots and her feet were beginning to blister. Neither Bill nor Karen voiced any complaints. They stoically kept putting one foot in front of the other.

David, on the other hand, was having a wonderful time shutter-bugging away with a large Nikon camera and a huge detachable lens -- until he fell. He wore a vest with multiple pockets for gear and attachments. The size of the camera and weight of the gear he was carrying combined with a little dizziness from the increasing altitude probably caused David to lose his balance. He'd hopped up on a little hillock for a shot, but slipped off and went ass over teakettle with gear-laden vest, camera, and lens flopping and flying as he went down. The trail was slick in spots from rain the previous night. His boots must have slipped on damp grass. David shook it off and continued to shoot away as we hiked on. But then he fell a second time.

I saw him take a stance on a rise beside a stream and then swing his camera around for a panoramic shot when he fell into the rocky stream. David hit hard enough that he was momentarily dazed. His right arm was cut and bruised. David laughed it off with self-deprecating humor while Sanga applied a bandage. He joked -- or maybe he was serious -- that denting his expensive lens hurt more than the bruised arm.

Carl galumphed along looking all around with an expression on his face which varied from wonder to delighted contentment. His beard was grey and he had a kind-looking and weathered face. He reminded me of the grey-bearded wise-looking and long-legged great blue-heron that inhabits the channel behind my house in Indianapolis. Another amusing thing about Carl was that he randomly chuckled as we walked along as if he was telling himself jokes or he just found humor in whatever his eyes lit upon.

Dax, David, and I hiked out ahead of the others a few times. When we came to a fork in the trail, we would find a pleasant stream to sit beside or a boulder to sit on, and then wait for the slower hikers to catch up. Sanga walked beside either Bill or Karen, whoever was moving the slowest.

Sanga was the only one who knew the trail, and there were no crew members to make sure we didn't take a wrong turn. So, Sanga reasonably asked us to hike together. But Karen and Bill were so painfully slow on any uphill stretch that the rest of us couldn't hike that slowly. Typically, trekkers can hike at their own pace, because the crew of porters, cook, kitchen boys, sirdar, and assistant sirdars are strung out along the trail. At a trail junction you wait for a crew member to point you down the correct trail. The sirdar usually assigns one member of the staff to be the "sweeper" and follow the last group member to make sure no one gets lost. If a client gets out ahead of the lead crew member and is uncertain of which direction to take at a trail junction, the client is supposed to wait for a staff member.

Patience is not one of my primary virtues and I've hastily made the wrong choice at trail junctions several times on Himalayan treks. Some of the first phrases in Nepali I learned were about asking directions. Whenever I became insecure, I could ask a local person for directions -- if there was anyone around.

On my first trek in the Khumbu in 1995, three of us in the group came to a fork by a little waterfall somewhere on the Base Camp Trail. Rather than wait for a crew member, we forged ahead on the trail we thought we were supposed to follow. A mile or so beyond the waterfall, we heard a voice calling desperately behind us. Our sirdar, Nyima, was running toward us.

When he arrived at the waterfall, Nyima noticed that our boot tracks went past the waterfall and missed the turn we were supposed to take. It was amazing that Nyima was so diligent in his duties he'd learned the boot tracks of his clients, and then to be so vigilant in looking after us that he noticed we'd missed a turn. There were many other boot tracks on the trail that day, but he found and followed ours.

When Nyima caught up, he gave us a choice of backtracking or scrambling over the top of the little mountain the trail was skirting. We chose the scramble climb. That was my first experience of climbing in the Himalayas. It was exhilarating! Getting lost that first time turned into a great experience. It was not the last time I got lost in the Himalayas.

Karen and Bill's slow rate of progress on the trail to Deorali was beginning to worry Sanga, Dax, and me. It was a relief when we came to a long descending stretch of trail leading down into a canyon. A river valley spread out below us. Beyond that was a lovely-looking village called Shivalaya. The village was our planned lunch stop. Sanga expected we'd be there by noon. It was almost 2:00 p.m. The group was already two hours behind schedule.

Approaching Shivalaya Village, 2008

Dax and I pelted down the trail and waited for the others to catch up at a suspension bridge which crossed the river to the village. Sanga led us over the bridge, which spanned a narrow stretch of the river Khimti Khola. (*Khola* is one of several Nepali words for river.) He led us to a teahouse in the village, where we ravenously wolfed down momos (dumplings), dal bhat (rice and lentils), and Orange Fanta. (I have been unable to track down the historical reasons why, but Fanta was the first bottled soft drink introduced in Nepal. It was the only soft drink available in many mountain villages until fairly recently. Fanta originated in Germany, but was bought by the Coca Cola Company in the 1960s. I don't know if German climbers introduced it, or for some strange reason the Coke Company chose to market Fanta in Nepal. Whatever, man, a bottle of Orange Fanta cooled by a mountain spring after a long, hot hike always slaked my thirst better than the water I carried in my pack.)

Sanga, Dax, and I huddled around a table to discuss how to adapt the plan for the afternoon to take into account the slow rate of progress the group was making. Dax and I were afraid we wouldn't get to Deorali until after sunset. We were not keen on hiking an unfamiliar trail after dark. It was especially worrisome thinking about how the first-time trekkers would handle a night hike the first day out. Sanga, upbeat as ever, assured Dax and me that the group would be able to handle it. He thought Karen and Bill would pick up the pace after a meal. He was confident they would "begin to get their trail legs." Whether the pace picked up or not, we had to get to Deorali that night. In order to get to Basa Village in time for at least a one-day visit, we had to stick to the schedule.

I was doubtful about the prospect of Karen and Bill increasing their hiking speed. Dax and I told Sanga we wanted to hike ahead with David. Our supposition was that at least the three of us could arrive in Deorali before nightfall, if we hiked hard and fast. Sanga could stay with Carl, Bill, and Karen and make sure they made it safely to Deorali, even if they had to hike after dark. Sanga agreed and gave us instructions on how to find Deorali.

After we finished eating and drinking a couple Fantas each, Sanga and I presented the plan to the group. No one seemed particularly concerned that the group would be splitting up for the rest of the day. Perhaps Karen and Bill felt some relief at not holding Dax and me back. The one surprise was that David decided to hang back with Sanga and the slower hikers. I wondered if his injury was worse than he'd let on. Or, maybe he thought it was wiser to stay with Sanga. I clapped David on the back and told him we'd see him in Deorali.

Dax and I took off humping double-time up the trail. We jogged whenever the trail was easy. I set the pace. Dax started to whine if I pulled ahead. I was selfishly fixated on reaching Deorali before nightfall. I pushed hard and barked at Dax to keep up or I'd leave him behind.

It felt good to be free of feeling an obligation to hike at a rate slower than what felt comfortable. I had conditioned well over the summer through daily workouts of bicycling, rollerblading, kayaking, or running up and down the Broad Ripple Park boat ramp. The last time I had visited Dax in LA, he put me to shame on the treadmill in his gym and then in street running around his neighborhood. But during the summer I had toughened up through fairly fanatical aerobic training.

In my experience outdoor workouts provide a better

conditioning base for trekking and mountaineering than gym workouts. Being outdoors creates a stronger spirit and willingness to handle physical stress more than the controlled conditions of weights and machines in a fitness club. It was ridiculous in retrospect, and violated my own advice -- that trekking is not a race to win -- but I was bent on proving to Dax that outdoor tough is tougher than gym tough.

The blood pumping through my veins, my lungs sucking hard for air, and my heart pumping rapidly felt great. All around was the pristine outdoors of lush hills and valleys in the Middle Himalayas. Pounding up or scampering down the trail, dancing across wood plank and log bridges over streams -- it all felt good! My senses were tuned in to the physical world around me and my own physiology.

I have loved and appreciated being alone or with a friend or two in the outdoors since I was a small child. When I was a little kid my best buddy, Baz, and I lay for long periods of time in his grassy backyard staring at the clouds moving across the sky. We looked closely at the different blades of grass and little creatures that crawled around in that tiny world. When I was a little older, nine or ten, my brother and I had a rowboat. I loved to row up and down the canal we lived on. I'd tie the boat to a tree and explore the woods along the canal by myself or with other kids in the neighborhood. There were always treasures to find in the woods, strange markings left by wood-boring bugs on a beech tree or a striated rock with lines of different colors.

Those experiences contrasted with another outdoor experience of my childhood, which was caddying for my parents while they played golf. Maplecrest Country Club's fairways and greens were well tended by the club's staff. The only natural areas were the few stands of trees left in the roughs. The most enjoyable experience caddying was when my dad would hit a ball into the rough. It provided an excuse to look around among the trees and high grass for more interesting things than a golf ball.

The wondrous beauty, oddity, and potential dangers of the outdoors have always turned me on. My senses perk up and I become more attuned to my surroundings than when I'm in the manicured safety of human devise. That is one of the reasons trekking the Himalayas kept pulling me back to Nepal. It was a spiritual release from the well-groomed environment created by human industry.

When I thought we were getting close to Deorali Village, I pushed even harder and left Dax behind. I arrived around six in the evening, just as dusk was settling on the village.

Sanga told Dax and me to go to the Highland Guest House on the right side of the stream bisecting the village. But when I went in and inquired, I was told by the Didi that there were no empty rooms. After some confusion, I learned that a group of porters had come to the lodge a little while ago and they were now at another lodge on the other side of the stream.

A bahini (little sister or young woman) led me out of the lodge and across a little stone bridge to the Sunshine Lodge. Our whole crew was at the lodge! As Sanga predicted, the guys took a shortcut. They didn't pass Dax and me on the trail. They hiked the day before from Phaplu to Deorali, spent the night in Deorali, and then left early in the morning to get to Jiri, pick up our duffels, and hike back to Deorali. They hiked double the distance Dax and I hiked that day, in less time.

A handsome young man introduced himself as Arjun Rai. He told me that he was our assistant sirdar. I was too tired and hungry for much conversation. I just thanked Arjun and each member of the crew and asked where they put the duffels. The duffels were organized and stacked outside of rooms awaiting the arrival of our group.

Dax arrived about fifteen minutes later and immediately demanded food and drink. We were both very tired after trail running and humping hard for over three hours. But I said, "You know, we have to go back and find the others after we finish eating." Dax told me to stuff it in less than polite language. He was not going to hike back down the trail in the dark. Sanga was with the group, and they didn't need us. Dax said that when he finished eating, he was going to bed. And he did.

After I finished eating and arranging my kit in a room with Dax, I headed back down the trail with a headlamp on. I did not tell Arjun what I was up to, and didn't ask him to accompany me. He and the guys were obviously pooped and some were already asleep by the time Dax and I finished eating.

The last stage of the trail into Deorali was weird. Deorali is built on a pass at about 9,000 feet. A stream ran down the middle of the village and then spread out and tapered off into a long shallow flow over the rocky trail leading up the incline into the village. The water was only a couple of inches deep, but it flowed over the trail into the village. My hiking boots got wet when I hiked into Deorali and again as I hiked back out to find Sanga and the members of our group.

About an hour outside the village I heard Carl's voice before I saw him. It was not totally dark, because there were stars shimmering above. Carl was out front of the others speaking in a loud encouraging tone. Bill and Karen looked fearful and fatigued. David looked wide-eyed and sort of shell-shocked. Carl looked no different than when we parted in Shivalaya. Sanga was bringing up the rear. He looked worried. Bill did not have a headlamp, so Sanga was shining his headlamp's light on the trail for Bill to follow. I had an extra headlamp, so I strapped it around Bill's head. He threw his arm around my shoulder and hugged me with gratitude and exhaustion.

I lied and told them the lodge was only about half an hour up the trail. The looks of relief were worth any extra time I'll spend in purgatory for the lie. I told them Dax and the crew were in a lodge and warm food and beds awaited.

I hung back and walked with Sanga. He whispered that the group was much slower than he thought they would be. He was especially worried about Bill. He did not think Bill could handle the pace we would have to keep up to reach Basa in time. He also thought Karen might not be able to handle it. I was even less optimistic. Based on the first day, I didn't think any of them could handle it, except Dax. We walked into the Sunshine Lodge about nine in the evening, three hours later than Sanga had expected.

Hypothermia, dehydration, blisters, pulled groin muscle, and muddy pants
Bill had one of the worst nights of his life in the Sunshine Lodge in Deorali. He was hypothermic and dehydrated. Sanga, David, and I nursed him through the night with bottles of warm water to drink. Sanga wrapped Bill in a sleeping bag and yak-hair blanket with a hot water bottle to restore his body temperature. In the morning Sanga assigned Soma Rai, a porter who spoke some English, to stay

with Bill and serve as his porter-guide. They were to take it easy and slowly trek to Phaplu. We could meet up again after the rest of the group visited Basa.

Three days later we arrived in Phaplu, another day behind schedule. David, it turned out, had pulled a groin muscle when he fell the first day. He hiked in increasing, and finally, excruciating pain by the time we arrived at the Numbar Lodge in Phaplu. Sanga made arrangements for David to stay at the lodge and await Bill and Soma's arrival.

We hiked after dark each of those three days, because of the slow pace. David was hobbled by his injury. Karen's feet were taped like little mummies in duct tape, because they were both covered in blisters. But the landscape of the Middle Himalayas we hiked through was beautiful and the night sky was iridescent above our tents. Despite our woes, the spirit of the group had been rising. David maintained his self-deprecating humor as he stumped along leaning on trekking poles like they were crutches. Karen was surprisingly sanguine about her foot problems, and said the duct tape "masked" the pain. She was actually getting stronger, so that Sanga's prediction that the group would be able to hike faster as the days went on was coming true in her case.

It started raining just before we arrived at our campsite the night before Phaplu and rained off and on through the night. But it was clear in the morning as we hiked into Phaplu and still clear after leaving David behind ensconced at the Numbar Lodge. The trail out of town was dirt, but it was packed so hard from foot traffic that it had developed a U shape. It became very steep and footing was difficult, because the previous night's rain made the trail extremely slick.

Dax started muttering and complaining, "I am not enjoying this one bit!" The trail rose more steeply and got more slippery. Dax fell down, skidded on his knees, and came up with mud on his pants proclaiming, "This is not working for me!" Then he announced he was not going any farther. He demanded that Sanga get his duffel and that he was going back to Phaplu and would stay at the lodge with David.

I tried to convince Dax not to quit the trek, but he was adamant. I was shocked. In Ladakh Dax was furious when John Roskelley ordered him to quit. Now, he was quitting just because he fell and got mud on his pants. It didn't make sense, but Dax waved away my imprecations. He demanded that Sanga order a porter to carry his duffel back to Phaplu. Sanga smiled and said he would carry the duffel and get Dax checked into the lodge. Luckily, our porters were just behind us. Sanga stopped the porter carrying Dax's duffel and pulled it out of the doko. Sanga slung the duffel over his back and strapped his own large backpack in front so it rode on his chest. After brief farewells, Sanga started down the trail with Dax following behind. I was very disappointed to lose Dax as a hiking partner and tent mate, but so it goes. Carl and Karen didn't seem too upset by Dax's departure.

Down to Three

Ten Americans signed up for the trek to Basa. We were down to three. Karen, Carl, and I followed Arjun. The trail became more difficult, like a slippery roller-coaster. But, after another hour of hiking it leveled off and became much easier. We passed a farmer carrying a bundle of hay in the typical Himalayan way. All we could see of him were two muscular legs chugging along under a mass of hay.

Around a bend, we discovered a little one-room temple just off the trail. The door was closed and padlocked. Carl and Karen were curious to see what was inside, so Arjun put down his pack and ran up a side trail leading to a couple of houses. He came back with a female caretaker who unlocked the door. A huge prayer wheel was the only thing inside. With the caretaker's permission, we turned the wheel. For some reason turning that gigantic prayer wheel released the stress that had built up from 12-hour hiking days and the loss of our companions. Karen and Carl turned the wheel faster and faster and began whooping with joy.

We thanked the caretaker and pressed a few hundred Rupees into her hand. Our packs seemed lighter and we walked with a new-found spring in our step. Arjun had Karen's pack in front and his own on his back, so he looked like a pregnant young man with a hump back. I patted his protuberant "belly" and asked if it was a boy or a girl. Arjun laughed like it was the funniest damn thing he'd ever heard. His clients were happy, so he was happy.

We hiked and bantered in good humor until we saw one of our guys, Rudra Rai, waving and calling to us. He pointed to a grassy field just off the trail. Our cook, Purna Rai, was cooking lunch in the open field. The crew spread out a tarp for us to sit on. Carl, Karen, and I plopped down and gratefully accepted cups of chilled Tang, bowls of peaches, and chapatti (thin, crisp, unleavened bread). We leaned against our backpacks, munched on the appetizers and gazed back over the country we had hiked through. White-peaked Mt. Numbar dominated the view towering over the now distant village of Phaplu.

While we were tucking into the main course of cooked sardines, veggies, and ham sandwiches, Sanga came huffing up, dropped his pack, stretched his arms, and looked at us quizzically. He could tell something had changed. We looked tranquil and joyful.

Getting off the treacherously slippery trail and spinning the big prayer wheel liberated us from any stress and anxiety we felt about the difficulties we'd faced on the trek to Basa. We were infused with the richness of living in the moment and the joy of being present in this picturesque place.

Trekking Home

Our crew consisted of 20 guys: sirdar Sanga, cook Purna, assistant sirdar Arjun, four kitchen boys, Pancha, Nirman, Kumar, and Rudra, and thirteen porters; a ridiculously large staff for three clients. Niru originally expected 10 clients, so he hired 21 guys (Soma Rai with Bill made 21) for the sweet job of working a trek in their own "neighborhood". Niru didn't welch on his offer of employment after he learned the group had shrunk to six. He knew what the extra income from working a trek meant to the families of these men. Subsistence farmers from villages in the Himalayas covet jobs on expeditions. The average income in Nepal in 2008 was about $2 per day. Working as an expedition porter paid from $8 to $12 per day, plus a tip.

Manke Rai carried the toilet and kitchen table; one might question the sanitary wisdom of this arrangement. 2008 Basa Trek.

We made quite the regal sight on the trail. Three sahibs escorted by a staff of 20. It was easy work for our porters, because their loads were relatively light. Divvied up among the 20 guys were our three duffels, the kitchen equipment, food supplies, four sleeping tents, one for each of the clients and one for Sanga and Arjun, a meal tent, a cook tent, a toilet tent, and a toilet seat with folding legs.

The trail leading to Basa continued to gain altitude. Carl's altimeter read 11,000 feet when we reached the crest of the Phurlung Pass atop the Ratnagi Danda, a long mountain ridge overlooking a huge plunging river valley. Somewhere below us on the other side of the river valley and around a few more hills was Basa. We couldn't see it yet, but the eager smiles on the faces of our crew members told us that home was not far away.

But the sun was going down. Sanga decided we should camp on the ridge, because it was too late in the day to hike on to Basa. He seemed untroubled that we were so far behind schedule that we would only be able to spend one night in Basa. "We can walk slowly and have a good lunch in the village tomorrow," Sanga assured us with a broad smile.

The view from our campsite was breathtakingly beautiful and intimidating. We looked out over a great valley we'd be crossing in the morning and then have to cross back the following day. We had to be back in Phaplu in two days for the flight Niru booked to get us back to Kathmandu in time for the flights home. It was daunting to realize that after tomorrow night we'd have to hike all the way back to Phaplu in one day.

The guys in the crew weren't the least bit daunted. They were ready to party. Purna made a fabulous multi-course feast of Sherpa stew with beef, rice, potatoes, veggies, chicken strips, fresh salad, canned fruit, and tapioca and rice puddings. Carl, Karen, Sanga, Arjun, and I lingered in the meal tent after dinner. The rest of the staff hung out in an out-building where the kitchen was set up. Happy sounds wafted across the yard of the guys laughing and singing while they drank their moonshine (rakshi) and chang (beer).

Arjun and Karen had become close friends from walking together every day since Deorali. He carried her pack each day. Carl was the staff's favorite. His endearing, mellow disposition was such a contrast to his gigantic size (especially in comparison to Nepalese men). His size-17-hiking-boots, six-and-a-half-feet-height, and grey beard earned him the nickname "Yeti" from the guys. Kumar Rai would point at Carl, pretend to look wide-eyed with fear, and whisper, "Yeti!" Carl would let out a roar and then the whole crew would laugh hysterically. This comedy routine was replayed several times each day, but no one tired of it.

I would not have guessed that, if the group was winnowed down to three, Karen and Carl would have been among the survivors. Carl was 59, the oldest member of the group. He admitted that he had not properly trained for the trek. Divorce proceedings and custody litigation had consumed his time and energy for several months prior to leaving Indiana for Nepal. Relaxing in the meal tent on the Ratnagi Danda, Carl said that, instead of being worn out by the trek, he felt reenergized. The psychic weight of the custody fight seemed to grow lighter each day during the long hikes.

Karen related that she'd opened her own psychotherapy practice just a month before the flight to Kathmandu. She'd spent the better part of a year wrangling with a former partner over the dissolution of the partnership. Resolving the partnership issues and then setting up her solo practice and office was so time consuming and draining Karen had not trained nor broken in her hiking boots.

Sanga and Arjun listened closely to Carl's and Karen's descriptions of the challenges they faced back home in their professional and personal lives. To what extent any of it made sense to them, I'm not sure. But they followed the conversations with rapt expressions. Sanga was always asking questions about life in America, so I'm sure he was cataloguing this new information about "our world".

When we opened the flap to exit the meal tent we looked up into an inky night sky filled with stars so bright they looked touchable. The three "white people" ducked into their individual tents. Sanga and Arjun hustled over to the out-building to join the party with the other guys from Basa.

Breaking camp to prepare for the final leg of the trek to Basa; Arjun is in the middle of the photo bending over the blue meal tent. His father, our cook, Purna, is behind Arjun, and Sanga is in the far right of the photo.

Basa Village Band, flowers, speeches, rakshi and more rakshi

There were countless switchbacks down the steep ridge to the river. I was so anxious to get to Basa Village I hiked out ahead of everybody. After crossing the Kaku Khola on a long steel-cabled foot bridge I walked through the market village of Sombare. Hiking hard for another hour I encountered a group of eight men standing by the trail. They were wearing topis (the colorful "national hat" Nepalese men wear for any occasion) and holding little drums, wooden flutes, and a brass horn. They signaled me to stop.

I asked in English whether this was the trail to Basa. No response other than befuddled expressions. I tried Nepali. "Yo Basa jaane baato ho?" (Is this the trail to Basa?). I couldn't tell whether these musicians understood my Nepali. Heads moved in various directions in response to my question. Nepalis tend to move their heads in a circular motion to indicate the affirmative and to look away to indicate the negative. The men's head waggling seemed to affirm I was on the correct trail to Basa -- then it dawned on me that

274

these men were the greeting party from the village. They were the Basa Village Band!

The men gestured with their hands indicating I should wait with them for the rest of the team. While we squatted beside the trail, I took several granola bars out of my pack and offered to share. The men chuckled but did not hold out their hands to take the snack. They seemed amused and pleased, but only the youngest fellow let me put one of the granola bars in his hand. He pocketed it. The guys smiled at me, but made no further effort to communicate. So I scrounged the book I was reading out of my backpack and read and snacked and waited.

About twenty minutes later, Sanga, Carl, Arjun, and Karen came hustling down the trail. As soon as the musicians saw Sanga, they jumped up excitedly. They briefly conferred with Sanga and Arjun in the local Rai language. Then, the men lifted their instruments with great dignity and began thumping on the drums, tooting on the flutes, and blasting on the horn. Sanga gestured for us to follow in single file.

Welcome to Basa Village; October 2008

The narrow trail descended about 500 feet with one long switchback and then the village appeared below us. It was astonishing to see a couple hundred people gathered to greet our party.

At the entrance to the village was a hand-painted "Welcome" sign atop wood poles ringed with flowers. As we walked under the arch, the band members, Sanga, and Arjun peeled off. A long line of women and children met us. Every person in line had a necklace made of marigold flowers. As Karen, Carl, and I walked down the line, the women and children placed these leis over our heads. When members of the greeting party bestowed a lei they would smile shyly or excitedly and then give the traditional Nepali "namaste" greeting with bowed head and palms placed together.

The leis piled up so high around our necks and over our faces that we had to take some off so we could see. It was a greeting like none I'd ever experienced. Poor Carl, he has allergies. His face turned red, his eyes were watering, and he sneezed repeatedly. Carl did his best to hide the discomfort he felt so as not to dampen the enthusiasm of the villagers' welcome.

At the end of the line of women and children, we were guided to a line of men. As we passed along that line, each man gave the namaste greeting or shook our hands. A few of the men took my hand and touched their forehead with my fore knuckle and then kissed my hand. Several placed white katas (silk scarves) over the flower garlands around our necks.

Sanga stood in the middle of an open area beside the school house. He indicated we should sit in chairs set up behind a table. The villagers settled onto benches set up around the grounds or squatted on their haunches in the dirt. After we were seated, Sanga made a brief statement in the local language to the gathered crowd and then sat down in the chair to my right.

Right to left: Carl, Karen, and the author after arriving in Basa Village; October 2008

A group of men, apparently the village elders, sat on a bench across from us. One of them stood up and began making a speech. Sanga whispered that he was the chairman of the School Board. Sanga didn't bother to translate the chairman's speech, but just explained he was speaking the local Rai language and was welcoming us and talking about the school.

While the chairman was talking, village women lined up to pour cups of their homemade rakshi for Karen, Carl, and me. It seemed that every woman in the village brought a pitcher of her best moonshine to the ceremony and expected each of us to drink a cup. The rakshi was wonderfully tasty in different flavors of corn, rice, millet, and plum. It was also quite potent.

After downing a couple of cups, I just took sips from the rest of the pitchers offered but exuberantly thanked each of the women for the rakshi. I whispered to Karen and Carl to follow my lead and just take sips or we'd get so drunk we'd fall out of our chairs. Karen immediately adopted my strategy. Carl had trouble turning down any gift and was three sheets to the wind by the time the chairman's speech was over. (Carl told me the next morning his memory of the

277

whole welcoming ceremony was "rather blurry".)

Next, the chairman of the Village Development Committee (a branch of local government) gave a speech. The rakshi kept coming. Sanga didn't bother to translate this speech. He just explained that Basa was one of six villages in the area served by an elected committee for development of the villages. He said the chairman was thanking us on behalf of the Committee.

After the second speech ended, Sanga told me he was going to introduce me and I would need to give a speech to the village. He would translate. In his long introduction, I gathered that Sanga was telling the villagers about the fundraising campaign for the school.

Sanga had not forewarned me I was to give a speech, but fortified by multiple cups of rakshi I had no fear. I figured one way I could score points with the villagers was to keep it short and sweet. So I thanked them for their wonderful welcome and told them that our friends from the United States who could not come with us sent their greetings. I said it was an honor and a privilege to be able to help finish the school. I related how I had become friends with Niru, Ganesh, Sanga, and many other men from the village who had served our trekking groups so well. I ended by thanking the families of Basa for producing such fine people.

When the ceremony ended many children and villagers came up to thank Karen, Carl, and me by kissing our hands or bowing to us. The three of us agreed that this was probably the closest we would ever come to being treated like celebrities.

Shocking condition of the Basa School

Next item on our agenda was supposed to be a meeting with the current teachers and inspection of the school. Sanga informed me that the teachers were too ashamed of the quality of their English to meet with us. That was disappointing, because I wanted to show the teachers sample workbooks I brought to see if the materials were appropriate for the school. A friend with the Indiana Department of Education arranged to donate educational materials sufficient to supply all of the Basa students with workbooks and supplies for math, social studies, science, and English. Sanga said he'd check out the materials and then explain to the teachers what could be shipped to the school. He assured me the teachers would be thrilled with whatever we could provide. After I saw the classrooms, I understood.

The only teaching materials were chalkboards with no erasers and handmade posters. There were no books or writing materials. There were a few rough benches for students to sit on, but no desks or chairs. It pulled at my heartstrings that the beautiful and eager children that welcomed us to the village with flowers had so little compared to the poorest schools in the US.

There was a three-inch wide crack in the floor. The walls were bare plaster. The wood frames of the windows were rotting. When Niru and I discussed how the donated funds would be spent, he said the first expenditure would be to patch the floor, paint and seal the walls and window frames, and build more benches so all the students could sit on benches. Next, the area behind the school would be cleared to create a playground with a rock wall for security. There is a 500-foot-drop-off at one end of the field where the playground was to be created, hence the need for a wall. The remaining funds would be used to pay the two teachers needed for fourth and fifth grade classes.

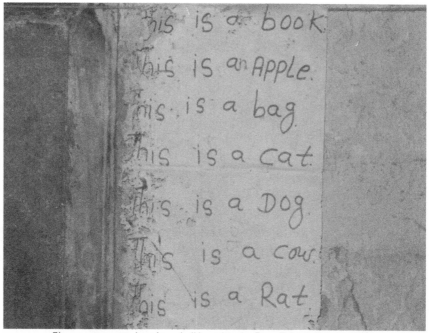

Classroom poster beside a chalkboard in the Basa School, October 2008

I discovered another issue. The charpe (outhouse) outside the school building was so disgusting it was padlocked and couldn't be used. From a previous project for another village, I knew that for a few hundred dollars a compost toilet could be purchased. The entire village could use it or reserve it for the schoolchildren. I added a compost toilet to a list developing in my mind.

Basa Hospitality and Local Customs
We spent the rest of the day walking around the village and visiting homes of the families of our crew members. We were followed everywhere by a gaggle of children who wanted to hold our hands and lead us to the next home. At each house, the matriarch of the family insisted we try her rakshi. Thankfully, we were also offered food at each house, such as fried potatoes, yoghurt with fruit, and plates of dal bhat.

The conversations with villagers were in the local Rai dialect with Sanga translating. Carl was almost sleepwalking from his intake of rakshi, but smiling happily and agreeing with everything anyone said. Karen and I were both feeling pretty tipsy, so my memory of what we talked about is a little fuzzy. But I was conscious of the warm glow of friendly hospitality from all the families we visited. We were asked polite questions about life in our "villages", such as, "Do people fly helicopters or airplanes to go shopping?"

I asked a few questions about the political situation in Nepal. The one that sparked the most interest was how the new national constitution would affect the village. I learned that the new constitution would require the election of a mayor of the village for the first time. The mayor would take over some of the duties of the Village Development Committee. I asked if Niru would run for mayor. Sanga laughed at the question and replied, "No, because Niru-ji ("ji" is added to a name to show great respect) does not want to live in village all the time."

Sanga explained that one of Niru's sisters lives in the family home in Basa. "Niru stays there when he visits the village, but his children are being raised in Kathmandu, so that is his home now." Sanga went on, "Niru and all of us who move to Kathmandu, we love the village side most. But there is no business here and children, they get better education in Kathmandu." Sanga confided that he hoped to move his family to Kathmandu when his son was old enough to begin school.

Families in every home we walked by asked us to come in and visit with them. Out of concern for our lagging condition, Sanga restricted our visits to six homes of crew members. But, at each house we passed the matriarch of the family importuned us to accept another cup of rakshi or a slice of bread or other food. We accepted most of the food offered, so we were stuffed as well as drunk. Our visit created a holiday atmosphere throughout the village. Most of the adults were getting tight on their own rakshi. People all across the village called out friendly greetings to us and each other as we strolled and weaved around from house to house.

In a Rai home the eldest woman in the family is in charge of all domestic matters within the household. Women marry into the husband's family, so in most homes the father's mother is the ruling matriarch. In each home we visited, grandmother welcomed us and offered food. The other family members helped serve the refreshments. After we settled on a straw mat on the floor, grandma would get a conversation started with Sanga translating. If there was a lull in conversation, grandma would instruct younger members of the family to make sure our cups stayed full and our plates were heaped with food.

Most of the houses in the village were made of shiny chiseled-stones light grey in color. The roofs were bright blue and made of tin or aluminum. A few of the houses had off-white plaster walls with wood shingled roofs or straw roofs. Sanga explained that the difference in style of houses reflects a difference in caste. (There is more information about the caste system in Basa later in this chapter.) The entryway doors were less than six feet high and Carl usually whacked his head on the lintel as he entered. The windows were open, but could be closed off with swinging hinged wooden casements in bad weather. Most of the houses had one central room. Each had a round fire pit dug into the dirt floor with three stones arranged around the fire pit. The fire pit was used for cooking and heating. Each house had a few straw mats for sitting on while dining and to sleep on. The floors were hard-packed dirt.

The families we visited each had a few sheep or cattle and terraced plots of wheat, hay, millet, barley, corn, or rice. Tall grass covered the uncultivated land between the houses. Footpaths through the grass connected one homestead to another. There were no commercial buildings and no marketplace. The villagers' sustenance came from the land they cultivated and the animals they raised. Each home we visited had a still for making rakshi.

The more prosperous homes displayed brass platters hung on the wall or placed on wood shelves. Sanga explained that, in addition to crops and animals, a family's wealth and status is revealed by the jewelry the women wear and the brass cookware in the home. All of the village women we met wore ornaments in their noses. Some of the women had just a simple nose ring or stud. Older women wore elaborate gold jewelry that looked like a small mobile hanging from their nose, called a "bullaki". The more prosperous women also wore gold and silver bracelets. All of the women wore long necklaces. Some of the necklaces were beaded and others made from gold coins. Another expression of prosperity and gratitude for good crops, called a "thangra", is a series of corn husks tied to a bamboo pole placed in front of the house. The thangra reveals a yearly history of the family's crop yield.

The men of the village wore much less interesting clothes than the women. They wore no visible jewelry or adornments. Other than the topi hat, there was no discernible customary style of dress. Men wore a mixture of handmade clothing and manufactured jackets and t-shirts. Presumably, the jackets and t-shirts were given to the men by members of expeditions or were purchased at the Sombare market.

Each home we visited was a working farmstead. But every home had a flower garden. How charming! These folks are subsistence dirt farmers, yet there is such an appreciation of beauty that every family cultivates a flower garden.

Outside a home in Basa Village, October 2008

School Dance

The villagers reassembled on the school grounds at dusk. Kids sat in a group against a stone wall. Sanga's wife, Nanda, was the senior teacher and principal of the school. She set up a battery-powered boom box on a table outside the school building. Nanda gave a brief description of the program, which Sanga translated for Carl, Karen, and me. A group of students began to dance, accompanied by instrumental folk music of drums and woodwinds on a cassette recording played on the boom box.

The girls wore brightly colored wrap skirts and multicolored checked blouses. The boys wore smart-looking pajama-style outfits with embroidered vests and brightly patterned topi hats. Most of the dances were coed, though a few were performed only by the boys and a few only by the girls. Two of the routines had driving drum beats from the boom box. The audience of villagers and three guests clapped along to the beat during those dances. Sanga explained that each of the dances told stories through the movements of the dancers. He said all the villagers knew the stories.

283

The youngest students furrowed their little brows and had very serious expressions as they carefully followed the dance steps and arm movements of the older students. The older kids moved very gracefully and danced with gusto and broad smiles. They strutted and swooned, their lithe limbs moving in perfect timing with the rhythm of the music. After the last set Karen, Carl, and I jumped to our feet and clapped and shouted, "Bravo! Bravo!" The kids bowed in the traditional way, then scampered over to be hugged by their beaming parents.

The caste system in "paradise"

Several kids hung around Karen, Carl, and me after the program ended. They held our hands and clung to our arms and legs. Chiding parents finally convinced the children to release us. Sanga asked if we were ready to go to bed and whether we needed anything. We told him to go home and enjoy the company of his wife and little son. Sanga's face was radiant with pride and joy over the success of the dance program.

Carl, Karen, and I were physically exhausted, but we weren't quite ready to crawl into our tents to sleep. We stood in silence outside the three tents set up in a line behind the school building. We listened to the village quieting for the night and gazed up at the huge sky lustrous with the sparkling swirl of the Milky Way. There was no electricity in Basa in 2008, so there was no light pollution to mar the perfection of the starry, starry night.

After we turned in I lay in my sleeping bag pondering whether I'd ever experienced a community as Edenic as Basa Village. It had to be a hard place to live, farming the little plots of land on steep terraces. Yet, the villagers were so sweet and had such a delightful sense of beauty. From the moment the eight men in the village band announced our entrance on their instruments we experienced a beautiful hospitality. We passed under a "Welcome" arch wreathed with laurels. A line of villagers covered us in flowers. From the trail above it, the physical appearance of the village was post-card pretty. Stone houses with bright blue tin-roofs were scattered across green terraced fields on the side of a great river valley. I wondered if the "religion" of the Rai people contributed to their appreciation of beauty. As animists, they supposedly sense spirit in everything around them. Does feeling the spirits of the natural world create a more fine-tuned sensitivity to the simple beauty of flowers, a star-filled sky, and other people?

But one aspect of the local culture that offended my own sensibility was the caste system. Ganesh and Niru had forewarned me before we planned the trek that the caste system is practiced in Basa. The way they described how it is practiced sounded relatively benign compared to orthodox Hinduism. Niru and Ganesh explained that low caste people are not allowed to enter the homes of higher caste people. The vast majority of people in the Basa area are Rai, but there are also Chettri, Damai, and Kami. Niru emailed me the caste demographics of Basa 6 (the official name of the village). The total population in 2008 was 357; 282 were Rai, 56 were Damai, 13 were Kami, and 6 were Chettri.

In Basa, Rai and Chettri are the high castes. In contemporary Nepal Rai people hold many different jobs, but most of them are still farmers. Chettri is the traditional Hindu warrior-caste. In traditional Hinduism, of the major castes only Brahmin is higher than Chettri. In Kathmandu Chettris tend to have white-collar jobs. Niru told me that a Chettri teacher was sent to Basa several decades ago by the government to teach local people to speak Nepali. The teacher's family eventually joined him and the family became part of the Basa community.

Damai are tailors and Kami are blacksmiths. In Basa they are the lower castes. Niru said that in addition to sewing clothes the Damai in Basa play traditional musical instruments at marriages and other ceremonies. The guys in the village band are Damai. Over time, Damai and Kami came to the area to offer their skills as tradesmen to the Rai farmers. Some stayed and acquired their own land, and some eventually married into Rai families. Niru said that there are several "mixed" families within the community.

While we were walking together on the 2006 and 2007 treks, Ganesh described comic incidents of his low caste friends having to jump out of a window or run out the back door when Ganesh's parents came home. Ganesh said he didn't personally agree with it, but the traditional rule was that when lower caste friends visited a higher caste friend's home, the lower caste friends were served food outside the house. His justification for honoring the rule was that it would upset his parents to ignore their traditions.

Niru and Ganesh claimed that the higher caste villagers in Basa do not treat lower caste people badly. Their claim was borne out from what I saw on our treks. Kami, Damai, and Rai worked together as porters without noticeable distinction. Although, I did note that all the guides for AGT that I met were Rai. Niru and Ganesh both told me that the younger members of the community do not believe the caste system is fair and would prefer not to follow it. They predicted it would die out within another generation or two.

I looked for it while we were guests in Basa, but did not observe people of different castes treating each other any differently. I didn't witness any detectable discrimination in the way people behaved toward each other. Sanga assured me that all the kids in the village attend the school and are treated the same by the teachers, regardless of caste. Still, I drifted off to sleep brooding on why these people who seemed so kind and gentle accepted an inherently unfair and oppressive system based on the randomness of birth and devised by people of a different religious tradition.

Leaving "Paradise"

Crowing roosters awakened me. Before I was out of my sleeping bag, little friends with gimlet eyes and devilish grins were outside my tent. They peered through the tent fly and chattered and giggled while I organized my kit and duffel for the day's hike. I zippered

286

the tent flap to dress in private. As soon as I emerged, several kids grabbed my hands to walk with me across the grounds to the school building where Purna was preparing breakfast.

The village children were fascinated by everything about their three American visitors. They were curious to see us eat. Nepalese villagers use the fingers of their right hands for eating. They don't use utensils. (They use the left hand for wiping themselves after a bowel movement, so it's usually wise to avoid greeting a local person by shaking the left hand.) The children were fascinated by our use of knives, forks, and spoons.

By the time we finished eating and packing our duffels, the village elders were seated once again at the table outside the school. The entire village assembled for a "departure ceremony".

Three members of the Village Development Committee gave speeches. Sanga was bustling around supervising the packing of duffels, tents, and kitchen gear. Arjun's English was not as good as Sanga's, but he tried to translate the speeches. The essence of all three speeches was that we were being thanked again for helping with the school and visiting the village.

I was more concerned about the hike back to Phaplu than trying to understand what the speakers were saying. It took over twelve hours to hike from Phaplu to Basa. Presumably, it would take that long to hike back. We needed to get out of town and get started up the trail! A little buzzing anxiety was beginning to erode the tranquil state I'd enjoyed since our welcome to Basa.

After each speech, the elders stood, smiled at us, and bowed in unison in our direction. The three of us returned the bow in unison. Despite the need to get going, it was difficult to leave. Children tugged at our elbows and shirtsleeves and wanted us to play and take pictures of them. Our departure was further delayed, because Nanda organized the women and children into a line with leis and katas to hang around our necks. At the end of the line, the three schoolteachers stopped Karen, Carl, and me. They pinned brooches of little figures made of colored straw on our shirts. Nanda said in perfect English, "Thank you very much for helping our children and coming to our village." Then she kissed each of us on the cheek.

The village band began thumping and tooting. But before we could start to hike up the steep trail out of the village, old women kissed our cheeks and old men and children wept openly as we slung our packs. Several of the men touched my hand to their foreheads and then kissed my hand and cheeks. They had tears in their eyes. Three leathered old matriarchs, led by Sanga's mother, Durga, stopped us a last time and kissed our cheeks and tried to push a last cup of rakshi into our hands.

Many of the villagers fell into line to hike up the steep trail out of the village with us. The band led the way with their drums thumping out a marching beat and the flutes blowing a triumphal tune. Children held our hands and clung to our arms and sides. I had never experienced anything so touching in all my travel experiences.

Threat to the community?
The hike back to Phaplu was even more wild and crazy than the hike to Basa. We ran out of water. Karen became dehydrated and hypothermic, and she began to hallucinate. The trail was still slippery where Dax fell. Carl slipped, slid down the trail, and came up covered in mud from head to toe. I, stupidly, once again hiked out ahead of the

group, got onto the wrong trail, and had to bushwhack my way back to the main trail frightening a farm family and their animals as I clomped across their property. But we made it back to Phaplu, amazingly, just after darkness fell.

I woke up once during the night and struggled out of my sleeping bag and tent to pee. A couple of water buffalos had come into our campsite and were snuffling around the tents. Carl was snoring rhythmically. I stood outside the tent in the darkness. The white peak of Mount Numbar glowed from starlight over Phaplu. This was my last night in the mountains for the year 2008. Being in the Himalayas inspires wonder, humbleness, and a quieting of the soul. I didn't want it to end.

Zipped up back in my bag, I lay quietly, enjoying the night sounds. Carl's snoring blended with the water buffalos snuffling. It had been an incredible day. Yet, the worry I'd had before visiting Basa that the community might be in jeopardy from too much outside contact continued to nag.

In a village like Basa, individualism is less important than identification with the community. Individual expression is allowed and encouraged to some extent. Women express themselves through their jewelry, men wear different clothes, and families display their prosperity through the lushness of their thangra and collection of brass trays. But survival depends on cooperation. If there wasn't a cultural tradition supporting a cooperative system within the community, when nature turns dangerous by storm, drought or flood, its powerful forces could destroy the village. In Basa the villagers are well aware of that danger. I wondered how cognizant they were of the danger to their cultural traditions by exposure to the different values of the modern world.

The harmonious equilibrium of such a tightly knit community creates a magnetic force which holds the community together. Will the force that holds Basa together be weakened or destroyed by outside influences such as exposure to consumer culture? In 2009, when I returned to Basa, this time with a much larger group, the first commercial transaction between a villager and a trekker took place.

Basa Heli-Port, Shaman Dance, and the First Commercial Transaction
Basa - Khumjung Trek 2009

I cannot say exactly how nature exerts its calming and organizing effects on our brains, but I have seen in my patients the restorative and healing powers of nature and gardens, even for those who are deeply disabled neurologically. In many cases, gardens and nature are more powerful than any medication. Oliver Sacks, neurologist and writer (1933 – 2015)

2009 was a painful year. Economies crashed worldwide and in the US retirement savings and jobs were lost in the Great Recession. In mid February I tore the anterior cruciate ligament (ACL) in my left knee playing volleyball and had to have replacement surgery in late April. It was uncertain whether the repaired knee would be able to handle the stress of a Himalayan trek five months later. It should have been a terrible year for recruiting people to spend three weeks and a couple thousand dollars trekking in Nepal.

But 2009 turned out to be a great year for a philanthro-trek back to Basa and beyond. Counting me, 19 Americans signed up to visit Nepal in October. We all met in Kathmandu for local touring, then three members split off on a fly-drive tour with AGT. The other 16 flew into the mountains to trek to Basa and then up into the Khumbu.

The Hillary-inspired idea from the 2003 Golden Jubilee was fully realized in 2009. My wife, whose ability with computer-tech far exceeds mine, created a website to help spread the word about inviting people to visit Nepal. Several articles I wrote about Nepal were published in travel magazines and different versions of the article about the effects of tourism on Sherpa culture were published in two literary journals. I began giving talks about the Himalayan region to Rotary and Kiwanis clubs and taught a course on the subject for IUPUI's Continuing Education Program and Oasis, an organization for "older adults". I joined Facebook and began posting about the wonderful experiences I'd had in the Himalayan region. These efforts helped to fulfill both aspects of the philanthro-trek idea. More Americans were inspired to visit the Himalayan region. The number of people joining a group I organized increased from just two in 2004 to 19 in 2009. The other piece, to engage in an ongoing effort to benefit Himalayan villagers was realized through the creation of a special bond with Basa Village.

The Basa School Project was completed, but that turned out to be a beginning rather than an end. Before the group left the States in 2009 to fly to Kathmandu, Niru reported that the 4th and 5th grade teachers were hired, the renovation of the school building was finished, the playground was leveled, a safety wall built, and additional benches were constructed for students. All of the work was performed by Basa villagers. The two new teachers were women from the village. Instructional manuals for the teachers and workbooks for all the students donated by the Indiana Department of Education were shipped to Kathmandu, delivered by air to Lukla, and then carried by a porter to Basa. There was even money left from the $6,000 raised to purchase and install a compost toilet for the school.

Despite the economic recession and my blown-out left knee, the dream of developing Basa that Niru and Ganesh began discussing with me in 2006 was starting to come true in 2009. The village school was transformed, but so was my relationship with Niru and Basa. One of the propulsive forces of transformation was the enthusiasm of many of the 2007 and 2009 group members to participate in an ongoing relationship with Basa Village. That enthusiasm was the impetus to create the Basa Village Foundation USA Inc., a US-based 501(C)(3) tax-exempt corporation with me as its first president. A sister organization, the Basa Village Foundation NGO, a Nepal-based nonprofit trust with Niru as chairman of the board was also formed.

However, as in 2006, 2007, and 2008 the experience the 2009 group had in Nepal was not unmitigated enjoyment. There was trouble enough to require a helicopter evacuation. And, several of us were plagued for a few days with personal evacuations of the diarrhea-type. Despite those discomforts, a core group of supporters emerged who were committed to do "culturally sensitive development" in the Basa area through a partnership with Niru's team and the Basa community.

The author presenting a check to Niru Rai for the Basa School Project, 2008

The biggest philanthro-trekking group yet

Word spread through my grapevine of friends, my writing, and social media about the extraordinary experience that Carl, Karen, and I had visiting Basa in 2008. Still, it was surprising that so many people wanted to join a trek to Basa in 2009, given the "casualties suffered" along the trail to Basa in 2008. I felt obligated to return in order to see with my own eyes the improvements to the school building and to meet the two new teachers. But I really wanted to experience Basa again regardless of that obligation. The magnetic attraction of Basa was pulling me back. I thought that a visit to the village and then a trek up the Base Camp Trail might attract some adventurous souls. Niru designed a programme for a local tour around the Kathmandu Valley and then a fourteen-day trek through Solu-Khumbu with two days in Basa and then up into the Khumbu along the Base Camp Trail.

Cousin David's wife, Melissa, who is blind, was so moved by David's and my descriptions of our experiences in Nepal in 2008 that she was determined to experience it herself. Niru designed a tour for her to travel throughout Nepal by van and domestic flights to the lakes of Pokhara, the jungle in the Terai (southern Nepal near the Indian border), and around the Kathmandu Valley. An eighty-year old friend, Joan, who I met through UChicago alumni activities, had trekked to Base Camp thirty years earlier. She made a threesome with David and Melissa for the tour.

Dr. John, who signed up for the 2008 trek to Basa but broke his ribs in an auto accident, made the trek to Basa in 2009. John is a big guy. He was a guard on the University of Wisconsin Football Team. "Dr. Yeti" succeeded Carl as the 2009 group's designated yeti. We had two other medical doctors in the group, Bill, another UChicago friend, and Joel the Elder (because a younger Joel was also in the group). Donna was a professor in the nursing school at Indiana University. Karen was a holistic healer, and Susan was a Pilates instructor. The 2009 group was chock full of healthcare professionals.

Two young guys, Chris and Max, are cousins and they graduated from college in the spring of 2009. Chris is still a nationally ranked long-distance runner and Max is a completive swimmer and swim coach. Fitness was not an issue with the two young guns in the 2009 group.

Joel the Younger and Leslie, a Korean-American, were friends of Cousin David's and Melissa's. (Joel eventually succeeded me as president of the Basa Village Foundation USA.) Jude worked with Joan and originally planned to travel with her on the fly-drive tour, but saw my photos of Basa and wanted to experience the village. Gregg is my neighbor and a very fit bike-rider and kayaker. He enjoyed riding around Thamel in a rickshaw while smoking a cigar as much as hiking Himalayan trails. Mike was a volleyball mate, Dr. Bill's UChicago roommate in college, Max's father, and Chris's uncle. Ursula is a philanthropist and experienced trekker, although ours was her first Himalayan trek. Ursula connected an Indiana elementary school with the Basa School to start a pen pal relationship between the two schools.

Bruce, Donna's husband and a Purdue prof, was also volleyball mate of mine. Poor Bruce; he did not have a good time in Nepal. Bruce is a big strong guy, over six-feet tall and an excellent volleyball player. It was not lack of fitness that cut him down, but the bad luck of ingesting a parasite in Kathmandu before the trek even got started.

I could not find any photo of the entire group of 19. So you'll know what we looked like, below is a chronological film-strip of photos of gatherings of group members as the trek progressed.

Pee stains, serendipity, and a heli-evac

The 16 of us who flew into the mountains were the first group of trekkers to fly to the two-year old Kangel airstrip. The pilot took a pass on the first attempt at a landing. He circled back and made an excellent and thrilling landing on the hump of graded dirt, which passed for a landing strip. The government later discontinued use of the airstrip for tourist flights.

The condition of some members of the group during the flight from Kathmandu to Kangel was a precursor of issues that developed on the trek. Bruce appeared to be suffering from a bad case of motion sickness. A few of the other guys, including me, had to pee something terrible on the plane. There are no toilets in a prop-driven Twin Otter. It wasn't that the flight was so frightening it scared the pee out of us so much as we probably drank too much tea before boarding. When I knew I was going to wet my pants, and sticking it out the window was not an option, I whipped out an empty water bottle and, as discretely as possible, filled the water bottle with yellow water. Other guys, whose names won't be mentioned here, either "tied it in a knot" (as my father used to order on family road trips) or left a stain on the Twin Otter's seat. These incidents are mentioned as "precursors", because Bruce's condition deteriorated and several of us developed more serious "bathroom issues" than just needing to pee.

Unlike the year before, when the trek to Basa started without porters, our crew was waiting for us at the Kangel airstrip. They greeted us with smiles and placed garlands of marigolds around

our necks. Ganesh quickly and efficiently organized duffels and gear. All of the stuff that 16 Americans require for 14 days of hiking and camping was packed into doko baskets and then hoisted onto the backs of our porters. Like a herd of turtles, we were on our way to Basa.

Near the end of the first day of hiking we walked into a market village called Neli. Serendipitously, the village was celebrating the festival of Diwali, which is a five-day Hindu festival to mark the victory of light over darkness. Like Christmas in the US, Diwali is not just a religious holiday for Hindus. It's a national period of celebration and partying similar to Dasain. It's customary to light candles and pans of flammable oil in and around residences and places of business during Diwali. There is a lot of singing and dancing in villages and parades in the cities. I'm not sure how it fits with the victory of light over darkness, but Diwali is also a celebration of dogs. In Kathmandu gangs of kids will stand outside of restaurants, hotels, and the homes of wealthy people and sing loudly until they are given food or money. The little rascals can be very persistent in their demands for treats.

The people of Neli invited our group and staff to participate in their festivities. Rakshi, chang, roti, chapatti, naan, and rice were passed around. (Roti and chapatti are flat unleavened breads made from wheat. Naan is leavened bread made with flour.) A circle was formed around a group of local musicians and dancers. Our group joined the circle. The crowd enthusiastically cheered the performers. Then everyone, villagers, trekkers, and porters joined in the dancing and singing. The Americans matched the locals in gusto, if not finesse.

One of our members who did not join in the fun was Bruce. He was so weak; he had a tough time walking from Kangel to Neli. His wife, Donna, and one of the crew members walked beside Bruce all day. At times they physically supported him while he rested leaning on his trekking poles. But he kept putting one foot in front of the other and made it to Neli while the festivities were still going on.

Ganesh ordered camp to be set up just outside of Neli. It was clear that Bruce could go no further. We got him situated into a tent as quickly as possible. Drs. Bill, John, and Joel the Elder, examined Bruce to try to diagnose the cause of his weakened condition. By the time we arrived in Basa the day after the street dance in Neli, Bruce's condition was even worse. He was unable to keep any food or liquid down. He either upchucked or couldn't swallow. He was getting seriously dehydrated. Ganesh sent a runner to the medical clinic in Sombare with orders of our Docs to bring back two IV bottles of saline solution. It was imperative to get liquid and nutrients into Bruce to prevent him from crashing any further.

The runner came back with one bottle of saline and a tube which did not have a needle attached. Dr. Bill rigged up a contraption with safety pins. But he could only get about two-thirds of the saline fluid into Bruce's vein. When Bruce's condition didn't improve by the second day in Basa, Dr. Bill was convinced a helicopter rescue was necessary. Ganesh concurred and called Niru by satellite phone to arrange the heli-evac. (Dr. Bill, a very successful internist with his own clinic in Albuquerque, took to this type of "rough medicine" like a duck to water. A few years later he retired and has done multiple volunteer stints in combat zones through Doctors Without Borders.)

This would be the first ever helicopter landing in Basa Village. Under Ganesh's supervision a bunch of villagers scurried around and labored to collect and lay stones to make a circle about 30 feet in diameter on a flat tract of land. They placed very-visible white stones in the middle of the circle in the shape of an 'H' to direct the heli-pilot to the landing area. The pilot circled over it, but then ignored the new Basa heli-pad and landed on a different terrace. So it goes.

Bruce and Donna boarded the chopper and flew back to Kathmandu. It was a bitter disappointment for both of them. Luckily, their travel insurance covered the cost of the helicopter, medical services in Kathmandu, and changing return tickets to the States. Bruce must have been exposed to an aggressive parasite in Kathmandu, since he felt weak and nauseous in the morning before we boarded the plane for Kangel. Once the bug was killed with the proper meds, Bruce made a full recovery. He was back on the volleyball court by the time I returned from Nepal. Despite their disappointing experience in Nepal, Bruce and Donna became supporters of the Basa Foundations.

Rai Culture in Basa Village

We arrived in Basa the day after camping outside of Neli. As in 2008, the village musicians met us on the trail above the village. The same guys led us down the steep trail into the open area beside the school house thumping, blaring, and tooting all the way. Once again, the reception by the villagers was amazing. Every child, woman, and man in the village lined up to place leis around our necks as we passed under the welcome arch. Senior members of the village gave welcoming speeches. Village matriarchs kept our tin cups full of rakshi and chang.

After the welcoming ceremonies wound down, we were given a tour of the renovated school building. Chris, Ursula, and I delivered school supplies, and Ursula gave Nanda letters from American school children to the children of Basa.

Then, it was time for fun with village kids. Max and Chris created the Basa air force by handing out balsa-wood airplanes and plastic flying-saucers, which took off with a sharp pull on a string. Basa kids had never seen anything like toy airplanes and flying-saucers. They were delighted with their new toys. Children scampered around launching and chasing after their airplanes and flying saucers. A few of the aircraft sailed out beyond the safety wall beside the school and down into the deep river valley. By the end of the day, the Basa air force was diminished by at least a quarter of its aircraft.

In 2008 I noticed that there were no balls of any kind in Basa. The kids played hackey sack with a bundle of leaves tied together with twine. They also used the bundle of leaves to play volleyball, although they didn't have a net. Mike brought a volleyball, soccer ball, and a hand pump as gifts for the school. Mike pumped up the balls, and for the first time in their lives, Basa kids had actual balls to play volleyball and soccer. They didn't have a net or goals, but they had a great time kicking and whacking the balls around their new playground.

We visited many homes around the village during the first two days of our visit. It was interesting to learn about the domestic customs of our hosts. Ganesh arranged for his parents to show us how they made rakshi in their still. We also learned how yeast was preserved for fermentation to brew chang. With Ganesh interpreting, his mother, Dila Maya Rai, showed us the herbs and spices she kept on shelves in the kitchen area of their house. Ganesh's dad, Rudra Prasad Rai, proudly pointed out the family's prized brass cookware. The house was one large room, about fifteen feet long and ten feet wide with a dirt floor. It had a loft reached by a wood ladder in which bedding, clothes, and other household items are kept. Dila Maya prepared rice in a pot and chicken strips in a pan over the fire pit for our entire group.

There were two objects in Ganesh's house, which we also saw in all the other houses we visited. One was a vessel, which is at least a foot tall and about five inches in diameter with a cap. It's made of dark wood. Ganesh called it a "mud pot". The other object is a tangle of rope hanging from the ceiling above the mud pot, which Ganesh called a "chikra" (cheek-ra). He explained that these two objects are sacred symbols to Rai people. "They are used in pujah" (praying). Ganesh said the mud pot and chikra signify the origin of the Rai as "born from the sea". "These things should have to be in Rai house. Otherwise, it could be very bad for the house."

It's always interesting to see how local people live, whenever you travel to a different place that has a culture different from your own. It's especially enjoyable when the hosts are as gracious as they were in Basa to their American guests. But whenever food was being cooked the house filled with smoke. The smoke stung our eyes and irritated throats causing several of us to cough. I can endure it for awhile, but before too long I have to go outside to get away from the smoke. The local residents, no matter their age, never seem to be bothered by the smoke enveloping them while cooking and eating around their fire pits. But they are affected. Cataracts and pulmonary disease are endemic in Himalayan mountain villages.

Dila Maya's food was delicious, but I was glad to leave the house so my eyes quit watering and the itch in my throat was relieved. Outside, Ganesh's father showed us how villagers plow small fields with a metal plow bolted onto wood braces with handles. The plow is pushed through the soil with human leg power. In larger fields a water buffalo can be harnessed to the plow.

Most of the homes we visited had chickens and at least one rooster clucking and pecking just outside the house. Some families had goats and cows tied with loose ropes to stakes. A few had pigs and several had water buffalo in pens beside their houses. Many kept cats as pets and mousers.

Children followed us around the village holding onto our hands. Copious amounts of rakshi, chang, and food were pressed upon us in every home we visited.

In the evening the school children performed a dance program. The headmistress, Nanda, brought out her boom box to provide the music. To share a bit of our culture, our volunteer song leader, Dr. Yeti, led our 15-voice choir in *America the Beautiful* and *Back Home again in Indiana*. Then, Ganesh and I led everyone in several rounds of *Row, Row, Row Your Boat*. It was a delightful evening of entertainment with no technological assistance except Nanda's tape-deck player.

Our cook, Purna Rai, took over one of the classrooms in the school to use as his kitchen. The kitchen boys set up tables beside the school house with place settings for 15. Purna served up a sumptuous feast featuring papadum, which looks like a turnover with a crisp shell. He stuffed it with lentils, chickpeas, and rice. He also made chicken momos for the carnivores. Potatoes, rice, canned peaches, green beans, carrots, peanut butter and jelly sandwiches, and tapioca pudding were the side dishes. For dessert Purna prepared kheer, which is made by boiling milk with sugar and adding rice, tapioca, and cardamom. We were amazed by Purna's ability to create such a feast from an outdoor kitchen. (It was technically not outdoors while we were in Basa, because Purna was using a classroom in the school for his kitchen. He prepared the multi-course meal using a kerosene-fueled camp stove for cooking and boiling.)

Children curious to see what and how we ate were run off by the kitchen boys while we dined. The kids were allowed to return when we finished eating. The Basa air force resumed flight training under Chris and Max's supervision. Mike and Leslie played net-less volleyball with the kids. Joel the Younger taught the kids some soccer moves with the ball, and they showed him how to play hackey-sack with a bundle of leaves. Less energetic trekkers sat along the wall sipping Tang from tin cups and watching the stars begin to populate the night sky. Gregg toked on a cigar. The crew set up our yellow North Face tents in a line on the terrace behind the school building. Group members began to toddle off to the comfort of their sleeping bags. Scolding parents finally hastened away the last of the lingering children.

A blue toilet tent stood at the far end of the terrace beyond the tent furthest from the schoolhouse. A toilet tent is about four feet wide, four feet deep, and six feet high. Inside is a metal frame with a toilet seat atop the frame and a hole dug in the ground below the seat. The hole (and its contents) is filled with dirt when the camp is torn down. A roll of toilet paper is, hopefully, hanging by a string next to the toilet seat. (Group members are encouraged to keep a roll of toilet paper in their backpacks.) There was about two feet of clearance between the stakes for the tent flies and the ledge of the terrace. Under a starlit sky with a headlamp it was only a minor challenge to make one's way down the line of tents to the toilet tent during the night. Still, there were a few incidents of members tripping over tent stakes while hurrying from tent to toilet during the night. But thankfully, no one pitched over the terrace ledge while hurrying to the little blue "restroom".

Mike demonstrating his juggling skills for village kids

Ganesh's father beside the family's trove of brass cookware

Religion and Commerce in Basa

The next day Ganesh showed us the two sacred places in the Basa area. One is a gigantic kapok tree southwest of the village and the other is a cave northeast of the village. There was a little concrete shelter near the huge tree and a few small metal objects that looked like upturned forks stuck in the ground around the tree. Ganesh said that ceremonies took place at the tree with a shaman. The cave was a rock hump about six feet high with a hidden entrance. The inside was not visible and Ganesh warned that no one was allowed to enter the cave, except a priest. I was intrigued, but didn't press Ganesh for more information about Rail religious practices. (I did, when I returned to Basa in 2010.)

Talking about the religious practices of the Rai people with both Ganesh and Sanga, while we trekked together, I had concluded that their "religion" was more a spiritual approach to life than an institutionalized religion. That was attractive to me, as I had become disenchanted with institutional Christianity. So it was surprising to learn that nine families in Basa called themselves Christian. But there was a unique Basa spin to their Christianity.

Tek Bahadur, a village elder and chairman of the school board, became interested in Christianity. He engaged in a personal study of the religion and then declared himself a Christian pastor for the village. Ganesh described Tek as "a very mentally curious and philosophical man." He said that Tek was not content just accepting Rai traditions, so he studied Hinduism, Buddhism, and Christianity. At different times in his life, Tek followed those different religions to some extent. Ganesh wasn't sure that Tek would remain a Christian the rest of his life. He said that Tek also "still followed the old ways." Anyway, the villagers supported Tek's desire to have a church in the village and helped him build the little one-room dirt-floor wood-frame church. Ganesh explained the tolerant attitude of Basa, "Everyone is happy for Tek Bahadur to have his church."

Tek proudly showed us the church. Since he didn't speak English we were spared from politely listening to a sermon.

The first commercial transaction in Basa Village between a tourist and villager occurred the second day of our visit. Gregg saw and coveted an antique-looking kukri knife in one of the homes we visited. I wasn't present at the time, but Gregg told me that he asked the owner if he could purchase the knife and its rugged leather-sheath. Although villagers who worked on expeditions earned money, it didn't have any particular use within the village. Rupees could be used to purchase goods at the Sombare market, but there wasn't anything for sale in Basa Village.

Gregg said that he paid the equivalent of one-hundred dollars in Rupees. He said that as much as he wanted the knife, he "felt sorry for how little the family had. I wanted to give them a donation. They were very surprised by how much I was willing to pay." Ganesh confirmed that the seller was pleased with the exchange. Gregg told me that he didn't put any pressure on the villager. "I just asked if he'd be willing to sell the knife."

I didn't think there was anything particularly wrong with the transaction, but I wondered if it might be the beginning of a slippery slope. Was this the first step toward developing a consumer economy in Basa? If Basa became a tourist-trekking destination, what else could the villagers sell, their treasured brass pots or the jewelry hanging from the village matrons' noses? It's understandable that the residents of Basa want electricity, plumbing, and an economy supported by tourism. Look what those developments have done for the Khumbu Sherpas. To paraphrase Ang Temba Sherpa, "You wouldn't want to walk a mile to fetch water, if running water can be piped into your house. Why should we?" Indeed, why should they?

Who are we, who have all the conveniences of modernity, to criticize the Sherpas for sacrificing some of "the old ways" for greater comfort and material wealth? Yet, I could not help worrying about whether a ball had begun rolling down a hill that would smash into this idyllic little community. Basa had sustained itself the way it was for hundreds of years. Would its people lose their love of flower gardens, if it became a tourist destination? Would villagers sell handmade leis, instead of graciously bestowing them on visitors?

Those dark ruminations had to be set aside on the third day of our visit. It was time to leave Basa and trek on. We were piped and drummed out of the village by the town band. Villagers again lined up to place garlands of marigolds around our necks. It was amazing that so many leis could be created by the villagers. But, every family did have a flower garden.

A few more scenes from Basa in 2009 ...

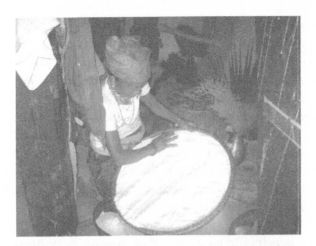

Shaman Dance

Our campsite the first night out of Basa was at a village called Adheri. Our cook, Purna Rai, lived nearby. Ganesh let it be known that Purna was not only a great cook but was one of the local shamans. The term for shaman in the local language is "purket". I asked if it would be possible for Purna to show us a shamanic practice. Ganesh explained that it wouldn't be proper for a purket to do an actual "healing" for the group. We were not Rai. However, if Purna agreed, he could demonstrate for us what he did during a healing ritual.

309

Purna's family invited our entire trekking group of 14 (16 minus Bruce and Donna) into the house. His wife and daughter served cups of rakshi, chang, and slices of naan (leavened bread). Once we were all settled around the fire pit in his house, Purna began his performance of a healing ritual. He entered a trance state and then began chanting, dancing, and performing ritualistic movements with various symbolic objects. He picked up one thing while dancing and after awhile exchanged it for another item. A kukri

knife, a small iron trident (like the "upturned forks" around the sacred kapok tree), leaves, and plants were incorporated into the dance. Purna's chanting varied from loud shouts to a quiet sing-song tone of voice. While Purna sang and danced, Ganesh, Arjun, and Ram pounded and beat on drums and shields.

Purna was soaked in sweat after the first half hour. The dance moves ranged from subtle movements of his hands to frenetically muscular bounds and jumps. He kept this up for two hours without a break. When it was finished, Ganesh told us that, "If Purna was trying to heal someone, it would have lasted six to ten hours." Ganesh also said that no other white people, so far as he knew, had ever witnessed the performance of a purket's healing ceremony.

310

Trail runs and the sweet sorrow of good-byes

The day after Purna's performance we parted company with Joel the Elder and Dr. John the Yeti. They didn't want to take three weeks away from their offices, so Niru planned a two-week programme for the two docs. They hiked over the Ratnagi Danda to Phaplu for a flight back to Kathmandu. The remaining group of 12 trekkers hiked on up through the middle-Himalaya region of Solu to enter the high Himalaya of the Khumbu.

Hiking through Solu was more peaceful than trekking the Base Camp Trail. The trail Hillary and Tenzing hiked to Mt. Everest actually began in Jiri Village, where our 2008 trek to Basa started. Our 2009 group's trek north from Basa up through the Middle Himalayas more closely resembled the early stages of the trek to Mt. Everest the mountaineers in the 1950s did than what has come to be called "the classic Everest Base Camp trek". Since the 1960s, most Everest Base Camp treks begin with a flight to Lukla Village. The original Lukla air strip was constructed in 1964 with funds from Hillary's foundation. It was renamed Tenzing-Hillary Airport in 2008.

Since far fewer trekkers hike through the Solu area south of Lukla, engagement with local people along the trail was more open and friendly. Villages along the trails south of Lukla are much less commercialized than along the Everest Base Camp Trail north of Lukla.

We avoided Lukla on our way north and entered Sagarmatha National Park at a place called Jorsale. From that point on we shared the trail with other trekkers and yak trains. The daytime temperatures in the lower altitudes of Solu got up to the high 80s. That made for sweaty hiking in the afternoons. The higher altitudes of the Khumbu brought the temperature down for more comfortable hiking. The beautiful wide and green-terraced hills and valleys of Solu gave way to the great white peaks and thrashing glacier-fed rivers of the Khumbu. Dust kicked up by yak trains on the Base Camp Trail brought out handkerchiefs to cover nose and mouth. Trekker traffic jams occurred at some of the swinging cable-bridges.

But the weather was gorgeous; not a drop of rain and clear skies everyday. When we crested Namche Hill, we were rewarded with a spectacular view of the Everest Massif and all the great peaks of the Khumbu Himalayas. We befriended a Tibetan shopkeeper in Namche. She had the best prices on Tibetan and Sherpa handmade goods, clothes, and gems in Namche Bazaar. Our group probably made her budget for the year with our many purchases.

The highest elevation of the trek was on a pass at about 13,000 feet near Syangboche and the Everest View Hotel. We stopped at the hotel for tea and to gaze appreciatively at Everest, Thamserku, Ama Dablam, Lhotse, Nupste, Pumori, and the other white-capped peaks along the border with Tibet.

Our northern terminus was the Sherpa village of Khumjung, where we visited an ancient Buddhist monastery, the Hillary School, and the nearby Kunde Hospital. While we were in Khumjung, our three fastest hikers, Chris and Max (the 20 somethings), and Gregg (our old-fart fast guy), hiked on to Tengboche Monastery for a visit to the monastery and to enjoy the magnificent view of the Everest Massif from the monastery grounds. They completed the 2-day hike in less than a day. I would have enjoyed visiting Lama Tenzing again, but the ACL surgery five months before the trek slowed my top-end hiking speed. So I didn't even consider doing the speed trek with Gregg and the youngsters.

When we left Khumjung, we said our good-byes to Dr. Bill. He and Himprasad, a porter-guide, hiked north to complete the trek to Everest Base Camp. They also hiked up 19,000-foot Kala Phattar, which offers exquisite close-up views of the Everest Massif. The classic picture of Mt. Everest seen in tourist brochures and posters is taken from Kala Phattar.

The day the remainder of the group hiked out of Khumjung a diarrhea-causing stomach virus attacked a bunch of us. I'm pretty sure it was a virus, because I took the antibiotic ciprofloxacin, and it didn't work its usual magic. Every time I've been in Kathmandu I purchase "cipro" over the counter, which is legal in Nepal. The antibiotic is manufactured in India and sold in every pharmacy in Kathmandu. It usually cures a case of diarrhea in 24 hours, but not this time.

Susan, who was a very fit distance runner, confessed she was so weakened by the attack her attention was not what it should have been in a charpe. Like Jim's camera on the 2007 trek, Susan's sunglasses went down the hole when she stood up. Unlike Jim's camera, which was recovered by a village search party, Susan's sunglasses rest in peace with the other droppings down the charpe's hole.

The three of us that were struck the lowest by the virus were Chris, Joel the Younger, and me. The trek down the trail from Khumjung to Monjo to Lukla should have been a piece of cake, especially for Chris, an elite distance runner, and Joel, an experienced trekker-climber. But we were dragging ass like the walking wounded. While we waited for the flight out of Lukla, the three of us spent most of that time in the airport's WC doing our best to eliminate any problems before we boarded the flight back to Kathmandu.

The night before we flew out of Lukla, the traditional farewell banquet was held in a lodge dining room. It was a rollicking affair with dancing and a lot of rakshi drinking. Purna outdid himself with another multi-course feast and chocolate cake for dessert. The 28 members of the staff were very pleased with the cash tips and many items of clothing and gear we gave them.

As the drinking and dancing wound down, the "good-bye party" became very emotional. Ganesh gave a speech thanking the group for "helping the poor, backward people of Basa." He expressed gratitude for the school project, but he also pointed out that the whole village benefited by the employment of these 28 men through Adventure GeoTreks. Ganesh explained that many of the village farms can no longer support the whole family for an entire year, because of the spike in infant survival. Outside employment had become essential for many families in order to make money to buy food after the food their crops yielded was exhausted. He said that Adventure GeoTreks, on account of Niru's loyalty to his home village, was the only employer that purposefully hired people from Basa.

My description doesn't do justice to the impassioned gratitude Ganesh expressed to the group for our support of the school and the village as a whole. He teared up, as did several members of our group and the staff.

Back in Kathmandu, we reunited with Cousins David and Melissa, and my intrepid octogenarian-friend Joan. They reported that they had a great time touring Nepal by plane, car, foot, and elephant with their guide, Raaj. They also said they'd reached TMI about the many incarnations and manifestations of Brahma, Vishnu, Shiva, and Buddha after visiting twenty different temples during the tour.

Melissa, David, Joan, and Raaj; the Annapurna Range is behind them in the distance

Philosophy of culturally sensitive development

Before I left Kathmandu, Niru, Ganesh, and I huddled once again to discuss what we might do next for Basa. While I was in Basa in 2008, Sanga talked about how the villagers could see lights at night twinkling on the other side of the valley. They knew those lights came from electricity and people in the village wished they too had electricity so they could have lights that twinkled at night. In 2009 Niru and Ganesh told me that the village elders requested our help to bring light to Basa. They said the teachers and School Committee members were especially interested in developing electricity for the village so kids could read after dark and the teachers could do lesson planning after sunset. Niru asked if I would conduct a fundraising effort to purchase the equipment to build a hydroelectric plant for Basa.

314

I had spent just over four days in Basa during my two visits, but the benefits to the village by reducing villagers' exposure to open fires was obvious from my own coughing and watering eyes. I thought developing ways to cook other than over their fire pits should be of greater priority than lights. Family planning should have been even more important in my opinion, given that the population explosion in the village seemed to be the underlying cause of many other problems. But another conclusion Niru, Ganesh, and I reached trumped those concerns.

We decided that the villagers themselves, not us, should decide what, if any, help they received from us. Our role would be to respond to requests for assistance from the village. We would not try to impose our views of how the village should develop on the community. My role, and that of the soon to be created Basa Village Foundation USA, would be to raise funds and provide any requested expertise. Niru's, and the soon to be created Basa Village Foundation NGO, would be to serve as intermediary between the village and the BVF-USA, to develop formal grant requests, manage distribution of funds, provide supervision for building projects, and report back to the BVF-USA on the progress and completion of projects. The village would provide all labor and would own and operate the completed projects.

The village built the school with local labor. It was staffed by teachers from Basa, and it had its own school board. All it needed from the outside was capital to purchase building materials and to pay teacher salaries. That was the model for development we decided to use for a hydroelectric project and any other future projects.

I called our philosophy "culturally sensitive development", because Niru and I agreed that whatever we did for Basa we wanted to have the least impact possible on the local culture. The formal creation of the sister foundations, I feared, would inevitably reduce the spontaneity of my commitment to philanthro-trekking. That was a correct assumption as developments over the next few years would prove. The Basa Hydroelectric Project and return to the village in 2010 drew me into a more significant relationship with Basa than I previously imagined.

Modernity sobered people up from the powerful but sweet

delusions and illusions that had made the misery of their lives bearable. Devoid of these fantasies, we would lead our lives without commitment to higher principles and values, without the fervor and ecstasy of the sacred, without the heroism of saints, without the certainty and orderliness of divine commandments, but most of all without those fictions that console and beautify." Moroccan sociologist Eva Illouz

Photos of trekking from Basa to Khumjung to Lukla in 2009 ...

Bringing Light to Basa; Blending Tradition and Modernity
Pikey Peak and Basa Village Trek 2010

The purpose of the 2010 philanthro-trek was two-fold: 1. to deliver equipment and finalize plans for a hydroelectric project in Basa, and 2. enjoy trekking through the Middle Himalayas and climbing Pikey (pronounced Peekay) Peak. I did not try to recruit members into this group, because of the first purpose. Just three of us were in the group. Mike Miller, a retired electrical engineer and entrepreneur, who became chairman of the BVF-USA, was the volunteer consultant in the planning of the hydroelectric system for Basa. Cathy Dawson is a retired teacher and agronomist, who volunteered to help the Basa School teachers with the instructional manuals that were delivered from the Indiana Department of Education and to consult with village farmers about farming techniques. Cathy is also a massage therapist. Her skill in massaging out kinks and strains was highly appreciated on the trek, and it came in handy in a delightful way at a 400-year-old Buddhist monastery.

We spent nineteen days in the mountains in mid November through early December. Before we left Indiana for Nepal, Mike reviewed plans for a hydroelectric plant prepared by a Nepalese engineer hired by our sister foundation in Nepal. Mike tentatively approved the plans, but wanted to see the actual site and meet the local engineer. Mike's family foundation provided most of the funds to purchase the parts for the hydroelectric plant. Many other "friends of Basa" made smaller donations toward the $22,000 goal for the project.

Like most Himalayan region dwellers, Basa villagers cooked and heated their homes with wood-burning fire pits. Cataracts and pulmonary disease caused by inhaling smoke each day is endemic to the Himalayan region. While I was visiting Niru in 2009 he informed me that the village leaders wanted to improve health conditions in Basa and one way they wanted to do that was to have electric lights in their homes. If they weren't dependent on fire for light in their homes after dark, it would reduce the amount of smoke that got in their eyes and was inhaled into their lungs. Villagers were also concerned that the forest near the village was threatened by the use of sticks as the primary fuel for the family fire pits. It is contrary to Rai ethics to cut down a living tree. So, the villagers are limited to picking up fallen sticks and cutting branches. But the forest was not providing a sufficient amount of fallen branches to meet the village's needs. The school teachers wanted electrical lights, so their students could more easily study after dark.

The villagers decided that they wanted to address these problems by developing hydroelectricity from the stream nearest the village, where they draw their water. Niru, the president of the BVF-Nepal, conveyed to Mike and me a proposal to purchase two hydroelectric generators and build a little power plant beside the nearby stream. So we raised the $22,000 for the Basa Village Hydroelectric Project.

The caste system distorts business dealings

Mike, Cathy, and I rode in a bus with our crew of porters, kitchen staff and guides, along with all the equipment to build the hydroelectric plant, from Kathmandu to the end of the road in Jiri Village. Guys from Basa carried over 300 pounds of equipment on their backs from Jiri to Basa. The three Americans with our trekking staff took a more circuitous route to Basa through the Middle Himalayas of the Solu region. But let me fast-forward to describe how the hydroelectric project went, and then I'll return to the trek.

In Basa Mike and I met with the local project engineer, Chandra Nepali. The three of us and village leaders hiked half an hour, mostly downhill, to the Mauri Khola, the little river below a waterfall, which is Basa Village's water source. Mike and Chandra eye-balled the site the village leaders had picked out for the power plant. They looked at the blue print Chandra drafted and talked through how the system should be built and could be operated. Chandra's English was excellent, so no interpreter was needed. The plan required construction of a small directional dam to narrow the flow of the stream to increase its power to turn turbines at the power station. After the generating plant was built, villagers would have to string wire from the power station to the village. Mike was satisfied with the plan as devised. Whether the villagers were capable of building the plant and stringing wire from the river uphill to the village over very difficult terrain was a different question than whether the plan "worked on paper".

When Mike and Chandra inspected all the equipment the

porters carried to Basa, they were very upset to discover there was only one generator. The BVF-USA had sent funds to Niru for the BVF-Nepal to purchase two. Chandra's plan called for the second as a backup to extend the life of the system. So what the hell happened to the second one? In 2010 there was no cell phone service around Basa, so Ganesh had to call Niru by satellite phone. Niru insisted that the full purchase price for two generators was paid with the funds Basa Foundation-USA sent. He faulted the Kathmandu-based supplier of the component parts, Techno Village Company. Resolution of the problem would have to await our return from Basa to Kathmandu.

When we finished our trek and were back in Kathmandu, Niru arranged a meeting at the Adventure GeoTreks office with representatives of Techno Village Company, the Basa Foundation-Nepal officers, Mike, and me. It was interesting to participate in a business meeting with the supplier-company representatives and the Rai guys from Basa Village, who now lived in Kathmandu and served on the Basa Foundation board. The meeting started with tea and the utmost civility. There was much bowing and thanking of everyone present by everyone else present. Civility, however, gave way as soon as the issue over the missing generator was broached. Voices were raised and faces began to turn red.

Ganesh told Mike and me, while we were trekking back from Basa, that we were needed at the meeting, because Techno Village was run by Brahmins. He claimed that the high caste Brahmins thought they could take advantage of the Basa Foundation-Nepal guys, because the Rai were lower caste. "They think we are nothing but farmers, even though Niru owns a successful business," Ganesh explained. "If our American sponsors are there, they will be afraid to take advantage of us."

Before the business meeting began I requested that it be conducted in English. But as soon as it got heated all the Nepalese guys reverted to Nepali. After awhile, I slammed my palm down on the table and demanded that everyone settle down and explain in English to Mike and me why a second generator was not delivered. Ram Devkota, the president of Techno Village, explained that only one generator was in stock and the second would be available for transport to Basa within three weeks. He said the delay was due to the fact that the Chinese manufacturer only had one in stock when he placed the order. The second one was being fabricated and would then be shipped to Kathmandu. Since he was unable to deliver both generators for transport to Basa together, Devkota promised that Techno Village would pay to transport the second generator to Basa.

It seemed absurd that this simple explanation and solution to the problem required a special meeting including Mike and me. I did not see any evidence that the high caste Brahmins of the company were trying to swindle the Basa guys. Yet, Niru, Ganesh, and the lower caste Rai guys distrusted the higher caste Brahmins to such an extent that they only accepted explanations and promises made with Mike and me as witnesses. Whether the distrust was based on current dealings or deeply held class resentment, I couldn't tell. But one of the take-aways for me was that the caste system distorts human relations in ways that are counter-productive to getting business done. It was interesting to see how Nepalis conducted a business meeting, although the contrast between the cordiality of the opening and how it descended into acrimonious shouting was baffling to Mike and me.

Of most importance, the second generator was delivered to Basa three weeks later.

The site along side the Mauri Khola, where the little power plant was to be built, is beautiful. The stream is fed by a waterfall. There is a sheer 100-foot rock wall beside the stream. Heavy jungle-like vegetation grows all around the other side of the stream and down the mountainside where the stream flows into a river 1,000 feet below. Consistent with traditional Rai ethics, as little harm as possible would be done to the environment in the construction of the power plant. Chandra calculated that during the dry season of winter the natural flow would be too slight to turn the turbine with sufficient strength to generate the needed power. So, a little hump of a dam was necessary to funnel a major portion of the stream into a pipe to increase the power of the flow. The river's course would not be changed. A portion of the water flow would be directed into the pipe aimed at a water wheel.

A cistern and shelter for the generator would need to be built beside the stream. Villagers would have to climb the rock wall beside the stream to pin wire to the cliff side. Poles would have to be planted to carry the electrical wire to the village.

Mike and I witnessed the two-day long village meeting at which plans for operating the electrical system were made. A committee was chosen to act as the utility board. A "code of conduct" was agreed to by the villagers to delegate responsibilities for the labor to construct and maintain the system. Everyone in the village would have a role from preparing food during construction to the hard work of pinning the wire to the sheer face and fashioning and installing the utility poles. A sliding scale for villagers to contribute financially to cover any future maintenance costs was worked out.

The power plant was expected to provide very modest electricity to the 62 homes in the village. Each home would have enough power for the equivalent of four low-wattage light bulbs. Each family would get to decide on a ratio of light bulbs to electrical outlets for other appliances such as a hot plate or small fan. The villagers don't have television sets, washing machines, refrigerators, or any high-power appliances. No disappointment was expressed about the amount of electricity each home would receive. Everyone seemed thrilled about the prospect of lights in Basa.

Back to the trek

We left the Nirvana Garden Hotel slower than a herd of turtles. Ganesh and his crew had packed an Indian-made Tata van with the hydroelectric equipment and camping gear before picking up Cathy, Mike, and me. With our duffels added to the small mountain of equipment the van would not fit under a sign hanging from another building just outside the hotel's driveway. The guys unloaded some of the gear, we rolled past the sign, loaded up again, and then -- a car blocked the street. After thirty minutes of searching, Ganesh located the owner inside a nearby shop. The car was moved and we entered the traffic of Kathmandu.

Driving through Kathmandu is rarely fun. It was horrific that morning. Streets were blocked, cars stalled, honking, beeping, rickshaws holding up traffic, rutted cobblestone roads, bicycles weaving in and out, cattle wandering through traffic. The air pollution and dust were so bad as our Tata van crept through Kathmandu, that Raaj, the driver, asked us to close the windows. He turned on the air conditioner, which drivers rarely do in Nepal.

Kathmandu traffic is crazy according to American sensibilities.

You drive on the left side of the road. There are very few signals or signs. Traffic cops at the major intersections give directions in conflict with the traffic lights. Stop, yield, and speed limit signs are considered advisory. It is customary to drive with a hand on the horn and a foot on the accelerator. Brake lights are optional.

The one enjoyable moment during the drive out of Kathmandu was a surprise. Niru, Sanga, and Arjun were waiting on a corner to say good-bye. They hung katas (silk scarves) around Cathy's, Mike's, and my neck as a good luck blessing for the drive to Jiri.

The drive was fun, thrilling and uncomfortable. The guys joked and laughed during the twelve-hour drive, even though most of them were sitting on tents, duffels, or hydroelectric equipment rather than seats. Leg room was an issue for Mike and me as the Tata van was not designed for six-footers. We snaked around s-curves and switchbacks on roads too narrow for two vehicles to pass as we made our way from the Kathmandu Valley into the foothills of the Himalayas. Raaj handled hairpin turns and steep mountain passes with the calm professionalism of a driver who has seen much worse. We arrived in Jiri late in the evening.

We spent the night in the same lodge where Cousin David and I peed off the balcony in 2008. I performed the act again, but solo this time. I was delighted to see two shooting stars in the night sky while peeing into the darkness below. Perhaps it would be a good omen for the trek (the shooting stars, not the pee).

Mike and I awoke at daybreak to the sounds of the crew chattering, equipment and gear being unpacked and organized, and Ganesh barking orders. Cathy, Mike, and I brushed teeth and watched from the second floor railing of the lodge as the guys spread out all the hydroelectric equipment and camping gear. The courtyard of the lodge was covered with the boxes, bags, containers, and crates that had been packed into and on top of the Tata van. Porters were dividing up all the stuff and packing it into their straw doko baskets. Three of the porters were going to carry pieces of equipment that weighed over 100 pounds in baskets hung on a rope and strapped around their foreheads. After the control panels, steel intake pipes, turbines, gear boxes, and all the rest of the parts for the Basa power plant were loaded into doko baskets, Ganesh patted the men on their shoulders. The porters trudged off in the direction of the mountains overlooking Jiri.

Packing up equipment for the power plant and supplies for the trek to Basa, 2010

Ganesh escorted Mike, Cathy, and me into the lodge's meal room for a breakfast of bacon, eggs, and pancakes. Ganesh explained that half the porters would take a direct route to Basa to deliver the hydroelectric equipment. The other porters, Ram the cook, and the kitchen boys would trek with us to Pikey Peak on a round-about way to Basa.

Our first day of trekking was a pleasant and unhurried contrast to the first day hiking toward Basa in 2008. Instead of the site for the first lunch break, Shivalaya was where we camped the first night on the trail in 2010. The Basa 2010 trek was not going to be another episode of "Survivor Nepal".

It was surprising to see that the road which ended at Jiri in 2008 extended to Shivalaya in 2010. It was a dirt track only fit for sturdy vehicles, but it was a road. We hiked alongside the dirt road for a short stretch, but we saw it in the distance a couple times as we drew near to Shivalaya. I wondered how the lives of the villagers would change with buses lumbering into town, lorries creaking and groaning with loads of cargo, and dirt-bike motorcycles screaming down the mountain road. I also wondered when the road would reach Basa and how that would change the village.

As we crossed the bridge over the Khimti Khola to Shivalaya we could hear the ping ping ping of steel hammers on rock. A new lodge was being built. In two years Shivalaya had grown. It had become a bustling commercial center. A couple new stone buildings, including a police station, had gone up since 2008. A six foot by four foot banner advertising "Cheese Trek" hung across the entrance to the town. Two lorries rumbled up and stopped.

Mike and I took a stroll around town and were quickly surrounded by kids who wanted us to take their pictures. We became the Pied Pipers of Shivalaya with our digital cameras, which provided instant gratification to the children wanting to see themselves in photos. We left the kids behind and hiked down to the river bank. I stripped down to my hiking shorts and washed in the chilly water. It was refreshing because the sun was quite warm. Mike passed on the opportunity for a river bath.

When we returned to town our camp was already set up behind a lodge across from the police station. A family of black and white goats patrolled our campsite. Ganesh arranged a drawing of lots among the staff for several pairs of shoes I'd brought, which were donated by Changing Footprints, an Indianapolis charity run by my Quaker friend, Carol. The winners happily compared their slightly-used shoes and laughed about their good fortune. Hamid, one of the kitchen boys, was especially proud of the pair he got. The shoes were soft black leather with ribbed rubber soles.

Even though we'd had an easy trekking day, Cathy, Mike, and I hungrily wolfed down the large meal of soup, potatoes, rice, veggies, and chicken Ram prepared. This was Mike's second Himalayan trek and Cathy's first. It was gratifying to see their amazement at the heaping and delicious meal Ram prepared. We rolled into our separate tents just after sun down with full and happy tummies.

Looking up at the yellow ceiling of the tent, I reflected on how different our experience on the trail was from 2008. Less than two months after back surgery at age 71 Mike handled the long, tough uphill hike outside of Jiri so much better than Bill and Karen had. It was amazing that Mike was even attempting the trek. He'd casually remarked that, "Ageing legs do better on uphill hikes than downhill." But Mike seemed to handle the down hills just fine. He was slow but steady uphill.

Cathy was ten years younger than Mike and a very strong hiker due to her training as a serious bike rider. She spent most of the day hiking ahead of Mike, Ganesh, and me. But she followed my advice and did not get out ahead of the entire crew. Our assistant sirdar, Buddhi, walked with Cathy most of the day.

Cathy, the author, and Mike during a rest stop; trekking to Shivalaya 2010

As sleep began to nibble at my consciousness I heard trucks rumbling by on the road just outside of town. It was a sound I had never expected to hear beyond Jiri. The modern world was following us to Basa.

Women's work and the hike to Namkhile

The hike from Shivalaya to Namkhile Village entailed one very long downhill and one very long uphill. Namkhile is in a beautiful river valley formed by the Likhu Khola. Huge hills rise up on both sides of the river. A prosperous clutch of farms are gathered in the bottom land along the river. Each of the homes had electricity powered by hydro-turbines. As we passed the little power station along side of the river, Mike remarked that it had about twice the output Basa's would have.

Before we crossed the suspension bridge over the Likhu Khola we paused to watch women threshing wheat and millet. They were still threshing after we crossed to the other side of the valley. They continued their work while we rested and ate lunch. They were still at it late in the afternoon. We lost sight of the women when we hiked over the opposite ridge.

A long mule train passed us just below the crest of the ridge. Cathy and Mike both moved quickly to the mountain side of the

328

trail as the mules clumped towards us. We hugged the hillside as the young mule masters whistled and threw rocks at the butts of any reluctant animals.

A group of about ten school children in tattered and dirty blue uniforms caught up to us after the mules passed by. The kids laughed and joked with us practicing their English. They wanted Mike and me to take their pictures. Cathy didn't bring a camera. She explained that she didn't want to look at Nepal through a camera lens.

One-by-one the kids peeled off to their homes as we hiked higher and higher, except one little girl. She hiked all the way to our campsite, which turned out to be her family's farm. Namkhile is not really a village. It is just a few farmsteads along the ridge line.

While we set up camp two little boys ran around our camp poking their noses into tents and duffels. After awhile the little guys settled into a game of running around and jumping into a puddle formed by a break in the water line between our tents and their house. When the younger brother was soaking wet up to his knees, he went indoors. Although the temperature was dropping and probably in the low forties Fahrenheit, the kids seemed unaffected by the cold and dampness of their clothes. Older brother finally called it a night after eating two marigold blossoms while I snapped pictures of him.

All through the evening the women of the house churned butter and ground barley to make bread. These two women and the others we'd passed on the trail worked so hard to harvest and prepare food. In "developed countries" we take grocery stores for granted. Food preparation can be as easy as unpackaging items and cooking the contents on a range or in a microwave oven according to instructions. Mountain people grow the plants that become their food. Every step from planting the seed in the ground to cooking they do themselves. Subsistence farming is a full-time job.

Mother and son churning butter, Namkhile, 2010

Sleep was difficult that night in Namkhile. A dog barked throughout the night. A loud drinking party in the house beside our campsite was even more disturbing. I wished we were invited to the festivities.

I was up early in the morning and asked Ganesh about the noisy celebration. He called it a pre-wedding party. He said that if I hiked a little further up the trail and over a rise I'd see the shelter being built for the wedding. While Ram was preparing breakfast I galloped up the trail to check out the shelter.

An elderly man was working at constructing the wedding shelter. He offered me tea, which I accepted. He spoke in his local Sherpa dialect and gesticulated to explain how he and the men in the family were preparing the shelter. I did not understand anything he said but intuited some of his meaning. A long green tarp was going to be fastened to a series of wooden poles, which the elderly fellow was fashioning and planting in the ground. I wished him and the wedding party well, and then jogged back to camp in time for breakfast.

Teachers, massages, 10,000 Buddhas, an ancient gompa, and aged lama
We stopped to eat lunch in a kharka (pasture) near Goli Gompa. The warm lemon juice Ram prepared hit the spot just right. We

drank the juice and gazed across the horizon at the white-capped peaks of Numbar and Jugla mountains. The aroma of chicken-vegetable soup wafting from Ram's cook stove heightened our appetites.

Goli Gompa is a picturesque sky-blue and white Buddhist temple-complex built on a steep hillside. Ganesh and Buddhi led Mike, Cathy, and me up a steep set of stairs into the main temple. We took our shoes off to enter the temple as is customary. Ganesh and Buddhi each lit candles and took a moment to pray while Cathy, Mike, and I slowly circumnavigated the interior in our stocking feet. The walls were covered with intricately detailed paintings representing characters and scenes from Hindu-Buddhist mythology.

After lunch, just down the trail from the temple we encountered two young European women. They were lying in a grassy field surrounded by a bunch of school kids. We chatted for awhile and learned that one was French and the other Austrian. They were working as volunteers in a program that provided teachers to Nepalese village schools. The young women told us they were serving six month stints. One was nearing the end of her service and was looking forward to trekking the Annapurna Circuit Trail before leaving Nepal. The other was just two months into her term of service.

They both related that they loved living in the village and teaching at the school with Nepali colleagues. But they were very disappointed over the lack of resources the school had. They also expressed concern about local teaching methods, organization, and scheduling. The women related that the Nepalese teachers they worked with "had true hearts for teaching" but were inconsistent in sticking to a regular schedule in holding class. The volunteer teachers said they were surprised by the number of holidays celebrated in Nepal with school closings. They also related that there is a far more relaxed attitude about starting the school day at a particular time. They expressed concern that the lack of a disciplined schedule jeopardized progress of the students. They worried that educational gains are lost due to inconsistent scheduling. The teachers described their experience as a combination of frustration and the most meaningful experience of their lives.

The two volunteer teachers and kids we encountered beyond Goli Gompa, 2010

Later that afternoon the trail became very steep and rocky. It branched off in multiple directions up the mountainside to Ngar Gompa, our destination for the night. Ngar Gompa sits atop a ridge line over 9,000 feet high. The trail up the mountainside tracks through a steep, boulder-strewn pine and rhododendron forest.

Mike seemed to get stronger as the trail got steeper and tougher. Cathy started up the steep climb in her "energizer bunny" mode, but began to struggle as the altitude increased. Just before sundown we crested the high ridge and looked out over a breathtakingly beautiful scene. We stood above the clouds on both sides of the ridge line. White snow-covered peaks thrust up through the clouds to the north while an ocean of cumulus clouds hid the land we'd just hiked through to the south.

The upper photo was taken from the Monastery grounds the evening we arrived facing north; the lower one is looking south.

Ngar is a modest little gompa with a small lodge and three houses hugging the top of the ridge. While we waited for Ram to cook dinner, Ganesh, Mike, and I sat around a wood burning stove drinking rakshi with a few local men. One older gent named Lakhpa Sherpa became quite voluble. He spoke some English and began proclaiming that he had climbed Mt. Everest three times and would guide us to the summit if we hired him. Despite telling him we were not father and son, Lakhpa insisted on referring to Mike and me as Poppa and Sonny. The other men laughed at everything Lakhpa said. Apparently, he was the local comedian.

Old Lama Paldung, abbot of the gompa, and his wife invited us to their little wood lodge after dinner. Cathy was wiped out after the last hiking stage up to Ngar, but she rallied after consuming the meal Ram prepared. She gave Mike, Kumar, the Lama's wife, and me massages. Kumar laughed gleefully during his massage. He rolled over at Cathy's instruction and accidentally stuck his bare toes into the coals in the glowing brazier. He didn't seem to notice.

Neither Kumar nor the Lama's wife had ever had a massage before. They loved it! Mrs. Lama, who was over 80 years old, smiled and chuckled with pleasure while Cathy kneaded her back and shoulders.

After breakfast the next morning Lama Paldung shared a poignant moment with Ganesh, Buddhi, Mike, Cathy, and me. He related how he wanted to find a successor to keep the gompa open for the next generation, but no other Buddhist leader wanted to live in such a remote place. With Ganesh translating, the Lama told us that Ngar Gompa was a 400-year old teaching monastery for Buddhist studies.

Lama Paldung's cheerful face drooped and the sparkle in his eyes seemed to fade. I could hear the sadness in his words even though I did not understand his Sherpa dialect. Only a few students had come to the gompa over the last several years. The Lama and his wife did not have any children. He worried that he would not find a worthy teacher to replace him before he died. "Life is too hard in this remote place," he said shaking his head. Lama Paldung had hoped that by opening a lodge it would create a revenue stream to help support the gompa, but very few trekkers came up to Ngar. He worried that Ngar's 400-year history would end with his death.

Lama Paldung showed us his study where he kept "the sacred texts that only lamas can read." He had a small solar cell for lights

in the house and study. He said he wanted another one for the gompa. The Lama explained hopefully that, "If the gompa was a more comfortable place for students, more might come." But his hope was dying as time passed.

Cathy massaging the Lama's wife

My heart was aching for the old fellow and his wife. They were over 80 and were living out their lives in this hard, remote, and beautiful place. They seemed so happy the night before entertaining us in their little lodge.

The mood lightened when Lama Paldung showed us "the 10,000 statues of Buddha" in the gompa's temple. Paldung's great uncle, a former Lama of Ngar, had vowed to do 10,000 obeisances (praying prostrations) to Buddha. But he got too fat to do the physically demanding prostrations. So instead, he ordered 10,000 clay statues of Buddha to be made. The former Lama placed many of the statues in the gompa. Buddhi and Ganesh laughed heartily as Lama Paldung told the story of the 10,000 Buddhas.

Before we left Ngar the Lama gave us slices of yak cheese to eat

on the trail and placed silk katas around our necks to bless our safe travels. Old Lama Paldung and his wife smiled and waved as we turned our backs on the ancient gompa and began walking toward Pikey Peak base camp.

Lama Paldung in his study, Ngar Gompa 2010

Spectacular view from Pikey

The hike to Pikey Peak base camp was an easy two-hour walk from Ngar. Mike calculated that we only gained 200 meters in altitude. A dense forest covered the mountainside above and below the trail. The woods were mixed spruce, pine, and rhododendron trees. Myrtle and tea plants covered the ground. The clouds that rolled in while we hiked up to Ngar the previous afternoon still hung above and below the trail to Pikey. I felt an eerie premonition hiking through the gray clouds.

What happened after we arrived at the foot of Pikey Peak is related in detail in the later chapter, "You Have to Get Lost before You Can Be Found". In brief, I got lost on the mountain, which I climbed alone, and spent the afternoon and early evening trying to find my way back to base camp. The next morning Ganesh woke Mike and me at 5:00 a.m., so the three of us could be on the summit (together!) by 7:00 a.m. My legs were pretty tired when we started the hike up on account of spending so much time wandering around the mountainside by myself the day before. I was thankful for Mike's slow steady pace up the mountain. I followed Ganesh and Mike back up to the summit for the second time in fourteen hours. Cathy did not feel well enough to hike up to the summit.

The sun was just peaking over the 14,000-foot-high crest of Pikey when the three of us stepped onto the mountain top. The wind was howling between forty and fifty miles per hour. Prayer flags attached to bamboo poles flapped maniacally. But the grey mass of clouds had cleared out and the view was spectacular. The sky was crystal clear blue with a few fluffy cumulus clouds floating regally above us. The Everest Massif looked surprisingly close for being 100 miles away. All the great peaks of the Khumbu were clearly visible. Ganesh named each of the white-capped mountains for Mike and me. We could even see Dhaulagiri in the far west of Nepal beyond Annapurna.

Mike struggled to keep his balance while he adjusted his camera lens to take panoramic photographs. I braced myself against the bamboo poles anchoring the prayer flags to keep my balance while taking pictures.

After we finished shooting photos Ganesh motioned us to come over and duck down just below the east side of the summit. We huddled together comfortably out of the wind and let the sun warm our wind-chilled faces. After meditating on the phantasmagoria of the High Himalayas for awhile, it was time to hustle downhill and trek on to our next campsite.

Mike Miller is to the right of the author on Pikey Peak, 2010.

Medicine, Tradition, and Modernity

We spent most of the day hiking upwards over the Salun Danda (11,400 feet). Ganesh told us that we would camp that night in "an even more adventurous campsite than Pikey base-camp." Ganesh's term for campsites outside of villages is "adventure camping".

High up on the Salun Ridge we stopped at a bhatti (tea house) for lunch. It was located at the convergence of two yak-herding trails. Ram bought potatoes, greens, and a chicken from the Sherpa family who owned the bhatti. Cathy and I played with the family's kids outside the bhatti while Ram cooked and our crew enjoyed a glass of chang inside.

The Aamaa (mother) didn't leave her bench seat the entire time we waited for Ram to prepare lunch, nor did she get up while we ate. A grey cat sat contentedly on Aamaa's lap. Her husband told

Ganesh and me that Aamaa had a condition that caused her muscles to ache and she had migraine headaches. He asked if we had any medicine to help her.

My mountaineering mentor, John Roskelley, told me that giving medicine to locals, unless you are a medical doctor or nurse, should generally be discouraged. The medicine could be sold or misused without proper supervision. John gave pain killers to an elderly Ladakhi woman we met when we were trekking through the Karakorum Range. She was so weak she was riding on a pack mule. She was clearly in pain and at her age it was unlikely she was a drug dealer.

I had observed Aama and her cat for the better part of an hour. She was obviously in pain and was not faking it just to wheedle medicine out of us. I asked Ganesh if he thought I ought to give her aspirin. He spoke to the woman and her husband in Sherpa and then concurred that it was appropriate in this case.

I gave her thirty aspirin pills in a baggy and Ganesh explained to Aama and her husband that she should take two at a time but no more often than every six hours. I thought the "placebo effect" might provide as much pain relief for her as the aspirin. Aama's husband thanked me effusively.

The Sherpa family lived in between the old and new, Eastern traditions and Western modernity. The woman wore a combination of traditional Sherpa dress and modern clothes; the colorful striped-apron of her tribe under a fleece pull-over and Nike sock hat. The family lived high up on a mountainside hours away from the nearest village. Yet, they knew about the benefit of modern medicine.

In Basa the villagers have learned to appreciate Western medicine without losing respect for the healing powers of the village shaman. In 2009 we learned how hard our cook Purna, a local purket (shaman), worked to heal villagers of illnesses. As sophisticated as Ganesh is, he told me that he had as much faith in Purna's ability to heal as Western medicine. He related that, when Niru's father was dying of cancer, the family utilized both Western and traditional healing to help the old man.

As medical facilities spread throughout Nepal in the late 1990s, life expectancy rose from 59 to 66 by 2010. During the same period of time unemployment and poverty significantly increased. The success of science-based medicine in reducing infant mortality and extending life expectancy resulted in many more mouths to feed for many more years. The availability of modern medicines was a double-edged sword.

Science-based agriculture might help to increase crop yields and thereby offset the problem of over-population. Family planning with birth control will certainly help. But will this process of two steps forward and one step back toward a developed nation actually improve the quality of life of the Nepalese people? To what extent will, for example, modern farming techniques decrease the family oriented and communal centered aspects of farming?

It is a conundrum. For every advance in structural development there is a risk of decline in the quality of cultural and social life.

Complementing the old with the new is the approach Niru and I agreed was the most sensitive way to approach development in Basa. Purna continuing to practice shamanic healing arts should not prevent establishing a medical clinic in Basa. Having a medical clinic should not prevent Purna from continuing his traditional healings. If the villagers want their traditional healer to continue practicing, and they want the benefit of science-based medicine, the two should be able to work in tandem. That's our philosophy, anyway. How well will it work out?

In farming, some aspects of modern agro-science could be incorporated into the traditional farming techniques of the Rai people. Using better seeds, rotating crops, improving storage facilities would not conflict with working their terraced fields with their traditional hand plows and water buffalo.

My hope for Basa is that the village will make wise decisions in its incorporation of some "modern" ways into village life. In 2010 and today I continue to have some confidence that Basa will develop an equilibrium of traditional and modern -- like the way the Sherpa Aama dressed.

Spirit of Nature at Salun Danda adventure jungle camp

Ganesh called the campsite where we camped the night after climbing Pikey Peak "an adventure jungle camp". He liked to give exciting-sounding names to our campsites. Since we camped at a site even further from any settlement than our "adventure camp" at the base of Pikey Peak, Ganesh designated our campsite on the Salun Danda an adventure jungle camp. The site he chose was at the apex of a rain forest. Ganesh called rain forests "sky forests". The adventure jungle camp provided a special treat -- a campfire.

We rarely make campfires in the Himalayas, because we don't want to contribute to denuding the forests nor do we want to use firewood needed by local people. Expedition cooks usually cook with kerosene. They will use the wood-burning cook stoves of local people, if we are camping in a village. But there was a campfire smoldering at the campsite Ganesh found; probably left by yak herders.

Cathy was juiced about having a campfire and began scouring the area for sticks to build up the fire. Mike claimed seniority and sat on his duff exhausted after a long day of hiking following the early morning climb of Pikey Peak. He "supervised" the rest of us while we searched the area for fire wood and then built up the fire with our collection of sticks and branches.

Unfortunately, there was no water source near the camp. Man Bahadur and Jusbir had to hike back uphill to a waterfall we passed twenty minutes before we made camp. They each filled and carried five gallon jugs of water back to camp for cooking and washing pots, pans, plates and utensils, and to boil for drinking water. The trail they hiked with the water jugs was steep, rocky, and slippery with a smear of wet snow. But Man Bahadur and Jusbir seemed untroubled negotiating the treacherous trail holding the big water jugs with both hands behind their necks. They chose to hike back uphill to a water source so they could carry the heavy water jugs downhill rather than hiking down to a river below our camp and then carrying the heavy jugs back uphill. They knew their business.

Our camp was in a lovely site. It was approximately 10,000 feet elevation on the east shoulder of the Salun Danda. A rain forest surrounded the campsite and a rocky ridge cut by a waterfall was above. A rushing river was below. Whenever I awoke during the night the sound of the waterfall above and the river below eased me back to sleep. The piney scent of the rain forest eventually overwhelmed the wood smoke of our campfire and the food odors of Ram's cooking. The huge night sky was lit up like Van Gogh's "Starry Night".

The ancients believed certain places, groves of trees, rocky summits, and craggy passes, were sacred. They experienced spiritual power in those places. Humans design temples and cathedrals to bring forth those same feelings of awe and transcendence. The Rai people of Basa do not use human-made structures to inspire awe and transcendence. The spiritual power evoked by Nature itself is sufficient.

That aspect of their way of life was very attractive to me. I am awe struck when I visit a magnificent cathedral or beautiful temple or church. Yet, the awesome beauty of Nature untouched by human intervention is especially soul stirring. Along the Himalayan Range there are so many places that inspire a feeling of awe and transcendence.

We broke camp in the morning and hiked down to the river. The sedge grass along the river bank was wet and marshy. Our hiking boots were soaked by the time we found a log bridge to cross. From the little river the trail took us downhill into Junbesi, the largest village we passed through during the trek. We stopped to visit the Hillary School, but school was not in session and there were no teachers around. We walked on through the town. The day ended with a hike up another high ridge, designated Sinsare Danda on my map. Our campsite was another beautiful "adventure jungle camp".

Buddhist chanting, a tidy town, berry munching, and lessons at the Saraswati School

The following day we ate lunch at a bhatti in the Sherpa village of Ringmu at just under 9,000 feet. The entertainment was a little

boy running around the teahouse yard with his pants falling down and his bum hanging out.

After lunch we visited Taksindu Gompa at 9,500 feet and witnessed the monks engage in a traditional Buddhist chanting ceremony. An ancient Lama Rimpoche presided over the ceremony. Ganesh told us that the Rimpoche is a very revered holy man who rarely leaves his study. Cathy, Mike, and I each gave a donation to the monastery. A young monk served dudh chiyaa (milk tea), but the Rimpoche did not give us an audience. The monk apologized and explained that the Rimpoche no longer met with visitors.

From Taksindu Gompa we hiked to a lovely village called Nunthala. Most of the homes and buildings inside Nunthala were white-washed stone with wood shudders painted sky blue. The roofs were matching blue tin. Nunthala looked very prosperous for a mountain village. It had a post office, medical clinic, and three lodges. In England the Tourist Board gives awards for "tidy towns". Winners proudly display their triumph with a sign at the entrance to the village. Nunthala deserved a tidy town award. It was so clean and pretty. But it was late November, so the trekking season was over and the lodges were empty. A few kids played around the cistern in the village center. If the kids weren't there, Nunthala would have looked like a beautifully preserved ghost town.

Nunthala Village 2010

Forty-five minutes beyond Nunthala we hiked past a smaller and more modest village Ganesh called Somdele. It was not marked on my map. Ganesh said that Somdele was somewhat unique because, "In this area Sherpa, Rai, Tamang, and Untouchables all live in mixed community."

Just outside the village we stopped to rest and eat berries that Hamid and Nirman picked from bushes along the trail. The berries were blue and a little sour tasting. Mike, Cathy, and I liked the taste, but we had never seen or eaten berries quite like these. The guys called them *chyasi* in Nepali. Ganesh didn't know whether the berry had an English name.

While Ganesh, Buddhi, Mike, Cathy, and I ate the berries, four farm girls flirted with Nirman (Ganesh's 16-year-old younger brother) and Hamid. Cathy whispered that Nirman was "as handsome as a matinee idol." No wonder the girls wanted to flirt.

The land around Somdele was gentler, less rocky and not as steep as most of the country we'd trekked through. We munched berries and gazed out across barley, millet, and buckwheat fields. Separate groups of three or four people worked in the fields.

Ganesh called a halt for the day at a school just beyond Somdele. Saraswati Secondary School was celebrating its silver jubilee (25th anniversary). Saraswati is the Hindu goddess of learning. Impressive silver and blue posters announcing the jubilee adorned the school. Our campsite was on the playground.

A few teenage boys shyly hung around the edge of our camp. I invited them over to show them my map of Solu-Khumbu. The young guys, along with Nirman and Hamid, gathered around the map talking excitedly and pointing at all the sites they recognized. They knew as many of the mountains on the map as villages. If your most likely job prospect to get out of town is to work for an expedition company, I suppose knowing the mountains is as important as recognizing other villages.

Cathy rounded up all the kids and began testing their English skills. She worked with Nirman and Hamid every evening she had sufficient energy after the day's hike. The familiar refrains of "These are my eyes. I have two eyes. I see with my eyes. This is my nose. I smell with my nose. This is my mouth. …" were recited by five local kids along with Cathy's two regular charges.

How community works in Basa Village; Saraswati School

Over dinner Ganesh and Buddhi answered questions from the three Americans about Basa. They told us that only five or six families own enough land to grow millet to sell. The other fifty-some families grow enough to feed themselves, so long as the weather cooperates to allow a full yield. The few families that are able to grow enough millet to sell normally sell the excess harvest in Sombare on market day. If they have an extraordinary crop, they might carry their produce in doko baskets for three days up to Lukla.

Ganesh related that his father liked to talk about the one time he

344

walked all the way up to Namche Bazaar "to get the very best price" for his millet harvest. Ganesh chuckled and said his dad spent so much money on food and places to sleep that he returned home after ten days without any money left in his pocket.

I asked whether there was a formal election in the community for positions on the Village Development Committee. Buddhi and Ganesh laughed at the idea that a formal election would be needed. They said that everyone knew who should be on the Committee. Although the interim Constitution of Nepal required a formal election, the Committee members were chosen in Basa by acclamation. Ganesh said it was the same for the School Board.

Buddhi explained that any dispute in Basa was settled by the "elder-leader". He expressed annoyance that proposed changes to the Constitution would require Basa to elect a mayor. He argued that it was unnecessary. Buddhi told us that Pungse Rai was the elder leader of Basa Village. Buddhi said Pungse was 86 years old and, "Everyone knows that he will settle any disputes within the village."

Buddhi and Ganesh claimed there is no crime in Basa. There are no locks on doors. Houses are left open while families are out working in the fields. They explained that, if a dispute arises within the community, the elder leader will act as a mediator and assert his moral authority to solve the problem.

Ganesh explained that all the family farms are owned as private property. There has never been a real estate foreclosure in Basa, but Ganesh said that, "In past years some villagers borrowed money and used their family's land for security." In Ganesh's view, mortgaging the family farm should not be allowed for fear the property could be lost. He said the village leaders now discouraged any borrowing that might create a lien on farm land within the community. Ganesh became quite passionate and exclaimed that no family should be allowed to lose land to a creditor. He worried that naïve villagers could be taken advantage of by "tricksters".

Before we broke camp in the morning we met with the headmaster, Angat Rai, and Shanti Chettri, the math teacher, of Saraswati School. The two men proudly showed us around the school and described the curriculum to Mike, Cathy, and me. It was a fairly typical school in my experience of village schools in Nepal. There were only a few books and the educational materials were minimal. The only English instructional materials were hand-made posters. It pained me to point out a couple errors in verb tenses and spelling on the posters, but I am married to an English professor. Angat and Shanti were embarrassed but thanked me for showing them the mistakes.

When we were gathering up our backpacks to depart the school, Angat gravely asked me to please write down for him the corrections that should be made on the posters. He solemnly promised to correct the grammatical errors. I asked if we could make a small donation to the school. A large smile crossed his face. Yes, he would be happy to accept a donation.

Angat barked an order in Nepali at Shanti, who fetched a receipt book. Cathy, Mike, and I each gave a few hundred Rupees. (At the exchange rate of 70 Rupees per Dollar, our total donation was probably around $20.00.) Angat and Shanti conversed excitedly in Nepali about our modest donations. Shanti carefully wrote out a receipt for each of us and then bowed gravely before handing over the receipts.

The two men stood outside the Saraswati School waving cheerfully as we trudged off toward Basa.

My third visit to Basa

All morning we hiked along the side of a huge valley cut between the rivers Dudh Khosi and Chhanga Khola. We finally crossed the Chhanga on a high suspension bridge and then hiked up a ridge to a village called Tholadungha. We were getting close; just one valley away from Basa Village and home to our crew.

We ate lunch sitting on a grassy knoll beside a school in Tholadungha. Ten boys were playing volleyball without a net in the school yard. A group of four girls who looked to be ten to twelve years old played hacky-sack with a wad of leaves tied together with a bit of string. Buddhi inserted himself into the volleyball game and demonstrated his awesome leaping ability. Since there was no net, jumping served no practical purpose, but it didn't matter. Buddhi and the kids enjoyed jumping and smacking the ball as hard as they could over the imaginary net. The hacky-sack players darted coy glances at Mike, Cathy, and me. They were hoping we would take their picture. Mike and I did. The girls pointed and giggled at the images we showed them on our camera screens.

After lunch we hiked along a trail which follows the curvature of a huge valley cut by the Dudh Khosi (Milk River). The Dudh Khosi's source is the glacier run-off from Mt. Everest at the Khumbu Icefall. It is the highest river on Earth. When trekking through the Khumbu on the Everest Base Camp Trail and then traversing east to hike the Gokyo Trail (as our 2006 group did), you cross and re-cross the fast-running Dudh Khosi. It roars past Basa too, but the river is just a thin grey line hundreds of feet below. We could hear a faint humming and hissing of water rushing downhill and thrashing over and around boulders as we tracked the ridge trail leading to Basa.

In late afternoon Ganesh called a halt at a trail-side bhatti. Like all the teahouses in the Basa area it was for locals not tourists. It was very rough, dirty, poorly lit, and only served tea and rice. I started to walk in with Buddhi and Ganesh to get cups of milk tea for Mike and Cathy, but Ganesh asked me to wait outside. I assumed he thought I would be offended by the squalor of the bhatti. But no, it was a surprise!

Ganesh and Buddhi exited the teahouse bearing cups of tea followed by the Basa Village Band. The musicians were beaming and holding their homemade instruments above their heads in greeting. After many namastes, hellos, bows, and handshakes, we drank our tea and then marched off toward Basa. We followed the musicians while they tunelessly, but with great gusto, thumped, tooted, and honked. Our procession of musicians, porters, kitchen staff, guides, and clients wound its way along the narrow ridge-trail leading to Basa Village. People working fields along the trail stopped, stared and smiled at the parade. It is not customary to wave in Nepal, but when Mike, Cathy, or I waved, the local people waved back.

The Welcome-sign arch, which the villagers had erected for my first visit in 2008, was still beside the school. Once again, as in 2008 and 2009, the entire village awaited our arrival with flower garlands.

The villagers showered us with flowers. Matrons pushed cups of rakshi into our hands. There were speeches by village leaders and dances by the students. During our three days in Basa we visited many homes. Mike and I asked many of the villagers how they felt about the hydroelectric project for Basa. Everyone in the village expressed anticipatory delight at the prospect of having lights in their houses.

Cathy taught the school teachers and the older students games, songs, and dances the purpose of which was to learn basic math and English grammar in fun ways. She showed the villagers how they could reduce spoilage of harvested crops by storing their crop yields on tarps rather than on the ground. I delivered a box full of pencils, pens, crayons, and writing tablets for the school. I also gave each student a bookmark made of ribbon. The bookmarks were handmade by kids in the Hamilton County Juvenile Detention Center through a program run by my friend, Jill Meisenheimer.

After the song and dance program by the school kids was completed, I expressed our appreciation to the student dancers by giving each one a Beanie Baby. But the activities that had the most significance for Basa were Mike and Chandra's finalization of the hydroelectric project plans and the community meetings in which the villagers worked out each person's responsibility for building and maintaining the electrical system.

Basa School students performing at the community gathering, 2010

Ancient stories and secret rites of the Basa Rai

Ganesh Rai, Buddhi Rai, and I sat by a campfire on the Ratnagi Danda, a 10,000 foot high ridge in the Nepal Himalayas the night of December 1, 2010. It was the night after departing Basa Village.

I asked Ganesh and Buddhi to tell me about the ancestral legends of the Rai people of Basa. They told me that their people "in the old days" had a written language and sacred texts, but the written language and the ancient texts were lost in the mists of time. The local language of Basa is a dialect of a greater Rai language spoken by the Rai people who inhabit the Middle Himalayas of eastern Nepal. The stories of gods and spirits and sacred things they learned from the village elders and their parents were similar to the ones passed down from generation to generation in other Rai villages.

Our camp was a clearing in a rhododendron forest. Mike and Cathy were asleep in their tents. The porters and kitchen crew were finishing their simple meals of rice, lentils, and tea. The crew had already cleaned up the kitchen and dining tents. As soon as the guys finished eating they would pile into the kitchen and dining

349

tents sharing body heat for warmth while they slept.

Before we sat down by the campfire, Ganesh and Buddhi spoke with our senior porter, Kumar Rai, about my request to be told the old stories of the Rai people. Kumar is a descendent of shamans and was the eldest member of our expedition staff. He doesn't speak English. Kumar assented to the request of "Jeff dhai". He reminded the younger men of some of the details he wanted me to learn.

I had become "the parent" of Basa village and "Dhai" (elder brother) to the men who staffed our trek. The guys knew I had written a book which described my experience of Basa in 2008. They agreed that I could take notes about what they told me.

Buddhi is the son of the caretaker of the Kali Devi shrine outside of Basa Village. It is the sacred cave mentioned in the previous chapter. Buddhi was expected to succeed his father after the old man's death. Buddhi confessed to me that he was torn between his sense of obligation to his family heritage and his and his wife's desire to live in Kathmandu. They are both college graduates and his wife wanted to find a job in a technology field. (By the time I returned to Basa in 2017 the issue was resolved. Buddhi had become chairman of the school board and was fulfilling his role as the Kali Devi priest.)

Buddhi sat on the other side of the campfire from me. He began to speak in the local dialect. His voice was low, resonant and had the sing-song quality of a chanting monk. It was a little unsettling, because Buddhi was in his mid twenties and was always smiling and joking while he bounded down the trail on springy legs during the trek. By the crackling campfire that night he was uncharacteristically solemn. He looked like a ghostly apparition through the smoke on the other side of the flickering fire. Iridescent moonlight completed the eerie atmosphere around the campfire.

Ganesh sat between us translating Buddhi's words into English. They stopped occasionally to confer, to make sure they got the story right. Ganesh's conversations with me were normally sprinkled with jokes and a ready laugh. But he wasn't laughing or joking as he translated Buddhi's narrative.

The flames of the campfire flashed and licked at the stack of sticks in the fire pit. Kumar had placed three stones around the edge of the fire pit as required by Rai taboo. The stones represented father, mother, and child. Red sparks wafted up into the great open sky above the Ratnagi Danda. The stars of the Milky Way and the constellations I'd learned as a child glimmered through the moonlight. I listened in rapt attention as Buddhi chanted and Ganesh translated the old stories and rituals of the Rai people of Basa.

Culturally Sensitive Development, Sacred Stones, Foiled again on Mera Peak
Basa – Mera Peak Expedition 2011

During the winter of 2011 the Basa hydroelectric project was completed. When the system was finished and lights were turned on in the village for the first time, the villagers celebrated with singing, dancing, and drinking rakshi and chang. I learned of these developments through emails from Niru, Sanga, and Ganesh. This was one of the e-mails from Ganesh:

> Dear jeffy dhai (big brother)! Namaste from Ganesh bhai (little brother)... I was a long time in the village so that I wasn't able to send mail. So for the electric project we finished completely and we got really very nice light... Every village people are really very happy with this and they feel like a dream this time and they can not express (with) mouth that happiness but they expressed from face how much they are happy nowadays for the light... I would like to give to you thank you very much for your great support for all and thank you very much for all our donors ... for your big support for the backward people and village. So I hope when you will be in Basa you will be satisfied for this project ... and it's going to be one of example for the remote area... So, dhai stay with good health and have nice time... With best regards from bhai.

The Basa Village Foundation USA was growing and taking shape as an organization. A friend and fellow attorney, Chuck Richmond, volunteered his time and talents to work through the IRS maze to obtain the final approval required for tax exempt status. The apron strings with First Friends Quaker Meeting were cut in 2012 after the BVF-USA became a fully independent nonprofit corporation. A group of twenty-some contributors signed on as initial corporate members. Mike Miller was elected chairman of the board of directors. I was approved as president. Jeanne Roue Taylor was chosen as corporate secretary. Melissa Hudson and Candace Vogel were voted in as co-treasurers, and Joel Meyers and Chris Taylor were chosen to be vice-presidents of the corporation.

The corporate structure took shape despite ambivalence on my part. I knew that burdens would be placed on volunteer officers that we didn't have so long as we operated as the Basa Village Project under the wing of First Friends. We would have to hold formal corporate meetings and take minutes. We would have to file taxes and deliver financial reports to members. We would have to pay filing fees to the federal and state governments. Nevertheless, most of the project supporters wanted to transition to a formal corporate structure. I reluctantly assented.

A helpful side-effect of people making long-term commitments to the Basa Foundation was that the officers and members created a core group interested in trekking to Basa as well as supporting future projects. That made it easier to recruit members into a trekking group in 2011. Several corporate officers and donors wanted to visit the village to see the school and check out the operation of the electrical system.

Niru informed Mike and I, when we were back in Kathmandu in 2010, that there had been an attempt to build a water system for the village, but it failed. He wanted to know whether the BVF-USA would consider funding the construction of a water system in Basa. That gave us another reason to visit Basa again -- to look into the possibility of funding a water system for the village.

Mike, Joel, Chris, and Jeanne were corporate officers with some level of mountaineering experience. They wanted to combine a trek to Basa with a mountain climb. The obvious choice for a mountaineering expedition after visiting Basa was Mera Peak. It is the closest peak to Basa for which the government of Nepal grants climbing permits. So, Niru designed a programme for a trek to Basa, then on to Mera Peak for a climb, and then over to Lukla to fly out of the mountains back to Kathmandu.

But, holy crap! The 2011 trek started out like the ill-fated, but wonderful, first trek to Basa in 2008. Two of our group of eleven members had to drop out before we left the States. Cousin David took ill in Kathmandu. Before he recovered a situation arose with the new position he'd just taken which required his presence back in LA. We lost a third member. Our flight up to Phaplu was cancelled and delayed for a day due to inclimate weather. Here we go again, I thought.

But the weather cleared and the cloud over the expedition seemed to lift the following day. The views out the windows of the Twin

Otter for our group of eight trekkers on the flight to the Phaplu airstrip were gorgeous. As soon as we disembarked the plane, the Adventure GeoTreks crew awaiting our arrival grabbed our duffel bags and climbing gear, stashed everything in their doko baskets, and led the eight of us out of Phaplu and into the mountains. That afternoon we hiked up the 10,200 foot high Ratnagi Danda and camped on the top of the ridge. In the morning we hiked down the other side of the mountain range and within a few hours were met outside of Basa Village by -- yup, the village band. Once again, and for me the fourth time, the entire village awaited our entry at the Welcome arch. The eight members of our trekking group were covered in leis as we entered the village.

The author after entering Basa Village, fall 2011

Welcoming speeches were given by village elders. The village matrons pushed their home-distilled rakshi in tin cups on us, each one insisting that we should at least try one cup. Our sirdar, Dilbal ("DB") Rai, gave an impassioned speech thanking each of us for coming and for the Basa Foundation USA's "great support" of the village through the school and hydroelectric projects. DB's gratitude was so heartfelt and sincere it brought tears to many eyes. DB went on to say that it was going to be his job to supervise construction of the water project, if we approved it. He was eagerly looking forward to working with "Basa's American friends" on a plan and budget to bring water to the village.

The welcoming ceremonies in 2011 had one significant difference from the other three I'd experienced. A delegation from the school in Sombare was in attendance. The head teacher gave a speech and then handed me two pages of handwritten script. The writing was in English and signed by the head teacher, Nwima Doma Rai. (I'm not sure Nwima is the correct spelling of her first name, because her signature was difficult to read. Her writing was otherwise quite legible.) She was tall for a Rai woman, with erect posture and lovely features. Nwima was dressed in a beautiful green full-length silk dress. She wore a black and silver-patterned silk scarf around her neck. Nwima conducted herself with dignity and just a touch of obsequiousness. She smiled and bowed trying to find the right balance of welcoming friendliness and neediness. A member of the school's delegation placed beautiful gold-colored silk scarves around our necks. The essence of Nwima's speech, and content of the two pages, was a request for $1,700 per month for five teachers' salaries and additional funding for a computer, science lab, and a student hostel at the Sombare School.

I handed the paper to Mike to look over. I'm sure the request was worthy in terms of the needs of the school. The school in Sombare was where Basa kids went to secondary school, if they pursued education beyond the village's primary school. A hostel would make the lives of students from Basa Village much easier, because it would provide housing for them during the week. Without a place to spend the night, they'd have to walk two hours to Sombare and two hours back home.

But Mike and I were taken aback and a bit offended to be hit with this additional request before we had even begun working on the water project. DB noticed our expressions of displeasure as we whispered to each other about being ambushed by the request. As soon as the speeches wound up, DB hurried over and apologized to Mike and me for the intrusion of the delegation from Sombare. He said he was unaware they had been invited to participate in the welcoming ceremonies.

DB was worried that the inadvertent offense might dampen our enthusiasm to partner with Basa on future projects. I reassured DB we were serious about helping with a water project for the village, but we were not prepared to consider other projects outside of Basa Village as yet. Later that day, I showed Joel, Chris, and Jeanne, the other BVF-USA officers on the trek, the written request signed by Nwima. We were all in agreement. Consistent with the original idea for "culturally sensitive development of Basa" that Niru and I had discussed in 2007, and the BVF-USA was founded on, we wanted to focus strictly on Basa Village itself and to do one project at a time. Even though Basa kids attended the secondary school in Sombare, it was not within our initial corporate purpose to help fund a school outside of Basa Village. At some point in the future, when culturally sensitive development of Basa was complete, we could consider using the Basa model to work with other villages. For the foreseeable future we wanted to focus solely on Basa Village.

I reported our decision to DB and asked him to respectfully inform the delegation from Sombare that we would not be able to respond to the request. I don't know what DB said to Nwima Doma Rai, but we never heard from her again. It was a little distressing to blow off such a nice lady. She'd come from Sombare with high hopes of meeting rich benefactors from America. Her cause was just and the need was undoubtedly real, but it would have distracted us from our intended purpose.

The next item on our programme for the day was to hike with a bunch of the villagers down to the Mauri Khola -- the river nearest the village where the hydroelectric power station was built. What we saw there was kind of amazing. When Mike and I left Basa the year before the component parts of the little power station were in scattered piles around the village. But here was a fully functional hydroelectric power station built with the labor of these subsistence farmers.

The construction was performed with as little impact on the landscape as possible. The equipment was housed in a six-foot by five-foot concrete-walled shed with a tin roof. Water flow was not blocked by a dam, which might adversely affect habitat. A small diversionary hump was built into the middle of the stream to direct part of the water flow into a pipe to turn a five-foot-diameter turbine (wheel). The spinning turbine generates the power. With their own hands the villagers built the entire system to generate electricity from the little river to their village. They strung wire up over the canyon wall by the riverside, and then planted poles into the steep and rocky terrain all the way to the village to bring light to its 62 families. Wow! Mike called the hydroelectric system "a feel good project". I certainly felt good about the part we played in bringing light to Basa.

Prakesh Rai had been trained in the operation of the power station. He proudly showed us how he could turn the power to the village on and off with a big lever which engaged and disengaged the turbine spinning in the current of the river beside the power station. I hoped no one was using lights or a hot plate in the village while Prakesh turned the power off and on several times to demonstrate his prowess in the operation of the system.

Mike switched on a light in Basa Village in 2011. Hallelujah, it works!

Five computers and 62 chulos in Basa

Chris Taylor obtained six laptop computers from his company for the Basa School. The computers were packed in our duffel bags and carried in the doko baskets of our porters to Basa. Whether it occurred while the laptops were being humped over the Ratnagi Danda or during baggage transfers on the flights to Kathmandu and Phaplu, one of the laptops was not functional when it arrived in Basa. But the other five arrived in working order. Chris and Jeanne spent much of the afternoon and part of the following day instructing the school's faculty and five hand-picked students in basic computer skills on the five working laptops. One of the teachers, Assam Rai, was already trained in user operations. He was licking his chops in excited anticipation of teaching Basa kids how to type and to master Microsoft Word and Excel spreadsheets. Assam planned to give each of the five classes two hours of computer time each week. That would allow each student about half an hour on a computer each week.

357

In 2011 there was no Internet connection in Basa. Furthermore, DB told us that the teachers did not think it would be wise to expose their students to the Internet; not yet, anyway. Googling and learning how to do online searches would not be within the curriculum of the Basa School computer lab for the foreseeable future.

Assam Rai and students on the laptops donated to the Basa School, 2011

Another project we were able to fund in 2011 with excess dollars left over from the hydroelectric fundraiser was for "smokeless stoves". Since the first time I visited Basa Village in 2008 I was concerned about health hazards caused by the villagers cooking, heating, and lighting their homes with wood-burning fire pits. Within a few minutes of sitting with a family by their fire pit my eyes would burn and water. My throat would get scratchy and my sinuses would begin to run from inhaling smoke. I researched alternatives and began bugging Niru by email about whether the villagers might be interested in trying alternatives to their fire pits. Niru shrugged off my inquiries.

I knew the fire pit and the three stones around the fire pit meant more to Rai people than a mere source of heat for food preparation and warmth on cold nights. I watched Kumar place three stones around each of the campfires we made on the 2010 trek. I thought Niru's lack of interest might be based on resistance to changing a traditional practice. Niru did not specifically use Tevye's *Fiddler on the Roof* "Tradition!" as the excuse for his lack of interest in my suggestions. He just politely changed the subject. I was trying to be careful not to explicitly violate our rule that the initiative for a project should come from the village, not from outsiders. But the health benefits for the villagers by reducing their intake of CO_2 was so apparent, it was difficult for me to let go of the issue. In 2009 and 2010 I asked a few people in Basa whether they were aware that cataracts were caused by excessive exposure to smoke as were lung and heart problems. One elderly fellow, who wore a patched-together pair of Clark Kent-type glasses, told me he that he was losing his sight. He said he thought it might have something to do with smoke getting in his eyes every day.

Niru and I had agreed that the initiative for any project should come from the village itself, not from him and not from me. I was caught between a rock and a hard place, because I was convinced that Basa villagers would benefit tremendously by cutting down on their exposure to smoke. And I was equally convinced that the best way for Basa to develop was on its own terms decided by its own people.

It struck me that it was kind of weird that I was so concerned about Basa villagers sitting around their fire pits. Like many American families, we have a fire pit in our backyard. Roasting marshmallows, smores, and hotdogs over an open fire is something I've enjoyed since I was a little kid. And I certainly enjoyed the campfires we had in our adventure jungle-camps on the 2010 trek. But there is a big difference in daily exposure to open fires and enjoying the occasional campfire.

I was delightfully surprised when Niru's response to my suggestions about considering alternatives to fire pits changed after he heard Mike express the same concerns on our return to Kathmandu after the 2010 trek. Whether it was Niru's culturally-determined respect given to the voice of an elder, or it just took another voice, Niru's attitude toward smokeless stoves changed after Mike weighed in on the topic. Niru agreed to find a model of what he called *chulo*. His sister, Ran Maya Rai, could test it out and let other villagers see it in operation. Then, the village could hold a meeting to decide whether smokeless stoves were desirable for the village or not.

In due course Niru reported that the experiment was a success. Ran Maya liked cooking with the stove, and the village decided to request stoves for each of the 62 homes. Niru had checked out various manufacturers of chulos and settled on one recommended by the Nepal Center for Rural Technology. The total cost for all the parts to assemble 62 of these chulos would be $3,000. Niru sent the specifications and budget to Mike and me. We were delighted with the proposal, because there was over $3,000 left from the funds raised for the school and hydroelectric projects. The BVF-USA board approved it, and the remaining funds in the account First Friends maintained for the Basa Project were transferred to the BVF-Nepal's account in Kathmandu.

Ran Maya and other villagers realized that an important benefit to the village was that, by burning sticks inside the enclosure of the stove, the amount of sticks used by a family for cooking would be dramatically reduced. A meal could be cooked by burning three or four sticks instead of nine or ten. Basa residents were already concerned enough about preserving there trees that they had planted 1,000 trees in recent years to maintain their fuel supply. Villagers also realized a chulo was a labor-saving device. They wouldn't need to collect as many sticks for cooking a meal.

After the 62 units were purchased, Niru dispatched a team of guys employed by AGT during the winter of 2011 to Basa with the component parts for the chulos. The team worked with each family to construct a stove with a smoke stack for each home in the village.

I was both gratified and worried to learn that stoves had been installed in each of the homes. My worry was that displacement of the traditional fire pit ringed by the three sacred stones was a violation of our ideal of "culturally sensitive development".

I visited many of the 62 homes during the days we spent in Basa in 2011. Some villagers had the stove placed in a corner of the house with the fire pit remaining in the center. These folks continued using their fire pit as the gathering place to eat and host visitors in the home. They continued to inhale CO_2 when they used the fire pit. But they did, at least, reduce the amount of cooking they were doing in the fire pit. They were cooking most of their meals in their chulos. I noticed that many of the homes with stoves in the corner were run by elderly women. Other homes, many of which were run by younger women, had the stoves placed on top of the fire pits. No matter where their chulo was located in the home, everyone in the village expressed happiness with the innovation.

It was great that everyone in Basa would be inhaling less CO_2 and would be getting less smoke in their eyes. And it was a good thing that fewer sticks were being burned. But weren't the families that placed their chulo on top of the fire pit losing a cultural tradition by covering the sacred stones? I confided my concern to Buddhi before we visited his house. He chuckled and replied, "We know where the stones are." His family maintained the custom of sitting according to placement of the Father, Mother, and Children stones. They just sat around the stove, which sat upon the three stones.

Buddhi's response kind of assuaged my immediate worry about the loss of a cultural tradition. But how many more changes would it take before the beautiful flower that was Basa reached a tipping point?

DB explained how a *chulo* (smokeless stove) vents the smoke out of Jasma Rai's house, 2011.

Eating, dancing, and the prospect of a road to Basa

Every member of the village wanted to show every member of our trekking group how the lights worked in their house and wanted to cook food for us on their new stove. We were treated to slices of giant cucumbers, roti pretzels, potatoes, chang, and rakshi, until our stomachs were ready to burst and we were drunk from the moonshine.

In the evening the school children performed a dance program they had been practicing for months in anticipation of our visit. Two individual dancers were featured, loose-limbed 12-year-old Sagar and beautiful 16-year-old Laxmi. All the kids danced barefoot on the dirt and pebble-strewn clearing by the school house. The skill and agility Sagar and Laxmi displayed leaping, bending, and twirling barefoot in perfect time to the music from Nanda's boom box was extraordinary. After the performance, Sagar told me he wanted to dance professionally in Kathmandu. But he also wanted to be a doctor or an airplane pilot. Laxmi said she wanted to practice medicine or become a teacher.

In the morning before we left Basa older members of the community performed a traditional "earth dance", which was led by Ganesh's father, Rudra Rai. Rudra and the other dancers chanted in low thrumming voices while they danced. The dance was slow with carefully stylized movements. Rudra waved a yak tail at the head of the line of dancers. DB described the attire the dancers wore as "traditional formal Rai clothing". Except for Rudra, they all danced barefoot.

Rudra Rai leading the "Earth Dance" flourishing a yak tail; Basa Village 2011

Joel filmed many of the events in Basa. He would like to create a documentary film about the philanthro-treks of the BVF someday. That hasn't happened yet, but Joel has posted a couple film clips on YouTube of the 2011 expedition. One of the clips includes our entrance into and departure from the village. If you watch it, you'll see that so many leis were placed around our necks our faces were hidden.

Many villagers walked with us and the "Basa Band" when we hiked out of the village. Kids held onto our hands. Many of the children and a few adults walked with us for an hour until we arrived at the trail crossing for Adheri. It was time to part ways with our friends in Basa. The musicians played one last tune. Villagers and trekkers danced to the music and embraced when it ended. It was a bittersweet parting, but we needed to make it to the campsite in Adheri that night.

There were spectacular moments of beauty our group of eight experienced during the remaining two weeks of our 2011 adventure, but we all agreed that the most rewarding experience was Basa Village. The gratitude expressed by the villagers for the contributions of the BVF was so heartwarming. Especially moving was the sweet and poignant way the children attached themselves to members of our group. Some of the kids shed tears when they had to part with their special friends.

Upper: Three of the village matrons watch our departure; Lower: departing Basa in 2011.

Another concern about preservation of the lovely character of the village was that a road was getting closer to Basa. The road passed Shivalaya the year before and was being clawed out of the rain forest and up the Ratnagi Danda. It was expected to reach Basa within a couple years. DB told us that most of the villagers were opposed to the road. He said, "The older people they fear the road will bring pollution and bad food and candy to Basa." DB described the purpose of the road as to make it easier "for agri-transport". But he scoffed at the idea that it would help the farmers of Basa Village. In DB's opinion construction of the road was being done very poorly. It was denuding hillsides of trees and causing erosion. He feared the erosion would worsen during monsoon season and cause landslides.

DB is a very thoughtful guy. His family is one of the more intellectually inclined families in the village. His sister, Deenah, was the Basa School's English teacher and Tek Bahadur is DB's father. (Tek was chairman of the school board and founder of the Christian church in Basa.) DB's antipathy toward the road reaching Basa resonated with my own fear for the community. However, DB admitted that many younger people looked forward to the road coming Basa. "They want interesting things to come to the village side," he explained. The younger generation didn't necessarily want to move away from the village, DB claimed, but they liked the idea that it would be easier to go to other places, especially Kathmandu. Ah, the lure of the big city.

Trekking to Mera Peak, jungle spirits, and good and bad progress
The next phase of the 2011 expedition was the trek to Mera Peak. So, dear reader, you should be introduced to the other three members of the group that have not yet been mentioned. Karlin and Ursi are Joel's brother and sister-in-law. They live in Switzerland, and were experienced alpinists and spelunkers. They added an interesting dimension to our discussions in the meal tent. It was a privilege to get a Swiss perspective on international affairs and to learn what the Swiss thought of US foreign policy and the never-ending wars in Afghanistan and Iraq. Karlin had great stories about caving adventures in South America.

Dennis is a childhood friend of mine from Goshen, Indiana, and was a professor of plant pathology at University of New Hampshire. Dennis was one of the best athletes of our cohort in Goshen. He was a three-year three-sport letterman in high school cross-country, wrestling, and track. He became an avid marathon ski racer and has participated in cross-country ski races all over the world. I called him Mr. Fussy during the trek, because he was the last one in the group everyday to get his tent and pack organized. He fussed over making sure everything was in its proper place. He couldn't abide just tossing stuff into his pack, and heaven forbid his sleeping bag and thermo rest were not neatly rolled up.

Although Jeanne, Chris, Dennis, Karlin, and Ursi had not done a Himalayan expedition before, we had a very strong and fit group in 2011; at the beginning of the trek.

2011 group without Mike; left to right: Joel, Jeanne, Ursi, Karlin, Chris, Jeff, and Dennis

As in 2009, we camped outside of Adheri Village near our cook Purna Rai's house. Purna plucked fresh green beans out of the family garden and cooked the beans as the veggies for our dinner. We ate with his family sitting around their fire pit.

After we hiked out of Adheri, the trail became much rougher. We crossed a swinging suspension bridge high over the Dudh Khosi, whose waters tear down through Solu Khumbu from the glaciers breaking off the flank of Mt. Everest. It rained in the evening when we were camping at a yak pasture called Lenji Kharka, which is near the monastery of Pangma Gompa. The dampness brought out blood-sucking leeches. The bastards harassed us by dropping from the ceiling in the meal tent and then finding ways to penetrate our sleeping tents. They seemed to prefer white flesh. All eight trekkers left Lenji Kharka with quarter-inch bleeding circular holes on our feet, ankles, or legs. The nasty little creepers ignored most of the porters.

We spent a night camped by a huge cave, which DB called Odare. Instead of curling up in the meal or cook tent, the crew slept in the cave. DB said the guys liked sleeping in caves better than tents, so long as they could make a fire in the cave for cooking and warmth. We practiced some rock climbing moves on the sides of the cave. On the cave's roof we found a stand of bamboo trees covered in moss. Exquisite little blue flowers grew out of the moss. The mossy ground cover was so soft and springy we did handstands, somersaults, and rolled around in the moss and flowers. We were full of vim and vigor, but that soon changed. We began exceeding the "no more than 1,000 foot increase in sleeping altitude" rule almost every night after leaving Odare Cave.

Members of the crew packing up after spending the night in Odare Cave; Subash is showing off his rock climbing skill.

The trail was very rugged for the next few days, but it offered up fantastical vistas and weird experiences to process. One hillside we hiked up was a slick and muddy bamboo forest. We had to grab hold of the bamboo stalks to pull ourselves up and then use them like rappel ropes to get down the other side. We ate lunch beside a magnificent waterfall. To cross the river below the waterfall we walked on a 30-foot long felled tree which served as a bridge. There were several trails up high passes that were so steep and rocky we had to pack away our trekking poles to scramble-climb up and then down the other side of the mountain. We hiked by more caves and camped by a waterfall, which roared so loud all night long it sounded like a jet airplane was flying overhead.

One of the kitchen boys, named Ganesh, fell and hurt his knee bad enough that DB and Purna decided he should return home to Basa. After Ganesh's fall, DB told me that we needed to be on guard for "jungle spirits". He related that, "One time when I was walking through a forest near Junbesi, jungle-forest spirits took away my ability to move." He was with two other guys, and all three of them were frozen in place. But DB winked confidentially and assured me we were lucky to have Purna with us on the trek. "Purna, he is a nature shaman." DB explained that Purna had more power than an ordinary purket (a Rai shaman with healing powers). "Purna is also a *jankla*. "He is a shaman who is in touch with jungle spirits."

When the trail was easy enough to permit extended conversation, DB and I walked together and talked about the situation in Basa Village. He was very anxious to get the go-ahead for the water project. If the village developed a water system with five reservoirs, he explained, then not only could each of the 62 homes have an outdoor tap each family could have a toilet with a septic system. DB's gentle voice turned hard with disgust. He related how the village had repeatedly requested help from the government to fix the unfinished water system. All they received in response to their petitions was silence or lame excuses. (Sanga and Ganesh told me the village had petitioned the government for help with the electrical system. The response to those requests was silence or excuses for the government's inaction.) DB exclaimed angrily that the government was not even paying the school teachers' salaries as promised. He claimed that only headmistress Nanda's salary was being paid by a government stipend. DB was angry and a little ashamed that his home village was dependent on

368

the largesse of donors "to make progress".

As with Ganesh and Sanga, I was impressed with DB's managerial skills as a sirdar. I was also impressed with his thoughtfulness about how Basa should "make progress". He was worried about how the coming road would affect the local culture. Yet, he was excited about the prospect of having tap water for each home and eventually toilets. He told me there was "a little conflict in the village" about the electrical system. There was a controversy over who should be chosen to become the power station technicians. But, he said, it made sense in the end to appoint Prakesh and his brother, because they lived closest to the power station. It also took some persuasion, DB said, to reach agreement that each family should pay a one-time charge of 20 Rupees per light bulb (less than 25 cents) for the first lights in Basa.

DB thought that working out these sorts of issues was all part of "good progress". The villagers debated the issues, and then made a decision by consensus (similar to how Quaker meetings make decisions). The road, on the other hand, might turn out to be "bad progress". The village had no say in whether it came to the village or not. The government controlled where the road went and how it was built.

Diomox debate and voluntary heli-evac

Kote (pronounced Ko-tay) was the last village we visited on the trail to Mera Peak base camp. Its elevation is around 12,000 feet. Three other climbing teams were already in the village, when we arrived in Kote. A climber with one of the other teams mentioned in conversation that his group's American guide required everyone in the group to take Diomox during the trek to Mera. Our group debated during dinner that evening whether we all ought to be taking Diomox. DB said that he was opposed to the use of Diomox prophilactically, and even discouraged it as treatment for AMS. If you definitely had altitude sickness, in his view the only thing to do is lose altitude by going back down to a lower campsite. My view was that it should be a personal decision whether you took Diomox or not. It shouldn't be a rule determined by a head guide. The one time I took Diomox prophilactically was on the Mera expedition in 1999 and it did not prevent me from getting altitude sickness during the trek to Mera Peak. Whether it helped relieve the symptoms in

1998 before climbing Pokalde Peak with Tom and Krishna, I'm not sure. But it sure made me pee a lot.

Dennis, Ursi, and I were suffering head colds and we coughed irritatingly through the dinner discussion. We took antibiotics, purchased over the counter in Kathmandu, hoping the pills would cure a head cold. Mike remarked that he was considering breaking away from the group and taking a porter-guide direct to Lukla and skipping Khare. (Khare is pronounced Car-ray. It is the name given to the Mera base camp, which was established sometime after Tom, Judy, Heather, and I were on the mountain in 1999. Our base camp in 1999 was at a different location.) Mike explained, "I'm tired of being tired."

The next day was a long walk across a huge moraine to what had been the village of Thang Nag. In 1997 there was an avalanche which burst a mountain lake. The water rampaged downhill and destroyed the village, killing most of the residents. Survivors rebuilt the village on higher ground. Alongside of the moraine beyond Thang Nag we passed by a Sherpa family's house, which was completely isolated. The family must have made a living herding yaks or working for expeditions, because there was no soil to plant crops in, just rocks for hundreds of yards. A teenage girl in traditional Sherpa dress sat on a rock not far from the house applying makeup with the assistance of a cosmetic mirror. What an odd juxtaposition of modern and traditional.

The next morning we were supposed to be on the trail to Khare at 6:30 a.m. But Chris was severely nauseous. He'd been up most of the night vomiting. He was very pale and sickly, but not much worse off than the rest of the group. Half of our members had symptoms of AMS. We were confronted with the same dilemma I faced when I was sick on the trek to Mera in 1999. The sensible decision is to hike back down the trail at least one sleeping stage to try to recover. As in 1999, the 2011 group decided to push on to Mera base camp. We wanted to have the maximum number of days possible to try to climb the peak. If we hiked back down the trail to a lower elevation, and spent at least a day and night there, that would probably blow our chance to climb Mera. It would take two days to hike to Khare after we recovered from AMS, so we'd be behind schedule by at least three days. By the time we got to Mera that would be the date we'd need to hike out to Lukla to catch the scheduled flight back to Kathmandu.

We were all on the trail by 8:00 that morning. Once again, good sense was over-ridden by the desire to try to summit a mountain.

It was a long, hard slog to Khare. We arrived after 5:00 p.m., but not too late for another delicious meal prepared by Purna and his kitchen boys. Pizza was the entree. Every one of our group members, except Karlin and Jeanne, had symptoms of AMS or a head cold. We took a rest day hoping that we would all recover before attempting the climb. The R & R helped, but it was not enough.

It was extremely cold in Khare at night, ten to fifteen degrees below 0 Fahrenheit. It was so cold you didn't want to get out of your sleeping bag once you tucked in; no stargazing at night. During breakfast Mike brought up a particular hazard due to the extreme cold at night. He said it was so cold he didn't get out of his sleeping bag to pee. "When using a pee bottle in your sleeping bag, it's a very technical operation," he muttered dryly.

Despite our weakened condition, after a rest day we practiced mountaineering skills on a hill with our climbing guide, Dendi Sherpa. Dendi met us in Khare. Dendi wanted to make sure that each of us knew how to tie a climber's knot and could rope up wearing a harness. He also tested our skills with ice axes and crampons. With a little practice and instruction, everyone passed Dendi's tests.

Everyone that is, except Mike, because he didn't try. Mike had not planned on climbing Mera and didn't bring any climbing gear. His plan was to hang out and do day hikes around base camp while the rest of us climbed Mera. However, he decided his septuagenarian legs had had enough and he didn't want to trek to Lukla after we finished with Mera Peak. As luck would have it, a helicopter evacuation had been arranged for an injured climber on another climbing team. Mike asked and was granted permission to climb aboard.

Before he left, Mike remarked, "I'm seventy-two. I wanted to set a personal altitude record. We're at 16,200 feet high. Goal accomplished. I'm rich enough to pay for a helicopter ride back to Kathmandu. See ya there." And off he went.

Mike thought he was going to have to pay $2,500 or more for the heli-evac, but Niru urged him to claim it on his insurance. Mike did have the classic symptoms of AMS, so he made a claim and the insurance company paid.

Foiled on Mera Peak for a second time; what's it all about?

As in 1999, all attempts to climb the mountain failed, because the weather conditions were so harsh. Karlin, Ursi, Joel, Chris, and Jeanne climbed up to high camp the day after our skills training. They were blown off the mountain by blizzard conditions along with all the other climbing teams. Many of the porters and kitchen staff, who were sent up to high camp with other teams, were not properly clothed for the severe cold and high winds. Karlin, Ursi, Joel, Chris, and Jeanne gave gloves and trekking poles to some of the Nepalese guys, who were not properly outfitted, to help them get safely back down the mountain.

Heading up to high camp; left to right: Jeanne, Joel, and Chris

In the meantime, Dennis and I were stuck in base camp suffering from Acute Mountain Sickness. It felt like an electric drill was boring into my forehead. I was mildly nauseous and slightly ataxic. In the moments when I felt strong enough to hang out in the very rough and grubby bhatti in Khare, I enjoyed chatting and playing cards with a Kurdish-Iranian climbing team. We talked about life in Iran and international affairs while warming ourselves beside a pot-belly stove fueled with yak dung. All five members of the team agreed the Ayatollah was "a crazy old fucker". The reply to my question about whether they thought the Kurds would ever have their own country was a sigh and a pessimistic, "Inshallah."

The following day Dennis felt strong enough to give the

mountain a go, and went up with Karlin. They were forced down by blizzard conditions. They came down the mountainside with Subash, DB's younger brother, who was in training to become a sirdar. Of all the members of our team, Subash had the worst time on Mera Peak. He spent a night in a tent by himself at high camp waiting for members of our group to make a second attempt to climb the peak. The wind was so strong Subash spent the entire night spread-eagle using his weight to hold the tent down and praying he would not be blown off the mountainside.

Subash looked like a puppy that had been beaten with a broom when he stumbled back into base camp. When I asked DB if Subash was okay, DB chuckled and said, "Subash got good training last night." DB was making sure that little brother was learning the hard way how to become a sirdar. DB related that his first job was portering at age 14. He had to carry as much as 120 pounds. DB felt little sympathy for Subash just because he had an uncomfortable night alone on a mountain.

After Joel's shot at the peak his symptoms of altitude sickness worsened. He too was experiencing excruciating headaches. We talked it over with DB and decided that Joel and I needed to lose altitude to get relief from AMS. Instead of improving with time in base camp, my symptoms were getting worse. DB assigned Subash, Krishna, and Baku to return to Kote with Joel and me. It took seven hours for the five of us to hike back to Kote. It was rather depressing to leave Mera Peak behind for a second time without seeing the views from its summit. The altitude-sickness symptoms of headache, nausea, and ataxia began to fade almost as soon as we arrived at Kote, which is 4,000 feet lower than Khare.

While Joel and I recuperated in Kote, he worked on editing the film he'd shot. I worked on strategic planning for the Basa Foundation. I drew up an organizational chart with multiple committees and made prospective personnel assignments to the committees. I wrote out a mission statement and a detailed explanation of the tenets of "culturally sensitive development". One diversion from my labors was being interviewed by Joel on camera about the history and purpose of the foundation. I looked and sounded terrible. The symptoms of AMS were fading, but not entirely resolved. I know how shitty I looked and sounded, because Joel posted the interview on YouTube. Thankfully, very few people have bothered to view it.

Kote is a striking looking village on a mountainside surrounded by rain forest and above a river. Sitting on a log across the river from the village rapping with Joel was a much more pleasant way to spend time than freezing our asses off in Khare or being whipped by blasts of wind during another failed attempt to climb Mera Peak. Still, I thought maybe I owed that damn mountain another shot some time in the future. Maybe three tries would be a charm.

That kind of thinking is symptomatic of egotistical mountain climbing. Standing on a summit is a worthy goal, but having a beautiful shared-experience is always more meaningful than merely checking off another item on a bucket list. Contrary to the ethos of the 20th Century British mountaineers, "conquering" a mountain should not be what it's all about.

(I can write that last sentence from the comfort of home and in a dispassionate mindset, but I have been guilty of that which I criticize. I also recognize a degree of hypocrisy in claiming that it's a better use of one's time just to enjoy the view and a comrade's company, when I was too sick to climb and now that I've decided I'm too old to train properly for a climb. As to younger, eager adventurers, as Lama Tenzing said, Do what you want to do.)

View of Mera Peak from Kote, October 2011

Another porter dies leaving Mera

Despite the blizzard conditions, there were no serious injuries or deaths on the mountain. Unfortunately, a porter died hiking down from Khare to Kote. He was employed by another group. The porter collapsed and died on the side of the trail, apparently due to cerebral edema. The story we heard was that he was sick in high camp, drank alcohol back in base camp, and then had a seizure on the trail between Khare and Kote. Karlin and Ursi, along with other climbers, tried to resuscitate him, but in vain.

Four porters died in the two times I'd been to Mera Peak. After the three deaths in 1999 I decided that it was unethical to engage in climbing expeditions that put high altitude porters at risk. I backed away from that position, because my Nepali friends argued passionately that the economy of Nepal was so dependent on mountain tourism that its benefits were worth the occasional loss of life of a porter or guide. Progress in protecting porters had been made since the 1990s through government regulations requiring that porters be issued proper cold weather clothing. I knew it would not come to pass, but I wondered whether an even better solution was to require climbers to carry all their own gear above base camp. In other words, outlaw the military-conquest style of climbing and only allow alpine style on the high peaks. Let the porters hang out in base camp, while climbers and guides climb.

The government of Nepal would never agree to that, because many climbers, especially on Everest, could not handle carrying the weight of tents and all their gear to camps above base camp. Fewer climbers would mean less revenue to the government in permit fees. The local people would probably oppose it too, because the pay is higher for porters and guides at higher altitudes. And the strong ones love proving themselves to be the current generation of Sherpa Tigers. (Remember Gheylsan saying the "best thing he'd ever done" was working as a high altitude porter for Hillary and Tenzing.) Nepalis will continue to get injured and die, so that wealthy people from richer countries can have a jolly good adventure summiting a peak. So it goes.

Photos of the trek to Mera Peak and in base camp at Khare ...

Over the Zatrwa La and party time in Lukla

One of the toughest challenges faced on the trek came after we were reunited in Kote. To get to the airport in Lukla we had to hike down the Zatrwa La. The Zatrwa La is the site of the avalanche in 1999, which killed three Nepalese porters when we were trekking from Mera base camp to Lukla. It's where our porters were trapped on the other side of the avalanche and our sirdar, Seth Chettri, rescued them with the help of senior porter Jid Baldoo. It did not bring back warm and fuzzy memories to return to that high pass.

Zatrwa La is actually two passes. The highest point is over 15,000 feet. When our 2011 group stood at the top of the high pass to rest and take photos before the descent, I had to get away from the group. It was a very emotional moment for me. I sobbed quietly for a couple minutes as the memory flooded back; seeing the three porters moving across the high ridge and then disappearing in a white tsunami of snow and ice. It was also disconcerting that I could not figure out exactly where they were in relation to where Seth, Tom, Heather, Judy, and I were when the avalanche struck in 1999. It didn't look the same and I couldn't figure out where the avalanche started. I had to push that feeling of discombobulation out of mind, because the descent in 2011 was also hazardous.

The steep mountainside was covered with snow and ice, but the trail down from the high pass was visible. In 1999 the snow was so deep we couldn't see the trail. The trail in 2011 was extremely slippery, because it was smeared with slick ice and snow. Trying to work your way down was like driving down a mountainside covered with black ice, and you have to negotiate hairpin turns without snow tires or chains. As soon as he started down the pass Baku slipped and fell down. His doko basket broke loose skittering down the icy trail and skidding to a stop ten feet further down the mountainside. I could barely keep my balance using trekking poles and wearing hiking boots with rugged soles. The descent was going to be especially dangerous for porters carrying loads, since most of them wore cheap Chinese-made sneakers. Chris and I shouted for everyone to stop!

We huddled with DB, who didn't seem too worried about the porters slipping and sliding down the rocky mountainside. But he agreed that the trekkers could lend trekking poles to the porters, so each porter had at least one pole to use on the way down. We trekkers could rely on the stability of our superior footwear. We could also use our ice axes, if we chose to, for additional support or for self-arrest, if we fell. I think everyone except Buddhi took at least one tumble as we inched our way down the switchbacks of the trail. Buddhi ran and slid down the mountainside like he was on skis.

Ursi working her way down the Zatrwa La, October 2011

All of our team members, staff and clients, made it safely down both passes of the Zatrwa La. There were several bumps and bruises, but no serious injuries. We crossed the three rivers on the way to Lukla without incident. The symptoms of AMS and head colds were left behind after we crossed the Zatrwa La.

Lukla seemed like a jewel of sophisticated civilization compared to the remote areas we'd experienced since leaving Basa. There was even a faux Starbucks.

We had a day to enjoy the local market and to gawk at trekking groups flying in to commence their treks up the Base Camp trail. Fresh faced trekkers disembarking from flights in to Lukla from Kathmandu looked so clean and peppy compared to how beat up and scruffy our group looked and felt.

None of the guys in our crew were flying with us back to Kathmandu. DB, Buddhi, Subash, Purna and most of the guys were planning to walk all the way back to their homes in Basa as soon as they saw us off from the airport. I mentioned to DB that it seemed unfair that we got to fly, while he and the crew had to walk. He laughed and said they would not be walking. They planned to run home to Basa, because they didn't want to miss the Diwali festivities. Some of our porters were supposed to meet another AGT group in Lukla after our departure. Clients from Germany were flying in to trek the Base Camp Trail; no rest for those weary porters.

No tears were shed the last night we were all together in Lukla. We had a rollicking going-away party. We engaged in the traditional singing and dancing in a lodge by our campsite. Our crew members were delighted with the tips and gifts we gave them. It had been a rough couple weeks since we left Basa -- so many of us got sick and no one summitted Mera. But we had bonded as a team. And we were still feeling enthusiastic about the future of the Basa Foundations. The affection and admiration we felt for the guys that carried our heavy loads, set up camp every day, and cooked great meals for us fired our desire to give back to the village that had produced such strong and kind people.

While Joel and I were away from the group recuperating in Kote, I witnessed how deeply he'd been touched by his two visits to Basa. The magnetism that kept pulling me back was working on him too. Chris and Jeanne were already planning a return visit for just the two of them. Basa magnetism pulled Dennis back again in 2017. When Mike returned in 2017 he brought three generations of the Miller Clan. My dream to develop philanthro-trekking as a way to involve Americans, and now Swiss, as well as South Africans, was meshing with Niru's dream to improve life in his home village.

It was also turning Basa into a tourist destination.

End of the trek party in Lukla, late October 2011

Murder-Suicide, Water for Basa, Rough Medicine, and the Caste System
Basa Trek of Marian University Students and Friends 2013

Namaste BVF members,
I want to let you know about the death of a dear friend, Ray
Schaefer. Ray gave $20,000 from his family trust fund to our
Water Project, which took us over the top for the $29,000 budget.
Ray killed his long-time partner and then took his own life. Ray
was fulfilling the clearly stated wish of his partner, Dr. Juan
Vigura, to have his life ended because of severe pain and
incurable medical conditions. Juan has been in nursing/hospice
care for over a year. The terrible choice Ray made was due, in
Ray's view, because the law allowed no other way to end Juan's
suffering. Ray told me and left notes to the effect that his life
had two purposes: to care for Juan and to give all his money
away to fund scholarships for Palestinian refugee
children. (Ray's scholarship fund has provided scholarships to
over 200 Palestinian refugees.) Ray believed the only way he
could finally fulfill his first purpose was to kill Juan and then
himself. And so he did what he considered a final act of love for
Juan and Palestinian students. Shortly before his suicide Ray
made the $20,000 donation to our water project for Basa Village.

I sent that email to the members of the BVF-USA and to Niru on
January 9, 2014; nine days after Ray shot Juan in the head and
himself in the mouth. Ray was 72-years old and in good health. Ray
was a dear, sweet person with a highly developed sense of justice,
compassion, and humility. His gift made the water project for Basa
possible. Construction began just before Ray killed Juan and himself
on New Year's Eve.
    A year before the murder-suicide Ray heard me speak about
trekking in Nepal and the development philosophy of the Basa
Foundation at the Mid-North Shepherd's Center, which is an
organization for older adults in Indianapolis. Ray button-holed me
after the meeting. He wanted to learn more about the prospective
water project for Basa the BVF-USA was considering. Ray was very
interested in the politics, history, and infrastructural development
of Nepal. We began meeting every month for lunch. Ray became so

well versed in the history of development efforts in Nepal that he was soon educating me about the subject. Ray spoke as a guest lecturer to the class I taught at Marian University spring semester 2013 and at Butler University fall 2014 about "doing philanthropy the right way".

Ray's terrible-beautiful act of killing Juan and himself pierced my heart and cast a dark shadow in my own mind over the water project. At our last lunch meeting Ray told me of his plan to do the murder-suicide. He said the only way he could put Juan out of his misery was to kill him – which Juan wanted him to do – because Indiana law prohibited euthanasia. Ray didn't want to live without Juan, and he wanted to give his $250,000 estate to the Palestinian cause rather than spending it on himself in his own waning years. Ray asked me to explain his reasons to the world. I told him that I didn't think the world would understand and probably wouldn't care.

After several email exchanges and phone conversations, I thought I had talked Ray out of his murder-suicide plan. Ray realized how upset and concerned for him that I was. He told me he'd changed his mind to make me feel better. He also sent me an email confirming our next lunch meeting. Ray realized that I was worried about being accused of failing to report a crime I knew he intended to commit. To give me moral and legal cover, he deceived me by telling me he'd changed his mind. If need be, I could use his last email to me as evidence that I reasonably believed he wasn't going through with the plan.

But the deed was done. The $29,000 needed for the Basa Water Project was raised, and DB's wish to supervise the project was fulfilled. There were, however, complications with the execution of the water project. A lot of work went into planning the water system before ground was broken.

Shortly after our 2011 group returned from Kathmandu, the BVF-Nepal team began working up a plan and budget for the water project. Niru emailed a detailed budget in February, 2012. Our BVF board thought it wise to get an engineer involved in the planning. By posting a notice on a Phi Beta Kappa message board I found an environmental engineer willing to volunteer for the project. Amleto had traveled in Nepal and was excited to help with the water project. He had worked on similar projects in Kenya. Niru sent a sketch that DB prepared showing his plan for piping water from the Mauri Khola into the village. Amleto developed a series of questions for Niru's team to answer about the flow of the river, the topography of the land, water usage habits of the villagers, quality of the water, etc. Amleto's list of questions was six pages long. For several months Niru and his team tried to gather the information Amleto requested. Emails were exchanged back and forth, but the Basa guys were unable to provide many of the details Amleto wanted. They didn't know the exact elevation of the water source or the multiple points in the village Amleto requested. They couldn't supply to Amleto all of the specifications of materials that he requested.

Over time Amleto and Niru became more and more frustrated with each other. The tone of their emails was always polite, but their frustrations were expressed to me as the "go-between". Niru explained that his team didn't have the knowledge or expertise to develop much of the information Amleto required. Amleto maintained that the requested information was necessary for him to design a system that would not fail. The "rough" proposal DB prepared was simply inadequate.

I was becoming exasperated with both sides. I hadn't signed up to be a moderator. Working out the plan for the hydroelectric system had been so much easier! Why couldn't we just get on with it?

The crucial difference was that BVF-Nepal had retained a local engineer to draw up the plans for the electrical system. Then, Mike Miller went to Basa and talked through the plans with Chandra, the local engineer. Niru didn't think a local engineer was necessary for the water system, since DB and his guys had drawn up a plan and priced out all the costs. At Amleto's insistence, Niru hired "the best available surveyor of this region" to perform a survey. Amleto was still not satisfied with the information received. He judged the photos and sketches sent with the survey inadequate. Amleto emailed me complaining that "the project hydraulic design is mostly based on a generic one that was provided by the Nepal Government."

If Amleto could have traveled to Nepal and talked through the plan with DB and walked with him over the terrain, I'm sure that would have broken the log jam. Unfortunately, Amleto's personal and professional situation didn't allow him that freedom. But, Halleluiah! I found a volunteer environmental engineer who was willing to go to Basa.

Ben Snyder was in the Army Corps of Engineers. He was looking for more adventurous outlets. Ben told me that he didn't have the personal funds to pay for a roundtrip to Nepal, but he thought he could raise the money to cover his airfare through an online fundraising campaign. It worked!

Ben needed a GPS rangefinder to properly survey the different elevation points for the water system. The BVF-USA paid $500 to purchase one, which was the only item added to the budget to help Ben perform an onsite study. Ben stayed at Niru's house while he was in Kathmandu. He trekked to Basa with Paul Rai, a porter-guide supplied by AGT.

In the meantime, Niru had hired a Nepali engineer, Bharu Man Rai, to prepare a project design to try to meet Amleto's requirements. With the GPS elevation measurements and his own survey of the water source and terrain, Ben was able to confirm that Bharu's plan should work. A major concern of Amleto was whether the force of the Mauri Khola's flow had the power to push the water to the village. And, if it did, was the system designed to reduce the force of the flow enough so it wouldn't blast out of taps at the villagers' homes so powerful it would blow out the bottoms of their buckets? So as not to bore (if you're not already) the non-engineers with the details, Ben determined that Bharu's plan handled those issues. He sent his comments to Amleto. They concluded that Bharu's design should bring water to the 62 homes controllable by turning the handle of a tap.

After Ben arrived back in the States he sent this email to Niru:

Namaste Niru! I made it back safely to the US. It was a wonderful visit to Nepal and I'm truly grateful for your hospitality and help with my trip! Although I'm happy to be back with my family, I miss Nepal already.

Ben was so stoked from his experience in Nepal that he joined the board of BVF-USA.

When Mike and I began discussing the water project with DB and Niru, we assumed there would be a filtration system to make the water safe for drinking. To our surprise, we learned the villagers did not want any type of filter for their water system. They drank water straight out of the river, and they wanted to continue drinking water from the Mauri Khola au natural as it came out of a tap. Ben was also surprised that filtration was not part of the plan, but he accepted that as the villagers' prerogative. He conveyed this in an email:

> It appeared that they don't tend to drink plain water the way we tend to. Mostly they drank chang, rakshi, tea, or yak milk. Sometimes hot water boiled in a kettle, like tea without the tea. My guide, Paul, had no concern with drinking straight from hoses draining rice paddies we encountered on the trail, although he recognized that I would be risking grave illness if I followed suit. There's definitely enough pressure to run a filtration system on the main between the source and the 10m3 tank. But is it worth it to treat all the water, when they'll use only a small fraction for drinking? Only they can answer, and without more data and/or education, it appears the answer is no for now.

During the winter of 2014 DB organized the residents of Basa into work crews. They built the water system that Amleto, Ben, and Bharu designed.

Professor Rasley

In May of 2013 I visited Basa and saw the stacks of PVC, bags of concrete, and other materials acquired for the water project. The trekking group I led to Basa that year came about in a unique way. In the fall of 2012 an old friend and fellow attorney, Jerry Williams, asked me to meet with his granddaughter Jessica and her friend Josh. They were seniors at Marian University. The two of them had read my book, *Bringing Progress to Paradise*. The book inspired in Jessica and Josh the desire to visit Nepal and trek to Basa Village.

I met with Jessica and Josh over coffee, and they asked whether I'd be willing to teach a work-study class at MU. Their idea was that we could design a class for their final semester before graduation in 2013. They'd get credit for the class and then travel to Nepal under the aegis of Marian University right after they graduated.

Their plan immediately appealed to me. I had spent so much time researching, discussing, and contemplating the right way to do philanthropy. The opportunity to share with college students what I'd learned from philanthro-trekking expeditions and the projects of the Basa Foundations was an exciting prospect.

I submitted a proposal to Marian's academic dean to teach a one-semester three-credit-hour International Studies course within the MU Honors Program. Josh and Jessica were both honors students. Students would have the option of writing a final term paper and not doing a service project in Nepal or writing up a proposal for a service project and then implementing the project in Nepal. The proposal was accepted. I began teaching my first college class as an adjunct professor spring semester 2013.

One of the most interesting features of the class was doing a comparative case study between Greg Mortensen's Central Asia Institute (CAI) and the Basa Foundations. The students first read Mortenson's *3 Cups of Tea*. The reaction of most of the students was awe of Mortenson. Like wow, man! He was this cool climber dude who got lost on K2 was rescued by a village and was so grateful he spent the next decade of his life running a foundation that built 200 schools in Pakistan and Afghanistan. (Please forgive the author for representing Millennial students with 70s slang.) Then, they read Jon Krakauer's *3 Cups of Deceit*. Bummer! That Mortenson dude is a lying hypocrite. He went parading around the country dressed in a robe and acting like some kind of guru, raised millions of dollars, and claimed he built 200 schools. His foundation only built half the number of schools they claimed and many of the ones built were never used. Mortenson and his board of directors got kicked out and he had to pay back a million bucks by order of the Montana Attorney General. That was doing philanthropy the wrong way, man.

I did not try to indoctrinate the students into my own way of thinking. I showed them the path I found by putting *Bringing Progress to Paradise* on the reading list and explaining the philosophy of culturally sensitive development Niru and I worked out. Aside from the lies Mortenson told, the significant differences between his approach and that of the Basa Foundations were:

1. Many of the locations of schools the CAI built were chosen by war lords and government officials. That is, many of the schools were built at locations by decree of powerful interests from above rather than where there was the greatest need. Many of the schools were not run by local people. BVF projects are all done at the request of local people, not the government or powerful people in Kathmandu. The school, electric system, and water system are run as cooperatives with the local people managing them by committee.

2. Mortenson paid work crews to come in to villages to build schools. The villagers themselves provide all the basic labor to build BVF projects.

3. Mortenson was paid a substantial salary and all sorts of expenses were paid by funds donated to the CAI. BVF officers and members have never been paid a dime and are not reimbursed travel expenses to visit Basa and check on our projects. We have paid the fees of Nepali engineers, charges for porters to transport materials, teachers' salaries, skilled stone masons, and we expect to pay the salaries of medical personnel at a planned medical center in the Basa area. So far we've managed to obtain free professional services here in the US. Before he unexpectedly died, our attorney, Chuck Richmond, worked pro bono, and even paid the federal fees for tax exempt registration. I've paid all state registration fees in Indiana, and Joel Meyers has paid Washington State fees.

4. Mortenson devoted a great deal of his time and the CAI's budget to promotion (mostly about himself and his book) and marketing. The BVF has not spent any money on marketing. We do fundraisers for specific projects. We don't do any marketing beyond having a website and what our members volunteer to do for specific projects. Being able to say that all funds raised go to the planned projects has been compelling enough that every project's budget has

been met.

It is noteworthy that Greg Mortenson did try to make amends for his deceit of donors and misuse of CAI funds. After he was forced to resign as president, he continued working for the CAI in the field for another ten years. He resigned in 2016.

What is also noteworthy is how easily Greg Mortenson was able to take advantage of so many good-hearted people who read his book or heard him give a talk. He looked, acted, and sounded so authentic. Without doing any sort of due diligence to check on how the CAI was operated and where the donations actually went, all sorts of people, from school children to major corporate donors, gave millions to the CAI. After Mortenson's misuse of funds and the many lies in his international best-seller, *3 Cups of Tea*, were exposed by Jon Krakauer's *3 Cups of Deceit* and in an investigative report on *60 Minutes*, the amount of donations substantially declined. Yet, some people had become followers of Mortenson as if he was their guru. They continue to believe in the self-created mythology of Mortenson and the CAI. Mortenson's story touched a deep place in his followers' hearts and some prefer to follow where their hearts lead them without engaging in rational analysis.

A fundamental principle I wanted my Marian U students to adopt when engaging in philanthropic endeavors is to do it with both their hearts and minds. Philanthropy means love of humanity, from the Greek *philos* (love) *anthropos* (humanity). If you are inspired to work for, or give to, a charitable organization or cause, doesn't it make sense that the cause or organization reflects your own values, what you truly care about? Then you should carefully consider whether the time or treasure you are giving to a particular organization or cause will achieve your philanthropic goals. Time and money are limited resources. Use them wisely. (That "wisdom lesson" is elaborated in my book, *Godless – Living a Valuable Life beyond Beliefs*, which was not on the reading list for the course.) "Be skeptical and watch out for charlatans" is a valuable lesson for the young and their elders. (A lesson US voters should have learned before the 2016 Presidential Election.)

Graduating seniors and senior citizen trekkers; the fire next door
Only three students out of twelve chose to go to Nepal in May 2013, Jessica, Josh, and David. The others opted to write final term

papers. I wasn't surprised that so few of my students were unable to travel to Nepal immediately after their graduation from college. It is unusual for young Americans to go trekking in the Himalayas. Few can afford the cost. Unlike some other countries in which a grand tour of the world after graduation is common, American graduates are expected to get on with life, go to grad school or land that first important job toward building a career. It isn't uncommon to see young people trekking from countries like Israel, New Zealand, Australia, the UK, and Western European countries; but young Americans, rarely.

Still, our trekking group numbered thirteen, counting me. Most of the group members fit into two different classes of seniors. There were the three MU graduating seniors plus two friends of theirs, Justin and James. Justin had just graduated from Marian and was Jessica's boyfriend. James just graduated from the University of Kentucky. The most senior members of the group were In Sook, a retired Indiana University pathology professor and Korean-American, and Jerry, Jessica's grandfather, who got the ball rolling for the MU class. Ole Dave (distinguished from the MU graduate David) was president of the Hoosier Backpackers Club and a retired design engineer. Dr. Patti was an about-to-retire family practice physician in her early 60s and a member of Hoosier Backpackers. Dr. William, a friend and UChicago classmate of mine and ER doc in Chicago. His friend Taissa was a few years younger than William and me. But all of us were old enough to be parents or grandparents of the students. The one outlier was Lauren, who was in her 30s. She planned to meet her friend, Mary, in Kathmandu after the trek to visit Tiger Tops and ride elephants.

Most of us flew to Kathmandu on Qatar Airlines, which was quite a change for me. I'd always flown Asian carriers, usually Royal Thai or Cathay Pacific, with layovers in Bangkok or Hong Kong. The airport in Doha was not as large and had fewer ways to distract oneself from the discomfort of a ten-hour layover than the more impressive airports I'd experienced in Asia and Japan. (A new airport has since been built in Doha.) It was also weird seeing men swaggering around in beautiful long flowing white cape-like-shirts (called a *thobe* in Arabic) and long, white headdresses (*ghutra*) held in place with a black rope, while two or three women followed in their wake. The women were completely hidden in their shapeless

390

black burkas.

A terrible design flaw in the airport (for god's sake I hope not replicated in the new one) was that the smoking room was right beside the sleeping room. The smoking room was very popular and the door was left open. Every time someone entered the sleeping room, smoke would get sucked in from the smoking room. Phuuh! It was difficult to fall asleep in a cloud of fetid cigarette smoke. After inhaling enough putrid smoke to drive my sleep-deprived body out of the sleeping room, I discovered an area on the upper floor that had lounge chairs and blankets reserved for tired travelers.

Ah, but the Kathmandu Guest House (KGH), with its pleasant courtyard and tea with my old friend Uttam the manager, would surely ease the irritating discomforts of the thirty-some hours of air travel. It did, until a fire broke out in a saloon next door to the KGH our first night in Nepal.

The phrase to describe comical incompetence should be changed from "a Chinese fire drill" to "a Nepali fire drill". A water truck showed up about 45 minutes after flames were leaping out of the windows and doors of the structure. The couplings for the hose didn't fit the truck. It left and came back about twenty minutes later. The second hose worked, but the water tank was only half full. When the truck returned a third time the restaurant had already burned to the ground. In the meantime, Pilgrims Bookstore, on the other side of the restaurant, caught fire and burned down. Pilgrims was a Kathmandu institution. It was a Mecca for book lovers, which also sold beautiful handmade Nepali stationary. It was the only place in Nepal one could purchase *Bringing Progress to Paradise*. Its entire stock of books and stationary was destroyed. What a loss!

The KGH staff ordered everyone to pack up and bring all bags into the courtyard. About half of the guests complied. KGH bell hops turned a couple garden hoses on the fire next door. A bunch of young men threw stones at the fire. It looked like fun, so I chucked a few over the KGH's wall at the flaming building next door. Josh and James acquitted themselves well, helping to drag hoses and joining in a bucket brigade to prevent the fire from leaping over the KGH's concrete wall. When the threat to the KGH had passed, they returned to the lobby covered in soot and looking quite the young heroes.

On the road and trail again

We passed work crews on the bus ride to Jiri. The road's surface was much improved since the first time I drove it in 2008. The road from Jiri to Shivalaya was not much improved. Our bus shook and rattled over potholes and unpaved stretches.

The only bridge over the Khimti Khola I remembered was a foot bridge, so I wondered how the bus was going to cross the river. The driver backed down the hill to the riverside. When we realized he was going to drive across the river, rather than let us unload and carry all our gear over the foot bridge, there was a little panic among some of our members. The river had a firm rocky bottom and was only about two feet deep at the time. The flow appeared to be about two miles per hour. I was familiar with this spot at the river, because in 2010 I'd bathed just on the other side from where the bus driver planned to drive across. I didn't think the bus would tip over in the current, but I wasn't one-hundred percent sure. Ganesh and I advised everyone who didn't feel comfortable riding in the bus across the river to get out and use the foot bridge. Josh and James, two of the more adventurous members in the group, whooped with delight at the prospect of riding across the river in a bus. And so we did.

Our crew of porters, kitchen boys, and Purna the cook were waiting for us in Shivalaya. The first meal of the trek cooked by Purna featured multiple courses of local veggies, roti, chapatti, rice, chicken, spam, and rice pudding and cake for dessert. A worrisome development was that Jerry and Dr. Patti both skipped dinner and retired to their tents without eating. David, Josh, and I explored the village and walked back down to the river. Shivalaya was coming into its own as a first or last stop for trekkers who wanted to do the classic Base Camp Trek. The new lodges had plenty of customers. Shivalaya no longer looked like a dying town out of an old Wild West movie set. The Sherpa couple who ran the lodge by our campsite did not have the gaunt look of yak herders. They looked well fed and prosperous.

The first full morning of hiking went well. The weather was clear and we enjoyed another Purna-prepared feast over lunch. The kitchen boys spread a flower-patterned table-cloth over a long folding-table. There were condiments to please every palate, honey, mustard, ketchup, horse radish, mayo, and even a bottle of Durkee

Sauce. Whatever anyone wanted to spread on a sardine, spam, or lamb-strip sandwich, or add to peanut butter and jelly, was laid out on the table.

Lunch the first day on the trail for the 2013 group; left to right around the table: Jerry, Justin, Jessica, David, Josh, In Sook, Ole Dave, Taissa, James, Lauren, and Jeff. Patti is missing, because she took this photo. Dr. William is missing, because...

William is not pictured because he didn't leave Kathmandu with the group. William was suffering from either plantar fasciitis or a chipped bone in his foot. He and Taissa argued so vehemently at the KGH about whether he could handle the trek or not they missed the initial excitement of the fire due to the intensity of their argument. William decided the medical advice he should give himself was to skip the trek and do some touring around Nepal. After two days of such pedestrian activities, William decided he had come to Nepal to run a temporary medical clinic in Basa, and he was going to do it. Although we had a two-day head start, William set out with DB as his porter-guide to catch up with the group.

Monsoon trekking, lost in rhododendrons, and return to Ngar Gompa
The weather turned during the afternoon hike to Bhandar. First,

dark-grey clouds rolled in and then it began to drizzle. Before we reached our campsite, the drizzle turned into a steady rain. Unfortunately, that was the weather pattern we experienced almost every day, until we arrived in Basa. The monsoon typically started no earlier than the second week in June. In 2013 the monsoon began in mid May. Wearing raincoats or ponchos and covering backpacks with a rain fly became a dreary part of the daily trekking routine for the 2013 group.

Ganesh and I were determined to make sure the youngsters and oldsters had a meaningful, not just a miserable rain-soaked, experience. We participated in a chanting ceremony with the monks at Namkhile Gompa, which is a small rustic monastery. The students were impressed and the oldsters moved. Our programme did not include spending a night at Ngar Gompa with old Lama Paldung and his wife, but I thought meeting Paldung and hearing his poignant story would be interesting to the group. Ganesh agreed. So we made the long and difficult detour up to Ngar. The rhododendron trees were in full bloom mid May. It was lovely hiking up to the monastery through a forest of flowering trees surrounded with their rich pungent odor. That is, until we discovered Taissa was missing. After an hour of searching we found her on the wrong path. She was so taken by the beauty of the

rhododendrons, with a little extra help from some hash she'd scored in Kathmandu, she was, like, wow man! I'm lost. Cool!

Rhododendron forest below Ngar Gompa; photo by Dr. Patti Binder 2013

At 9,000 feet Ngar Gompa was above the rain. It felt good to dry out while taking in the dramatic view from the monastery of the cloud-covered valley we'd trekked through that afternoon. I sat by myself outside of the monastery grounds on a boulder just enjoying the view for fifteen or twenty minutes, until Taissa joined me. She apologized for causing trouble by getting lost. I reassured her that it was little trouble, and the crew was used to us silly Westerners losing our way in the mountains. Being high on hash and digging the beauty around her was a better excuse for getting lost than the excuses I had for the several times I'd managed to get lost on a trek.

Taissa and I sat awhile and watched the clouds moving across the huge valley below and sweep around a mountain ridge in the distance. On the other side of the monastery the clouds crashed like waves into the great white peaks to the north trying to breach the wall of mountains between Nepal and Tibet. Then it was time to introduce the group to Lama Paldung and his wife.

From Ngar Gompa, May 2013

It was a poignant experience to witness old Lama Paldung's joy in hosting our group, especially our fresh-faced college graduates. I imagined he wished he could keep them as his own students. Recall the tale of woe he related during our visit in 2010 about the likelihood that the monastery would close when he died. There were no novice monks studying under him and no other lama was willing to live in such an isolated place. Still, he enjoyed showing us the gompa's collection of wood carvings of Buddha. Paldung related the story of his lazy great-uncle, who had the Buddha images made for the gompa instead of fulfilling the physically demanding vow he'd made to do 10,000 prostrations. Our youngsters and oldsters laughed at the story. They were also impressed by Lama Paldung's little solar-powered generator, which provided enough electricity to light his study.

Left to right: the author, Lama Paldung, and Ganesh Rai; some of the carved Buddhas are in the background. Photo by Dr. Patti Binder.

Finding William, losing Jerry, and over Lamjura La

The hike from Ngar to Pikey Peak base camp was depressing. The clouds rolled in again and the afternoon drizzle returned. We donned rain gear for the fourth day in a row. The cloud cover was so thick we could barely see the flowering rhododendron trees lining the trail. Pikey Peak was completely invisible.

There was a delightful surprise, which ameliorated the gloominess of the weather. Just before we left Ngar William came hobbling into the monastery leaning heavily on one trekking pole. He was followed by DB carrying William's duffel. Even though William limped all the way on his injured foot, they caught up to us in four days, despite our two-day head start. DB looked almost fresh in an unstained white, long-sleeved polyester shirt. William, on the other hand, was pretty bedraggled looking in dirty blue jeans and a rank-looking work shirt. But William smiled broadly and shared hugs all around. He was psyched up with deserved pride for having ignored the pain in his foot to trek the distance in two days it had taken the group to hike in four.

As we set off for Pikey base-camp, DB waved good-bye. Then, he set off on his solitary hike back to Kathmandu. He hoped to hitch a ride in Shivalaya or Jiri.

Our programme scheduled a hike up to the summit of Pikey Peak before sunset. The views and photography would be fantastic! But Ganesh decided it would be too dangerous and all we'd be able to see was the inside of a cloud. The heavy fog around the base of Pikey Peak allowed about ten feet of visibility.

Another depressing development was that illness struck down two of our comrades. The second day of the trek Josh and I had raced the last hour or so to see who could be the first to the campsite at Bandar. He won, but he got sick that night. I suspected he'd over-exerted himself, lowered his resistance, and caught a bug. Or, maybe he had AMS, given the rapid altitude gain we'd made in the last 24 hours. We exceeded the "no more than 1,000 foot altitude gain for sleeping" rule at Ngar. Josh was a big, strong guy, a standout high school football player with a mass of red hair. By the time we got to Pikey base-camp he was puking and runnin' on empty.

Even more troubling, Jerry had symptoms at Shivalaya which appeared to be food poisoning. Instead of improving after two days on antibiotics, his symptoms were getting worse. He couldn't eat or drink. Even tiny sips of water came back up. He was getting ataxic and had a hell of a tough time hiking the few hours from Ngar to Pikey. His condition looked very similar to the parasitic infection Bruce developed in 2009. Although Jerry was a lowland-dwelling Hoosier, he had climbed Kilimanjaro and trekked through the Andes without altitude problems. So it seemed most likely he picked up a nasty bug in Kathmandu same as Bruce. After a miserable day and night in Pikey base-camp, and after consulting with Drs. Patti and William, Ganesh decided he had to call in a heli-evac for Jerry.

It was a crushing blow. In a way, Jerry was the force that brought us all to that place. He had connected Jessica and Josh with me. He encouraged us to submit a proposal to the dean at Marian University for the international studies course. Yet, he was the sole member of the group who did not make it to Basa. Prakesh looked after Jerry, while they waited two more days for a helicopter. How they were both not driven mad with boredom, I can only imagine. Jerry reported later that he did have a good time while recovering in Kathmandu at a beautiful resort hotel with a swimming pool and gorgeous views overlooking the Kathmandu Valley.

Our hopes for cloud clearance by the morning were dashed. The fog was still so thick around Pikey there would be nothing to see from the summit, and the climb up would be too risky in Ganesh's opinion for so many novice trekkers. With Josh leaning heavily on trekking poles, we waved good-bye to Jerry and Prakesh as we hiked out of base camp through fog and drizzle toward Junbesi.

The weather was so crappy and rainy and our progress so slow we didn't make it to Junbesi as planned. The day wasn't all gloom and doom. A moment of levity occurred at a stream crossing. Logs were laid across it as a bridge. However, In Sook declared that at 70-years-old with her short, little Korean legs she was not going to risk falling off the logs into the stream. Ganesh nodded at Santosh, a sirdar in training. Santosh dropped his load, picked up In Sook with her pack still on her back and waded across the stream with In Sook hanging on for dear life. The group clapped and cheered.

The rain let up as we hiked up the Lamjura Pass, which is about 10,000 feet high. The trail up and over the la is not particularly steep and it is well marked and well worn. It's just high and a long slog. There is even a bhatti near the top, which offered a much appreciated rest stop for a warm cup of dudh chiyaa. Unfortunately, it was still foggy. What we hoped would be another photo op of mountain views was another disappointment.

Down the other side of the pass and we were below the clouds and once again hiking in the rain. Ganesh called a halt just before dusk at an isolated lodge, which looked like a Nepali version of the witch's cottage in the Hansel and Gretel fable. The location was identified on my "Jiri-Pikey-Everest Map" as Toktor.

Another unpleasant aspect of the early monsoon was that it brought out the dreaded bloodsucking leeches. Wherever there were trees overhanging the trail, leeches dropped onto our caps, rain hats, and shoulders. Ganesh's decision to spend the night in a lodge was partly based on pity for our delectable white flesh. The lodge had a few small rooms and a big open bunk room on the upper floor. Patti and Ole Dave hung their hammocks up and William set up a tent inside the bunk room for privacy. The rest of us doubled up in rooms and the crew prepared to sleep in the dining room.

The evening's entertainment consisted of gathering around the lodge's potbelly stove, drinking Orange Fanta, and playing with the Didi's little tyke. He was quite a curious little fellow. He touched our noses and pulled gently at our ears. He was especially fascinated with Josh's mass of red hair and Jessica and Lauren's blond hair.

Lama on ice and Donkey Shit Trail

The rain god was merciful the following day on the short hike to Junbesi. It was overcast, but pleasantly temperate in the mid 60s Fahrenheit. James and I played volleyball with high school kids at the Hillary School. But one of the most interesting and marvelous experiences of the trek was spending the day at Tutenchholing, aka Choling Gompa.

Choling is a Tibetan-Buddhist monastery complex which had over 400 resident nuns and 100 monks in 2013. Most of the nuns and monks were Tibetan refugees. We visited the gompa's medical school and hospital, where both Western and traditional Tibetan homeopathic-medicine is practiced. Our monk-guide gave us a basic lesson in Tibetan medicine. He explained that the practitioner learns the routes of energy flow within the human body and seeks to balance and harmonize mind and body working with the "chakras", which are the vortices of one's life energy.

The interior of the monastery's main temple is covered with fantastical paintings of demons, gods, and spirits in bright colors. The body of the founder of Choling Gompa,

Rimpoche Trukling, is kept on ice with the expectation that he will arise when a new age comes. In a side room of the temple 2,000 candles burn at all times. One of the monks we met said it was his job to replace each candle before it burned out, so 2,000 are always burning.

I made a vow years ago at Tengboche Monastery that I would not visit Tibet or China until the Dalai Lama is allowed to return. Tutenchholing may be the closest I will come to experiencing Tibet in this life.

Photos of Choling Gompa:
The one to the right is of a portion of an internal wall in the temple. The internal walls are painted with sacred scenes of Tibetan-Buddhist mythology and legends.
Above right is of the room with 2,000 candles. It was taken by Dr. Patti Binder.
The tomb where the body of the founder of Choling Gompa, Rimpoche Trukling, is kept on ice is pictured above on the left.

We were blessed with another day without rain on the trail to Nunthala. But the trail turned into a mud slide near Ringmu Village. That was station of the mule-train transport-industry in the region. We followed and dodged long trains of mules on the way in and out of Ringmu. Hundreds of mules decided the best time to defecate was while we were sharing the trail with them. I don't remember whether it was David or Josh, both of whom had considered the priesthood as a vocation, who christened the trail to Ringmu "the Donkey Shit Trail".

What a joy to be back in the beautiful town of Nunthala with its white-washed homes and sky blue roofs after spending most of the day hiking through mud and mule feces. I told the group to be on the lookout for *chyasi* berries, which were the delicious berries Nirman and Hamid picked and shared with Mike, Cathy, and me in October 2010 outside of Nunthala. Unfortunately, late May was too early in the season for ripe berries. That evening Prakesh came huffing into our campsite. He ran all day from Pikey base-camp after seeing Jerry off in a helicopter. That was unfortunate enough, but we also discovered that Ringmu is the union station of the mule-train transport-industry in the region. We followed and dodged long trains of mules on the way in and out of Ringmu. Hundreds of mules decided the best time to defecate was while we were sharing the trail with them. I don't remember whether it was David or Josh, both of whom had considered the priesthood as a vocation, who christened the trail to Ringmu "the Donkey Shit Trail".

What a joy to be back in the beautiful town of Nunthala with its white-washed homes and sky blue roofs after spending most of the day hiking through mud and mule feces. I told the group to be on the lookout for *chyasi* berries, which were the delicious berries Nirman and Hamid picked and shared with Mike, Cathy, and me in October 2010 outside of Nunthala. Unfortunately, late May was too early in the season for ripe berries. That evening Prakesh came huffing into our campsite. He ran all day from Pikey base-camp after seeing Jerry off in a helicopter.

David and Lauren on the Donkey Shit Trail

Basa family history and a temporary medical clinic
The following day we arrived in Basa. And yes, we were met by
the village band on the trail above the village. They thumped and
tooted and led us down to the Welcome arch, which was wrapped
in fresh pine branches. Fewer villagers turned out to welcome us
than had lined up with flower garlands for my previous visits. But
there were more than enough well-wishers to drape marigold leis
around the necks of our group members until our faces were hidden
by flowers.

It turned out that the timing of our visit was unfortunate.
Ganesh informed us that all of the teachers were at a conference in
Sombare, and many of the men were attending "the festival of full
moon at the cave temple". He said, "Men will return tomorrow, but
won't see teachers for two days."

Tek Bahadur and a couple other village elders gave the
traditional welcoming speeches. The grandmotherly rakshi pushers
insisted we sample their best rakshi. The crew set up our tents, and
Purna cooked up another feast. We walked around the village and
visited the homes of many of our staff members. It was good to see

the hydroelectric system functioning well, the smokeless stoves being used, and the computers appeared to be in good working order. All the school supplies provided by BVF members and the Indiana Department of Education were neatly stacked in the principal's office. We delivered a batch of children's picture-books BVF member Jane Rubesch donated to the school. Ganesh showed me the stacks of PVC pipe and bags of cement to be used for the water project. Yet, for all these "improvements" the village looked the same as when I first saw it in 2008.

My image of Basa as a delicate flower, which needed protection, was changing. The village's culture and the strength of its community were proving to be more impervious to outside influence than I feared. My worries about harming the local culture were somewhat, but not entirely, assuaged.

Santosh Basnet was especially well liked by the members of our group. He was training to become a sirdar. Santosh was better dressed and better groomed than any of the other members of the crew. His hair was a finer texture and his features were more delicate than most of the Rai men I knew. He looked more like a Brahmin or Chettri. So it wasn't too surprising to learn that Santosh's family caste is Chettri rather than Rai. I asked Santosh how it came to pass that his family lived in Basa. He told me that, according to the oral history of his family, over 300 years ago five Basnet families came to Basa, but only his family still lives in Basa. He feels as much a part of the community as his Rai neighbors. He knows the Rai family histories as well as his own.

It was interesting to visit Santosh's home and see the generational contrast between him and his very sweet 78-year-old grandmother, Lali Maya Basnet. She served us tea and potatoes, while Santosh and her doted on each other. Their bond was so strong, yet Santosh seemed so worldly in comparison. He had been to Kathmandu and exposed to the ways of Westerners by working on trekking expeditions. Especially since he was Chettri by blood, would he be content to live in Basa and follow the old ways? My worries were not entirely put to rest.

Village grandmothers pouring a cup of rakshi for the visitors; Santosh and his grandmother; Basa Village 2013

One of the most interesting projects the Basa Foundations sponsored occurred during our visit in 2013. While the rest of us were visiting homes our first day in the village, William and Patti turned a classroom in the school into a temporary medical clinic. Niru informed the local grapevine that two American medical doctors were coming to Basa to offer medical services. The clinic wasn't supposed to open until the following day, but villagers started lining up while Patti and William organized their supplies and instruments. They began seeing patients that evening.

A steady stream of local people from all around the Basa area were examined and treated by William and Patti to the extent the rough circumstances allowed. They couldn't perform surgeries that required an IV or general anesthetic, and they couldn't cast broken bones. But they had an extensive supply of prescription meds, bandages, and splints. I was unable to spend any time other than a few quick look-ins at their clinic, but they were at it all evening and the following day. Some of the people that showed up had serious conditions. In those cases all the docs could do was to strongly encourage the patients to go to a hospital. Patti and William were able to treat numerous infections. Giardia was one of the most common ones they diagnosed. Not surprising, since the parasite inhabits soil, food, or water that has been contaminated with feces from animals or humans that are infected with the bacteria. (Given the risk of giardia infection, I thought the village was making a big mistake rejecting a filtration system for the water project. But it was the village's, not my, choice to make.)

William later told me one of the most difficult decisions he made in Basa was for a man from another village, who had a gigantic abscess in his jaw. The patient clearly needed surgery to remove the seeping abscess, which William was capable of doing. But it would have been too risky to perform the surgery in the rough setting of the classroom, so William decided against removing the mess from the guy's jaw. He cleaned and drained it, and gave the patient antibiotics. William thought the man would need reconstructive surgery because the guy's jaw was so badly deformed.

It was a good thing William made the hike to Basa despite the pain in his foot. I think Patti, working by herself, would have been overwhelmed by the number of local people in need of basic medical treatments. The clinic was also a good experience for James. He was taking a gap year, but had been accepted to medical school. He had worked with a medical-mission team in Africa, and was interested in "third world medicine". His dilemma was whether to start med school in a year or to accept the invitation from a rock band to travel the country playing gigs from town to town. Which path do you think he chose?

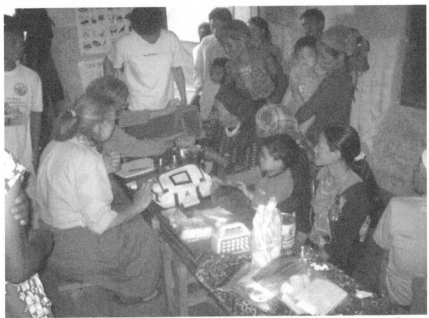

Drs. Patti and William at work in the medical clinic they ran out of a classroom in the Basa School, 2013

Pig Slaughter and Mangled Music

The second day the medical clinic was in operation, on the other side of the village a pig was slaughtered. The local custom is that a sick or dying animal will be put out of its misery. Meat from the animal is cut into portions and distributed to each family in the village. Although private ownership of farm animals is customary, that type of ownership does not extend beyond the life of the animal. What an interesting, and different from the Anglo-American, understanding of property rights and communal values! In Basa the responsibility of caring for an animal is entirely that of the owner, but the animal's meat belongs to the whole village.

Ganesh claimed that he killed the animal with one shot from a bow and arrow. I didn't see the execution, and Ganesh was in a playful mood. I'm not sure whether his claim was accurate or not. The pig was owned by his uncle's family. Those of us with strong enough stomachs watched Ganesh's uncle cut the meat from the dead pig's body. A group of men cut the larger slabs up into portions and handed the slices out for delivery to homes throughout the village. Ganesh capered about brandishing the bow

406

and arrow pretending he was a fierce warrior.

The pig is being butchered to share its meat with all families in the village, while Ganesh played the fierce warrior for the benefit of onlookers, including In Sook and James. Basa Village 2013

The school children performed their traditional dances and songs the evening of our second day in Basa. Perhaps it is a sign of aging, but the kids looked cuter and sweeter each year I returned to Basa. They take the performance so seriously and they are very proud of their handmade outfits. (I wondered how often the students get to perform, since visitors to the village are such a rare treat.)

Our students planned to give something back to the village by singing a series of American folk songs. Justin is a classically-trained musician. Per my encouragement, he volunteered to pick out songs, which our group would sing as part of the evening program. We had planned to practice before we arrived in Basa, but we never found time, and no one felt like singing after trekking through an afternoon of rain and dodging leeches falling out of trees. Before we arrived in Basa Justin handed out copies from a songbook of a few songs he thought would impress the village with the beauty of traditional American folk singing. But, because we'd hiked through so much rain, most of the copies got wet and were unreadable. It was dark by the time we were supposed to sing. So it was difficult to make out the lyrics on the blurry, surviving copies. To make the situation even more challenging, most of us were three sheets to the wind from all the rakshi pushed on us by the village grannies.

I don't even remember what songs Justin wanted his choir of

angels to sing, but I'm sure his voice was the only one that could have been pleasing to the villagers' ears that night. My recollection of what the half-drunk Americans sounded like was more that of a bunch of frogs croaking and geese being strangled than a worthy rendition of American folk music. To whatever extent Basa villagers might think Americans are better off than them, based on the evidence they've heard, they must think we really suck at singing.

Shaman healing performance and the caste system explained

Ganesh and I arranged for Purna to perform a shamanic healing ceremony in Niru's house later that night when it was pitch dark. As in 2009, Purna would not actually be healing anyone. Outsiders are not allowed to witness a healing. It is unusual to have a clutch of American youngsters in a trekking group. Purna and all the other guys in the crew were delighted to have our fresh-faced youngsters as clients. When Ganesh and I approached Purna about demonstrating how a Rai purket healed an ailing villager, he immediately agreed to do so. Purna understood that the experience was primarily for the Marian students as part of their cross-cultural education. However, the member of our group most fascinated with Purna's performance was Dr. William.

As an experienced camp cook Purna knew the English words for many food items. Beyond those labels, he spoke almost no English. So there was little conversation between him and William. Yet a bond of interest about their different modes of healing grew between the two of them. Purna looked in on William and Patti's work in the medical clinic, and William was thrilled that he was allowed to see how Purna practiced shamanic healing.

Purna first drank rakshi and inhaled incense to warm up. Then, for four hours late into the night he danced and chanted. It was eerie, entrancing, and amazingly athletic. Purna walked with us from Shivalaya to Basa. He'd carried a pack with kitchen supplies much heavier than our backpacks, and he worked every day preparing three meals plus afternoon snacks for thirteen hungry trekkers. And he still had the energy to dance and leap and chant for four hours.

Purna prepares to act as a *purket* (Rai Shaman) to demonstrate a healing ceremony.

William, Taissa, and In Sook had to leave on the third day we were in Basa. Their schedules didn't permit them as much time in Nepal as the rest of the group. They had to get back to Kathmandu to catch their flights out. In Sook was flying off to visit family in South Korea. William and Taissa were bound for home in Chicago. Before William left, he and Patti organized medical supplies they were leaving in the village. They boxed and labeled different types of bandages and over-the-counter pain meds and health aids. William instructed Ganesh and Santosh on how to store and use the supplies. Purna presented William with a necklace, which he indicated had healing powers. It was a string of hollow nutshells. They were brown in color and each shell was about two inches in diameter with a hard surface. (William hung the necklace on a model skeleton he keeps in his home office. In June 2019, when I was staying at his house for a weekend visit, William showed me that the skeleton still wears Purna's necklace. The skeleton appeared to be quite healthy.)

I hated to see the three of them leave the group. Tai had a great brassy sense of humor and lit up the meal tent with her deep booming laugh and sarcastic commentary. In Sook was an inspiration on the trail. She was over 70, but light on her feet and quick down the trail. She has a sly sense of humor and enjoyed pointing out to our youngsters how much easier their lives were than what life was like in Nepal. In Sook grew up in pre-industrialized Korea. She loves America, but thinks most Americans are sissies. William and I had become close friends after bonding at a college class-reunion. As an ER doc on the south side of Chicago, he had a lot of interesting stories to share. Before they hiked off, William told me that doing the Basa med clinic made him "feel five years younger". He said it was "one of the most gratifying things" he'd done as a physician.

I later learned that our three early departees had a very exciting drive back to Kathmandu. Two days after they left Basa they met the driver Niru sent to pick them up in Salleri. (Salleri is the administrative center for Solukhumbu Province, just a mile south of Phaplu.) He drove the better part of 24 hours to get to Salleri from Kathmandu. William asked the driver whether he wanted to sleep before heading back to Kathmandu. The fellow insisted he didn't need any sleep. After he nodded off a couple times and William jabbing the driver in the side and grabbing the wheel, William, Tai, and In Sook demanded he stop and sleep. He refused and started to pull back onto the road. William jumped out of the truck and blocked the driver from going any further, unless he was going to run over William. The driver acquiesced and slept soundly for several hours. They made it back to Kathmandu without crashing. I don't know how well William, Tai, and In Sook tipped the driver.

On the fourth and last day in Basa Ganesh led us around the village once more. He pointed out the differences between the "dukey" houses and those of the farmers. "Dukey", Ganesh said, is the slang term for the lower caste members of the community, the tailors, *Damai*, and blacksmiths, *Kami*. Ganesh explained to the group how the caste system works in Basa. It was adapted from the dominant Hindu culture and is occupational based. Since the Rai farmers first inhabited Basa and occupied the land, they were the dominant caste. When Hindu tradesmen came and were welcomed into the community, they accepted a lower status. The last name of all members of the Rai ethno-tribal group is "Rai". Damai and Kami have different last names, "Nepali" being a common one. The exterior of most of the Dukey houses is light-brown-colored cement. The exteriors of Rai houses in Basa are either exposed white stone or they have a white cement exterior. Some of the lower caste people's houses also have a white cement exterior. The roofs of the Rai houses are blue or green in color and made of tin or aluminum. Dukey house roofs are made of wood planks or thatch.

One of the most interesting aspects of the caste system in Basa is that the Rai families give a fixed portion of their crop yield to the Dukey families. The tailors and blacksmiths own small plots of land, but not enough to provide a sustainable diet for their families.

The Rai farmers make up the difference needed for the Damai and Kami to remain in the village. The mutually beneficial exchange is that the tailors and blacksmiths do not charge any money or goods in barter when clothes need to be made or mended and tools need to be fabricated or repaired. They perform their work for anyone in the village in need of the skills of a tailor or blacksmith. The amount of crops set aside for the Damai and Kami families is recalculated every few years to make sure the system is sustainable.

Ganesh said it had always worked this way in the village, but he wasn't sure it would always be that way in the future. He said, "Now that men work for the Niru, they have money and can buy a shirt or pants." Villagers can buy Chinese-made clothes, or even tools, at the market in Sombare. Ganesh opined that the Chinese-made goods were usually better quality than what the Basa Damai and Kami made. He thought the system of providing food for the services of the tailors and blacksmiths might have to change, if the Rai members of the community preferred to buy most of their clothes and tools at the market.

I asked Ganesh whether he was worried that the Damai and Kami might starve, if the Rai decided they no longer wanted to maintain the traditional system. I was surprised at his sanguine response. It was a Nepali sort of que sera. He was confident it would all work out somehow. I hoped he was right, but warning bells once again went off in my mind about threats to the communal equilibrium of Basa.

The reaction of the American youngsters and oldsters to Ganesh's explanation of the caste system in Basa was similar to mine, when I first learned about it in 2008. The immediate reaction was shock that such kind, sweet people would engage in such open and obvious discrimination. Any version of a caste system violates egalitarian principles and cannot be considered right and just by post-Enlightenment Westerners. Yet, it seems to work. The Damai and Kami seem as content with their lives in Basa as the Rai farmers. Still, it's hard to accept. Our youngsters were pleased to learn that most of the young people in Basa want to let go of the caste system.

If you have an open mind, learning about the caste system as it operates in Basa should help develop an understanding that there is no monolithic right way that should be applied to all people everywhere. This lesson is not just an antidote to ethnocentrism. It is also a lesson about the limitations of every political ideology and all religious doctrines. Anyone who believes that Marxism, fascism, socialism, democracy, Calvinism, Catholicism, Buddhism, Islam, Hinduism, or whatever the religion or ideology may be, is the best one for all of humanity should consider how well Basa Village works as a community. One of the purposes of the class I taught at Marian University (later at Butler University) was to expose American college students to a different way of understanding human relations. I wanted them to consider that something as alien and abhorrent as a caste system might work just fine for people in a different culture. The American form of democratic-republicanism with its hybrid capitalistic-socialistic economy might not be the shining example every tribe and nation should emulate.

Several people in Basa told us that they resent being told by the national government that the village will have to engage in an election to choose a mayor and members of the Village Development Committee. Village leaders have always been chosen by consensus. "Why should we have to change our traditional ways?" they lamented. Holding elections was not a practice that made sense to these villagers. Their tradition of holding village meetings to talk through issues and then make decisions by consensus made perfect sense to them, and to me.

The house on the left is owned by a "dukey" family; the one on the right by a Rai family. Basa Village 2013

Breaking up was hard to do

A feeling of lethargy spread within our group after four days in Basa. It was probably a combination of drinking too much rakshi and chang, eating too much without doing any strenuous trekking, and a dread of trekking through rain and leeches back to Jiri. Leaving Basa was like Adam and Eve getting kicked out of Eden. All our needs were taken care of and it hadn't rained and there were no leeches in Basa.

Three of our Marian students, Jessica, Justin, and Josh started muttering about how they would like to get a ride back to Kathmandu from Salleri, like In Sook, Taissa, and William did. Ganesh told them that, if they were serious, he would try to arrange it. They were.

I was rather peeved at the three of them for wanting to poop out on the rest of the trek. Doing a trek in Nepal was, for god's sake, Josh and Jessica's idea! True, the weather was miserable and the leeches disgusting on the trek to Basa. Poor Jessica, she even got a leech bite on her lovely cheek. But it was disappointing to me that the three of them wanted to quit before reaching the finish line. On the other hand, they planned to go down to the Terai (jungle area in southern Nepal) to do a safari and ride elephants. The sooner they got back to Kathmandu, the sooner they'd be able to go on safari. I couldn't fault them for wanting to do that.

I took Ole Dave aside and told him I thought he should consider driving back to Kathmandu with the three youngsters. Dave is known in the Hoosier hiking community for his slow, steady pace. He was the last into camp every day on the trek. Dave never complained and seemed to enjoy his slow, steady rate of hiking on the way to Basa. But I was concerned about his ability to keep up on the way back. Niru's programme required 7-8 hours hiking each of the four days from Basa to Jiri. Dave's rate of speed had been getting slower rather than faster on the way to Basa. A 7 to 8 hour day per Niru's programme would probably be an 8-10 hour day for Dave. And, he'd gotten sick while we were in Basa. Another factor was that James, David, and Lauren were very fit, fast hikers. They liked to trail run whenever possible, and that was definitely not Ole Dave's style. Patti and I would be challenged to keep up with those three youngsters. Of course it would be Dave's decision, but I thought he'd have a better time riding with the students than trying to keep up with faster trekkers on the trail back to Jiri. Dave agreed.

In the Nepal Himalayas one should never assume things will go exactly as planned. Our departure from Basa was a lovely experience as expected. Villagers lined up and placed leis around our necks and the grannies tried pressing a few last cups of rakshi and plates of potatoes on us. Children grasped our hands and didn't want to let us go. Parting with Basa is a sweet sorrow, because the villagers are so affectionate toward their visitors.

All of the sweetness of the parting was displaced with sorrow to be back on the trail, because it started raining while we hiked up the long, steep, and winding trail on the Ratnagi Danda. It is rarely pleasant to hike in the rain. This was particularly unpleasant because of that lethargy we were all feeling from excessive eating and drinking. We managed to drag ourselves up to the top of the 10,000-foot-high ridge. There is a very rough teahouse on the ridge. It is filthy and the roof leaks. It's more of a yak shelter than a teahouse, but a family lives there and ekes out a living selling tea, rakshi, and rice to porters. Having a trekking group camp on the grounds probably doubled the annual revenue for the bhatti.

It rained all night and leeches found their way into all of our tents. The hike down the other side of the Ratnagi Danda next morning had the advantage of being down, instead of an uphill slog, and the rain diminished to mist and drizzle. But the trails were so slick we had to downhill ski in our hiking boots. Everyone, porters, trekkers, and even Ganesh took at least one muddy butt slide on the way down.

By the time we skidded onto the level trail between Phaplu and Salleri any remaining doubt about the decision of Jessica, Justin, Josh, and Ole Dave to abandon the trek was resolved. It was tempting to join them.

The unexpected twist was that they arrived back in Kathmandu less than a day before the hikers did. Jessica, Justin, Josh, and Dave traded hiking for boredom and frustration. They waited two days in Salleri for the truck to arrive. It didn't. On the third day they hired a guy who was driving to Kathmandu to give them a lift. Dave got stuck riding on a makeshift seat in the truck bed under a camper shell. His ass was directly above the rear axle, so he took a hell of a beating. When they arrived in Shivalaya the river was too high to cross. Around 4:00 p.m. on the second day waiting by the river, the truck was loaded on a ferry barge. The four Americans crossed the river on the foot bridge and loaded up for the day-long drive to Kathmandu. The truck broke down before it got there. They called

Niru, and he sent a van to pick them up. Our weary compatriots arrived at the KGH after midnight, four days after we parted from them on the trail outside Salleri.

One might think as high a rating on the misery quotient as Ole Dave experienced he would have no desire ever to return to Nepal. Nope. Dave organized a group two years later to trek in Langtang on what is now called the Tamang Heritage Trail. Near the end of the trek, Dave took a freakish fall and broke his ankle. He was helicoptered to Kathmandu to have temporary screws put in the ankle. A US surgeon had to go in and re-screw the bones. After all that Dave would surely never want to return to Nepal. Nope. Despite the pain and suffering, as with so many of us, Nepal touched Dave very deeply. He joined the BVF board and is looking forward to his next trek as I'm writing this.

The truck being ferried across the Khimti Khola; photo by Dave Culp, Shivalaya 2013

Last stage of the trek, aesthetic hiking, oldest Everest climber, and partying

Dr. Patti, James, David, Lauren, and I were the remaining members of our initial group of thirteen. After a night out of the rain inside the Numbar Lodge in Phaplu, it was back on the trail for the five of us with a reduced staff. The rain held off until late afternoon. It was actually a lovely day for hiking. Cirrus clouds scudded along the horizon. The temperature was in the high 60s Fahrenheit. The landscape was very green and reminded me of the Alps of Switzerland and Austria. Dzo bells tinkled mimicking alpine cowbells.

That day on the trail was typical of trekking the Middle Himalayas. We hiked through three long river valleys by the Junbesi Khola, Marbu Khola, and Khimti Khola. Hiking up the Lamjura La was the only really tough hike. But we were feeling so good about being back on the trail in sunshine, James, David, Lauren, and I raced down. I kept up, but every joint from my toes up through my hips hurt. This must be what old age feels like, I thought. I did not share that thought with my young companions.

One of the most delightful aesthetic experiences was waking up to the silly sounds of cuckoo birds cuckooing each morning. Monkeys called across the rain forest at night. The coolest animal sighting was of a five-foot tall white lemur scrambling down the trail toward us about 50 yards ahead. It broke off and leaped into the rain forest to join four others. I wasn't quick enough with my camera to get a good shot, damn it!

One of the most interesting human contacts was in Shivalaya with Yuichiro Miura. He set the record, at the age of 80, for the oldest person to summit Mt. Everest. His team was staying in the lodge that we camped beside. They were partying every night on the long hike from Base Camp to Jiri. The evening we met them in Shivalaya was their last night on the trail. They were having a hell of a good, loud time. We were privileged to join in a toast to Yuichiro. But I wished his team of Japanese and Nepalese climbers would have quieted down so we could fall asleep in our tents that night.

We had one more day of hiking to get to Jiri and meet up with the AGT van and driver Niru sent. Some members of our crew planned to leave from Shivalaya to hike back to Basa. So we held an evening and morning going-away party in Shivalaya. The feast with a cake was held in our meal tent, since Yuichiro's party occupied the lodge. The evening party was more somber and pensive than the usual good-bye party. I suppose that was because only five of the thirteen were there to enjoy it. Maybe we were intimidated by the raucousness of Yuichiro's party. Purna's chocolate cake with vanilla icing was, of course, delicious. Ganesh wrote on the cake with green food coloring: I Hope Every Body Enjoy The Trek.

The morning party was more fun. Before we split up, clothes were collected from the whole group and saved in a duffel bag to distribute to the crew at the end of the trek. Because of the rain and mud there was a lot of discarded clothing. Ganesh and Prakesh carefully divided all the clothes and donated camping gear into equal piles. Lots were drawn by the guys from numbered strips of paper.

What really pleased the crew was the amount of the tips. I was concerned that our young folks might not be able to afford to give a decent tip. As I always do, I'd informed the group that a minimum of $100 was the recommended tip. But I'd warned Ganesh the total might be lower because of the lower age of half the group members. I received wads of Rupees from each group member before we split up as their contribution toward the total tip. When Ganesh and I sat down to count out the total amount of the stash, we were cheered that it was over 125,000 Rupees. In 2013 that was around $1,700, and it didn't include a large tip from Jerry.

The five Americans even redeemed our musical reputation somewhat by belting out a very strong rendition of *The Star Spangled Banner* in response to the crew's singing and dancing during the morning good-bye party.

The crew gathers for a toast on the last night of the trek. Shivalaya 2013

It was a wonderful end to the 2013 trek. But our troubles were not actually over. The last hour or so hiking into Jiri was on a road which was covered in mud two feet deep. It was impossible to walk through. Luckily, there was a fence with a concrete base running along side the road most of the way into town. We struggled along trying to keep our footing on the concrete base; at times grasping the chain-link fence to avoid falling into the mud. Prakesh slipped and fell flat on his back. He went down hard on the concrete right in front of me. I was sure he was seriously injured, but he popped right up embarrassed to have fallen.

In Jiri, Ganesh received a message that our van was stuck in a town called Cherokat. The Maoists were on strike and not letting any traffic through. We had a boring few hours waiting for the van, but it did arrive around 5:30 p.m. We drove through the night arriving at the blessed Kathmandu Guest House at 2:30 a.m.

We met up with Ole Dave and Lauren the next day. We just missed Josh, Jessica, and Justin. While we were sleeping off the long ride from Jiri, they flew off for views of the mountain lakes of Pokhara. Lauren, Patti, and Dave met up with the youngsters in the Terai for elephant rides and a safari in Chitwan National Park. Before Patti, Dave, and Lauren left Kathmandu we had one last feast at Niru's house. My god, there was so much food! We probably gained back all the weight lost on the trek.

And so it ended. Fat and happy we went our separate ways.

More photos from the 2013 Basa trek ...

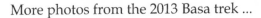

Chapter Postscript

One of the most touching "thank you" notes I've received from a member of a trekking group came from James. It reads:

> Jeff Dhai – I could not have asked for a better/cooler trek leader. I thoroughly enjoyed my time with you, and the conversations we had together. As you probably recognized I'm sort of a wandering soul, which can be scary when trying to figure out what you want to do w/ your life after graduating college. After trekking with you I'm less worried about that b/c I realized you kind of are too. I mean who would bike to Mexico, become a lawyer, go to Nepal to climb and save a village, kayak by himself in Palau ... write books, have a family, teach college classes... For reasons like this I drew similarities b/w us, and I find it comforting that you've made it work. I'm excited to see what the future holds for me. Thanks again for opening up such an incredible experience to me and the rest of our fellow trekkers. I will always remember Nepal 2013.

James dramatically exaggerated my impact in his phrasing, "save a village". Basa didn't need saving, just some help; for which I've received much in return.

James chose not to enter med school. As of this writing, he is still touring with his band, C2 & The Brothers Reed.

Earthquakes, Wedding, Loss of a Friend, Glasses, Solar-Powered Lights, Evolution or Revolution
My Last Philanthro-Trek, Basa and the Royal Trek 2017

I planned to return to Nepal in 2015 to co-lead a trek to Basa with Joel Meyers and try Mera Peak for a third time. Joel agreed to succeed me as president of the BVF-USA in 2016. As a prelude to the leadership handoff, Joel and I wanted to visit Basa together with other BVF supporters. We also wanted another shot at climbing Mera Peak. Our plan was to do a mountaineering expedition to Mera after spending a few days in Basa. The plan was dashed by the earthquakes that killed over 9,000 people in Nepal and injured another 22,000 in the spring of 2015. The first of two major quakes struck on April 25, 2015. Its magnitude was 7.8. Many buildings and historic temples were toppled in Kathmandu. It also destroyed numerous mountain villages. Hundreds of after-shocks followed and a 7.3 level quake occurred on May 12th. The two major quakes and after-shocks caused landslides and avalanches across the Himalayan region.

The epicenter of the 7.8 quake was 140 miles east of Mount Everest. There were hundreds of people in Base Camp when the quake happened. The government had issued over 350 Everest climbing permits for the spring climbing season. All those climbers plus their support staff were on the mountain or in Base Camp when the quake struck. It triggered an avalanche on nearby Pumori. Ice and rocks crashed down into Base Camp killing 22 people. Expedition tents were blown into the Khumbu Icefall.

Sir Edmund Hillary's demand in 2003 for a moratorium on climbing Everest was finally achieved in a bloody way. A year before the 2015 earthquakes sixteen Sherpas were killed in an avalanche while they were setting ladders over the Khumbu Icefall to prepare for the spring 2014 climbing season. Climbing on Everest was cancelled that season, because all the surviving Sherpa guides refused to repair the ladders or lead anyone up the mountain. So for two consecutive spring seasons climbers were forced to let the mountain brood alone in singular austerity.

I helped plan a Base Camp trek for a father-son duo in April 2015 through Adventure GeoTreks. The two of them were on the trail near Namche Bazaar when the first earthquake struck. They were uninjured and praised their AGT guide, Gom Rai, for leading them safely out of the mountains. But they had a hell of a time getting out. They could not fly out of Lukla as planned. They hiked with Gom all the way down to Basa Village. It took a few days, but Niru was able to send a car to Salleri to bring them back to Kathmandu. This is from an email the father-member of the duo sent after he and his son were back in the US:

Jeff, I wanted to drop you a note to express my sincere thanks for coordinating our trip to Nepal in April. Our trip was an adventure of a lifetime despite the earthquake and resulting damage and chaos. We developed a new appreciation for simple pleasures and living in the moment, and I could not have enjoyed myself more. Both my son and I trained hard for the trek and I do feel that conditioning prepared us well for the physical side of the trip. I was not prepared for the culture shock and immersion of events, nor the breathtaking landscape and views. Words cannot express the feelings of accomplishment after hiking for 9 hours in such beauty with such effort, and I cannot say enough about the Nepalese culture, its welcoming people with their honest, humble and innocent nature. I only hope they maintain these qualities as long as possible. I swear I had a grin on my face nearly the entire time, despite the challenges, and I plan to return in the near future with the goal of reaching EBC this time. Once again, many thanks for making our trip so memorable. Please feel free to use me as a reference for future trekkers! Doug

From his son:

The trip was a blast and due to the quake we got to make it to Basa. When we got there we looked at 17 of the houses. There were 5 that were damaged enough for people to sleep outside... Now that there was a larger quake a few days ago closer to Basa things might be much worse, but hopefully the initial damage puts your mind somewhat at ease... We were hiking back to Namche when it hit. The hiking was much harder than I thought because I've never done anything like it but I loved the challenge every day and want to go back to make it to EBC! By the way our guide was

Gom Rai who was Niru's Wife's Sisters Daughters Husband ... or something like that. He had not met you but was an excellent guide and hiking partner. Jesse

Internet was down in Nepal, so I did not hear from Niru for several days after the April 25 earthquake. I sent him several messages as soon as I learned about the earthquake. Before we even heard from Niru to know what damage the earthquake had done in the Basa area, BVF-USA board-member Leona Hamrick established a GoFundMe account to begin fundraising for an earthquake relief effort. This was the message she sent to her contacts to announce the relief effort:

Namaste,

Most of you remember that I visited Nepal in the fall of 2012. My trip deeply impacted me and my love for the beautiful country runs deep. It was most important to me that every dollar I spent in Nepal benefit the country because of the widespread poverty. In other words, I did not want to book a tour with an American company. The search for a Nepalese company led me to Jeff Rasley, author and founder of Basa Village Foundation USA. This foundation works directly with the Rai people and a small remote village (Basa) only accessible by trekking. Niru Rai, originally from Basa, owns a travel company in Kathmandu. I worked directly with him to plan my trip. His sister and brother-in-law, along with their two children, opened their home to me while I was there so I could truly experience Nepal.

I now serve as a board member for Basa Village Foundation USA. Along with the other board members, we created a donation page to gather funds that can be sent directly to Nepal to help in relief efforts following this devastating earthquake. So far everyone we have spoke to in Nepal is okay but the effects from this tragic event are widespread and long lasting. If you have felt compelled to donate to help with the relief efforts in Nepal I encourage you to consider donating to our not-for-profit organization. Every dollar donated will go directly to Nepal. Thank you all for taking time to read my email.

425

Kindest Regards, Leona Trent Hamrick

This was the first email I received from Niru:

Dear Jeff,

Namaste and many greetings from Nepal! Thank you very much for your so kind message and your kind concern. We are very happy to hear from you. Yes unfortunately, we had a really terrible situation with one of the big and destructive earthquakes after a long time in history of Nepal and lots of damage with it. But luckily so far we are safe (all our family and team) and we are staying in safe area and are mostly out of house. We have no electricity since the incident and so limited access to internet and phone for the moment. We are hoping the situation gets better day by day and everything will go back to normal soon and we can recover and continue with our normal lives.

Here in Kathmandu, most of the old houses and old monuments were completely destroyed and new and strongly built houses survived but with some damages. In Basa also almost all the homes are damaged or destroyed but luckily there also people have survived and living outside house for safety. We really hope this will now stop and we will have no more earthquakes and we can recover from what we have already lost.

We really appreciate your kind wishes and concern during this hard time. And also thank you very much for your kind supports.

With best regards, Niru

The earthquakes completely changed our philanthro-trek planning. Niru advised Joel and me that it would be unwise to visit Nepal in 2015. The country needed to focus on recovery and rebuilding, not hosting tourists. The projects we'd discussed with Niru about toilets and a medical clinic were dropped. We kicked into high gear fundraising to purchase materials needed to rebuild and repair homes, the school, electrical lines, and the water system in Basa. Niru sent estimates of the costs to rebuild and repair the village, which varied from $40,000 to $100,000, depending on how many structures were rebuilt or repaired. The BVF-USA quickly

426

raised the low estimate of $40,000 from our members and donors. But we didn't send it to our sister foundation's bank account in Kathmandu for several months.

The national government of Nepal began seizing earthquake-relief funds. When a bank in Nepal received a wire-transfer of funds from foreign donors, the bank was required to report it to the National Treasury, which then seized those funds. The government decreed that it would distribute all earthquake funds on an as-needed basis according to its own criteria. We were not about to let the central government screw Basa out of the funds we raised. The BVF-Nepal board members were positive that, if the government got hold of the $40,000, not a penny would be spent on Basa Village.

Niru and I discussed various schemes to get the funds to Nepal in a way that would circumvent the government from claiming the money for itself. Just before we dispatched a person to Nepal with the funds, the government gave in to the howls of protest and pressure from other countries and major foundations. The policy to seize earthquake-relief funds was revoked. We wire-transferred the $40,000 in October 2015 to the BVF-Nepal's bank account. Niru tapped another source he'd developed, the French NGO Sol Himal, for a donation to help rebuild the school. Enough money was raised from the two organizations, plus money donated by AGT and board members of BVF-Nepal, to purchase all the cement, stone, wood, and other materials needed to repair and replace the damaged homes, the school, and the water and electrical lines. The complete restoration project was finished by the end of summer in 2016.

We exceeded our $40,000 fundraising goal, so for the first time we gave grants outside of Basa Village. One of our board members, Sydney Frymire, had a connection with New Hope Women's Shelter in Kathmandu. The shelter needed to repair its walls, so our BVF-USA board agreed to purchase and donate to the shelter a brick-making machine. It cost $2,000. With the brick-making machine the only materials the shelter's staff needed to rebuild its walls were mud and water. They had plenty of mud and water. It was a pain in the ass to get the machine through the red tape of Nepal's customs office. I won't bore you with the details, but it was maddening that the government kept putting up roadblocks which slowed down rebuilding the country. The machine was eventually delivered and the shelter's walls were rebuilt.

We also received a designated donation of $4,061 to help rebuild another village, Ramati. That donation was raised by Mary Schuller, the sister-aunt of Doug and Jesse, the father-son duo who took shelter in Basa after the April 2015 earthquake. Mary was involved with an NGO in Nepal called Hope and Peace Foundation, which was working on developing a water system for the 50 families in the village of Ramati when the earthquakes struck. Hope and Peace Foundation didn't have a US sister foundation to accept tax-deductible contributions. The BVF-USA agreed to act as its fiscal agent, so Mary's US donors would be able to claim a charitable deduction on their taxes. We released the funds to the Hope and Peace Foundation after receiving proper documentation of its nonprofit status and mission work in Ramati Village.

Kasia Jamroz was a member of one of the Himalayan mountaineering groups my old friend Elliot led. She met Niru in Kathmandu and got to know the Basa guys that staffed her

Old Damaged House

New House

*under Construction

expedition. Kasia loved Nepal and was quite taken with the strength and goodness of the guys from Basa. She wanted to do something to help their families. Elliot referred her to me. I suggested she do whatever she could to contribute to the BVF's earthquake relief fund. Kasia took a unique approach to fundraising. She set up her own GoFundMe account and asked donors to contribute based on her competitive

428

running. She ran three half marathons and one full marathon and raised $7,000. Our board was so impressed with Kasia's enthusiasm that we asked, and she accepted, to join our board.

Marriage the Rai Way

We're going to backtrack one year from when the earthquakes struck Nepal. In between the end of the 2013 trek and the 2015 earthquakes a joyful event occurred in Basa. On March 7, 2014 Niru's oldest son, Milan, was married in Basa Village. The celebration lasted a week. I knew Milan from the many meals I had at Niru's house and because he picked me up from the airport in

Kathmandu several times and drove me around Kathmandu when I needed a driver for BVF or AGT business. Milan worked for his dad in the AGT office and handled correspondence whenever Niru was unavailable. We exchanged numerous emails over the years. It would have been a wonderful and interesting experience to participate in the wedding celebration. But alas, the photos Niru sent had to suffice.

Weddings in the US are a big deal too. In a small American town, when a prominent citizen's son gets married, most everyone in town would probably be invited to the wedding reception. In Nepalese villages, not *most* everyone, *everyone* in the village participates in the wedding. The host family provides food and drink for the

whole village. During the following days of celebration every family in the community contributes food, rakshi, and chang for the festivities, as well as gifts to the newlyweds.

A more significant distinction in traditional marriage customs is that in Nepal, whether the couple is Hindu, Buddhist, or Rai animist, the marriage should be arranged by negotiation and agreement of the parents. *Meet the Patels* was a popular 2014 romantic-comedy-documentary in the US. The film portrays a generational conflict over arranged marriage within an Indian-American family. The parents of 30-year old Ravi expect their son to conform to tradition and to allow them to arrange his marriage. Ravi loves and respects his parents, but has fallen in love with a woman unacceptable to his parents. That conflict is an ancient one in Nepal. But my Nepali friends tell me that few children bucked the authority of their parents to arrange their marriage, until recently. "Love marriages" are becoming more common and more acceptable as the culture becomes more westernized and less traditional.

By email, I asked Niru whether Milan's marriage was arranged. His reply to my question:

> About Milan, it was kind of mixed. They were introduced by their uncle and got chance to know each other for about 4 years before they were married. So it's not like traditional arranged marriage, where the couple does not know each other before they marry.
>
> In traditional arranged marriage the partners are selected by family and all the arrangements are made by the family, community. Now days it's more common that the younger people have love relation then they share with their family when they are ready for marriage.

Niru's own marriage was arranged the traditional way by his parents. So were the marriages of the AGT senior guides, Sanga, Ganesh, and DB. All four of those Basa guys have told me that their marriages are successful, loving unions.

Sanga Rai sent this email in response to my question about the status of arranged marriages in Nepal and among the Rai people:

> Arrange marriage system was more active until our previous generation and just partly touched to our generation. Under the arrange marriage just parents from

both side (bride and bride groom) were making a marriage plan between boy and girl. Bridegroom might know about his coming marriage but bride was completely unknown. Only she would have known on the day of their final inauguration, we call it "SAGUN". At the SAGUN party, bride and bridegroom know each other as husband and wife.

Bride used to live with her own parents and bridegroom used to live with his own parents... Most couples were living with own parents for years and years, men were working in own village or out of village in another place/country.

Mostly bride and bridegroom visited each other on certain occasion or their parents were making appointment of visiting. For important occasion bridegroom had to take some souvenir to the bride. If bridegroom was not available at home then some family member of bridegroom had to take that souvenir to the bride.

In middle of Monsoon time there is one festival call "Sawane Shankranti". On this occasion bridegroom had to give new GHUM (made by bamboo) rain cover including some fresh meat, rice, rakshi and possibly some butter and clothes to the bride if she was still living with her parents. Bridegroom himself had to bring those things to his bride in her parents' home.

Their marriage took final cultural ceremony (authority) after years and years later or could be after they have got kids. After the final ceremony bride lives with husband or husband family, if he is working in other places. But their life was always interesting, loving, caring and full of curiosity.

Whether we make arrange marriage or love marriage we (Rai) community have to make 2 wedding ceremony. One is called "Sagun" at the beginning and "REET" the final ceremony. After the REET bride gets completely full rights from the husband side, for example family name, over property, societal and all kinds of other conditions. Before the REET she mostly belongs to her own parents' side.

Nowadays Marriage system among Rai community has been changed to modernize. Bride and bridegroom know each other already by themselves.

Some aspects of the marriage customs Sanga describes may seem weird and outlandish to Americans and other "modern" folks. What's the point of being married, if the wife still lives with her parents? Why have two stages to finalize marriage? Isn't withholding property rights and other legal rights from the wife, until the second stage is completed, sexist and repressive?

On a superficial level the marriage customs Sanga describes seem very different from modern "Western" marriage customs. However, if you think of the *Sagun* stage as the engagement phase and the *Reet* ceremony as the wedding, the differences are not all that significant. What struck me, as I learned about the traditional Rai marriage customs, is that the essential purpose of marriage is similar across cultures. A couple is united and that union is celebrated by the wider community. How the couple gets together and how the family and community celebrate the union varies among different cultures. The fundamental purpose, or the ideal, is living in a loving partnership and starting a new family. That purpose/ideal is shared by almost every culture. That essential aspect of marriage applies to same-sex marriages. It even applies to cultures that permit polygamy. It's all about creating a new relationship, hopefully a loving one, no matter how it begins or is formalized.

Differences in customs might strike a narrow, inflexible person as odd, offensive, or even immoral. But when we look past the superficial differences the essential values underlying cultural norms and customs often turn out to be similar to the values we cherish. Isn't establishing a loving partnership and starting a new family at the heart of most all the forms of marriage humanity has conceived? It's enjoyable to participate in a meaningful celebration with friends and family, to eat, drink, and be merry.

Loss of a friend to the BVF

Chuck Richmond was a rare bird as an attorney. He entered the law as a second career. His first was as a hospital administrator for Riley Children's Hospital in Indianapolis. Chuck's law practice took second place to his charitable activities. His father was US Surgeon General under President Jimmy Carter. Chuck came from a privileged background. He believed that, "To whom much is given, much will be required." (Luke 12:48) Chuck was the long-time director of the Panther League, which is the youth basketball program for Washington Township Schools in Indianapolis. My boys played ball in the program every year of their eligibility from third through eighth grade. I served as a coach for the program for seven years, and that's how I got to know Chuck. He was also the chairman of the board for the local Ronald McDonald House.

When I asked Chuck to act as the BVF's attorney in applying to the IRS for tax exempt status, I intended and expected to pay him for his services. Chuck did not charge us for his legal time. He paid the filing fees, and he prepared and filed the first couple corporate tax returns. He never charged a penny to the BVF. Chuck agreed with the approach to philanthropy Niru and I worked out for our sister foundations. Chuck spoke as a guest lecturer to the classes I taught at Marian and Butler Universities about the legal requirements for nonprofit corporations. He thought the BVF should be a model for other organizations and wanted to help spread the word about how to do philanthropy the right way.

Chuck, Candace, the original corporate treasurer for the BVF, and I met every month or so for coffee to discuss BVF business, world affairs, and any weird legal case that crossed Chuck's desk. We called our meetings the Basa Coffee Circle. Chuck suffered from pulmonary disease. The last two years the Basa Coffee Circle met, Candace and I had a hard time hearing what he was saying. Chuck's lung capacity was reduced so much that his voice was very soft and almost inaudible. Still, it was a shock to learn that Chuck died on August 30, 2017.

To let the members of the BVF know about Chuck's death, this was included in an email I sent to our members:

I just posted this tribute on the memorial page for Chuck's funeral: Chuck had the most generous and philanthropic spirit of anyone I know. I got to know Chuck as a coach in the Panther Basketball League and witnessed his tireless work to make basketball a character-building and fun experience for kids. We became friends, and so I was delighted when he agreed to handle the legal work for the Basa Village Foundation, which I founded and does culturally sensitive development projects in Nepal. Chuck refused to charge any fees for the many legal hours he spent to help make the BVF a success. Many families in the Basa area of Nepal will never know how they benefited from Chuck's generosity, which was critical in the development of their schools, water and electrical systems, and the other projects funded by the BVF. I always enjoyed telling the many civic groups I have spoken to about the BVF how our attorney never charged a penny for his work, so we could truthfully claim that 100% of donations went to our projects and not to professional fees and overhead. Yes, there was an honest, loving, and generous attorney. I will miss my friend, Chuck.

Achilles strain, jeepsters and trekkers to Basa 2017

Once Niru reported that the rebuilding of Basa was complete, Joel and I resumed our planning to visit the village and then trek up to Mera Peak for another attempt on the mountain. I urged BVF members and supporters to join the trek and come with us to visit Basa. Counting Joel and me, we had a group of fifteen to trek to Basa in November 2017.

Our flight to Phaplu was delayed a day and a half, because of weather. But the big, personal disappointment was that I was injured three weeks before the departure date. I sent this email to group members:

Namaste Group, On a personal note, last night playing volleyball I suffered a strained Achilles tendon. My physical therapist advises it's a 4-8 week healing period. (I'm supposed to use a walking boot/cast the next week or so.) My plan is still to attempt the Basa-Mera trek. There is a possibility I won't be able to handle the Mera portion of the trek/climb. Just wanted to let you know, so you won't be surprised if I'm a bit hobbled on the trail.

One of the training regimens I used for many years to prepare for a climb or high altitude trek was to run up and down a boat ramp in Broad Ripple Park, a half mile from our house. The "ramp runs" were in addition to my ordinary workouts. On the 19th of the 20 up/down ramp runs I was doing on a Thursday afternoon, I felt a twinge in my right calf. Instead of finishing and running home, I quit the run and walked home. I iced my calf, and by that evening I thought it was fine. Thursday night is a volleyball night for me. During the first point of the first game I jumped up to block Big Bob. When I came down I felt a pop in the right calf area of my leg. I knew it was my Achilles tendon. Thankfully (sort of), it was strained, not torn.

I got in as many physical therapy sessions as possible before the flight to Kathmandu. The recommended period of physical therapy was eight weeks. I could only do three weeks before the departure for Nepal. So it goes. I flew to Kathmandu on schedule with the hope that I'd be able to limp through the two-day hike from Phaplu to Basa. While in Basa, I could determine whether the leg could handle trekking for another week up to Mera Peak to attempt the climb.

That injury in October 2017 was further evidence that my spirit might still be strong but my ageing body was rebelling against the hard training I expected of it to prepare for a climbing expedition. Joints, tendons, ligaments, and muscles were not as cooperative as they used to be. Mentally and emotionally I still enjoyed the perverse high of a hard physical workout. But there was a growing psychological rebellion within my own ranks, along with the physical deterioration of my troops. Air travel in general, and long international flights with transfers in particular, was increasingly dreadful to me. The discomfort of cramped economy-class seats, the insecurity of whether scheduled flights would depart on time, and baggage loss fears, were minor concerns when I was younger. After turning 60, they were major complaints. I was less the adventurer and more the grumpy old man by 2017. Initially, I only told my wife (she didn't believe me) and Joel that 2017 would be my last visit to Nepal.

My sore leg was a minor disability compared to that of three members in our 2017 group. My sight-impaired cousin, Melissa, was a supporter of the BVF from its inception. She was a donor, board member, and served as co-treasurer with Candace for six years. She toured Nepal by van and plane with husband David in 2009. Melissa also has rheumatoid arthritis. Trekking was out of the question for her. She yearned to visit Basa, but we assumed it would never happen. Until, in 2017 the road which was slowly creeping toward Basa reached the village. At least one good thing about the road was that Melissa could be driven to Basa.

Another member of our group, who seemed an unlikely candidate for a Himalayan trek, was Hal. He was 85 in 2017 and had arthritis in his hips and back. He'd heard me speak about the BVF and had become a donor. After Niru informed me that Basa could be reached on wheels, a "jeep trek" was arranged for Melissa and David. Hal jumped (not literally) at the chance to visit Basa. His son, David, signed up to accompany dad.

The fifth member of the "Jeepsters" was Gordon Mendenhall, whose age and health made trekking over the 10,000-foot-high Ratnagi Danda too daunting. But Gordon had a special mission to perform in Basa. In retirement Gordon's "thing" was to do mission trips to Africa and Central America to distribute reading glasses in remote villages. Gordon gave a talk in 2014 to the Indianapolis Scientech Club about his unique mission. After the program I asked Gordon whether he'd be interested in doing his thing in Nepal. He said he'd love to go to Basa to distribute reading glasses to villagers who needed them.

The way Gordon's mission works is he takes hundreds of pairs of reading glasses to a village. He trains a local person in vision testing. The two of them begin testing the vision of local people and fitting those in need with reading glasses. Gordon leaves any extra glasses with the person he's trained so the mission can continue after Gordon's departure from the village. In correspondence with Niru about planning a 2015 philanthro-trek (before the earthquakes), I described Gordon's mission and asked about the possibility of doing it in Basa. Niru's initial reply was surprising. He claimed no one in Basa needed reading glasses. I knew that could not possibly be true. I wondered if it was Niru's way of reminding me that we did not suggest projects for Basa. Our policy was to respond to requests from the village, not recommend projects.

We had made minor exceptions to the rule in the past. School supplies, clothing, shoes, soccer balls, and the flying machines of the Basa Air Force were brought to the village without requests for those things. Delivering those items could be interpreted as gifts to the school and individuals in the village rather than development projects. Money wasn't raised by the BVF to pay for the gifts. Individual trekkers brought the items on their own volition.

The issue of eye glasses for Basa was put on hold along with visiting Nepal when the earthquakes struck in the spring of 2015.

When planning for a 2017 trek began, Gordon again offered to do his thing in Basa. I conveyed the offer to Niru, and for some reason still unknown to me, he was now enthusiastic about reading glasses for Basa. Perhaps Niru had talked with people in the village about the prospect of getting free reading glasses and the response was positive. The BVF-USA purchased 400 pairs of reading glasses at Gordon's discount rate of $1,650 (about $4 per pair). We bought the glasses through A Bridge to Kenya, the NGO Gordon worked through. Gordon became the fifth member of the Jeepsters.

Niru's programme for Melissa, David H, Hal, David S, and Gordon was a drive from Phaplu to Basa and then back to Kathmandu from Basa. I doubted whether any group had ever driven that far on recently constructed back roads in eastern Nepal. I figured the Jeepsters were in for a wild ride.

Another contingent within our 15-member group was the Miller Clan. Mike brought his son-in-law, Brian, grand daughter and Brian's daughter, Rachel, and grandson, Jake. Rachel was a recent graduate of Syracuse University. Jake was a student at IUPUI. Mike was stoked that subsequent generations of the family wanted to visit Nepal. He hoped they would love the experience of Himalayan trekking as much as he did. He also hoped that they would get involved with the Basa Foundation. After Basa, the Miller Clan planned to hike to Pikey Peak, climb it, and then trek to Jiri Bazaar.

Steve and Suzanne had recently become a couple. They thought a Himalayan trek would be an interesting bonding experience. They had read *Bringing Progress to Paradise* and were impressed with the Basa Foundation's approach to culturally sensitive development. Steve and Suzanne are both social activists, and we hit it off immediately when we met for coffee. Steve served for many years as the director of the Indiana Civil Rights Commission and wanted to sign up for the 2015 trek after he retired. It was cancelled because of the earthquakes. Steve knew Ole Dave and attended a program Dave gave about the Tamang Heritage Trail trek Dave did in the fall of 2015. The programme Niru planned for Steve and Suzanne was to drive back to Kathmandu with the Jeepsters after the Basa trek. Then, they would drive up to Langtang to trek the Tamang Heritage Trail.

The guys planning to do Mera Peak were a fourth sub-group of our 15-member group. My childhood-friend Dennis, along with Joel and me, wanted to try Mera Peak again. A new friend through Scientech Club, Andy, also signed up for the Basa-Mera programme. He is an experienced outdoorsman. Andy had done lots of hiking and climbing out west and in South America. He was looking forward to adding a Himalayan climb to his bucket of outdoor adventures. I was supposed to be the fourth member of the Mera sub-group, but the Achilles strain jeopardized my chances for a "third time's a charm" on Mera Peak.

Trekking to Basa again

Joel arrived in Nepal several days before the rest of the group and trekked to Basa with a porter-guide. He spent four days in Basa before the rest of us arrived. He surveyed villagers about past and possible future projects, and immersed himself in getting to know Basa without the distractions of other trekkers. It was reassuring to see how seriously Joel took his new responsibilities as president of the BVF-USA (my baby!).

Our AGT crew met the rest of us when we landed at the air strip in Phaplu. They hauled our baggage to a cow pasture on the edge of town. Purna prepared a picnic lunch for the group, which we ate while sitting on tarps to avoid sitting in cow dung. Our crew organized the baggage, while we ate. After lunch the Jeepsters and their bags were loaded up and they rumbled off on the dirt road to Basa. The trekkers slung our backpacks and the crew strapped on their doko baskets. We walked out of Phaplu to mount the flank of the Ratnagi Danda.

I'm guessing the distance between Phaplu and Basa on the road is less than 50 miles. I can only guess, because no map I've been able to find as of this writing, including Google's satellite map, shows the road. When I searched "Phaplu to Basa Village" in Google Maps, the two locations appear, but when I requested "route options" this text appeared: "Sorry, we could not calculate directions from *Phaplu Airport, Dudhakunda 56000, Nepal* to *Basa, 56000, Nepal.*"

The condition of the road, scraped out of the mountainside, is so rough that the driving speed ranges from five to fifteen miles per hour. The drive from Phaplu to Basa takes four to five hours in a 4-wheel drive vehicle. A dirt bike (motorcycle) could probably do it in a couple hours. Hiking the most direct route takes about eight

438

hours, if the hiker is fit and moving at a steady clip. A trekking group will take considerably more than eight hours to make the hike. There will be meal and snack stops, photo ops, and members hiking at varying speeds. Our group of trekkers started off after lunch and we expected to arrive in Basa around lunch time the following day.

It did not take long on the trail up the 10,000-foot-high Ratnagi Danda before my not-entirely-healed Achilles tendon was screaming for attention. The pain was sharp whenever I stepped down. When the trail was flat, if the surface was hard rock, each step was painful. Surprisingly, the pain was minimal when hiking uphill. That was just a dull ache. The first day was mostly uphill to our campsite high on the Ratnagi Danda, so the pain was constant but endurable. The second day was much more painful, because it was mostly downhill.

Steve was having an even harder time than I was. In early June, five months before departing for Kathmandu, he crashed riding his bike. He broke his clavicle and cracked two ribs. He had surgery in late June. Steve was determined not to miss a second chance to trek the Himalayas and visit Basa. He did his best to train for the trek, but was still treating with a physical therapist right up to the date of departure for Kathmandu. (I know that, because by sheer coincidence we had the same PT guy and bumped into each other in the clinic.)

Steve was very slow the first day, but made it up the ridge looking beat and red-faced. Early the second day on a steep downhill section he slipped and fell. Steve was about fifteen yards ahead of Sanga and me when he fell. Suzanne was somewhere ahead of us. Sanga and I hustled up to check on Steve and saw that his arm was scraped and bleeding and he bruised his shoulder. While Sanga and I were talking to him and cleaning the cut, Steve said he felt dizzy and disoriented. It was clear that he'd lost his balance due to dizziness brought on by dehydration.

Sanga decided that it would be unsafe for Steve to continue the hike to Basa. Steve would probably be fine once he was re-hydrated and rested, but Basa was four hours away of steep and tough downhill hiking. Sanga wanted to get Steve off the trail and into a vehicle to finish the trek to Basa. I hiked ahead to find Suzanne, who was sitting on a boulder ten minutes down the trail waiting for

Steve to catch up. She was unaware he was hurt. Suzanne hurried back up the trail to find Steve and Sanga after I told her Steve had fallen. Steve downplayed his injuries, but Sanga convinced him and Suzanne to come with him over to the road and finish the trek to Basa on four wheels. I'm not sure how, but Sanga managed to fetch a vehicle to drive Steve and Suzanne the rest of the way to Basa Village that day.

The rest of the trekkers made it to Basa without any serious incidents. Andy and Dennis were as strong and fit as they needed to be to attempt Mera. Brian was also a notably strong hiker. Rachel and Jake were surprised hiking up and down a massive Himalayan mountain ridge was as tough as it was. I suspect their already tremendous respect for Grandpa Mike rose even higher. Tired as the two youngsters in the group were, their spirits shot up when we received the traditional greeting in Basa and they were deluged with flowers.

Rachel is part way through the reception line of greeters. Jake is next in line, and Grandpa Mike is behind him. Basa 2017

We were happy to see the Jeepsters, Melissa, David H, Gordon, Hal, and David S, along with Joel, among the crowd of villagers welcoming us to Basa Village. The Jeepsters survived "the slowest,

440

bumpiest ride" of their lives. Melissa was carried piggy-back style by a young porter down from the road into the village. As tiny as she is her porter might have been grateful for such a light load, as compared to carrying stones and lumber down from the road during the rebuilding of Basa after the earthquakes.

Three Active Days in Basa

Time was limited and we had much to accomplish during our three days in Basa Village. We were hosted and entertained in the customary ways. The school children danced and sang. We visited many homes and consumed too much rakshi, chang, and food. We inspected many of the houses that were rebuilt or repaired using earthquake relief funds raised by the BVF-USA. The cheerful gratitude of the families whose houses were rebuilt spread a warm feeling through our group. That hearts of the BVF veterans, Mike, Joel, Dennis, Melissa, David H, and me, expanded with pride as we saw villagers using their smokeless stoves and filling water buckets from the taps outside their houses. It feels good to be thanked. It feels really good to see lives changed for the better, because of your efforts.

Next, we inspected the new school building. Its most impressive feature was the combined computer lab and library. Sydney Frymire is a trek leader/organizer, who connected with me in 2011 and joined the BVF-USA board the following year. She also started using AGT as the outfitter company for her treks. Sydney organized a drive for additional laptops to replace three that died. Sydney's 2016 trekking group delivered six laptops to Niru for the Basa School, bringing the functioning total to seven for the five-grade school.

Osan Rai succeeded Sanga's wife, Nanda, as principal of the school. He thought three of the original computers gave out, because they were exposed to so much dust. The earthquakes exacerbated the problem of excessive dust in the old building. In the new computer lab tarps covered the computers when they weren't in use. The library consisted of a few shelves containing the books, manuals, materials, and school supplies BVF philanthro-trekkers had delivered to Basa since my first visit in 2008.

By American standards the schoolhouse was still very rudimentary. But it had so much more to offer the children of Basa in 2017 than when I first visited in 2008. Then, the only educational materials the teachers had to work with were a few handmade posters and chalkboards with no chalk. In 2008 the kids wore old, threadbare uniforms of white shirts/blouses and blue cotton pants/skirts.

A month before we left for Nepal in 2017 the BVF-USA filled a grant request from the village to purchase new uniforms for the school kids. The uniforms are very cool-looking nylon track-suits; the same for girls and boys.

The kids pictured with Hal are wearing their new uniforms. The boy on Hal's lap is wearing a new pair of glasses received from Gordon. Basa Village, November 2017

We also approved and sent a grant to pay the salaries of the teachers the government wasn't paying. The government was only paying one full salary and one-half salary for the six Basa School teachers. Four of the teachers had worked without pay for a full school year. When we learned from Niru that the teachers were not being paid, the BVF-USA quickly approved and sent $6,080 to pay the unpaid four and one-half salaries for one year. (Do the math and marvel at how low the pay is for the Basa School teachers.)

The school children wore very fancy new outfits for their song and dance performance in 2017. They still danced barefoot, but on a tarp instead of on the pebble-strewn dirt playground.

One of the holding tanks of the water system was damaged in the earthquakes and had to be replaced. With impressive leg-strength Joel leaped onto the tank and pulled off the cast iron cap to look down into the tank. He confirmed the new tank was holding water that appeared clear. Mike and I once again asked Sanga about developing a purification system. And once again he confirmed that the villagers liked their river water as is and didn't want it to be filtered. Since there are no human habitations above the water source, human pollution of the water is unlikely. Few animals of any size inhabit the mountainside around the Mauri Khola, where the water is piped out of the river for the village. So, animal feces are unlikely to pollute the village's water. But I still thought the villagers made a mistake not including a filtration or purification component in the system. But, Basa villagers have drunk water from the Mauri Khola for 500 years, so who am I to suggest they change.

Sanga led the group down to the power station on the bank of the Mauri Khola to show us that the sturdy little building survived the quakes. The squat, little concrete-block building with a corrugated tin roof looks out of place in the wildly beautiful setting. There's a waterfall just up-river and the dense vegetation of a rain forest surrounds the power station. Mike proudly showed Brian, Rachel, and Jake the hydroelectric system that he and Chandra designed. And Prakesh proudly demonstrated how he can disconnect and reconnect the turbines. (I hoped no one in the village was too upset that their electricity was momentarily off/on during the multiple times Prakesh showed off his power over the system.) Sanga related that a couple of the electrical poles were knocked down by the big quake. The villagers set the poles back up and reinforced the bases with concrete.

Another interesting development Sanga reported was that the government had finally extended rural electrification to the Basa area. The village receives additional power to supplement the BVF system. And, cell service reached the village in 2017. Sanga pointed out several people in the village who owned cell phones. With a satisfied smile he said, "These people, they use the electricity for their phone chargers."

Man, talk about changes in the village. Just a few years ago nothing much had changed for 500 years. Now, computers, cell phones, running water, electricity, and even a motorized vehicle; we saw a motorcycle parked in a goat pen in the village.

One of the coolest activities during our stay was Gordon's eye glasses gig for Basa. Gordon trained Assam, the school teacher in charge of the computers and library, to do vision exams. Then, the two of them set to work. Chairs and vision charts were set up beside the schoolhouse. The tool Gordon and Assam used was a contraption with four pairs of reading glasses attached to it. The glasses had different levels of magnification. Any villager who had trouble seeing the figures on the chart tried out each of the four pairs of glasses to determine which one worked best. The "patient" received a pair of glasses which provided the optimal level of vision. Gordon and Assam tested over 200 villagers in two days. About half of the people tested received reading glasses. Assam was left with about 300 pairs of glasses. He planned to train someone in each of the nearby villages to give eye exams. The ultimate goal of the project is to give reading glasses to anyone in the Basa area who needs them.

We held a shoe and clothing drawing, which Sanga presided over like a carnival barker. He called out the lucky winners to receive coats, clothing, and school supplies that members of our group brought to the village. The shoes were donated by the Indy-based Changing Footprints. Seeing little kids and elderly folks, mostly from the lower caste families, receive their first pair of decent shoes is a very sweet experience.

The final give-away was for solar-battery-powered LED lanterns in compact inflatable containers. At a Scientech Club program I learned about this amazing product created by a company called LuminAid. The company was started by a couple of Columbia University graduate students who did volunteer work in Haiti after the 2010 earthquake. They designed and received a patent for the device. Leave the little plasticized packet with its solar battery in the sun for seven hours and the LED light will have power for up to fourteen hours. I thought the lanterns would be excellent supplements to Basa's electrical system. Because of the low level of power the little generator delivers, there are no outdoor lights on homes in Basa.

The school classrooms don't have lights. Purchasing replacement light bulbs is a hardship on the poorer members of the community. LuminAid lanterns could be placed anywhere, and they radiate light in all directions. They can be carried around to light up the narrow, treacherous paths through the village at night. Students and teachers could place the lanterns right beside their workbooks to read at night.

I could imagine many uses for the lanterns in Basa, so I sort of deviated from our rule of letting the village tell us what it wanted and not telling Basa what it should do.

I emailed information about the lanterns to Niru and asked whether he thought they would be useful and desirable in the village. I justified asking the question as a legalistic dance around our core principle. The village wanted lights when it made the original request for help with the hydroelectric system. The lanterns were a supplemental

response to that request. That's how I rationalized it, anyway.

Niru replied positively enthusiastic about lanterns for Basa. So I proposed and the BVF-USA board agreed that we should purchase 80 lanterns from LuminAid. We were able to buy the lanterns at a cost of $10 per unit; a $5 discount, because the BVF is a nonprofit corporation. I had to fill out a "Charitable Use Subsidy Application" and promise to send photos of the lanterns being used in Nepal. (The picture at the bottom of the previous page is one of the photos I sent.)

We handed out lanterns to each of the families at the end of the party the last night we were in Basa. Sanga opined that, "Man working in distant field after dark, he can carry lamp out there. Lamp can be used to herd animals at night. Lamps will make some work safer." One of the scenes I treasure in my Basa memories is seeing lights streaming through the village as families made their way back to their homes late at night after the festivities ended.

The celebration during our last night in Basa was especially meaningful for Sanga, Joel, Mike, and me. Sanga presented Mike and me with letters of appreciation from BVF-Nepal. The letters were embossed on brass plates and framed in beautiful hand-carved wood frames. I gave the longest speech of the several I've given in opening and closing ceremonies in the village. I explained the handoff of the presidency of the BVF-USA from me to Joel. I gave a brief history of the sister foundations. I mentioned how wonderful it was that three generations of the Miller family were there and what an important role Mike and his family foundation had played in the BVF projects. I ended by thanking the villagers for their extraordinary hospitality to me and the friends I had brought to the village in my six visits to Basa. I said that I did not expect to see my friends in Basa again with my eyes, but they would always be in my heart.

Sanga was translating my speech. When I said this would be my last visit to Nepal, he started crying. We were both choked up. I

waited for him to regain his composure, so we could finish. Sanga was my guide the first time I visited Basa. I was glad he was there when I said good-bye to the village.

Good-bye Basa, Never Again

A depressing sense of finality took hold of me the next morning. This would be the last time a cheerful kitchen boy brought hot tea and *taato pani* (bowl of warm water) to wake me up from a night's sleep in a North Face tent. It would be the last time I'd hear Purna rustling up breakfast, and then my rumbling stomach lurch with delight when I pushed the flap back on the meal tent and sniffed the aromas of sausage, eggs, muesli, pancakes, and apple sauce with cinnamon. Never again would I see villagers lined up with garlands of marigolds to place around our necks. This would be my last chance to accept a tin cup of rakshi from one of the village matrons, who were so eager for the departing guests to taste their best moonshine.

My languorous mood abruptly ended when I saw a slight young man from the village hoist Cousin Melissa on his back like a sack of potatoes. Hiking up the steep, rugged trail out of Basa covered in flowers accompanied by the atonal tweeting, thumping, and blaring of the Basa Village Band always amused me. Seeing little Mel carried on a porter's back in our snake-like parade dispelled my melancholy.

On the trail out of Basa with Melissa on a young porter's back for the 45 minute hike to the bhatti, where our group split up.

Sanga halted the troops by a teahouse 45 minutes up the trail from Basa. Children swarmed around to hold our hands and get a hug or hair tousle. This was where the group split up. The Mera climbers headed north with Sanga as sirdar. The Miller Clan, led by Santosh, trekked with the Mera group for a day and then turned west toward Pikey Peak. The rest of us waited for two Jeeps to arrive to haul us back to Kathmandu. Before parting, Sanga formed us up with the village band and Santosh for a group photo.

Band members are in the front row. Santosh is on the far right. "White people" left to right: Steve, David H, Suzanne, Brian, Rachel, Joel, Jake, Melissa, unidentified interloper, Jeff, Hal, Andy, David S, Gordon, and Dennis. Sanga took the photo.

A long and winding road

I laughed and groaned at the expense of Ole Dave and my students in 2013 after they bailed out of trekking back to Jiri Bazaar and had such a terribly uncomfortable experience getting back to Kathmandu. What comes around goes around. Suzanne, Steve, and I joined the Jeepsters for the drive from Basa to Kathmandu. We didn't get stuck for a day waiting for the river to subside in Shivalaya, and our vehicle didn't break down. It was just the longest, dustiest, and bumpiest drive on the crappiest road I've ever experienced. The worst stretch was the new section from Basa to Phaplu. Hal, David S, Steve, and Suzanne were in one vehicle. Melissa, David H, Gordon, and I were in another. Ekha, a cute little sirdar-in-training, rode with us. (I don't remember the make and model of the two vehicles, but I think they might be the India-manufactured Mahindra Thar. I refer to the vehicles as Jeeps in a generic sense.)

I'm a little ashamed of how I treated Ekha. Since I had the longest legs of the four riding in the second vehicle, I claimed the front passenger seat. Gordon, Mel, and David had sufficient room in the back seat. Ekha chose to ride in our vehicle, and started to get in the front to share the single bucket seat with me. I stopped him, and informed him in no uncertain terms that I would not be squeezed against the door for the 16-hour-long drive to Kathmandu. I told him to ride in the truck bed with our duffel bags and backpacks. He could make a bed for himself back there, and we'd both be more comfortable. He meekly obeyed. When we stopped for the first pee break, Ekha crawled out of the "trunk" coated in dust from head to toe. He looked like a coal miner at the end of a day-long shift. Ekha weakly asked again if he could sit up front with me. I declined his request, but helped him figure out how to have a less dusty and more comfortable ride.

The Jeep had a canvas cover over the luggage-storage area, which could be snapped shut from the outside to keep the road dust out. Dust was kicking up from the tires and blowing into the back, because the cover had not been snapped shut. David and I helped Ekha rearrange the baggage to create a "bed" that Ekha could lie in for the duration of the ride. When it was time to take off, Ekha clambered in. He spread out, smiled sheepishly, and turned on his little cassette player to listen to Nepali folk music. Our driver snapped the cover shut. When Ekha emerged at the next stop, he was not covered in dust and proclaimed cheerfully that he had the most comfortable seat in the Jeep.

We tried to make the drive to Kathmandu less painful and boring through conversation. At one point, when conversation began to lag, I proposed that each of us share an embarrassing experience we'd had in Nepal on this trip. Melissa and David had a mutually embarrassing tale. They spent the night before the trekkers arrived in Basa in Niru's house. Melissa had to pee really bad during the night. As she's blind, Melissa couldn't risk venturing outside for fear she might tumble down the mountainside. (Remember, houses don't have toilets in Basa.) David found a bowl and gamely held it for Mel to pee in. She peed all over his hands. That was their embarrassing story.

The dusty, crappy dirt road from Basa to Phaplu

Next up, Gordon told us that he went out for a walk by himself one of the nights we were in Kathmandu before we flew to Phaplu. A pretty young woman struck up a conversation with him on the street in Thamel (the old-town area where the Kathmandu Guest House is located). He said that she seemed very nice. He was eager to talk with local people to learn about their culture, so he was happy to engage in conversation with her. When she asked Gordon to buy her a drink in the bar they were standing outside of, he wasn't too concerned. When they went in, he discovered it was a strip joint. Pretty, young Nepalese women were dancing in itsy-bitsy-teeny-weeny bikinis. He paid for the drink, thanked his new friend for her company and exited as soon as it didn't seem too impolite.

Well, Melissa, David, and I howled with laughter at Gordon. You see, Gordon is rather saintly. He's a retired teacher who has travelled all over the under-developed world performing free eye exams and giving reading glasses to needy villagers. We gave the saintly Gordon hell for patronizing a strip joint. Melissa and I needled him the rest of the drive claiming we didn't believe he was so naïve as to be talked into buying a stripper a drink. We actually did believe it. (As to my tale of embarrassment, the privilege of authorship grants me the power to remain silent on that score.)

The drive from Basa to Kathmandu was very uncomfortable, but there were some fantastic views, like this, at rest stops.

Pokhara Touring

My disappointment in being denied a third try on Mera Peak was mitigated somewhat by doing the "Royal Trek" with Steve and Suzanne. Why is it called "Royal"? This is the answer given by

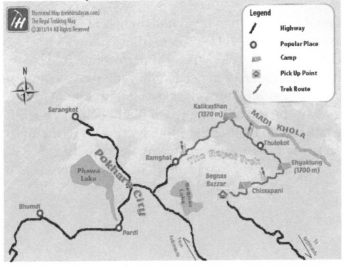

Mountain IQ, an online directory of mountain guides: "The Royal Trek in Nepal is so named because Prince Charles and his 90 camp followers

explored the route in 1981 shortly before he married Princess Diana. It is also used by Nepal's royal family, making it a very royal route indeed."

I had helped groups plan scenic tours to Pokhara and around the nearby lakes and solo hikers and group trekkers to do the Annapurna Circuit. But I had not visited that area. All of my Nepal trekking and climbing was in the Solu-Khumbu and Langtang areas in north-eastern Nepal. All of my touring was around or near the Kathmandu Valley. Pokhara is located in the very center of Nepal. The Annapurna Range is north of Pokhara on the border with Tibet. The Royal Trek follows a route that begins just outside of Pokhara to the northeast. It loops around Begnas Lake and tracks along a river called Madi Khola, as shown in the illustrated map by Trek Himalayan.

Our flight from Kathmandu to Pokhara took off and landed without a hitch. Pokhara is Nepal's second most populous city after Kathmandu. Its elevation of 5,700 feet is about 1,000 feet higher than Kathmandu. The waterfront in Pokhara is mystically beautiful. Mist rises from the grey water of Phewa Lake. I watched little boats paddling and scudding around the lake. Larger boats with canvas canopies loaded with pilgrims and tourists motored slowly out to an island in the middle of the lake. Barahi Temple, devoted to the female goddess Shakti, dominates the island with its large pagoda. I was told by a boatman that goats, roosters, and chickens are regularly sacrificed to Shakti at the temple. I declined his offer to row me out for the gruesome show. Phewa is 1.7 square miles in size; much larger than the little lakes I'd seen along the Gokyo Trail. It looked more than twice the size of the

lakes we camped by in Gosainkunda. The great white monsters of the Annapurna Range rise up in the distance miniaturizing all the manmade structures around the lake front.

Suzanne, Steve, and I spent a couple days in an attractive lodge with a grassy courtyard across the road from the lake. I limited my exploration of the city to the waterfront; in part, because my calf still ached and it screamed at me when walking on a cement sidewalk or paved street. The other reason was that, away from the lake, the air quality in Pokhara was almost as bad as Kathmandu. Both cities are in valleys, so the exhaust spewed by tens of thousands of vehicles without catalytic converters remains in the air you breathe, until it is blown out by favorable winds.

Ramesh Rai, Ganesh's younger brother, was our Adventure GeoTreks guide. He allowed us one day and night to enjoy the sanctuary of the lodge and to leisurely explore the lake shore. The next day began a whirlwind of tourist activities before commencing the Royal Trek. Ramesh shepherded the three of us to Davis Falls (aka Hells Falls), an impressive waterfall which pours down into a tunnel of caves (hence the nickname). We slipped and slid through the cave tunnels with busloads of school kids. We visited the Peace Stupa, which is a brilliant white stupa in the shape of a pagoda (presumably because it was initially funded by Japan). It is intended to encourage "people of all races and creeds within the world and to help unite them in their search for world peace." World peace is promoted from a Buddhist perspective. Statues of Buddha figure prominently in the interior of the stupa. We visited another cave, called Mahendra Gupha, famous for its stalactites, stalagmites, and bats. Next, we motored to Bindhabasini Temple, a white dome-like structure with a stone courtyard outside the old-town bazaar of Pokhara. This temple is also dedicated to Shakti and has animal sacrifices on special occasions. We finished off with a visit to the Tashiling Tibetan Refugee Center. I bought a little handmade rug woven by an elderly Tibetan woman for my cat, Bandit.

Ramesh was indefatigable in his desire to show his three charges everything of interest around Pokhara. We were, however, beginning to tire of playing the role of ogling tourists after two days of waterfalls, caves, temples, and shopping at bazaars. But we weren't finished. The next two days were less touristy and more edifying.

We spent several hours at the International Mountain Museum outside Pokhara. It is a world class museum. The many diverse tribal-ethnic cultures of Nepal are exhibited with art installations and historical documents. The diversity of this nation the size of Arkansas is mind-boggling. The 2011 national census listed 123 different native languages spoken in Nepal. The museum also displays and documents the history of Himalayan exploration and climbing. I knew a fair amount about the famous climbers and first summits of major Himalayan peaks from the 1950s through the present. The exhibits about the initial exploration of the Himalayan region by Europeans and the first attempts to climb Mt. Everest by the romantic hero George Leigh Mallory helped fill a gap in my knowledge about earlier contacts between "the West" and Nepal. The museum even has a 31-foot high model of Manaslu you can free climb (which I did).

Our last touristy activity was the most enjoyable. We spent the night up on Sarangkot (it's marked on the map above). It is a steep mountain ridge north of Pokhara, which is lined with shops, restaurants coffee houses, and lodges. The road up is so steep our 4-wheel drive "Jeep" moaned and groaned on the way to the summit. Several vehicles had to pull off the road, because they didn't have the power or low enough gear ratio to handle the steep incline. We spent the night in a lodge near the summit, just under 6,000 feet. The panoramic views of the Himalayan range and looking back over Pokhara and Phewa Lake were breathtaking. But the coup de gras for sight-seeing was watching the sun rise along the Annapurna Range. Over 100 people crowded the viewing stands to watch the sun

gradually turn the sky red as it crept up the backs of distant mountains to the east. The massive white flanks of the Annapurna Range sparkled brilliantly when rays from the sun reflected off the snow and ice. Oohs and ahs rippled through the crowd while cameras clicked and snapped at the sunrise.

There were three options for coming down the mountain after sunrise. Steve took the most exciting way down; he paraglided. You had to fly with an instructor. I have solo skydived and flown a glider and Piper Cub, and I'm a bit of a control freak. So, being strapped to another male body, who is controlling the flight, did not appeal to me. I probably made a mistake. Steve said it was "absolutely thrilling sailing out over the mountainside and then down into the valley and out over Lake Phewa." The landing was on a sandy beach beside the lake. Damn! That would have been beautiful. Suzanne took the putzy way down; by car in very slow-moving traffic down the very steep mountainside. Ramesh and I hiked for three hours down the mountain, out to the beach, and then along the lake shore back to the lodge in Pokhara. I wanted to test my gimpy leg. We had not done any strenuous hiking in the five days since we'd left Basa. It hurt, but the pain level was endurable.

Royal Trek

As soon as the touring phase ended and the trek began Ramesh transformed from an eagerly solicitous tour guide into a sirdar. Sanjay Rai was our Adventure GeoTreks porter. Sanjay carried all three of our duffels, but they were relatively light, because it was only a five day teahouse trek. Sanjay didn't have to carry any kitchen or camping gear.

The Royal Trek was the easiest trek I've done in the Himalayas. We stayed in teahouses and lodges instead of tents. The altitude of the trails we hiked varied from 3,000 to 7,000 feet. Hiking hours during the day were usually two hours in the morning and two to three hours in the afternoon. Compared to high altitude trekking and mountaineering expeditions, it was very leisurely. We even imbibed in a few glasses of wine one evening, while we sat outside our lodge and watched the sun set. For two novice trekkers, one still recovering from a bicycle crash, and a gimpy-legged trekker, it was well suited.

The white-capped peaks of Annapurna I, Annapurna II, Annapurna III, Annapurna South, Fishtail, Langtang, and Dhaulagiri were in view every day. We hiked through a few small villages and across several rice paddies. Hiking across the rice paddies was an interesting challenge. There is a ten-inch wide track between the flooded fields. If you're not careful and trip on a tuft of grass, to catch your balance you might have to step off the little ridge dividing the flooded fields. If you do, you'll be hiking in soggy boots the rest of the day. (I won't divulge which of the three trekkers squished down the trail most often in muddy boots.) Domestic scenes of families working together in the rice fields made a lovely pastoral contrast to the gigantic mountains in the distance.

We ate most of our meals in teahouses. Rice was, of course, the staple. Our diet was healthier than the typical meals of a camping trek, because all the food we ate was locally grown. Camp cooks have to rely to some extent on pre-packaged food, because expeditions often trek through remote areas where there are no farms or food vendors. Ramesh solicited samples of food direct from farmers we met along the trail. One farmer sold us the largest cucumber I've ever seen. Others offered small bananas right off the tree.

The dominant tribal-ethnic group in the area of the Royal Trek is Gurung. I knew very little about the Gurung people. Ramesh's English was not as fluent as older brother Ganesh"s, so it was difficult to hold an in depth conversation with him about local customs and culture. The following is from the website *Indigenous Voice*:

> Gurung is one of the 59 indigenous nationalities in Nepal residing on the foothills of Annapurna mountain range. The name Gurung is derived from the Tibetan word 'Grong' which means farmers. Gurung call themselves 'Tamu' which means horseman in the Tibetan language... According to 2011 Census, the total population of Gurung is 522,641. They are animists or followers of the Bon-religion, which is Shamanistic and animistic in nature...

> Their Tibetan Sojourn pre-dates the introduction of Buddhism there in the 7th century as the Gurung religious traditions are basically animistic. They celebrate their feasts

and festivals and carry out the ceremonies and practices related to worship, birth, death and marriage in accordance with the Bon and Buddhist religion...

Their main occupation is animal husbandry, including the raising of sheep and hunting. Lately they have a fame of joining British army and renowned as Gorkha soldier. In terms of their living, Gurung are divided into highlanders and lowlanders. Highlanders are those who are living on the slopes of Himalayas who still rely heavily on a pastoral and agricultural way of life. They resemble that of Tibetans in terms of religious beliefs and cultural practices. The lowlander Gurungs are more influenced by Hindu religion, who have migrated to the plain lands in the Terai...

Gurung have their own mother tongue called 'Tamukwyi', which belongs to the Tibeto-Burman language family.

Steve, Suzanne, and I agreed the low light of the trek was staying in one of the filthiest, dingiest, most primitive lodges I've ever slept in. If Prince Charles or the King of Nepal visited Shyaklung Village, I don't think they stayed in a lodge. I whined about it to Ramesh, but it was the only teahouse in the area. We did enjoy sitting outside the teahouse, observing the comings and goings of villagers and talking with a government official who was passing through Shyaklung on a fieldtrip. He wore a white shirt and tie, which he removed to wash and shave in a trough beside the teahouse. As I carefully unrolled my sleeping bag on the musty mattress, where I was obliged to sleep, I noticed a gigantic spider on the clapboard wall. I called Steve and Suzanne to come look at the monster. They were in another room separated from mine by a little creaking wood hallway and a filthy drape. With a monster spider on the loose the prospect of falling asleep in that place ratcheted up from dismaying to horrifying. I started looking for a bowl or some object the creature could be trapped in and thrown outside. But then, I heard a bang and squeak from Suzanne. Steve took off his shoe and -- Bam! Bam! Bam! -- smashed the spider on the wall. He removed the remains from the wall and shoe with a rag, and that was that.

In addition to the stunning mountain vistas and picturesque pastoral scenery, we had several serendipitous experiences on the trek. Two came the day we ended the trek at the lakeside city of Chisopani (which means "cold water" in Nepali). Just before dinner we met a local musician who played the sarangi, which is a traditional Indian-Nepalese musical instrument. It has four strings and can be finger-picked or played with a bow. Our new friend, Arjun, was extraordinarily talented. We invited him to dine with us. Throughout dinner he played Nepali folk songs, Beatles tunes, and Dylan songs. We bought his dinner and tipped him well.

After dinner, Sanjay, Ramesh, Suzanne, Steve, and I walked along the waterfront of Begnas Lake. Beyond the commercial area  several women were bathing and washing clothes in the lake. That's a common sight around any body of water in Nepal. Here, the water was clear enough we could see minnows swimming in schools just off shore. So I said, "Come on, let's go swimming!" Ramesh laughed and replied, "Nepalese, we don't swim!" But the five of us took off tour shoes, rolled up pants legs, and waded out into the water. It felt like the water temperature was around 70 Fahrenheit. I have bathed in lakes and rivers many times in the Himalayas, but I had never actually swum around in a body of water. I was the only one in our group wearing short pants. I pulled off my shirt and tossed it to Sanjay. Then I ran out and dived into the cool but exhilarating water of the lake. I showed off my skill at the four competitive swimming strokes, butterfly, back, breast, and free. Suzanne, Steve, Sanjay, and Ramesh cheered as I swam back and forth and out into the deep water.

Revolution or evolution to increase happiness
Walking back to our hotel in Chisopani, I began to shiver and my limp was more pronounced because my injured Achilles ached after the swim. Steve and Suzanne left us for a romantic walk along the lake shore. Ramesh hurried ahead to take care of some business at the hotel. Sanjay walked close by my side as I limped along the water front. In broken English he told me his career goal was to become a sirdar, but he knew he had to improve his English and learn at least a little of the major European languages, as well as Chinese, and Japanese. Sanjay is a handsome and strong young man with a winsome personality. He might become an asset to Adventure GeoTreks as a sirdar. But man, what a tough challenge he faces. How many head guides can Niru employ?

I have met many fine young people in Nepal, like Sanjay, who would like to improve their financial situation. My heart strings were similarly tugged by a young clerk in a shop in Thamel, where I bought some purses as gifts to bring home. Raaj left his mountain village to complete his education in Kathmandu. He was paying a few Rupees each week to stay with a family in their apartment. He shared a room with a couple of their boys. Raaj's bed was a straw mat on a concrete floor. His dream was to become a pilot or doctor. He was skinny as a rail and looked hungry. Yet, he smiled throughout our conversation. Raaj asked nothing of me except to practice his English in conversation. He wanted to learn popular American slang words and phrases.

Nepal is the poorest country outside of Africa. At last check the average household income was just over $3,000 per year. When I first visited Nepal in the 1990s, the average household income was about one US dollar per day. And yet, so many of the economically challenged people I've met in this poverty-stricken country are warm and gracious. I have met unpleasant people in the cities, and some of the porters Hari and I interviewed on the Base Camp Trail were not happy with their lot. I recognize that believing in the happy-native stereotype is a trap tourists can fall into through superficial experiences in a country like Nepal. With that cautionary note, I am still impressed by the sweet and winsome personalities of the many financially challenged Nepalis I've met over the last 25 years.

When I was the president of the Indiana Tenants Association

461

(ITA) and worked as a staff attorney with Legal Services Organization (LSO), I dealt with many poor people in central Indiana. Most of my clients were bitter, resentful, and expressed no appreciation for receiving free legal services or aid from the ITA. There were some exceptions to that generalization. Most of the clients were getting sued or suing someone, which is not a happy situation. But the difference in the response to living in poverty between Nepalis and Hoosiers, or Americans generally, is striking.

The history and personal experience of racial and class injustice may explain in part the unpleasantness of so many of the economically deprived people I dealt with through the ITA and LSO. But there is wide-spread ethnic and class injustice in Nepal because of the caste system. I think a major factor in explaining why poor people in the US are more unhappy (if you accept that generalization) than poor people in Nepal is a cultural difference in expectation and acceptance.

The sign on the trail-side vendor's hut states: "Being happy is a habbit (sic). Being sad is a habbit. Choice is yours." Royal Trek, 2017

The religions and cultures in Nepal emphasize accepting

circumstances and fate. American culture, especially the historically-dominant mainline-Protestantism, emphasizes individual striving, ambition, and success. In the US, if you're poor, (as President Trump would say) you're a loser. And that feels pretty crappy regardless of the reasons. In Nepal, if you're poor, that's what you're supposed to be. Only recently has the capitalistic ethic begun to change the culture in Nepal. If there is a cultural revolution happening in Nepal on the heels of the political revolution, I hope it does not result in "them" just becoming more like "us". I don't think it would change Nepal for the better to become more Americanized in a cultural sense.

I think there is an alternative way forward for Nepal, which is neither Americanization nor the Marxist-socialism originally advocated by the Maoist revolutionaries. Changing religious and cultural traditions, which have provided meaning and stability for hundreds of years, should be done carefully. Take the extreme examples of the caste system, arranged marriage, and animal sacrifice. Each of those traditions is anathema to those of us enculturated in the West. Many older people in Nepal want to hold on to those traditions, while many young people want to discard them. The arguments against those customs are strong. It's unfair to discriminate in employment, housing, etc., on the basis of caste. It's repressive and violates personal freedom for parents to arrange marriages. It's cruel and wasteful to kill animals as sacrifices to gods. More and more young people in Nepal are buying those arguments. If these traditional practices are allowed to change evolutionarily, they may fade away in another generation or two. On the other hand, if traditional norms and customs are discarded willy nilly for the sake of aping secular-Western culture, the transition will probably not improve the happiness quotient of Nepal. If the transition is made by government decree and enforced brutally against traditionalists, there will be resistance, conflict, and probably violence.

An example of the most destructive approach to modernizing development is the approach Maoist China took during the Cultural Revolution. Any tradition not in accord with Mao's interpretation of Marxism was suppressed and practitioners were brutally punished. China continues its program to destroy traditional cultures through its repressive policies in Tibet and its use of re-education institutes, i.e., concentration camps, for Uyghurs. Another shameful example of cultural repression (along with genocide) is the treatment of Native Americans by the US during the 19th Century. Not only were tribes massacred and survivors "relocated" to reservations, their tribal customs and mores were systematically suppressed.

Nepal survived its recent civil war and is working its way through dramatic political reforms following the abolition of a 240-year monarchy. The most recent version of the national constitution does require, to a certain extent, proportional ethnic-tribal representation in Parliament and government bureaus. But in other ways it ignores the unique customs of Nepal's many tribal-ethnic groups in the attempt to create a modern, democratic republic. For example, why not let a village which has always chosen a leader by consensus, or by age, or any other method, maintain that tradition rather than forcing a mayoral election? Why force a community to cease a traditional practice, which is working, when the community doesn't want to change?

Infrastructural development should proceed cautiously, and the local people who will be most affected should be the decision makers. That is one of the key lessons of the (so far) successful development of Basa. As much as possible, let local communities decide what infrastructural changes they want. Contract with local companies and professionals and hire from the local community. Local communities will happily accept and cooperate with outside investment and help with development, so long as they can maintain local control and ownership.

The most pressing issue is not how to lift up poor people out of poverty as quickly as possible. How to help people live happier, more meaningful lives is the salient issue. If I'm right about that, when we look deeper into the soul of the country, not just at economic metrics, Nepal might not have so far to go to catch up to the developed nations.

I've learned a lot from my friends in Nepal and from my association with Basa Village about living meaningfully and happily in a community. Some visitors to Basa, as well as other mountain villages, are so impressed by the warmth of those communities, they think we modern people should try to be more like them.

In the US, and in other "developed" nations, we have our own issues to grapple with. There are some parallels with remote

Himalayan villages struggling with the tension between tradition and modernization. But it is romanticism and a mistake for Americans to try to mimic a way of life which has not organically evolved here. We should not try to be like them.

America is chaotically free, crazily violent; its culture is constantly changing and fantastically creative within a divisively diverse population. As grand and troubled as it is, America is us. We need to own it. Let's figure out how we too can promote meaningful change to increase our local and national happiness quotient. Significant threats, like global warming and dangerously high income inequality, might require us to pick up the pace of change. But, if you've studied the violent and bloody history of revolutions, you must know that there should have been a better way to move forward than killing and jailing those on the other side.

(Please forgive my sermonizing. But I find my fellow UChicago alumnus Bernie Sanders' rhetoric about revolution discomfiting, given my knowledge of the death and destruction dealt by the revolution in Nepal. On the other hand, President Trump's willful, or calculated, ignorance of climate change and income inequality is even more alarming. Advocating for pragmatic analysis to determine the best ways to evolve our communities to a happier state can feel like crying in the wilderness.)

Reports from the Mera Team and Miller Clan

By the time Suzanne, Steve, and I arrived back in Kathmandu, the Jeepsters had departed the country. We hooked up with the Miller and Mera groups, not at the Kathmandu Guest House, but at the Moonlight Hotel. My old friend Uttam resigned his position as senior manager at the KGH and opened his own hotel, The Moonlight, just down the street. I asked Niru to book us in the Moonlight to help Uttam's new business venture. The Moonlight has a beautiful internal courtyard, rooms with all modern conveniences, and a sumptuous breakfast buffet. Our group members were not disappointed with the new hotel, and I was delighted to resume my regular philosophical and political chats with Uttam over a pot of tea.

It was also delightful (mixed with envy) to learn that two of the three Mera climbers summitted. Finally! I didn't get a third chance, but Andy and Dennis made it to the top of Mera in perfect climbing weather. I was surprised and alarmed to learn what happened to Joel. He was the youngest and strongest of the climbers, but he strained his back, which exacerbated a chronic condition, while the team was practice climbing in base camp. By the time the guys set up high camp on Mera, Joel could barely stand up his back pain was so intense. He was also dehydrated and had AMS symptoms. In Kathmandu he was still feeling so beat up he spent the better part of two days in bed. Joel related his "adventure" from high camp to Lukla in a subsequent email:

Seems my pushing myself along with some pain meds and just plain difficulty being at high altitude created extreme fatigue and my (chronic) back pains were exacerbated. It took all I had to get to high camp and I knew immediately upon arrival there would be no summit attempt for me.

We all retired early and Andy and Dennis were to depart at 2am or after, weather permitting, to work on up to the summit. They finally departed around 3:45 and they both summitted about 4 hours later. Dennis threw up a couple times but made it.

I crawled out of my sleeping bag finally, after zero sleep, headache and feeling incredibly fatigued and dehydrated. I was escorted back down to Khare by a porter, arriving slightly delirious and extremely exhausted. I had some liquids, some soup then crashed hard for a few hours. Andy and Dennis made it back to high camp and then started down, both arriving early afternoon. We then all hiked back down all day to arrive in Kote, back around 12,000 ft. Then next day would be a hike up to a pass called Zatrwa-la, a high traverse and camp then a hike back down some very steep and snowy/icy dangerousness to Lukla. I decided I would not be able to do this so chartered a helicopter to fly me to Lukla that morning. The heli ride was amazing, flying high over the passes then dropping steep down to the Lukla valley. Exhilarating (and I was thankful). A few porters who were also having altitude sickness joined the ride. The rest of the team arrived two days later and we then had a great celebration in Lukla with the porters and Sanga.

Dennis and Andy's summit bid was not without challenges, especially for Dennis. This is Dennis's description in an email sent to the group:

> After a night of fitful sleep, and several cold but necessary trips outside of my tent, Andy and I were woken at 2:30 AM to have some porridge and prepare for the ascent to the summit. I put on my multiple layers as well as a pair of down mittens and plastic boots with crampons that I had rented, and with the help of our climbing guide I also put on my climbing harness. The water bladder for my backpack wasn't working because it had frozen during the night so I only had my water bottle to which I had already added powdered Gatorade. By the light of our headlamps we made our way to the trail and clipped ourselves together along a rope with guide Dandy in the lead followed by Andy, myself, and then our porter Ravin.
>
> I was definitely not feeling my best. We headed up the glacier in the darkness with wind and face coverings making communication difficult. I seemed to be having considerable difficulty breathing effectively. I would try to count 50 steps before I would have to stop and lean on my hiking poles while I regained my breath. Unfortunately my stopping meant that Andy would get jerked backward as our connecting line went taught and eventually our impatient lead guide would start tugging at the line on Andy in the other direction to get us moving again. Eventually a deep red sunrise began to light up the eastern sky but I was in no mood to try to get my camera out. Even with the down mittens and polypro glove liners my fingers started to feel numb and I made efforts to wiggle them around to enhance blood circulation. As morning light increased the headlamps were no longer necessary and we could see the trail ahead and hope that the summit would be just over the next rise.

Finally the sight of fluttering prayer flags indicated the summit was near. As we took a rest before attempting the last ascent up a fixed rope to the summit, I drank some of my Gatorade and felt nauseous. I thought I would not be able to attempt to climb the last 70 ft. of elevation to the summit. After seeing Andy go up I decided that I could try to make that last climb and got myself to the top. We stayed long enough for a few photos and a spectacular 360 degree view of that region of the Himalayas with Everest in the distance.

[Left to right: guide Dandy, Andy, and Dennis. Photo by Dennis, Mera Peak 2017]

(Dennis continues)
I felt somewhat better but extremely tired as we made our way back to the high camp. I felt there was no way I could make it all the way back to base camp that day, especially after experiencing another bout of nausea and hoped that I could spend the remainder of the day recovering in my tent and head down to base camp the following day. However, the tents at high camp were not ours but available by reservation and I didn't have one reserved for that night. So, after some lunch and a bit of rest I was escorted back down the glacier and on to base camp by Rudra and several porters later sent to assist him. I arrived at base camp on fumes and crashed in my tent shortly before sunset. The crew had prepared a nice dinner but I only got part way through it before another attack of nausea struck.

Sanga's recommended cure was a Coca Cola, which I tried. It must have worked, because I was able to eat the apple pie dessert and had no subsequent stomach problems.

(hiking out to Lukla) ... one of the highlights of this day was when Sanga detected the odor of what he suspected were nearby wild goats, his nose proved to be accurate as two large, brown furry animals came crashing through the vegetation crossing our path at breakneck speed a short distance ahead of us...

Our last day of trekking was another long one involving several climbs before reaching the Zatrwa La. The descent on the north-facing side of the Zatrwa La was snow covered but not as treacherous for those of us with crampons as for members of the crew who did not use them. Even after descending to an elevation where there was no longer continuous snow cover, the trail itself was a mixture of dirt, ice, and rocks that made for tricky footing; and in my case a bruised bum. Eventually we descended low enough that there was no longer any ice and we were passing fields of green barley and houses with blooming flowers. After 8 hours of hiking we reached Lukla and were delighted to stay in an unheated hotel room with its own attached bathroom and a water line to the shower that could be heated with an in-line gas heater. We enjoyed a last dinner with our crew and distributed some of our donated gear and tips to individual members.

The Miller group had a less challenging adventure on their Pikey Peak expedition. Mike was not feeling well the day the group arrived at Pikey base-camp. Since he'd climbed it with Ganesh and me back in 2010, he gave it a pass in 2017. Brian, Rachel, and Jake hiked up the "fourteener" with Santosh. They reported that the views were spectacular. After Pikey, the Miller Clan trekked through the scenic "sky forests", high passes, and gigantic river valleys of the Middle Himalayas on the way to Jiri Bazaar. Jake described the drive back to Kathmandu in an email as "the longest, scariest bus ride back from Jiri."

Over breakfast at the Moonlight Hotel Jake, Rachel, and Brian told me that they enjoyed the challenge of Himalayan trekking and the magnificent views, but the most meaningful experiences were meeting local people and learning about the way of life of Nepalese villagers.

Left to right: Rachel, Jake, and Brian (photo provided by Jake)

The elevation in Basa is less than 7,000 feet, but spending time in the village was the high point of the expedition for the second and third generations of the Miller Clan.

This is how Jake expressed that sentiment in an email to me:

Hello Jeff,

I started reading "Bringing Progress to Paradise" yesterday and finished it today. What a wonderful read. I got choked up and my eyes and nose burned slightly when reading about Sanga, Purna, and Rudra and remembering meeting them, and the parade into Basa Village. Just by reading your words my heart filled with the love and feeling I had walking into Base myself. One of the most amazing experiences of my life. I can still taste the rakshi and smell the marigolds. Thank you for all you have invested into this village and for bringing my family into this wonderful work, experience, and extended Nepali family as well. You captured the spirit and mental roller coaster of a Himalayan trek well, along with the warmth and love of Basa Village. It was wonderful reading this book and being taken back to my time there. It is very insightful and inspiring, not to mention has me seriously thinking about when I can go back. Hope you are doing well and are enjoying the start of

summer. Look forward to seeing you soon I hope.
Best Wishes, Jacob Miller

Wandering Kathmandu and a the last visit to Monkey Temple
I spent my last afternoon in Kathmandu wandering around
Thamel by myself. A beneficent air current lifted much of the

polluted, acrid air out of the city. Despondency similar to what I felt
my last day in Basa set in. I needed to walk with a purpose. So, I set
off for Swayambhunath, the famous "Monkey Temple". The
monkeys never fail to amuse, and I wanted to buy a string of prayer
flags and a "singing bowl" to bring home as my last souvenirs from
Nepal. Vendors and artisans line the 350 steps up from the street to
the temple complex, so I was confident I'd be able to find and
purchase the desired items.

The following is quoted from the **Wikipedia** entry on
Swayambhunath (I took the photos in 2017):

Swayambhunath ... is an ancient religious architecture atop a
hill in the Kathmandu Valley, west of Kathmandu city. The
Tibetan name for the site means "Sublime Trees" for the
many varieties of trees found on the hill. For the Buddhist
Newars, in whose mythological history and origin myth as

well as day-to-day religious practice Swayambhunath occupies a central position, it is probably the most sacred among Buddhist pilgrimage sites. For Tibetans and followers of Tibetan Buddhism, it is second only to Boudha.

The complex consists of a stupa and variety of shrines and temples... The stupa has Buddha's eyes and eyebrows painted on. Between them, the number one (in Devanagari script) is painted in the fashion of a nose. There are also shops, restaurants and hostels ... a long staircase leading directly to the main platform of the temple, which is from the top of the hill to the east... The first sight on reaching the top of the stairway is the Vajra. Tsultrim Allione describes the experience:

'We were breathless and sweating as we stumbled up the last steep steps and practically fell upon the biggest vajra (thunderbolt scepter) that I have ever seen. Behind this Vajra was the vast, round, white dome of the stupa, like a full solid skirt, at the top of

which were two giant Buddha eyes wisely looking out over the peaceful valley which was just beginning to come alive.'

After taking photos of the temple complex, monkeys, and monks, I bargained with a couple vendors and purchased prayer flags and a singing bowl with just a little haggling over price. Then I strolled back toward the Moonlight Hotel along the Bagmati River. On impulse I purchased a pink shawl I saw in a shop window. It had colorful patterns in purple, blue, and orange sewed onto it.

Alicia didn't particularly like the shawl. She had a couple other shawls I'd brought home on previous trips. So, I sold it at a fundraiser to benefit the BVF sponsored by All Souls Unitarian Church in Indy.

My relationship with Nepal as an exotic destination started with a bang, when my wife told me to go take a hike. It sort of ended with a whimper, because I didn't get the chance to return for a third try on Mera Peak. But the end of the trail I am walking with my friends in Basa and the Basa Village Foundations is not yet in sight.

Sundar shanta Nepal. "Beautiful, peaceful Nepal."

You Have to Get Lost Before You Can Be Found
Pikey Peak 2010

I had a funny experience on Pikey Peak in 2010. Reflecting on and writing about that experience inspired the statement, "You have to get lost before you can be found." I first wrote about the experience in a 2012 e-book titled, *Light in the Mountains*, which had a chapter title, "You Have to Get Lost Before You Can Be Found". I've also written a couple articles using that statement as the title of the articles. The phrase has caught on with some online marketers. If you google that statement, the search will not reveal an earlier publication of those exact words. It will reveal numerous uses of the statement by graphic artists in digital art, banners, and posters. At least one other author co-opted the phrase for the title of an article. Several international travel companies use the statement on their websites. Some credit me and others use it without crediting anyone. A vendor of coffee cups and baseball caps was using the phrase on products sold on Reddit. I asked the vendor to credit me for the phrase. I didn't ask for compensation. My request was ignored, so I complained to Reddit. In response to my complaint, Reddit removed the sales page of the cups and caps when the vendor failed to respond. I've never requested compensation from advertisers and vendors for their use of the quote, just credit for it.

The sentence has particular meaning to me. When I first tried to make meaning out of the experience on Pikey Peak by writing about it, that statement was what I came up with to express the major theme of the story I wanted to tell about my personal evolution from adventure traveler to philanthro-trekker. The story could start when I was nineteen, dropped out of college, and stuck out my thumb on State Road 15 to begin hitch-hiking from Goshen, Indiana across the country. That story would take too long to tell in this book. In these pages I've described the transition of an adventure traveler into a committed philanthro-trekker. Age-related physical decline has brought me to another fork in the road. The trail chosen is a continued commitment to *philos anthropos* (love of humanity) but to leave the trekking part of philanthro-trekking to younger legs.

Pikey Peak base camp is a yak herding station, a *goth* in Nepali.

Our group of three American philanthro-trekkers and crew of seven Nepalis from Basa established our tent campsite around the goth before lunch time. We planned to hike up to the summit of Pikey (just under 14,000-feet high) the next day. We were on our way to Basa Village in the Middle Himalayas of eastern Nepal. The "philanthro" part of the trek had to do with projects for the Basa Village Foundations. Mike Miller was our consulting engineer on the design of a little hydroelectric plant for the village. Cathy Dawson planned to work with teachers and students at the village school on English instruction and with farmers on increasing crop yields. She is a retired teacher and a farmer. As president of the US foundation my principal task was to report to foundation members and donors on the projects we'd funded and discuss possible future projects with villagers.

Hiking up to the summit of Pikey Peak to enjoy the views was supposed to be the high point of the "trek" part of our philanthro-trek.

A yak calf nuzzled Cathy and me while we explored the campsite. After the kitchen was established and the tents were set up, Ram, our cook, signaled lunch was ready. It was early afternoon. While we sated ourselves on roti (bread), dal bhat (rice with lentils), and dudh chiyaa (milk tea), I asked our sirdar, Ganesh Rai, whether we could hike up Pikey today rather than wait until morning. It was a cloudy day. The view from the summit might be limited by clouds. But I didn't want to sit around in camp the rest of the day with nothing to do except read and play with the baby yak.

In the programme Niru planned for our trek, it stated that the hike from base camp to the summit of Pikey Peak could be accomplished in two hours. The elevation of base camp was around 9,500 feet. I figured we could make the 4,000-foot hike to the top and be back in camp before dinner time. During lunch, Cathy began to feel nauseous and feared she was getting altitude sickness.

The expedition started with the drive from Kathmandu at 4,600 feet to Jiri village (6,250 feet). We'd crossed several high passes but our sleeping altitude gain was less than 4,000 feet since we started trekking. Basa village was still three hiking days ahead of us. Porters had already transported on foot in doko baskets all of the parts and materials to construct the Basa Village hydroelectric plant.

Ganesh agreed to lead Mike and me up Pikey that afternoon.

Cathy opted to stay in camp hoping to better acclimatize. She pulled out her pack of playing cards intent on beating the guys in our crew in another game of Fish, which she'd taught them over the last few days of the trek. Mike, Ganesh, and I headed up the mountain.

First, we made our way through a pine forest, which we broke out of about 200 yards above base camp. Ganesh pointed to a rocky trail winding upwards. Scree, clumps of tea plants, and dense vegetation hid the trail from view as it snaked up the mountainside. But portions of the trail reappeared in rocky clearings higher up the mountainside.

Mike began to slow down after we left the pine forest and the trail became steeper and rockier. I signaled that I was going on ahead. After fifteen minutes I looked back and saw Mike sitting on a boulder taking a rest break. Ganesh and I waved to each other. I pushed on upward. The next time I looked down they were out of sight.

I felt strong and was moving well. It was a steep hike, but a hike not a climb. I'd suffered from AMS so many times in the Himalayas; it was a blessing to feel good on a high mountain trail. To make it more challenging, I hauled myself up on a boulder the size of a VW Bug and jumped from that boulder to another and then another, until I began to tire. I took a swig from my water bottle and looked up. Large, grey cumulus clouds were rolling across the sky beyond the summit. I capped the water bottle and hurried up the trail. Below the crest of the mountain was a series of stones set into the ground creating a "stairway" to the summit. Beyond the last rocky-step was a rounded green hump with an arch of prayer flags -- the summit!

Most high passes and Himalayan mountain-tops are rocky. Pikey has a green dome, which looks like a putting green rather than a craggy Himalayan rocky-top. There wasn't any snow or ice on the summit, even though its elevation is well above the typical snow line of 10,000 feet in November. Pikey's summit was a surprisingly pleasant place, unlike other austere and forbidding mountains I'd climbed in the Himalayas. Prayer flags hung between two opposing bamboo poles anchored with piles of rock. Gusts of wind made the prayer flags flap crazily. The slappity slap of the prayer flags was the only noise. The view of the great white peaks from Kanchenjunga and Makalu in the east to the Everest Massif dead ahead and the Annapurna Range in the distant west was awesome.

Standing alone on that mountain was a "mountain top experience". All those trails I had hiked since 1995, the hills, valleys, glacier-fed rivers, mountains, and villages of the Khumbu and Langtang were just out there. I could see all the way to the border of Tibet. For 15 years the Himalayas had been my refuge from the walls of ordinary life closing in. Feeling at one with the vastness of space for that moment in time was the essence of the escape I sought.

And then it was gone.

After just a few minutes a grey cumulus cloud enveloped the green dome of Pikey Peak. Visibility was reduced to a few yards. I had not taken a photo; I was so caught up in that metaphysical moment. The wind was picking up. Prayer flags began flapping violently. I spent a few more minutes sitting in the grass in solitary meditation. Then I hopped up and snapped a photo of my trekking pole balanced beside the prayer flags. I hoisted my backpack and walked over to the edge of the summit to try to see whether Ganesh and Mike were still hiking up to join me on the summit. I couldn't see diddly. Most likely they'd given up and returned to camp. If my guess was wrong, I'd run into them on my way down the mountain. There was nothing to see up here and no point in waiting around any longer.

I looked over the crest of the summit for the stone steps. The highest one should've been right below. The fog was so thick I couldn't see the big, flat stone. I carefully edged my way over the crest, but the "stairway to heaven" had vanished in the fog. Okay, I must have gotten turned around during my magical moment on the summit. I walked back across the green dome and looked over the edge on the other side. No stone steps there. The density of the fog was increasing and visibility was down to ten feet or less. Wind velocity was also increasing. Gusts slashed at my Gore-Tex jacket. I walked all the way around the dome of Pikey peering over the edge trying to find the stone steps. They had disappeared by some magic trick of the fog.

What the hell! I felt fit and strong. It would be fun to break my own trail down the mountain. I started bushwhacking my way down rather than spend more time searching for steps the mountain faeries were hiding. Hubris out-ranked caution.

The trail from Ngar Gompa tracked around the side of Pikey Peak to base camp. So, whether I went down the same route I came up or another shouldn't really matter. I would run into the trail to base camp somewhere down this side of Pikey. When I found it, I'd follow the trail back to our campsite. I had a compass in my backpack, but hadn't taken a compass reading on the way up Pikey; so the compass was of no use in finding the trail. But no worries, the main trail back to the campsite had to be somewhere below.

My attention hiking up the mountain had been on the ground and the boulders immediately in front of me. I had not even made a mental note of which side of the mountain the Sun was on. The fog was so thick I couldn't see the sun anyway, as I began to bushwhack my way down the mountainside.

A thick patch of scrub pine rose up out of the fog. I wanted to descend in as straight a line as possible on the assumption that a straight line down would intersect with the trail which encircled the base of the mountain; simple geometry. However, descending in a straight line with no trail to follow was more difficult than zig-zagging up the mountain on a well-marked trail. It also seemed like the incline of the mountainside was a steeper angle than the trail up.

I had to move from tree to tree, hanging on to branches or trunks, to keep from falling. The philosopher-poet-artist William Blake wrote, "The tree which moves some to tears of joy is in the eyes of others only a green thing which stands in the way." I love trees and would normally claim kinship with those moved to tears by the beauty of trees. And I was grateful for the purchase the trees offered on the steep shoulder of Pikey, but I would have much preferred they got out of my way, and let me find the trail to base camp.

The patch of scrub pine suddenly ended on top of a rocky crag. I carefully peeked over the edge of the cliff, but couldn't see the bottom of the sheer rock wall through the fog. Without a rope it would be too risky to try to down climb the cliff in the fog. So I worked my way along the ledge of the cliff until a frozen waterfall appeared through the fog. Water was trickling under several inches of ice hugging smooth rock. The frozen waterfall was at a slight angle projecting outward from the cliffside. It looked like a ten-foot long icy slide. The view was gauzy through the fog, but it looked like solid ground at the end of the frozen water trough.

I held on to the granite edge of rock along side the ice, swung my legs out over the ice, and dug my boot heels into the ice to slow my descent. With my backpack pressed against the icy trough I let go. Whoosh! I slammed into solid ground. The impact was jarring, but I kept my balance and wasn't hurt. I smiled with satisfaction. Spraining an ankle or a knee alone on the mountain would have turned this fun little adventure into a painful, scary misadventure.

A forest of rhododendron trees spread out below the waterfall. Continuing downward by grabbing branches for support, after fifteen or twenty minutes I was atop another rocky outcropping. The density of the fog had diminished enough that I could see edges and cracks for secure foot and hand holds on the rock face. I crouched down on the ledge with my backside out so I'd be facing the rock wall as I descended. I got a good grip on solid rock near the edge of the drop off and extended my right leg downward. The toe of my boot found a crack wide enough for support. Still gripping the edge of the overhang, I extended my left leg downward until my boot found protruding rock wide enough that I could securely release the ledge with my right hand while still gripping it with my left hand. I found a seam in the rock face with my right hand wide enough that I could let go of the top of the ledge with my left hand.

Free climbing is a blast. Only rappelling and glissading of all the activities associated with mountaineering rival it for fun. This solitary adventure was definitely more fun than sitting around in camp playing cards.

The mountainside at the base of the crag was covered with tea bushes. Working my way through a mass of tea bushes was like walking in deep mud. Every inch of ground was covered with tea plants and other ankle grabbing vegetation. I could barely pull and push my feet and legs through the mess. I gave up after struggling for ten or fifteen minutes. I couldn't see the perimeter of the vegetation through the fog. I worked my way back to the edge of the vegetation under the rocky outcropping. I tracked along the base of the crag until it petered out and I was back in the rhododendron forest.

It was irritating that the detour forced me to veer off from the straight-line descent I'd planned. But no worries; I knew the trail to base camp had to be below. The detour would just extend the adventure a little longer. I resumed the tactic of grasping tree limbs for purchase to keep my balance as I struggled down the steep mountainside.

Sunset was more than two hours away and I still had plenty of energy. I had two granola bars in my pack for snacks and some water left in my water bottle. I didn't have any cold weather clothes or a sleeping bag with me. The total time from Pikey base-camp to summit and back down was only supposed to take three or four hours. Bushwhacking might take longer than hiking back down the path to base camp, but I'd gotten to the top pretty quickly, so I figured I'd still make it back to camp before dinner time. I had not expected to be out after dark, and was determined not to be. Both of my headlamps were in my tent.

The fog was still thick enough that I couldn't see down the mountainside to get my bearings from landmarks I might recognize. No problem; stick to the plan and I'd eventually intersect the main trail.

When I broke out of the rhododendron forest, I found myself among tall spruce and pine trees. Tall trees are typically lower on a mountainside than the scrubbier rhododendrons. Most of the trail from Ngar Gompa to Pikey base-camp tracked through a pine forest. The trail should be nearby.

The slope of the mountainside was less steep. It was easy truckin' through the conifers with a piney aroma all around. My stride became free and easy, and yippee! There it was -- the trail. Stepping on to a well-worn path after bushwhacking and scrambling down the mountainside felt like re-entering the civilized world. My solitary time in the wild was about to end, I thought.

My sense of direction told me that I needed to go left on the trail. The campsite would be that way, and shouldn't be too far. Boot and shoe prints marked the path wherever rocks gave way to dirt on the surface of the trail. They were probably our prints from the morning hike from Ngar, I reasoned. We had not seen anyone else on the trail.

I strode down the trail feeling bold and confident. My trekking poles remained in my backpack. They would've been more a hindrance than useful bushwhacking and scrambling down the mountain. The trail was level and I felt good, so just leave 'em in the backpack. Hiking through a pine forest on the side of a Himalayan mountain with a tasty meal cooked by Ram at the end of the trail – that was going to be a great finish to another cool adventure in the Himalayas. I might as well eat one of the granola bars, since I had two. Pulled it out of the back pocket on my backpack, tore the wrapper off and stuck that in my pants pocket. Umm, yum.

Not far down the trail I knew something was wrong. The trail kept descending. I clearly remembered the trail to base camp gradually ascending, not descending. Mike took an altitude reading and remarked that Pikey base-camp was 200 meters higher than Ngar. But this had to be the right trail. The boot prints pointed this way.

I followed the trail another thirty minutes before I was absolutely convinced that I was walking in the wrong direction. The trail continued to trend downward, not upward. This made no sense. Who else would have made the footprints I was following? But I must be going the wrong way. We had not gone down from Ngar; we had gone up!

Turning back and going the other direction was the logical solution. That way, the trail would be ascending, instead of descending. I must have erred when I found the trail. Instead of turning left I should have turned right. The Himalayan fog-faeries tricked me again. Or, my sense of direction was 180 degrees off.

I back-tracked the half hour I'd spent walking left. I picked up the pace and ran a hundred yards or so every few minutes. Sun down would be at six o'clock. Dusk was coming in an hour or so. I needed to make time. Without a headlamp, hiking after dark would not be pleasant. Stupid! I was out here without a guide, no cold weather clothes, and no flash light or headlamp.

I jogged past the spot where I'd found the trail. The fog was finally starting to clear. I could see fifty yards ahead. Twenty minutes later the trail came to an abrupt end. A rock slide had wiped out a football-field-size stretch of the trail. What the hell!? No section of the trail was avalanched when we'd hiked it that morning.

Could I pick my way across the rock slide to gain the trail again? Lots of loose rocks on a very steep incline -- without a rope or a partner it would be dangerous. Traversing across the loose rubble of a landslide was a dicey proposition with a team of climbers. Trying it solo would not be a wise decision. I could see splotches of color through the fog on the side of an adjacent mountain. It might be Ngar Gompa. I couldn't tell for sure. If I could not find our campsite, I could walk back to Ngar and spend the night at the monastery. But I'd have to scramble across the land slide. A little tingle of panic spread through my limbs. Where the hell was I? Which was more dangerous, trying to pick my way across the loose rubble of the landslide and hopefully make my way to the monastery, or continuing the search for the right trail to base camp?

I had to make a choice. If I was not on the trail to base camp, there must be another trail, which I had missed on the way down the mountain. When I came down through the trees was it possible I didn't see a trail that ascended instead of descended? The trail I'd been hiking could not be the trail from Ngar. There was no section destroyed by a landslide. My instinctive turn to the left when I found the trail was probably correct. There must be another trail I'd missed in the mist of the fog. Crossing an avalanched section of the mountain was too risky. I turned around and hurried back toward the point I'd found this trail. There must be another trail! I ran.

I shot glances from side-to-side as I ran back down the trail. I was looking for caves and places I could possibly take shelter for the night in case I couldn't find the right trail.

My pace slowed to a walk as I neared the spot where I'd originally found the trail. I scanned the trees looking for a sign of another trail. A little way further I noticed a break in the trees above the trail. I stopped to check it out. There was a little clearing in the woods. As I walked toward the clearing I saw a broken down fence and the remains of a couple bales of straw. It was a small pasture for yaks. Yes! I remembered this scene on the way to our campsite. On the other side of the little pasture was another trail. And thank god, there was a Buddhi arrow!

It was customary that Buddhi or Ganesh, whoever was in the lead, drew an arrow in the dirt with a stick or trekking pole to mark the direction to take at any trail intersection or whenever it was difficult to see which way the trail went. Buddhi led our team on the hike from Ngar to Pikey base-camp. The line in the black dirt with an arrowhead at the far end was definitely a Buddhi arrow pointing toward base camp.

Dusk was rapidly approaching. I alternated from jogging to speed hiking every couple hundred yards. I came to another trail intersection. There wasn't an arrow, but I was sure I should take the upward trail. Without hesitation I turned to the left heading uphill. Another twenty minutes and I was back at the pasture where I'd started. Aargh! The cursed mountain faeries had run me around in a circle! I wanted to gnash my teeth and tear my hair.

Instead, I stopped and breathed, then ate the other granola bar. Need to regain composure. Time for a mantra. I'd chanted to myself off and on throughout the afternoon the ancient Buddhist mantra: *Om mani padme hum*. But I was lost and needed to be found. I began to hum and then sing the old Christian hymn:

Amazing Grace, how sweet the sound,
That saved a wretch like me.
I once was lost, but now am found,
Was blind, but now I see.
T'was Grace that taught my heart to fear.
And Grace, my fears relieved.
How precious did that Grace appear
The hour I first believed.
Through many dangers, toils and snares
I have already come;
'Tis Grace that brought me safe thus far
and Grace will lead me home.

Like grace, Buddhi's arrow would lead me home to the safety of our campsite. Calm was reclaimed. I headed back down the circular trail at a steady pace. The faeries hadn't moved the crossing trail. I stopped and looked closely at the trail to the right. The fog was gone, but the sun was down behind a mountain. In the gathering dusk I could make out boot prints beyond the crossing point. I leaned over to scrutinize the prints. Yup! There was Hamid's unique print. I brought a batch of shoes to Nepal from Changing Footprints to give away in Basa. When he saw the duffel bag full of shoes when we were in Jiri Bazaar, Hamid asked if he could have a pair of shoes. He replaced a beat up pair of sandals with a cool pair of soft leather shoes which had ribbed soles of hard rubber. Hamid's tracks were easy to recognize.

Just over five hours had passed since I lost sight of Ganesh and Mike on the trail up Pikey. Most of the time I was alone on the mountain was enjoyable. Only when I feared that I was lost and might not find my way back to my companions did the adventure feel like a fool's errand that had gone awry. I was lost but now I was found.

Night settled on the mountain by the time I could see the lights at our campsite. I knew Ganesh and the crew would be worried and upset, so I began yelling as I approached the camp. No one answered. I poked my head into Mike's tent. He was asleep. Cathy was moaning in her tent, nauseous with altitude sickness. Ram came out of the stone shelter where he'd set up the camp kitchen. He pointed up toward the summit of Pikey, waved his hand, and said, "Ganesh, Buddhi, Nirman, Hamid, up." Shit! Of course, they were up there looking for me. What did I expect?

Ratanbir appeared next. I signaled for him to come with me. We ran up to the trailhead Yelling and hollering. After jogging and shouting for about fifteen minutes we saw Ganesh waving down at us. He started whistling loudly. Then we saw Buddhi higher up the mountain. He waved and answered Ganesh's whistle with his own.

When all the guys were back down and gathered in the meal tent, Hamid exclaimed that he hiked all the way to the top and looked all around for me. He said there was an English word he didn't know that described what he was looking for that would lead him to me. "Clues, evidence?" I suggested.

"A clue! That is word I'm thinking of." Hamid was pleased that he remembered the word that explained how he conducted his search for me on the summit. I told him I was watching him the whole time, but the fog faeries hid me, so that he couldn't see me. A sly smile crept across his young face. The guys laughed uproariously. Hamid's riposte was, "Jeff dhai has some special power to convince mountain spirits to hide him all day." More laughter.

Ganesh congratulated me for creating a new trail down the "wrong side" of the mountain. He joked that it would be named for me, but no one else would ever find it. More laughter at my expense. But then Ganesh turned serious and complimented me for recognizing the tall trees were nearest the trail and for finding Hamid's shoe print. Ganesh said, "Jeffy dhai is becoming Nepali mountain man. He is learning to see."

Plates of dal bhat were passed around along with glasses of rakshi and a pot of hot tea. The mood in the meal tent was that of a party. It was very good to be back in the bosom of our little community.

The next morning Mike, Ganesh, and I hiked up to the summit of Pikey. Then, we had a very long and arduous day of hiking to a "wilderness camp". The guys who had to hike up Pikey looking for me got their revenge, because I was thoroughly beat after summiting Pikey twice in less than 18 hours and then hiking another 8 hours. Mike took this photo with my camera. Ganesh is in the background. Mt. Everest is at the far left of the range of mountains in the distance.

Being alone and feeling lost on the mountain created several moments of near panic. A person can feel very small when alone on a Himalayan mountain. When feeling lost, no matter where you are, there is an erosion of confidence, increasing insecurity, and downright fear. My misadventure on Pikey Peak was more aggravating than terrifying. But it reminded me of how much we humans are social beings. We need community. It is unnatural and inhumane to live in isolation. Being human is to give and to receive from others.

I enjoy hiking alone and many other solitary activities, like reading, solo-kayaking, and meditating. But I need community. Sliding down the frozen waterfall was exciting. Free climbing down the crag above the huge field of tea bushes was fun. Being able to share those experiences with the guys in the meal tent and later with family and friends at home gave those experiences, and my life, more meaning.

If you live out of fear, life is not much fun. If you wear a belt and suspenders your pants are much less likely to fall down. But some folks are so concerned with safety and reducing risk that they do not experience the real juice of life-giving adventure. Shimon Peres, explaining how Israelis were able to build a nation in the desert surrounded by hostile neighbors, said, "The most careful thing is to dare."

Risks shouldn't be incurred stupidly, and age does diminish the thrill of adrenaline highs, but continuing to live life as an adventure has given me much in experience. I have learned how I react when out of my comfort zone by getting out of my comfort zone. I have experienced how strong my will to survive is when running from an avalanche, when lost at sea alone in a kayak, and when confronted with a man holding a handgun as I slid into the front seat of the car that stopped when I was hitch-hiking. The willingness to dare, whether it is climbing a mountain or entering a deeper state of meditation, is the first step toward living adventurously.

I am happy I took that step when I was young. I am content with where many other steps have led. One of the places adventuring in the Himalayas led was to a little village called Basa, "a place of rest". What the Basa Village Foundations, USA and

486

Nepal, have done as partners with the community of Basa means far more to me, in this stage of my life, than any mountain climb or other exciting experience.

When I first went to Nepal, I was feeling lost. My wife and I both diagnosed the feeling as the mid-life crisis of a 40-year old whose life had come to feel too confining. Trekking the Mt. Everest Base Camp Trail was the prescribed therapy. Many wonderful adventures followed, and coming home eventually became more exciting than leaving on another trek, climb, or kayaking expedition. Home was where my heart was. The connection with Basa made it worthwhile to continue to philanthro-trek in Nepal. But now, with Joel and others taking leadership responsibilities for the BVF-USA, and Sydney and Elliot leading groups for tours, treks, and climbs through AGT, my physical presence in Nepal is no longer needed.

I am happy to be home with Alicia and to let the next generation strike out into the unknown until they are lost and need to find their way home. And the same for the generation after that and after that...

Afterword

The approach to "development" projects Niru Rai and I worked out in 2007 is still followed by the Basa Village Foundations. The primary labor for each project is provided by resident villagers and the projects are owned and managed by the residents of Basa Village. Sensitivity to the traditional culture of the Rai people has been paramount in our minds in trying to accommodate the stated wishes of the village to achieve a higher standard of living while maintaining a high standard of happiness.

The village school, hydroelectric and water systems were built by the villagers and are governed by committees of villagers. The model Niru and I established through those initial BVF projects became a model for culturally sensitive development, which the current leadership of the sister foundations is encouraging other villages in the Basa area to follow.

For more information about and how to contribute to the Basa Village Foundation USA Inc. go to **https://www.bvfusa.org/**.

The End

Every night I take my cat on a leash out into the backyard. We pee in the grass and look up at the paltry number of stars shining through the light-polluted sky of Indianapolis. It makes me long to see again the fantastic starlit Himalayan night sky. I do not plan to go back. The children growing up in Basa can see a night sky filled with stars and in the daytime can look up the huge river valley of the Dudh Khosi to see the magnificent mountains in the distance. They have a school, electricity, running water, smokeless stoves, solar-powered LED lights, reading glasses, school uniforms, running shoes, laptops and a library, competent teachers, a community center, and soon, a medical clinic. Their village has become a model for culturally sensitive development for other villages in Nepal. I am satisfied that I had a part in what I hope has changed those children's, and their children's, lives for the better.

Made in the USA
Coppell, TX
05 November 2020